The Formation of the Colonial State in India

In the period between the 1770s and 1840s, through the process of colonial state formation, the early colonial state in India was able to harness and extract vast amounts of agrarian wealth in north India. However, little is known of the histories of the Indian scribes and the role they played in shaping the early patterns of British colonial rule.

This book offers a new way of interpreting the colonial state's origins in north India. It examines how the formation of early agrarian revenue settlements exacerbated an extant late Mughal taxation tradition, and how the success of British power was shaped by this extant paper-oriented revenue culture. It goes on to examine how the service and cultural histories of various Hindu scribal communities fit within broader changes in political administration, taxation, patterns of governance and a shared Indo-Islamic administrative culture. The author argues that British power after the late eighteenth century came as much through bureaucratic mastery, paper and taxes as it did through military force and commercial ruthlessness. The book draws upon private family papers, interviews and Persian sources to demonstrate how the fortunes of scribes changed between empires, and the important role they played at the height of the British Raj by 1900.

Offering a detailed account of how agrarian wealth provided the bedrock of the colonial state's later patterns of administration, this book is a unique and refreshing contribution to studies in South Asian History, Governance and Imperialism.

Hayden J. Bellenoit is Associate Professor of History at the US Naval Academy, USA. He is the author of *Missionary Education and Empire in Late Colonial India, 1860–1920* (2007) and has published in journals such as *Modern Asian Studies* and *South Asian History and Culture*. He holds a DPhil in modern history from Oxford University, UK.

Routledge Studies in South Asian History

The State and Governance in India
The Congress Ideal
William F. Kuracina

Gandhi's Spinning Wheel and the Making of India
Rebecca Brown

Gender and Radical Politics in India
Magic Moments of Naxalbari (1967–1975)
Mallarika Sinha Roy

Bureaucracy, Community and Influence in India
Society and the State, 1930s–1960s
William Gould

A History of State and Religion in India
Ian Copland, Ian Mabbett, Asim Roy, Kate Brittlebank and Adam Bowles

Hindu Mahasabha in Colonial North India, 1915–1930
Constructing Nation and History
Prabhu Bapu

Cinema, Transnationalism, and Colonial India
Entertaining the Raj
Babli Sinha

Environment and Pollution in Colonial India
Sewerage Technologies along the Sacred Ganges
Janine Wilhelm

The Kashmir Conflict
From Empire to the Cold War, 1945–66
Rakesh Ankit

Hindu Nationalism, History and Identity in India
Narrating a Hindu Past under the BJP
Lars Tore Flåten

The Formation of the Colonial State in India
Scribes, Paper and Taxes, 1760–1860
Hayden J. Bellenoit

The Formation of the Colonial State in India

Scribes, Paper and Taxes, 1760–1860

Hayden J. Bellenoit

Routledge
Taylor & Francis Group
LONDON AND NEW YORK

First published 2017 by Routledge

2 Park Square, Milton Park, Abingdon, Oxfordshire OX14 4RN
711 Third Avenue, New York, NY 10017

Routledge is an imprint of the Taylor & Francis Group, an informa business

First issued in paperback 2018

British Library Cataloguing-in-Publication Data
A catalogue record for this book is available from the British Library

Library of Congress Cataloging-in-Publication Data
Names: Bellenoit, H. J. A. (Hayden John-Andrew), 1978- author.
Title: The formation of the colonial state in India : scribes, paper and taxes, 1760-1860 / Hayden J. Bellenoit.
Description: Milton Park, Abingdon, Oxon ; New York, NY : Routledge, 2017. | Series: Routledge studies in South Asian history ; 18 | Includes bibliographical references and index.
Identifiers: LCCN 2016038675| ISBN 9780415704472 (hardback) | ISBN 9780203762011 (ebook)
Subjects: LCSH: India–History–British occupation, 1765-1947. | India–Colonization–History–18th century. | India–Colonization–History–19th century. | Scribes–India, North–History. | Government paperwork–India, North–History. | Taxation–India, North–History. | Revenue–India, North–History. | India, North–Politics and government–18th century. | India, North–Politics and government–19th century.
Classification: LCC DS475.1 .B44 2017 | DDC 954.03/1–dc23LC record available at https://lccn.loc.gov/2016038675

ISBN: 978-0-415-70447-2 (hbk)
ISBN: 978-1-138-34757-1 (pbk)

Typeset in Times New Roman
by Sunrise Setting Ltd, Brixham, UK

Contents

	List of figures	vi
	List of tables	vii
	Acknowledgements	viii
	List of abbreviations	x
	Introduction	1
1	Revenue administration and scribal skills in late Mughal India, c. 1650–1750	12
2	The pensmen and scribal communities of Hindustan	33
3	Revenue and state formation in the Doab, c. 1780–1840	67
4	'Accounting for every grain': the origins of the colonial archive in north India	118
5	Kayasthas, 'caste' and administration under the Raj, c. 1860–1900	155
	Conclusion	190
	Glossary	203
	Bibliography	205
	Index	214

Figures

1.1 A revenue-agreement (*bandobast*) form used to enter contracts between zamindars and *sarkars* 22
2.1 King Chitragupta (*Sri Chitragupta ki Maharaj*) and his 12 sons, from whom the north Indian Kayastha sub-braches trace their lineage 35
2.2 Demographic distribution of Kayasthas in South Asia 37
2.3 A Kayastha scribe 44
3.1 The Doab and the 'Ceded and Conquered Provinces' after 1805 78
3.2 Codex used to correlate the Fasli calendar (*taghvim padishahi*) with the Gregorian calendar (*taghvim-i-ingilisi*) 93

Tables

2.1 Selection of various Perso-Islamicate names adopted by Kayasthas 48
2.2 Selection of Perso-Islamicate names and titles adopted by Kayasthas reflecting profession 49
3.1 Revenue collected in Bengal, Bihar and Orissa, 1766–9 71
3.2 Changes in assessment in north India, 1805–18 97
3.3 Changes in assessment in north India, 1805–18 98
4.1 Rent-roll (*hastobud*) – required statistics, c. 1850s 126
4.2 'Weekly and monthly returns' for Settlement Officers, c. 1840s 127
4.3 'Weekly and monthly returns' for Settlement Officers, c. 1840s 127
4.4 'Weekly and monthly returns' for Settlement Officers, c. 1840s 129
4.5 'Rules for Tehsildar's accounts' 130
4.6 'Circular order for the Sadr Board of Revenue' 131
4.7 Overview of the *khusrah* survey 133
4.8 Weekly and monthly returns required to be filed by treasuries 137
4.9 Requirement for 'Register of Landed Property' in CCP, c. 1810s 145

Acknowledgements

One incurs many debts in writing a manuscript of such length. As academic publishers breathe a sigh of relief upon receiving their slab of meat, one hopes for a product of reasonable academic merit. This project started as a spin-off of my previous work on educational sociology in north India, where Kayasthas made their mark as a prominent 'service caste'. Their noticeable prevalence in the administration of Awadh and, as I increasingly learned over the years, in the rest of the Doab and Bihari country got me thinking about the history of scribes and how they fit into the transition to colonial rule under the East India Company after the 1780s. I was also fortunate to have gotten to know a good number of Kayastha families in my travels to India. For all the literature on the transition to colonialism, surprisingly little was made of mundane paperwork, fiscalism and taxes. I decided therefore to follow this broader group of pensmen between the Mughal and British empires. So while this book is somewhat of a distraction from my overarching interest in religious encounters and interactions, I can only hope it proves a persuasive one that stimulates further discussions on paper and scribes in India's history.

I would like to thank Richard Barnett, Ian Barrow, Ananya Chakravarti, Joya Chattrjee, Nandini Chatterjee, Frank Conlon, Faisal Devji, Michael Dodson, Sanchari Dutta, Carl Ernst, Ravindram Gopinath, Angma Jhala, Justin Jones, Dilip Menon, Afzar Moin, Ilhan Niaz, Mubbashr Rizvi, Aparna Vaidik and David Washbrook, all of whom provided gentle guidance and constructive feedback and reviewed chapters. I would specifically like to thank Karen Leonard for reading a few chapters and offering valuable feedback and insights on the cultural fashionings of Kayasthas. In Lucknow, Naheed Verma generously opened her home to my curiosity, and her late husband Raj Verma openly shared details about Kayasthas over the years. Vibhuti Rai and his father, Sampal Rai, taught me more about Kayasthas than I could imagine and were gracious enough to share a very valuable family history. I particularly am indebted to the late Ram Advani in Lucknow, a true gentleman who linked me up with Kayasthas in the city, its environs and Unao. I only wish he could have seen this final work. Feedback at seminars in Cambridge, Delhi, Oxford and Lucknow helped in navigating the early contours of the project. A visiting fellowship at Clare Hall, Cambridge enabled me to hammer out final details and discuss my findings with faculty at the Center for South

Asian Studies. Special thanks should be given to David Washbrook. He not only encouraged me to follow up on the histories of scribes but also (in an unsurprising Marxist analysis) to examine the impact of revenue administration upon the agricultural economy. I also would also like to thank Dorothea Schaefter and Jillian Morrison at Routledge for their help in preparing the book's final details, both vexing and less so. The staff at the Library of Congress, the British Library, the National Archives in Delhi and the Uttar Pradesh State Archives in Lucknow all provided immeasurable assistance in tracking down material and errant files. A special mention should be made of the late Chris Bayly. Over the years, he gave so much warm support and encouragement in pursuing the histories of a scribal group he always wanted to investigate more. Hopefully this work will do justice to the scribes he often referenced in his work on Benares and north India.

This book, though, is ultimately dedicated to my wife Sara, our daughter Noor and our son Kian. Sara corrected my fumbling Persian (mis)translations, and our *dokhtar-Noor-ilahi* endured travels to India and the UK while daddy was off at the archives in work that must seem remarkably pointless to a three-year-old. She is the 'light' that guided this book. They have all opened my eyes and heart to the wider Indo-Persian cultural world and its luminance.

Hayden Bellenoit
Annapolis, October 2016

Abbreviations

ARP – Agra Revenue Proceedings
BBRP – Bihar & Benares Revenue Proceedings
BL – British Library, London
BORPB – Board of Revenue Proceedings, Bengal
CCP – Ceded & Conquered Provinces
CCPRP – Ceded & Conquered Provinces Revenue Proceedings
CPRP – Ceded Provinces Revenue Proceedings
DRONWP – *Directions for Revenue Officers in the North-Western Provinces of the Bengal Presidency*
IESHR – Indian Economic and Social History Review
IOR – India Office Records, British Library
KS – Kayastha Samachar
MAS – Modern Asian Studies
NWP & O – North-Western Provinces and Awadh (UP)
PRLTRSO – *Papers related to Land Tenures and Revenue Settlements in Oude*
RRSNWPBP – *Reports on the revenue settlement of the North Western Provinces of the Bengal Presidency, under Regulation IX*
SAHC – South Asian History and Culture
SRB – Sadr Revenue Board
SRRNWP – *Selections from the Revenue Records of the North-West Provinces*
SVN – Selections from Vernacular Newspapers
UPSA – Uttar Pradesh State Archives
WPRP – Western Provinces Revenue Proceedings

Note on transliterations and translations

I have largely tried to avoid using modern Iranian Persian transliterations, with which I am more familiar, and have attempted as much as possible to stick to Indian Persian (*istimal-i-hindustan, nama* vs. *nameh, madrassa* vs. *madrasseh*). Regarding words of Arabic origin, I have avoided using various *alef* notations and distinguishing between long and short vowels (such as *bad* vs. *baad*). I have attempted to be as consistent as possible. Any errors in translations (of which there are bound to be a few) are solely mine.

Introduction

The famed ICS ethnographer William Crooke and Ram Gharib Chaube, a major contributor to the *Linguistic Survey of India*, noted in their co-authored *Folktales from North India* the story of a Kayastha clerk who started a quarrel with a soldier (*sipahi*). The soldier badgered and threatened the humble Kayastha clerk: 'I will knock out your teeth'. The protocol for dispensing pay included establishing a physical description of each soldier. So the un-amused Kayastha military paymaster (*mir bakshi*) inserted in the margins 'two teeth missing'. When the verbally abusive soldier returned to collect his pay, the Kayastha refused, pointing out that his appearance did not match the form's requirements. Frustratingly, the soldier was only able to collect his pay after he smashed out his own two teeth.[1] This was, perhaps, the scribe's preferred method of resolving conflict: vicarious, passive-aggression through the pen.

While anecdotal, Crooke and Chaube's tale points to a frustrating dynamic that would have faced any visitor to India in 1900. It was the power of middling scribes and bureaucrats to frustrate the lives of countless peoples. A zamindar's claims to tax-free assessment dashed; a Nizam's embarrassment when papers revealed his financial dealings; a revenue farmer's tax liability ramped up when faced with compromising documents. Paper in India possessed a unique ability to level the playing field between high and low, pure and impure, landed and the landless, and ruler and ruled. Much of this had been built up during the seventeenth, eighteenth and nineteenth centuries. Its most pronounced manifestation, the British Raj by 1900 was a true paper raj (*kughaz raj*). Colonial India had become one of the most procedural, paper-intense administrations on the planet. Paper and ink were used to administer the lives of hundreds of millions of subjects across a large swathe of southern Asia. In administering the Indian subcontinent, to use the old cliché, the pen was often mightier than the sword.

Literature on colonial state formation

Of course, the building up of such a paper-driven administration was a complex, jagged process that spanned centuries. From the seventeenth century onwards, Indian rulers began to employ more procedural, paper-backed administrations, which sought to regularly tax and assess their subjects. Starting with the reforms of Akbar and Todar Mal, the Mughals built up what Jadunath Sarkar first called a paper raj. The infusion of Islamicate values of the pen, paper and writing, bolstered by the Persian traditions of accountancy and record-keeping administration, gave the Mughals a deeper 'paper foundation' than any rulers in India's history.

The British and the East India Company, from the 1700s onwards, stepped into this administrative culture of paper. Within two generations, by the 1810s, the British had become the dominant power in India. This was a significant change. And, perhaps accordingly, historians have attempted to describe the transition from the Mughal to the British empires largely in macro terms, examining 'the state' and other larger institutions and factors, such as landholding, warrior classes and economic change. Over the past few generations, the accumulation of this literature has done much to enrich out understanding of the emergence of British colonial rule. We now know so much more about how merchant families, warrior scions and new British institutions all shaped the colonial state and, indeed, modern India. It is a much more colourful and richer picture than the view that prevailed all the way up to the early 1980s of a 'chaotic' eighteenth century, which only recovered with the 'settling' aspects of British rule and administration.

The literature on the eighteenth century in India, for its part, has largely been based on explaining two important aspects: the state of eighteenth century India and the subsequent 'transition to colonialism'. Our historical literature now sees a much more dynamic and culturally and economically vibrant century between empires, along with more sophisticated eighteenth-century political systems. Muzaffar Alam's classic work has examined the first half of eighteenth-century north India. Looking at Shia-ruled Awadh and Ranjit Singh's Punjab, Alam has argued that by the 1740s north India saw economic growth that was accompanied with a strong assertion of zamindari rights.[2] He has pointed, though, to a '*jagir* crisis', whereby the proliferation of feudal land grants (*jagir*s) hampered the ability of the Punjabi and Awadhi states to centralize their administrations. For his part, Richard Barnett has taken a much more positive view of eighteenth-century Awadh. He has argued that eighteenth-century Awadh was remarkably successful and pragmatic. The strength of its political institutions lay in its ability to keep as much of its agrarian wealth and prosperity in the kingdom as possible.[3]

Looking west, Stewart Gordon has enriched our understanding of precolonial Maratha country. He has demonstrated that Maratha governance and administration were sophisticated and paper-driven, and the Peshwas administered a state that taxed efficiently and with a light touch that enabled broader agricultural prosperity.[4] The late Chris Bayly painted one of the most dynamic and positive pictures of eighteenth-century north India. He argued that while war, dislocation and famine punctuated large swathes of north India, overall there was steady, albeit inconsistent, economic growth. Trade and revenue farming expanded, and in many ways India possessed many of the 'capitalistic' aspects that would emerge later under colonial rule.[5]

The real historical debate over eighteenth-century India, though, has for the past generation lay in the 'transition to colonialism' and the nature of the British impact upon Indian forms, culture and economy. Much of this work has been focused on examining the shift from late Mughal forms of sovereignty and governance to British forms, attempting to explain how the East India Company managed to establish itself as an Indian power by the 1830s. This debate has been, as Ian Barrow and Douglas Haynes have noted, really a debate over change vs. continuity.[6] On the one hand, some scholars have tended to see more rupture and change in the emergence of colonial rule. In looking at landholding structures in colonial Bengal, Ranajit Guha has argued that British conceptions of property fundamentally altered the nature of landowning in Bengal through Cornwallis' Permanent Settlement (1793).[7] Rather than reflecting an Indian reality, Guha has shown how the imposition of the landed settlement was essentially an extension of European discourses about the nature of property that were removed from existing Indian reality. Shifting towards ethnography and caste, Nicholas Dirks has more controversially argued that colonial ethnography resulted in the creation of caste in a form that was different from precolonial traditions and practices.[8] Similarly, Sudipta Kaviraj sees a radically different colonial state that emerged from Indian eighteenth-century forms. He argues that the Company state 'did not emerge out of the internal logic of evolution of earlier Indian society, and had little by way of internal relation to do with the state it came to succeed in India'.[9] In these analyses, rupture and break from the eighteenth century characterize the emergence of the British colonial state, which jettisoned Indian forms and an ethos that were incompatible with its joint-stock-military nature.

On the other hand, a number of historians have detailed a great deal of continuity between the late Mughal and early British empires, emphasizing how British rule built upon extant Indian forms and trends. They have tended to emphasize Indian resilience and economic dynamism, seeing Indian seeds in the roots of British rule. Seema Alavi, for example, has argued for the primary role of the army and military organization in understanding the transition to British rule. She argues that the Company's standing as a military force offered stability and employment in an eighteenth-century India where armies and soldiery were already a prominent economic influence and that this helped to shape the dynamics of civilian society and provide a framework through which the Company encountered Indian society. To Alavi, the army was vital to the construction of colonial state apparatus.[10] Bayly, again, perhaps made one of the most novel arguments in explaining the rise of British power. He argued that north India's merchant and trading communities, who contributed to the broader patterns of eighteenth-century economic growth, slowly withdrew their support from Indian rulers and worked with the Company state in its initial generations. Bayly argued that the great merchant families of Benares played a significant role in moulding the early Company state and its patterns of administration.[11] In these examples, much has been made of continuing forms of governance and culture which, variously, shaped the emergence of the colonial state.

Yet, perhaps ironically, for our sophisticated understanding of the eighteenth-century transition to colonial rule, politics and economics, one of the most significant changes has been taken as axiomatic: increased taxation. This is surprising, for it affected everyone from cultivators to kings. Our historical literature is rather mute about changes in revenue administration and the more mundane, daily rhythms of fiscal administration. It is seen as axiomatic to the point of not requiring investigation. But there is a promising opportunity here. Muzzaffar Alam, for example, has argued that the Nawabi and Sikh kingdoms were hamstrung by gaps between calculated assessment and the actual revenue collected.[12] This is a crucial gap that begs explanation. How and why was this so? Did this change later under the Company? Chris Bayly noted briefly how scribal castes – mainly Kayasthas – served as crucial pensmen for eighteenth-century states.[13] But how were they crucial? What happened to their positions and skills after the 1780s? Ranajit Guha's analysis, again, fails even to consider how agrarian wealth got from the ground to the treasury.[14] Who was involved in the process? How were taxes assessed? What documentation and ideals guided the process? These are all crucial questions, for they open a window into the world of the scribe and how they linked agrarian tracks with large townships, urban capitals and, ultimately, imperial treasuries. The increased tabulation and collection of revenue from India's lush agrarian tracts between 1770 and 1830 was, for all its mundaneness, the single greatest contributor to the Company's power in India and indeed for wider British imperial might. The vein of fiscalism was the lifeblood of the army, the legal system and the eventual apparatus of colonial administration. In a way, larger debates over landholding, caste and society have all overshadowed these tedious yet crucial developments.

This book therefore aims to contribute not only to our understanding of eighteenth-century precolonial India but also to reassess the broader transition to British colonial rule. It deepens our existing literature by taking a novel look at how patterns of fiscalism changed between the late Mughal and early British empires and at the dynamics unleashed by these very changes. The book seeks to delineate how revenue assessment and collection were actually enacted through groups of paper-managers and literate, subordinate pensmen. It will analyse the dynamics of eighteenth-century revenue collection, how they were shaped and adopted by the East India Company, and emergent forms of 'bureaucratic' administration and governance – for it was in revenue collection that the early pillars of colonial rule were built. Since our collective literature on eighteenth- and nineteenth-century state formation largely overlooks fiscalism and taxation, the book seeks to redress this imbalance and argue for a more central role for the colonial state's ability to tax in the process of its formation. The book focuses on the material workings and rhythms of day-to-day revenue administration and how they shaped, and were indeed shaped by, dynamics within Indian society.

Rescuing the subordinate: scribes, paper and state formation

In arguing for a more central role for fiscalism in understanding the emergence of the colonial state in India, this book also aims to contribute to an emergent body of literature on the scribe in India's history. The tale of the Kayastha clerk and the soldier's teeth, combined with the power bureaucracy exerts in contemporary

South Asia, have encouraged scholars to explore more fully how scribes and paper managers have shaped India's past. In a way, the recent development of work on scribes as 'middling' castes might be the result of the trajectories of India historiography itself. Scribes fit neither an elite nor subaltern category. Further investigation into their histories therefore promises only to enrich our historical literature. Historians have started to fill this gap by exploring the social, cultural and political worlds of India's various scribal groups. There is a growing body of literature on the scribe, which ranges from examining Tamil clerks to Persian-literate Brahmins. Starting in a special 2010 edition of the *Indian Economic and Social History Review*, a collection of authors began to explore the roles that scribes and pensmen played as agents of historical change and how they supported Indian rulers. Rosalind O'Hanlon, for example, has shown how competition for service posts often revolved around, and was indeed determined by, the perception of the caste's 'social worth'.[15] The late Kumkum Chatterjee, similarly, showed how scribal skills sustained political regimes and shaped social and ritual status in Muslim-ruled Bengal up until the 1700s.[16] Both Chatterjee and O'Hanlon have made a strong case for a greater appreciation of the significance of the scribe in India's history.

More recent works have further deepened our understanding of the cultural, social and political worlds in which scribes lived and operated. Rajeev Kinra, for example, has given us a fresh new look at the cosmopolitan worldview of the Mughal court through the Brahmin munshi Chandar Bhan. Tracking Bhan's rise from a provincial clerkship to become the chief secretary (*mir munshi*) of the Mughal Emperor, Kinra gives us a novel perspective through the eyes of a scribe in seventeenth-century India. Bhan's career shows how the values traditionally associated with Akbar's court – of civility (*akhlaq*) and mystical awareness (*marifat*) – lasted well into the seventeenth century.[17]

In a similar vein, though focusing on a different region and period, Bhavani Raman has also greatly enriched our understanding of the scribe's role in Indian history. Looking at south India in the transition to colonial rule, she has demonstrated how accountants and scribes (*karnam*/*kanakkam*) ported their skills from a late precolonial system to a colonial one. Raman argues that scribes' skills were transformed by the colonial state, jettisoning their mnemonic ability for paper-based, attestable knowledge that could be made procedural (and hence governable). Less focused on the cultural and spiritual worlds of scribes, Raman emphasizes the processes of attestation and verification of paper documents that transformed 'native scribes' into something very different from what they were under Indian rulers.[18]

These more recent contributions to our historical literature studies have done much to shed new light upon how groups with literary and paper-management skills fit within the broader contexts of social order and administrative reach. They have also shown, in varying degrees, how scribes could act as powerful agents of historical change. But there is still so much more to explore in this budding literature on the scribe. For one, Kinra's focus on the Brahmin Chandar Bhan, while illuminating, only gives us a narrow slice of the fairly elite world of the chief secretary of the Mughal court. Raman's analysis of the colonial 'document raj' could do more to connect the changing value of paper with broader transitions in judicial authority, state formation and transformations in scribal careers, lives and marriage patterns. For example, it is one thing to look at how the 'teeth' of paper changed under colonial rule. But we can learn so much more if we look at how these newly coloured teeth actually 'bit' into the agrarian economy and affected the rhythms of daily administration. Documentation was an important development for sure. But the process of increased fiscal extraction and revenue administration made possible by a new type of valued paper had even wider implications. An analysis of scribes also begs the question of voice: what were their voices? How did they fashion themselves in light of broader processes of change? What were their cultural fashionings? These are questions worthy of further exploration and which can tell us so much about the nature of the emergence of colonialism in the Asian subcontinent.

A real opportunity exists therefore to cross-fertilize an emergent literature on the scribe with colonial state formation. Scribes such as the property registrar (*qanungo*) and the village accountant (*patwari*) in north India often possessed material, paper-based records of valuable fiscal information: rent rolls, historical rate payments, names of cultivators and classifications of leases. For any eighteenth-century ruler – Indian or British – this information was increasingly the foundation of rule and authority. The ability to tax meant the ability to wage war, to coerce recalcitrant groups into settled agriculture and to give greater procedure and consistency to one's kingdom, be it the Maratha lands, Nawabi Awadh, Ranjit Singh's Punjab or Bengal. These scribal families and their skills were already proving themselves indispensable for more revenue-hungry regional states in the eighteenth century. They assisted regional states' taxation penetration deeper into the countryside over the course of the eighteenth century.

Specifically, this book aims to explore the broader histories of a collection of scribal families known as Kayasthas. Along with smaller numbers of Khattris, Kayasthas were a group who the late John Richards called the 'technicians of the state,'[19] who had integrated themselves into the middling ranks of paper managers, copyists and letter writers. Some had reached the heights of respected munshis and *diwan*s, authoring administrative manuals (*dastur ul-amal*s). Yet, strangely enough, historians have paid scant attention to Kayasthas in Indian's modern history. There may be charitable explanations for this. Hindustan's scribes, for example, rarely engaged in revenue farming and advances for cash-crop production. The liminal *patwari* and *qanungo* only occasionally graced a Mughal court or Governor-General. Kayasthas also possessed a fairly ambiguous caste rank, especially in their 'twice-born' status. These may be the reasons why these more 'humble' officers have escaped the eyes of historians. The only work to substantially engage with Kayasthas as a group is that of Karen Leonard. Leonard has pointed to the continuance of a flourishing Indo-Islamic culture in Hyderabad, demonstrating how Kayasthas were essential for the Nizam's administration.[20] Other scholars have cautiously hinted at a far greater role for Kayasthas than they have been afforded. Kumkum Chatterjee noted that they provided eighteenth-century rulers with what she called the 'nitty gritty of administration': tax rates, assessments, installment payments and records of debts.[21] In other words,

Kayasthas, through these fiscal aspects, increasingly shaped regional kingdoms, their accounts and, above all, their abilities to wage war. By the early 1700s Hindustan's scribes provided invaluable reach for the Mughals' revenue tentacles and the regional successor states of Awadh, Bengal and elsewhere; and by the late eighteenth century they offered similar services to the East India Company's sprawling military-commercial regime. It is in this trend towards more paper-oriented forms of political authority that we can situate the cultural and service histories of Hindustan's various scribal groups.

Since Kayasthas were so notable as a 'clerical caste' under the late Mughals and then the British, their social histories can tell us much about how the colonial state was formed by the 1840s. The examination of Hindustan's various scribes – through the processes of revenue collection and management – can offer new and refreshing perspectives on the origins and emergence of British power in India. Largely overlooked, some historians have given us nuggets and clues as to the importance of such intermediate men. Eric Stokes once suggested that in the early days of colonial rule *qanungo*s and *patwari*s were the only real sources of information on revenue traditions available to British Settlement Officers.[22] Kumkum Chatterjee hinted similarly in her work on eighteenth-century Indian administrative traditions.[23] The present book continues in this spirit and seeks to rescue the less known 'intermediate men' of Hindustan and to make a case for the significance of their agency in the days of Mughal decline and the rise of British power. It takes these observations as its starting point and goes much further and deeper, investigating how revenue administration functioned in the late seventeenth century, how it changed in the eighteenth century and then under the Company in the early nineteenth. In doing so, the book also aims to give a social history to Hindustan's pensmen, examining their marriage patterns, ritual traditions, cultural posturing and worldviews, and how they changed under colonial rule. It seeks to delineate the changes in Kayasthas' occupations between empires, demonstrating how they were partially transformed from *qanungo*s into clerks. In spite of not belonging to any influential economic, religious or landed elite, north Indian Kayasthas became, and would remain, influential paper managers for Muslim and then British sovereigns in India. Their histories can therefore enrich our understanding of major changes in the subcontinent from the early 1700s onwards. The book is therefore written in this spirit of rescuing the scribe from the historical shadows and the literal cramped writing room. It attempts, as much as possible, to write a social and cultural history interwoven within a broader process of colonial state formation, shedding light upon how intermediate scribes served in the interstices between ruling overlords and the local structures of power and revenue. It aims to provide a refreshing examination of the emergence of the colonial state by injecting the processes of revenue administration and scribal history into its arteries.

Outline and aims of this book

This book argues that our understanding of the emergence of colonial rule can be enriched by tracking the lives of Hindustan's scribes, and how they shaped, and were shaped by, colonial state formation. Specifically, it examines changes in the revenue-collection systems in north India between 1750 and 1850 by looking at the paper and record-based mechanisms by which wealth was actually extracted from India's hinterlands. It looks at how such increasingly paper-based sinews of rule enabled the state to communicate with cultivators and collectors through scribes. It examines Kayastha pensmen as *qanungo*s and *patwari*s and how the markedly increased intensity of revenue assessment, extraction and collection after the mid 1700s was assisted by means of pen, paper and ink. After the 1770s the East India Company utilized this extant culture of paper to push through savage revenue demands in its agrarian revenue settlements in north India. The pensmen provided the Company's early state with crucial skills, physical records and legitimacy to garner the agrarian wealth which would fund Britain's Indian empire. This established more regular patterns of paper-oriented administration, which, in turn, engendered a process of bureaucratic communication, systematization, and the emergence of a modern colonial state that could extend its writ deep into the countryside via written orders. Perhaps inevitably, then, this book is also partially a history of the emergence of modern 'bureaucracy' in India.

This book draws upon various sources in painting a broader picture of change between 1760 and 1860. It includes settlement reports, personal memoirs, Persian treatises on taxation and rule, the personal family papers of Kayastha families and a cumulative set of interviews undertaken with Kayastha families in Lucknow between 2003 and 2012. Of course, oral histories can prove problematic when seeking to illustrate historical events and facts. This book couches the use of oral histories within a framework offered by Jan Vansina. Vansina, an anthropologist of Africa, has argued that oral histories must be treated with a healthy degree of caution. But when they are gleaned against the backdrop of historical records they can be useful: not as sources of historical fact but of historical trends.[24] This book does precisely that. Vansina also argues that oral history needs to be treated with caution when dealing with 'paperless' and 'archive-less' groups. But this is clearly not the case with Kayasthas and scribes. They were literate, paper-savvy and possessed written 'voices'. These interviews therefore are not treated as historical record but as corroboration of general trends in hard archival evidence. For example, I have only referenced oral interviews with families when what is communicated is confirmed by more than one party – an extra layer of caution when gleaning observations and historical insight. This combination can provide rich, illuminating insights into the historical experience of the pensmen's communities and their service histories.

The use of interviews is also located within conceptual work of Marcia Hermansen and Bruce Lawrence. Hermansen and Lawrence argue that Indo-Persian *tazkira*, a prominent form of Persian and Urdu writing, cannot be treated as a simple, factual historical source, but that they can be treated as 'memorative communication' and as a 'representation' of broader historical trends and changes.[25] This can usefully, albeit carefully, be applied to interviews with Kayasthas and private family papers. They are treated as representations of broader historical trends, general representations that have to be corroborated by the archival record. So while oral interviews and private family papers may not be *tazkira* literature, they nevertheless require a similar approach: a judicial and prudent use of oral histories serving to enhance the investigated historical record when measured against archival evidence. Lastly, the danger of self-representation in oral interviews and private papers can easily complicate objective historical analysis. But since this book largely focuses on Kayasthas as a *functional* group, rather than as a *caste* category, bias is less of a concern. As historians of caste in late-nineteenth-century India know all too well, it is in discourses about a caste group's 'twice-born' status, varna lineage and overall 'worth' where self-representation and bias can quickly muddle objective historical analyses.

This book draws upon settlement reports, but it is not focused on British imperial ideas and debates on landholding and the value of agriculture. These debates are of little interest and indeed of lesser relevance to this book. They were, as Baden-Powell noted, really a debate on political economy: 'I know of no idler and less interesting war of words'.[26] The reports of Settlement Officers are used here to identity larger fiscal trends, track looser scribal families and, most crucially, to examine the roles scribes and their documentation played in the Company's emergent colonial state.

This book is organized into five main chapters. The first chapter provides a broad overview of the role of paper and procedural administration in late-Mughal India. It looks at how paper became tied to the rhythms of revenue collection, and how, after the early eighteenth century, fiscalism and taxation were becoming increasingly vital to the Mughals and their eighteenth-century avatars. Chapter 2 proceeds to look at the broader families of Kayasthas across the Doab and Bihar. It examines their origins, marriage patterns, rituals and customs, and how they increasingly inserted themselves into the Indo-Islamic cultural and administrative world through their service professions, shared experiences with Sufism and the forms of learning they acquired.

Over the next three chapters, the rest of the book shifts gears into the early colonial period. Chapter 3 proceeds to examine the emergence of Company rule in the Doab, how it built upon an extant tradition of revenue administration and scribes, and the effects of this new fiscal regime across the north Indian economy. Chapter 4 moves on to examine the by-products of this new fiscal raj, looking at the archival accumulation of knowledge that was a result of the Company's penetration of the north Indian economy. It also examines the 'materiality' of rule through paper, pen and ink, looking at how the colonial state tapped an extant 'writing economy' for its fiscal authority. Chapter 5 moves into the late nineteenth century and examines how Hindustan's scribes shaped the Raj's administration by 1900. It looks at how their careers were refashioned and how, as a result of this, Kayasthas were subject to newly emergent debates about their caste status, consumption patterns and public instruction.

In the process of this broader analysis, the book will engage with a wider literature on paper and bureaucratic rationalism. As we will see, Max Weber's concept of 'bureaucratic rationalism' finds some echoes in the Indian case. So while engaging with some of Weber's useful insights,[27] this book attempts to move beyond a purely Weberian framework, by treating 'bureaucracy' as less a monolithic *entity* and more as a *process* shaped by social actors, economic dynamics and cultural values. In doing so, it identifies the origins of 'bureaucratic' patterns of governance, administration and the steady accumulation of taxonomized knowledge, providing alternative interpretations of modern, rationalized 'bureaucracies'. The book also engages with recent work by Matthew Hull, who has argued that 'bureaucracy' is less a static, immovable behemoth and more an entity that responds to, and is shaped, by local events and characters.[28] The transition between late Mughal and early British rule is studded with such examples. The book also engages with the recent work of Ben Kafka. Examining the proliferation of a bureaucratic paper administration accountable to French citizens after the Revolution, Kafka argues that historians have traditionally looked *through* paper but not *at* it.[29] Chapters 1 and 4, which examine the materiality of administration under the late Mughals and then the British, takes this approach of looking *at* paper and how it shaped, and indeed was shaped by, the larger social and cultural forces that surrounded it – and the book as a whole looks at the material histories of paper, pen and ink, looking at methods of production, distribution and how the Company's taxation patterns drew upon them. The aim here is to give a broader, material history to humanize larger process of historical change, demonstrating how paper and pen, seemingly insignificant and distant, welded together taxation and governance and reverberated across Hindustan to affect the lives of millions.

Notes

1 W. Crooke and R.G. Chaube, *Folktales from Northern India* (Santa Barbara, 2002), pp. 376–7.

2 M. Alam, *Crisis of Empire in Mughal North India: Awadh and the Punjab, 1707–1748* (Delhi, 1986).

3 R. Barnett, *North India between Empires: Awadh, the Mughals, and the British, 1720–1801* (Berkeley, 1980).

4 S. Gordon, *Marathas, Marauders and State Formation in Eighteenth Century India* (Delhi, 1994).

5 C.A. Bayly, *Rulers, Townsmen and Bazaars: North Indian Society in the Age of British Expansion, 1770–1870* (Cambridge, 1983).

6 I. Barrow and D. Haynes, 'The colonial transition: South Asia, 1780–1840', *MAS* (2004).

7 R. Guha, *A Rule of Property for Bengal: An Essay on the Idea of Permanent Settlement* (Chapel Hill, 1996).

8 N. Dirks, *Castes of Mind: Colonialism and the Making of Modern India* (Princeton, 2001).

9 S. Kaviraj, 'On the construction of colonial power: structure, discourse, hegemony', in D. Engels and S. Marks, eds, *Contesting Colonial Hegemony: State and Society in Africa and India* (London, 1994), p. 28.

10 S. Alavi, *The Sepoys and the Company: Tradition and Transition in Northern India, 1770–1830* (Delhi, 1995).

11 C.A. Bayly, *Rulers, Townsmen and Bazaars: North Indian Society in the age of British Expansion, 1770–1870.*

12 Alam, *The Crisis of Empire in Mughal North India: Awadh and the Punjab, 1707–1748*, p. 315.

13 Personal communication (Cambridge, 2014). Also see sections of Bayly, *Rulers, Townsmen and Bazaars: North Indian Society in the Age of British Expansion, 1770–1870*.
14 Guha, *A Rule of Property for Bengal: An Essay on the Idea of Permanent Settlement*.
15 R. O'Hanlon, 'The social worth of scribes: Brahmins, Kayasthas and the social order in early modern India', *IESHR* 47, 4 (2010), pp. 563–95.
16 K. Chatterjee, 'Scribal elites in Sultanate and Mughal Bengal', pp. 445–72.
17 R. Kinra, *Writing Self, Writing Empire: Chandar Bhan Brahman and the Cultural World of the Indo-Persian State Secretary* (Berkeley, 2015).
18 B. Raman, *Document Raj: Writing and Scribes in Early Colonial South India* (Chicago, 2012).
19 J. Richards, *The Mughal Empire* (Cambridge, 1995), p. 71.
20 K. Leonard, *Social History of an Indian Caste: the Kayasths of Hyderabad* (Berkeley, 1980).
21 K. Chatterjee, 'History as self-representation: the recasting of political tradition in late eighteenth century Eastern India', *MAS* 32, 4 (1998), p. 918.
22 E. Stokes, *The English Utilitarians and India* (Oxford, 1959), p. 85.
23 Chatterjee, 'History as self-representation: the recasting of political tradition in late eighteenth century Eastern India', p. 918.
24 J. Vansina, *Oral Tradition: A Study in Historical Methodology*, H. M. Wright, trans. (London, 1965).
25 L. M. Hermansen, 'Indo-Persian Tazkiras as memorative communications', in Gilmartin, ed., *Beyond Turk and Hindu: Rethinking Religious Identities in Islamicate South Asia* (Gainesville, 2000).
26 B. Baden-Powell, *The Land Systems of British India* (Oxford, 1892), p. 280.
27 A. Henderson, T. Parsons, trans., *The Theory of Social and Economic O* (New York, 1947).
28 M. Hull, *Government of Paper: the Materiality of Bureaucracy in Urban Pakistan* (Berkeley, 2012).
29 B. Kafka, 'Paperwork: the state of the discipline', *Book History* 12, pp. 340–53; also see, more recently, B. Kafka, *The Demon of Writing: Powers and Failures of Paperwork* (New York, 2012).

1 Revenue administration and scribal skills in late Mughal India, c. 1650–1750

Introduction

The late Mughal Empire is perhaps best known for its creation of a composite, Indo-Islamic culture and broader system of governance. This chapter offers an outline of the mid-to-late Mughal period, its political and revenue administration, and looks at the parameters, reach and patterns of its bureaucratic and revenue administration between the late 1500s and the early 1700s. It examines patterns of revenue administration within Indo-Islamic governance, how they were buttressed by non-Muslim scribes and administrators such as Kayasthas and Khattris and how they were integrated into the looser 'system' which by 1700 arguably boasted the world's wealthiest and most sophisticated paper-driven agrarian enterprise. It argues that paper became a more permanent feature of government in South Asia under the Mughals, and that this helped generate an Indo-Islamic culture of proto-bureaucratic governance which bound non-Muslims scribes into a pattern of revenue administration and its concomitant culture.

The literature on the Mughal state has, broadly, focused on larger trends of the Empire: its decline, resilience and ultimate eclipse. Less examined have been the normative conditions that shaped revenue collection, especially when it came to distinction in ideas of property, the constitution of objects and rights over objects. This chapter therefore explores a more neglected aspect of what made such broader changes in the Mughal empire possible: taxes, paper and ink. The Mughals in the seventeenth century achieved a high level of centralization and control over revenue. This was assisted greatly by the mechanisms and officers they used to extract such wealth, and it does seem that revenue per cultivated acre was as high in remote provinces as in the centre. In a way, this chapter builds upon the work of Irfan Habib, who argued that the Mughal system was fairly regulated and procedural. His examination of the careers of Mughal revenue officials shows that provincial postings were consistent across north India, usually around two and a half years. This would suggest that remote provinces were well integrated into the imperial machinery.[1] This broader paper context also served as a check upon local officials. Most Mughal officials were rarely local potentates. They were bound by a looser regulatory and administrative framework, which was not rigid but flexible and, above all, paper bound. For the Timuri fiscal state, which extracted up to 40 per cent of agrarian surplus, a sophisticated paper-bound and procedural fiscal system was as crucial as courtly ritual, millennial sovereignty[2] and sheer military might.

The pen, paper and learning in Mughal India

The connections between learning and government clerical service in the Indo-Islamic world were forged largely in the sixteenth and seventeenth centuries. Under the Mughals, the structures, contours and ethos of the court were influenced by the wider Persian cultural universe, which drew heavily upon a mixture of Persian, Turkish and, to a lesser extent, Arab cultural and ethical norms. This all ensured that both Persian vocabulary and the forms of learning it engendered – the local primary school (*maktab*) and the shared social experience of the poetry (*ghazal*) – percolated beyond the court and into medium-sized townships of north India and beyond. It also engendered residual forms of Persian administration, and ruling cultures reverberated into the plains of north and east India. This 'percolation of Persian',[3] as Muzzafar Alam has termed it, was particularly noticeable in the great *qasbah* townships of the Punjab, the Doab and upper Bengal. As a result, most words in Hindi, Urdu and Bengali which deal with the nuances of revenue collection and its 'culture of politeness' are of either Persian or Arabic origin: forgiveness (*maf*), assessment (*jama*), rent roll (*hast-o-bud*), agreement (*qabool/manzur*), spring crop (*kharif*) and fall crop (*rabi*). When ink was put to paper to document sovereigns and the affairs of government and revenue, it was usually in Persian. This was meant to give amplification to a wider political culture which celebrated the Mughal sovereign as the shadow of God on earth.

The expansion of the Mughal revenue-collection apparatus between the mid sixteenth and late seventeenth centuries went hand-in-hand with a ballooning of new forms of learning and the related values of penmanship, calligraphy and paper. The expansion of Timuri authority and administration served as a boom for the culture, and indeed production, of pen, paper and ink. The Mughals brought with them an increased appreciation for pen and paper, due to the inherited traditions of calligraphy as both an administrative and an Islamic spiritual art form.[4] Timuri administration and courtly ritual infused Indian governance with the more regular use of paper. Paper, therefore, ultimately became a technology of sovereignty. Paper was needed for tabulating rent, the ranks of military nobles (*mansabdars*), the Department of Letters/Composition (*dar ul-Insha*) and the *wasti* pens of Hindustan's pious and poetic. The Islamic tradition of calligraphy, particularly the Persian-influenced variant (*nastaliq*), was a practice considered second only to reading the Quran,[5] seen as much as a pious as it was a meritorious act. Importantly, calligraphy as an artistic form transcended religious 'community' and region and took prominence over mass print.[6] It created valuable bonds of patronage between Indian sovereigns, writing communities and poets. Indeed, the value of the written word, and the ethos it embodied, was not limited to the refined and literate but broadly appreciated by all, even the illiterate. Calligraphy's anchoring to the Mughal court stimulated a wider appreciation for pens, paper and the value of written words. Mir Panjab Kash, a resident of Delhi in the 1740s, entered the bustling bazaar of Chandi Chowk without any rupees on him. But he quickly scripted up a few samples of calligraphy that were immediately accepted as currency by the bazaar's shopkeepers.[7] Writing therefore was not only an administrative technology central to the court: its concomitant cultural fabric was appreciated by a wide swathe of Indian society.

In the seventeenth and eighteenth centuries, the Mughal Empire also made paper a more permanent feature of government in South Asia. The House of Timur was as much a standing military cantonment as it was what the Bengali historian Jadunath Sarkar called a paper empire (*kaghaz raj*). It is hard to assess what fiscal traditions existed in north India previously, but it does seem that paper became crucial to the new Timuri rulers and more important to Indian sovereigns than ever before. The Mughals' larger revenue, political and military functions required volumes of paper to account for illuminated books, copies, dispatches, accounts, letters and reports from spies, military nobles (*mansabdar*s) and paymasters. Secret correspondents (*khufia navis*) often had to report once per week and with multiple copies of their digests.[8] The Department of Letters/Composition (*dar ul-Insha*) was rumoured to be one of the largest areas of Mughal governance, from which receipts were sometimes granted to peasant cultivators. Paper was needed for military paymasters, celebrations, court ceremonies and sermons (*khutba*s) that pronounced the Mughal sovereign's name across Hindustan. Personal communication between the Mughal Court, provincial governors (*subahdar*s), deputies (*naib*s) and nobles consumed substantial volumes of paper. Forms of correspondence could also be complex and sophisticated. Different forms of paper and composition styles were expected for communication between equals (*raqima*), from respectful persons (*sahifa*) and between friends (*kitabati*).[9] At a more ceremonial level, voluminous detail was put into the illustrated copies of the stories of shahs and sovereigns, such as the Institutes of Akbar (*Ain-i-Akbari*) and the Book of Shahjahan (*Shahjahannama*). These kingly anthologies and the compendiums of the Mughal 'King of Kings' (*Shah-en-Shah*) projected the image and authority of Mughal sovereigns into the circles of the learned and the ears of the illiterate. But above all, patronage was crucial. Writers and political secretaries personified not only a gentlemanly ethos but also the bonds between sovereigns, secretaries and subordinates. For the Mughals, like the British later, something as simple as pen and paper, as much as intelligence, political suasion and military force, guaranteed legitimacy over a large swathe of the rich agrarian fields of Hindustan.

These traditions of learning and calligraphy also possessed demographic dimensions that mirrored the cultural universe in which they flourished. They were largely located in urban cities and the great *qasbah* townships of the north and east Indian plains: Mirzapur, Allahabad, Bilgram and Kakori. Delhi was a natural magnet for Muslim scholars, the *ulama*, and those loosely connected with the Mughal centre. Lucknow was another equally attractive township. The Persian-born Nawabs lavished huge patronage upon *maktab*s and calligraphy after the 1740s,[10] infusing the court and its culture with an appreciation of the pen. In Lucknow and Faizabad literate Kayastha Hindus and learned Muslims shared experiences which extolled the virtues of pen, piety and Sufi guides (*pir*s). Farther southeast, Jaunpur was known as the 'Shiraz of India' (*Shiraz-i-Hind*) for its Persian poetry, *ghazal*s and prominent gentry-service families.[11] Perhaps this *qasbah*'s most famous resident was Maulvi Roshan Ali (c. 1700–40). Ali was reputed to have commanded the following of hundreds of Hindu and Muslim students[12] as the city's pre-eminent scholar (*ustad*), teaching in *maktab*s and *madrassahs* and instructing Hindu scribes such as Kayasthas the intricacies of *insha* and *nastaliq*, making them full participants in the culture of association in Jaunpur, Mirzapur and Bilgram. This constituted a shared experience with their Muslim peers, which revolved around the local *maktab*, Sufi shrine and, ultimately, gentlemanly skills of the pen.[13]

The whole Indo-Islamic system of governance, revenue management and artistic expression was reflected in the forms of learning they engendered. *Maktab*s were a key component in the whole interconnected chain. They were usually attached to mosques and therefore benefited from endowed charities (*waqf*),[14] which generated regular patronage. Indian *maktab*s seem to have largely lacked Quranic learning and jurisprudence (*fiqh*), as far as they could be separated. Here, Persian was usually the medium of instruction. The skills of penmanship and letter writing (*insha*), necessary for working in various Mughal departments, were the mainstay of the 'curriculum'.[15] Unlike in the structures which emerged under the British, learning was voluntary, particularistic and defied standardization. It could vary in standards and regularity between townships. Nevertheless, pieces of the great works of Sadi's *Gulistan* ('Land of Flowers'), the *Mirzanama* ('Book of the Gentleman') and the *Amundnama* ('Conjugation')[16] seem to have been common readings, although it is tough to gauge the consistency of such instruction. More importantly, accountancy (*siyaqi*) was taught.[17] Various Kayasthas and Khattris had started to learn Persian and forms of its accountancy in local *maktab*s in significant numbers under Emperor Akbar's reign and his personal encouragement.[18] Kayasthas became conversant with and literate in the wider Perso-Arabic fiscal lexicon. These included papers relating to area (*taqsim*), copy of record, (*tasdiq-i-yaddasht)*, realization of revenue (*hal-o-hasil*), last ten years' revenue collection (*dawazina*), taxes (*akhrajat/kharaj*), realization (*wusul*), expression of consent (*razinama*) and cultivators (*muzarian/raiyat*). Hindu scribes, it seems, particularly excelled in the art of copying manuscripts (*manqualat*). Kayastha families from Lucknow's environs, such as the Navreens, Rais, Vermas and Srivastavas,[19] and from the east Gangetic plain and Bihar, were particularly adept in seizing advantage of *maktab* learning and landing subordinate posts as surveyors, accountants and particularly as registrars (*qanungo*s). Crucially, such career trajectories brought these Hindu pensmen into a shared cultural experience with Indian Muslims. For example, the financial pool for *maktab*s often came from the endowments of Sufi shrines, which linked them up with *pir*s, wandering devotees and the Muslim faithful who adorned these shrines with prayers.[20] And while these traditions were never explicitly meant to reproduce the prerogatives of the state, as it would be under the British, *maktab*s and *nastaliq* could but not help but glorify and engender a paper and pen tradition that glorified the culture of the Mughal sovereigns.

The materiality of administration in late Mughal India

This centrality of pen and paper enabled the late Mughal state to maintain a fairly extensive and sophisticated paper-based administration. Max Weber famously characterized the Mughal Empire as 'patrimonial-bureaucratic' model.[21] Of course, it was not a modern bureaucracy that was depersonalized; personality and relationships sustained the patronage and workings of the court and army. But if we look deeper, we see that the whole edifice of collecting revenue between Dinapur and Delhi bound the Mughal court, ledger and scribe with markets for pen, paper and ink. When it came to the Mughals' fiscal priorities, administration was remarkably paper-infused and materially shaped.

This Indo-Islamic administrative culture, and the forms of learning it engendered in the *maktab* and Persian 'curricula', was dependent upon manufactured technologies of learning. There was a substantial 'materiality' to administer the Mughals' fiscal might. Whether they were literary compositions, news (*khabar*) or coded conveyances, they required pen and paper, which connected many different communities of procurers, refiners, producers, customers and transporters.[22] It required groups of those who could procure wood, rags and tree leaves to make pulp, starch and dye. This involved numerous skilled vocational communities, commercial stakeholders and distance-based trade routes, connecting Delhi with the Doab, the Punjab, Kashmir, Bihar and Bengali country. Some of these networks, as Stephen Dale has recently demonstrated,[23] linked up with Hindu and Jain merchant communities in Central Asia. The *wasti* pen, made to draw out elaborate *nastaliq* calligraphy, was produced by specialized craftsmen who were recipients of patronage from Muslim sovereigns and landed Muslim gentry. Sialkot, in particular, was a major centre, which produced one of these major 'technologies of administration'. This Punjabi city's paper and ink were used, along with other inks from Kashmir, to feed the pens of maulvies, *qazi*s and secret-letter writers (*khufianavis*) as far afield as central India and Bengal country.[24] These two material technologies kept the Marathas' ledgers (*daftar*s) up to date, and were used to document payment of the quarter tax of produce (*chauth*) in the west Indian plains. Pen and paper were also crucial for surveying and assessment across a great swathe of Hindustan. Sialkot's paper production was particularly reputable, producing a renowned and durable silk paper laced with gold at its edges,[25] often used at ceremonial readings from the *darbar* and in poetry gatherings (*mushairah*). Sialkot and other cities supplied the Delhi court and the pens of maulvies, *ghazal* sessions and accountants.[26] From these locales, men of letters and stylistic expression spanned generations. It should be no coincidence that the famed poets 'Allama' Muhammad Iqbal (1877–1938) and Faiz Ahmad Faiz (1911–94) were born and raised in Sialkot. They were latter-day manifestations of a culture connected to the sinews of an Indo-Islamic culture of the pen, bolstered by Timuri authority.

Paper production after the 1500s also bolstered the Mughal fiscal state, and gave it the paper sanction it needed to organize and to extract revenue. On the surface, India in the sixteenth and seventeenth centuries, unlike Ming-era China, lacked a substantial manufacturing economy, something tightly bound up with, and dependent upon, regular patronage. It was, crucially, localized and particular. This larger paper network was bound up with longer-distance trade routes, for Islamic political culture was largely 'acquainted with no substitute for paper'.[27] Families who specialized in paper production (*kaghazi* families) tended to be overwhelmingly Muslim,[28] which put them in a precarious, but also profitable, position. *Sawakar* families were the muscle of this production process. They beat and pulped paper before it was poured into blocks to be strewn out and dried.[29] The strength required to produce such reams often required workers to eat 25 *chappati*s and one large *lassi* per sitting. In Dinajpur in Bengal, for example, coniferous trees were used to supply paper to various regions in Bihar and the lower Doab.[30] Rangpur was another example. Its paper quality tended to be not as starched and firm as from another famous 'paper city' farther west, Arwal.[31] Arwal possessed over 70 houses and employed over 240 men who produced paper to the annual value of Rs 32,000.[32] One single family produced up to 24,000 sheets of paper per year.[33] Paper production, it seems, was particularly prominent in upper Bengal and Bihari country, much of which went on to supply the *daftar*s of Bengal and even into the records of Awadh further upcountry. It was noted that Arwal's paper was 'commonly used by Persian writers all over Bengal'.[34] The trade and production was so profitable that the mostly Muslim families who produced the rolls lived 'in easy circumstances'.[35] Patna (Azimabad) was another paper-production centre. It exported close to Rs 5,550 of paper annually[36] to feed the books of pensmen, *pir*s and *padishah*s. Nepal was also part of this broader market for processed paper. Its largely coniferous hilly tracks possessed abundant amounts of bark from the *daphne cannabina* (known in India as *mahadeva*), from which pulped paper was produced. Nepali and Hindu merchants carried its supplies from the Himalayas and into production centres in Sialkot, Delhi and Arwal, which, in turn, injected a paper that was said to be 'immune from the ravages of insects'[37] into sinews of Mughal administration.

Ink (*samghi*) was another component of this tradition integrated into the Indian 'paper economy'. It was essential for Mughal government and later for eighteenth-century regional successor states. Kashmiri ink was reputedly the finest in India, supposedly because it was the region through which the Persian techniques of paper production were introduced into India.[38] And the region's inks fed the ledgers of the Mughals and later eighteenth-century kingdoms. The production of ink was a commercial and multilayered process. For one, the Indo-Islamic traditions of learning required ink that was carbon and plant-based to ensure posterity. Ink production came from the soot of lamps and other burnt forms of carbon, combined with other ingredients such as indigo, gallnuts and rice powder. Gum and water were usually mixed to enhance consistency, especially with the fine *qalam* pens, which were supposed to be 'long and fleshy' and were to vibrate gently when put to paper.[39] Once this initial concoction was mixed, it was boiled and settled for two to three days. Aloe was added, and would sit for 100 hours, and then strained though silk. Often it was topped off with a touch of saffron[40] for artistic refinement. The process for producing a pot of ink could take weeks and the availability of gallnuts, saffron, gum and soot was dependent upon the agriculture economy and the blessings of the monsoon season. This was a recipe for what may have been the finest ink used in India, but it was loosely followed across India in various cities that produced it. Documentation also took longer, which restricted the overall supply and reach of calligraphic work, because of the desire for posterity. Writers employed a technique of rubbing black powder into the incisures, which, it seems, gave these documents a longer shelf life than the inks used on contemporary wood pulp paper in Europe and North America.[41].

Copyists were also part of this wider materiality of paper culture. There were not particularly large numbers of copyists, as there would be under the more regulatory colonial state, with its 'copyist-babus'. But copying was nevertheless a form of technical reproduction that reaffirmed the value of the calligrapher. Srinagar, for example, probably possessed close to 800 copyists, who transcribed the Persian epic Book of Kings (*Shahnama*) and the poetry of Hafez.[42] Rs 60 could easily purchase a copyist for hire,[43] who could work on hundreds of finely illustrated pages for reproduction, ranging from Sadi's *Gulistan* to the administrative manuals (*dastur al-amal*s) that were increasingly being written by Hindu pensmen and munshis after the late 1600s.[44] Thus a profitable – but by no means mass – market in copying manuscripts of kings, shahs and holy men was bound up with a broader tradition of appreciation of the culture of pen and paper. It was only later under the British, with their obsessive desire to check 'native corruption' through regular paperwork, that copyists would come into their own as a subordinate bureaucratic class.

This whole Indo-Islamic world of learning was both a by-product and an affirmation of an existing political and administrative culture. It should be stressed that this world was in contrast to the 'mofussil world' of learning. Here, the village *tol* and *pathshala* 'schools' were far less connected to existing political orders, save perhaps in eighteenth-century Maratha territories. Their purpose was to reproduce Brahmanical and vocational norms regarding proper social and ritual conduct according to dharmic norms. There were also crucial economic differences with the Indo-Islamic world. In contrast to the central role paper played in *maktab*s and the Muslim courts, palm leaves and soil writing were less useful for accounting, ledgers and the affairs of kings, sultans and maharajas.[45] *Tol*s and *pathshala*s did more with less, as they often used bound volumes with palm-tree leaves as pages.[46] In Bengal, Bihar and the lower Doab, these schools used soil (*mitti*) to draw in the earth.[47] These palm leaves were often procured locally and were not bound up with long-distance trade, production and shipment.[48] This meant that *tol*s and *pathshala*s were less liable to disruption in supply. To the bulk of rural Hindustan, it made no difference whether Sialkot's paper made it to the great *qasbah*s of north India or the court of the *Shah-en-Shah*. There was always Hinduism (*sanataana dharma*) and the holy pilgrimage sites of Benares, Haridwar and Allahabad, which made paper, Persian and the pen seemingly irrelevant.

Increasing extraction: law, revenue and debt in the eighteenth century

This whole paper economy and culture of the pen bore immensely upon government in late Mughal India. Land revenue and agrarian wealth for Indian sovereigns, from the Pallavas all the way to the Mughals, were the main sources of revenue. What the Mughal Empire did was to put revenue administration on a more consistent and rule-bound footing.[49] And the Mughals, like their eighteenth-century successors, used pen and paper to do this. As the 'one great customary source of fiscal wealth in India',[50] agriculture accounted for at least 80 per cent of all revenue and assessment (*jama*).[51] The three traditional sources of revenue were usually land and salt revenue (*mal/maliyat*), customs and tolls (*sair*) and miscellaneous fines (*bazi jama*). But it was always agricultural taxation that held the lion's share of revenue going to the court. As one of the main functions of the late Mughal state, revenue administration was a complex and sophisticated machine. For the eighteenth-century regional successor states of India, revenue administration acquired even more importance. Increasing revenues had become a central priority for eighteenth-century regional polities. Ali Vardi Khan, the Nawab of lush and commercially vibrant Bengal, was constantly 'at his wit's end for money'[52] when facing border disputes with Awadh and periodic Maratha incursions. Most regional eighteenth-century Indian courts and kings were driven by a 'desire of the State for more and more revenue',[53] which meant that well-oiled fiscalism could determine regional success or failure in the flux of eighteenth-century Indian politics. Indeed, the eighteenth century was the century of the 'fiscal state'.

While it is hard to make broader generalizations about revenue collection in north India, given the differences between districts, soil qualities and planting patterns, we can still ascertain some commonalities and measure how they changed under the Company. One of the reasons the late Mughal revenue traditions were so complex and paper driven had to do with the monsoon season. They varied in practice regionally, but some common features can be drawn out. Unlike other western Islamic lands, large parts of the Indian subcontinent received two harvests, and in south India sometimes three. For north and east India, the *bhadoi* millet crops were harvested in August and September in Bihar. All of this could theoretically double the relative amount of paper, documentation and personnel needed to collect agrarian revenue. The autumn (*kharif*) crop usually stretched between the onset of monsoon rains and early autumn, producing much of India's millet, rice, sugarcane and *bajra*. The spring (*rabi*) crops came in the dry cool seasons of the winter and usually included various forms of wheat, barley, sesame, mustard, peas and pulses. The central Doab was known for a three-circle crop-rotation system, which boosted agricultural yields, even in more sandy soils (*bhoor*). And the connections with revenue collection and the state were immediate and expedient. In some parts of north India, for example, grains were measured quickly to prevent vagrant idols (*bhuts*) from stealing them.[54] This hastened the connections between agrarian output and bringing grain to market, which, by extension, increased the speed of collection, paperwork and the pensmen required to manage what was likely the largest agricultural extraction of any Muslim-ruled empire by 1700.

Eighteenth-century Awadh and Bengal

This same culture of revenue, albeit in greater intensity, greatly coloured eighteenth-century regional states' orientation and their forms of state organization. We can glean some general trends of how revenue administration worked in the Doab, Bihar and, to a degree, Bengal before British conquest. Pre-British Awadh provides a good starting point for analysis, from which we can draw some initial comparisons. Richard Barnett has pointed to a general trend of increased cultivation and taxation in pre-British Awadh and an increased intensity of fiscal penetration by the Nawabs.[55] Further exploration of the historical evidence suggests that Awadh between 1770 and 1830 witnessed a significantly ramped-up revenue administration, made possible by north India's scribal groups, notably the Saxena Kayastha families of Unao. What we see in pre-British Awadh, as in Bihar and Bengal, is that revenue traditions were more 'corporately interconnected' than their more legalized and procedural manifestations under the Company. For Awadh, the whole system of harnessing *kharaj* involved a constellation of intermediary groups, exceptions and flexibility that allowed the Nawabs not only to achieve fiscal might but also to maintain a veneer of legitimacy that kept local stakeholders and rural magnates content.

One particular Persian work, 'The Composition of Muhammad Faiq' (*Insha-ye-Faiq*), gives us rich insight into how revenue collection worked in Awadh before the British conquest. The author, Muhammad Faiq, lived in the late 1700s around Sultanpur and worked as a minor official for the Nawabs. His son Abdul Ahmad (d. 1851) later worked as a *sheristadar* for the British Resident at Lucknow.[56] Faiq described the middle Doab district of Sultanpur in the 1820s, a liminal period when Nawabi authority was being sandwiched by increasing Company demands and the Nawabs' penetration of the countryside. What Faiq seems to have offered was a moral template for revenue administration. It was one that taxed more intensely but was sensitive to the constellation of interconnected middlemen and individuals that made the harnessing of agrarian wealth possible. This interconnectedness was a form of 'moral binding' that made people stakeholders in a broader process. Faiq argued that for any locale to be 'inhabitable' (*adabat*), peasants and cultivators (*raiyat*) needed to pay agricultural taxes. For this, sophisticated and accurate records were needed, and the volume could be stunning.[57] These documents detailed a number of categories: who paid, when payments were made and, most importantly, who defaulted.[58] Prompt taxpayers were equated with dignity, subjects who glorified a Muslim sovereign. And in a nod to entrenched realities, Faiq understood the powerful fabric of local village society. He advised that it took time to persuade zamindars to reveal their full holdings, knowing full well that their fellow Hindu *qanungo*s and *patwari*s played a mischievous role in helping them shield their lands from the taxman. But the 'system', if it was one, seemed to be effective. This is best seen, for example, in the overall revenues from the Unao District, where the Saxena Kayasthas held significant sway. Under Akbar in 1600, Unao yielded Rs 452,242. By 1855 under the Nawabs it yielded Rs 963,930, a doubling of the overall taxation.[59] Both revenue farming (*ijara*) and direct collection from cultivators (*amani*) were used. It was a flexible system, but it does seem that *ijara* revenue farming increased in prominence over the late 1700s. Some tracts in and around Awadh, for example, grew *shali* rice, which was harvested roughly three months before the normal *kharif* harvest,[60] often around July or August. To further encourage increased cultivation, taxes paid in advance were rewarded with discounts (*takfif*s)[61] on future and current assessments. Overall, this kept the pulse of revenue administration and assessment constant and regular, connecting the court at Faizabad (and later Lucknow) to the rhythms of the monsoon.

Another precolonial insight can be gleaned from the north Indian scribe Chattar Mal. His grandfather Bhakht Mal (born in Thuri Mal) wrote administrative manuals (*dastur ul amal*s) in the time of Emperor Muhammad Shah (1719–48), and Chattar's 'Guide to the Treasury' (*Diwan-i-Pasand*) dates from the 1820s. Mal's *Diwan* was a sophisticated system for accounting and agrarian taxonomy and outlined a whole process of revenue collection that was nuanced, granular in detail and punctuated by paper and procedure. Mal seems to have written this manual for the Company, with the aim of providing a guide to the British Collectors who were fanning out across north India after the early 1800s. It was a complete regulatory guide, offering complex accounts of agriculture, farms, farmers and the laws related to sharing and renting farms. It included methods for calculating the share of each farmer and described the best periods of the year for planting specific seeds. Mal described specifically the methods for calculating harvests (*ajnas-i-mazarah*). This involved regular forms, which had specific tables indicating the net produce of seeds, wheat and eggs. Each good contained a number index (*raghan*), which was used to multiply the different good by its weight. In this sense it was procedural. But the forms were not inflexible. For example, tax collectors (*malguzar*s) were required to make inquiries to cultivators through zamindars about failed or rotten crops, the point being to give as accurate an estimate of net produce as possible and underscore the fairness of the assessment. But there was also a personal dimension. Discussion and consultation, with a significant degree of leeway for local 'sovereignty' via zamindars, characterized the sinews of revenue collection. For example, both district authorities (*sarkar*s) and *malguzar*s were required to engage zamindars to ensure they were not displeased (*narazi*) with the arrangement and the claimed loss. Before the finalized revenue schedule (*bandobast*) (Figure 1.1) could be drawn up, zamindars had to be in agreement (*mouvafegh*) in order to mitigate future disagreements between district authorities and landholders.[62] Since it was one of the most sensitive and contestable dimensions to assessment, the personal interactions mattered. The calculated loss was incorporated into the final rate before taxes were collected. And the terms were usually, at least in many parts of north India, set on multi-year bases. Mal described a regular tradition of revenue contracts based on five-year terms (*bandobast-i-panjsala*).[63] With the vagaries of the monsoon complicating projections for sovereigns, Mal noted a simple solution. If a harvest had suddenly more than a prior year, which would have been written down, then the tax rate could be historicized, based upon the ten-year average. This, in turn, required volumes of paperwork to track and detail historical rates of return.[64] This averaging was, in a way, a narrow preview of the later British obsession with historical 'averages' of agricultural yields.

When it came to the nitty-gritty of enforcing payment, Mal's *diwan* gives us further insight. The Mughal state was characterized by John Richards[65] and Irfan Habib[66] as extractive and centralized. But Mal, like Muhammad Faiq, painted a picture of a system that might have *appeared* centralized but that, upon closer inspection, was revealed to be locally flexible. Mal showed that the teeth of enforcing payment came not through law courts, as it would later under the British, but though the coercive power of community and relationships. Mal noted that when payment was due negotiations between the district *sarkar* and the zamindar would revolve around one of two procedures: advance payment or installment agreements (*kistibandi*). Both were based upon the agreed five-year contract (*bandobast-i-panjsala*).[67] Zamindars were given an incentive to pay the total in advance (*yekja*) through a reduced rate. In a way, the advances were meant to maintain revenue flows to the centre through the provinces (*subahs*). The teeth of this 'system' was also seen when it came to assessing surpluses. For example, at the beginning of a new *fasli* year the surplus was calculated and written down. Small annual surpluses which went beyond the estimated, and agreed upon, yields

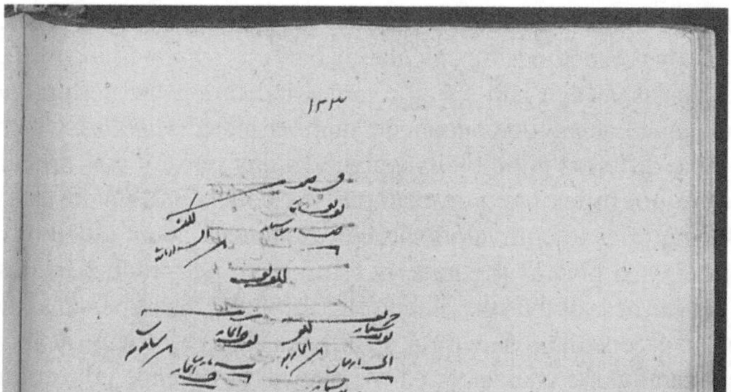

Figure 1.1 A revenue-agreement (*bandobast*) form used to enter contracts between zamindars and *sarkars*, from 'Diwan-i-Pasand', Chattar Mal, c. early nineteenth century. Reproduced with permission of the British Library.

would be compounded into a total sum. After five years these smaller amounts would be rolled into a category of net produce, and the assessment (*jama*) would be based upon this with a with a clear, specific date (*tarikh-i-roshan*) set for payment. Mal described a process that sought to account for every grain by working with the existing local authority in landholding and, when possible, using incentives to encourage advance payments. This was meant to keep revenue flows constant. But, above all, it was interconnected and based on personal relationships.

Military force and collections

Another defining component of eighteenth-century kingdoms' fiscalism was the role of the soldier. Military force was becoming increasingly bound up with the enforcement of revenue demands. In the military-fiscalism of eighteenth-century Indian states, sepoys and *subahdar*s did not merely divert revenue towards military expenditure.[69] Sovereigns increasingly deployed soldiers and artillery to collect taxes. The powers of steel, horses and gunpowder were used by regional and local rulers to coerce cultivators and zamindars into payment of taxes, especially when they fell into arrears. This was particularly noticeable when default loomed. And it seems to have been a trend that extended into west and central India. As Stewart Gordon has demonstrated, the Marathas' territories increasingly used physical coercion to realize payment by defaulters to collect the quarter agricultural tax (*chauth*).[70] In many cases, the solider was the taxman.

This trend can be seen across north India, and Benares is a good example. In the 1770s the Raja of Benares, Balwant Singh, regularly deployed armed soldiers to coerce resistant cultivators to cough up. Singh had to make 'constant use of both Horse or foot to overawe his turbulent subjects and to realize his collections, and making constant circuits through is territories'.[71] This was particularly the case in the contested border regions between Awadh and Benares, where armed horsemen were usually needed to collect taxes. In areas northwest of Benares, often in tussle with the fiscal jurisdiction of the city's Raja, by the 1760s it

> was the constant practice in this and the neighboring country of the Nawab Vizier to carry on the collections by military aid, the habit was so rooted that if the Amils had not a party of sepoys with them, the Zemindars and Ryots were inclined to contemn their authority as thinking they had not the support of the Residency.[72]

Similar trends were seen in Awadh. Muhammad Faiq, who had earlier outlined an interconnected system of revenue administration, had much to say about default and enforcing payments. Delinquents, Faiq argued, needed to be 'persuaded' to pay. Not through law courts, as they would be under the British, but with military force. Faiq suggested the arrival of fifty armed horsemen would be enough to persuade any debtor to pay up.[73] In areas between Bengal and Delhi, the punishment (*tanbih*) to be meted out for non-payment involved soldiers dragging the defaulter to the central government office (*nazim*) in the local neighbourhood (*muhalla*).[74] Of course, this fiscal violence was caste- and rank-sensitive. Lower-caste cultivators were physically transported. Those of higher status and rank could settle behind closed curtains. Yet violence, at the same, was tempered. It was believed that if Collectors (*malguzars*) and not soldiers used force (*shalalat*), zamindars and the *raiyat* would naturally evade or ignore established rules. This would create the problem of 'tax evasion'.[75] It also seems that courts were rarely involved. *Faujdars* mostly issued military threats to defaulting zamindars with the arrival of horsemen and could take a zamindar as collateral (*asir*, equivalent to a prisoner of war).[76] Another eighteenth-century commentator, the Kayastha Shitab Rai, outlined a broadly similar role for violence. He argued that the reckless use of violence to coerce payments forced cultivators into hiding, which, in turn, affected overall assessable produce, ultimately impacting the treasury.[77] It was this accepted reality, that violence was a necessary resort, that would later be derided by the British. It would greatly colour their conceptions of a 'turbulent, violent' era of Mughal 'decline' which could only be overcome through the 'peace' of British administration and legal procedure.

Islamic law and the fiscal state

The late Mughal revenue tradition was firmly rooted in a confluence of Indian agriculture and armed Timuri power. But it was also, upon closer inspection, firmly rooted in Islamic jurisprudence and legal anchoring. Revenue (*kharaj*) for the Mughals, as for many other Muslim-ruled empires in the Safavid and Ottoman domains, was defined in the classical Islamic legal sense as 'taxes on the vegetative powers of the soil'.[78] By the late seventeenth century, the legal and juridical sanctioning of agricultural taxes, in a largely non-Muslim land ruled by Muslims, was of paramount importance. Indeed, one could read Emperor Alamgir's commissioning of the *Fatawa-i-Alamgiri* as an attempt to give Islamic legal interpretation (*fiqh*) and sanction to a widening Mughal agrarian tax base.

India's revenue administration was firmly moored in the Hanafi judicial tradition of interpretation. In spite of its largely Hindu-coloured cultural syncretism, including overwhelming staffing by non-Muslims, the whole system was 'Islamic' in the strictest legal sense. For example, the *jagir* that Robert Clive received from the famed 24 parganas in 1756 was confirmed by the Mughal Emperor according to Hanafi precedent.[79] The Hanafi tradition was already the major branch of Sunni legal thought in north India, and it borrowed heavily from Ottoman legal reforms under Suleiman the Magnificent (1494–1566). A few broader insights can be drawn here. When it came to cultivation, Hanafi law seems to have encouraged the equivalent of 'venture capitalists'. These were the great revenue farmers (*ijaradar* is the most specific term in the Persian lexicon) of the eighteenth century, who increasingly assisted Nawabs and Nizams in cultivating more lands, one of the best examples being Sheo Lal Dube of Jaunpur.[80] They were to be given protections and safeguards to maintain their proprietary rights and were rarely dispossessed of their holdings.[81] Hanafi jurisprudence and the *Fatwa-i-Alamgiri* both say much about default, largely holding that those who fled to evade tax did not lose their rights to the land. They were given protections, and the sovereign could not, legally, seize the land in question. But the ruler could lease it out to a community (*quam*) for a set, stated period or use it for the public good in order to maintain its vegetative and productive capabilities. It was only in the death of a defaulter where this revenue–legal tradition approached anything close to liquidation. Hanafi scholars alluded to the notion that the sovereign could appropriate the lands of a dead defaulter, but it was never clearly addressed.[82] The legal handling of debt seems to have been based partially on religious law (*shariah*). In areas of Bihar the local judge (*qazi*) would often hear cases of default in the 'court of moral judgment' (*katcheri-ye-ghezah*).[84] In this sense, Hanafi revenue law treated questions of default on Islamic principles, seeing it as a moral shortcoming rather than – as later, under the British – a strict legal category divorced from ethical considerations.

Hanafi conceptions of default and its moral dimensions were not only stitched into the fabric of revenue administration and taxation patterns but also into that of landholding, which itself was part of this broader 'system'. Islamic jurists largely framed land and its productive use not as a commodity but as a relationship between individuals, bound together by norms of ethical behaviour (*akhlaq*) backed up by *shariah*. Hanafi law theoretically painted the leasing of contracts for cultivation (*muzaraut*; *patta*) as invalid and against Islamic law. But Emperor Alamgir sanctioned it, seeing it as practical and necessary in lands with such marked agricultural volume and productivity.[85] Hanafi law over the seventeenth century in India also seems to have shifted tax responsibility away from lessors of land and towards tenants and cultivators, which partially explains the hasty British conflation of proprietary rights with tax responsibility – most tragically seen in Bengal after 1793. Though compared with the other great centre of Hanafi scholarship in the Islamic lands, the Ottoman Empire, Mughal India remained legally decentralized. Scholars have demonstrated how after the late 1500s the Ottoman Sultans centralized their fiscal power by slowly chipping away at status of endowed (*waqf*) lands and peeling away at cultivators' right to private property, seen mainly in the 1553 'Book of Custom' (*Qanunnama*).[86] In Mughal India, by contrast, a more regionalized eighteenth century polity emerged, which empowered local elites and revenue farmers. This prevented the rapid fiscal–legal centralization seen in the Sultan's domains. Mughal India, after all, lacked the residual Byzantine heritage to enable such centralization in the first place.

'A moral fiscalism': tempered taxation and default

The late Mughal revenue tradition was relentless and paper-driven when it came to assessing agrarian surpluses to fund its larger military and courtly expenditures. But it was also fairly 'collaborative' and less centralized in its executive decision making than the practice that would emerge under the British. This can be seen in the case of addressing cultivators' grievances. For example, if disagreements emerged over rates of payment or making payment installments (*qist*s), grievances were shared with the local official (*mukhtarkar*, someone with authority to make decisions). They would then would convene a meeting of a village's *malguzar*s and zamindars. It was recommended that this be done in a quiet place, where an investigation could be done collaboratively.[87] Here, we see a revenue tradition that bound various stakeholders into a process that guaranteed the wealth of the sovereign and, to borrow Max Weber's phrase, its patrimonial-bureaucratic nature. Paper made much of this possible. It greased the wheels of an interconnected, personnel-driven method of assessing and collecting revenue, where documents and proof would be shared and assessed. It also served to temper the human relationships between *qanungo*s, *mukhtarkar*s, *qazi*s and zamindars. Testimony was checked against written record with an aim of finding either a discrepancy or a continuation of the *qist*s. But later, under the British, paper's function would be transformed. It would not so much serve as the binding glue between various officials as represent the top-down centralized fiscal authority of the Company state, emanating from Leadenhall Street and extending via Calcutta to various villages across Hindustan.

When it came debt and default of payment, the mid-eighteenth-century traditions possessed a marked degree of fiscal flexibility. The Nawabs of Awadh and Bengal were, as historians have demonstrated, increasingly ruthless in extracting revenue. But at the margins they were also flexible when it came to 'chasing down debtors' and collecting payment. The guidance of Shitab Rai, a Saxena Kayastha with roots in Delhi and Bihar, who navigated the late Mughal and early British periods, tells us much about how late Mughal sovereigns treated debtors. Rai drew upon a not untypical Kayastha experience and pedigree of scribal and administrative service. Rai argued that if the contract for the land (*bandobast-i-mulk*) was not paid within three to four years, barring a complete investigation, zamindars were not to be 'disrespected'. What this meant was that their holdings were to be maintained. But a further investigation (*taftish-i-moffasal*) should follow, which would check the testimony and numerous records from *qanungo*s and *patwari*s. Again, this was couched morally. Forcing zamindars to compel their cultivators to pay up quickly, Rai argued, resulted in poisoned relationships between *malguzar*s and zamindars and weakened the latter's image in the eyes of cultivators. More broadly, the moral reverberations would lead to what Rai called 'bastard-ishness' (*haramzadegi*). And if *malguzar*s could still not collect the agreed rates within five years, then defaulters would have to pay through installments (*qist*s) on terms decided by their zamindars alone. This seemingly propped up zamindars as the local enforcers of fiscal procedure. But it also provided a great deal of flexibility, with the moral character of zamindars being weighed almost equally with regularized procedure and paper. It also operated on the assumption that revenue was most effectively harnessed by maintaining the moral interdependency of a locale, from the *nazim* all the way down to the cultivator.

This human-oriented and interdependent conception of fiscalism was also seen in the treatment of fleeing defaulters. Public orders and warrants (*hukum*s) were rarely issued. It was believed that they took away from the humanity (*insaniyat*) of individuals. Respect for the individual's dignity was paramount, though it obviously varied depending on perceived caste status. Shitab Rai again argued that public *hukum*s did little to actually solve the original problem of payment and that wisdom (*hekmat*) should guide the *mukhtarkar* to talk to the zamindar of the absconder and help make an individual, private arrangement for repayment, all the while keeping it out of the public view. If there was severe disagreement, then the *mukhtarkar* should listen to both the zamindar and the cultivator in person (*ru-be-ru*, or 'face to face').[88] It was only later, under the Company, that the moral component was jettisoned – immediately. The only face later debtors would see was a British magistrate who ruled in legal not moral terms, disregarding an extant concern for the dignity and character of the accused, in a language they did not understand.

The possible liquidation of defaulters' assets also deserves mention. The trend towards liquidation seems to have started in areas upcountry in Awadh after the 1770s. But it was, it should be stressed, only piecemeal. On the whole, proprietary rights were rarely auctioned off to fulfil revenue demands. As with confronting debtors, the whole process was moored in a moral harbour. Poor zamindars who did not promote cultivation affected the entire neighbourhood (*muhalla*). When zamindars could not meet revenue demands, *malguzar*s were allowed to give the rest of the revenue contract (*bandobast*, 'bound and closed') to partners or people who would inherit lands through the traditional patrilineal method, namely sons or other male relatives. They would all meet to discuss and determine who would be the most worthy candidate to take on the *bandobast*. The old zamindar did not lose his proprietary rights like he would later under the Company in east India, but the responsibility of the *bandobast* would be taken on by a worthy male relative. This created an incentive, Shitab Rai again argued, to extend cultivation by instilling fear (*khauf*) in lazy landholders to promote agriculture and the moral authority and leadership of the zamindar (*umarat-i-zamindari*) within a family. Families could not be dispossessed of their lands, for it was argued that the treasury (*khazaneh*) only benefits if payments are made. The whole aim was to work around existing actors and families to get the payments, not to replace them with more 'creditworthy' candidates. Of course, in theory and in practice, lands could be sold. But on the whole they were largely sold by the zamindars themselves and not through compulsion by the state.[89] This was famously jettisoned in Bengal after the 1793 Permanent Settlement and, as we will see, punctuated the first few generations of revenue administration in the Doab after 1803.

The Mughal 'paper raj'

While the late Mughal revenue traditions were based upon personal and moral pillars, it was paper that held them together. Thousands of documents were used in assessment, confirming payment and providing written receipts. Here, again, Shitab Rai gives us a peek into the paper intensity of revenue collection. In Bengal and Bihar revenue contracts (*bandobasts*) that had stipulated collections *had* to be written down. There was no room for oral testimonies and recollection. This was based on the reasoning that a final decision (*faisala*) over adjustments could only be mutually agreed upon if there was paper (*kaghaz*). *Bandobast*s were only legitimate if they were written down; the value of orally committed contracts was seen as empty. Paper was needed to determine the schedule of instalments (*kistbandi aqsat*s) to ensure that tax rates were based on written laws. This again was seen through a moral rather than a legal prism, for it was meant to avoid unnecessarily punishing people.[90] Revenue reports usually started from the first day of the Fasli year, and if there was disagreement over how long a contract was, the *malguzar* was to consult with zamindars and *mukhtarkar*s by drawing upon five years' worth of prior records.[91] Here, we can see that eighteenth-century fiscalism already possessed a slight degree of 'archival depth'. So paper, aside from serving a bureaucratic-state function, also served a moral purpose: to prevent unnecessary shaming or individuals via spurious claims. Paper had a moral as much as an administrative and technical dimension.

Paper also buttressed various other aspects of revenue administration in the late Mughal fiscal state, from registrars to the treasury. The amount of paperwork stitched into the fabric of revenue administration was remarkable. Every treasury (*khazaneh*) of a province had to have a letter writer (*kaghaznavis*), who would check daily to see what liquid cash was available and write a daily report.[92] *Qanungo*s, the registrars of a pargana, wrote and maintained the *kistbandi* agreements that bound sovereigns and subjects in paperwork.[93] This not only created hundreds of pages of documentation but also gave *qanungo*s, in particular, privileged knowledge and a repository of the adjudicating papers within a locale. Defaulters also generated volumes of paperwork. They often had to give their residential locations to the neighbourhood office (*daftar-i-muhalla*) and would be visited daily by the police chief (*darogah*), who then filed written reports. Defaulters who lived further into the mofussil were contacted by the zamindar's representative (*vakil*). Within three to four days *qanungo*s wrote down all the details of the defaulting claim, including payments made, payments due and the circumstances of the individual that should be considered. Here, we can ascertain some early trends in eighteenth-century India that would later be exacerbated by British administration. Often enough, the acquittal or arraignment of a defaulter hinged upon the paperwork of a subordinate paper manager, who, as a lettered few among unlettered masses, could often wield life and death over cultivators. As late as the 1740s the Mughals kept these subordinates truly subordinate. But the British, as we will see, empowered these local officers greatly, much to the wistfulness of observers such as Ghalib and Tabatabai.

Conclusion

This chapter has outlined the broader contours of revenue administration and taxation in late Mughal India. It has argued that pen and paper were made a permanent feature of Indian governance under the Mughals, and that this connected broader realms of experience, from the *maktab*, where Persian was learned by Hindus and Muslims, to the ink and paper-producing microeconomies of north India, Kashmir and the Punjab plains. By the mid 1700s, the increasing tabulation and documentation of receipts and management was a marked feature of statecraft, which facilitated the swelling coffers of regional states. Awadh, like the Maratha territories, Bengal and Ranjit Singh's Punjab, was moving towards more paper-based forms of political authority via increased agrarian taxation. War and horses were not only motivating factors for this increased fiscal scope but were increasingly used to extend a kingdom's fiscal reach. At the same time, the late Mughal and eighteenth-century 'systems' were fairly flexible and moored in moral conceptions of interdependence, all the while backed up by paper and pen. So by the mid 1700s the various revenue traditions of India, while not standardized, do seem to have moved towards greater uniformity in terms of 'materiality', paper-ness and overall levels of taxation and administrative practice. It was already moving in a direction which the British would later take it further.

Some more general observations can be made about how revenue was collected in eighteenth-century precolonial India. First, it seems the late Mughal traditions of revenue administration were already moving towards greater assessment and its concomitant policing, though not through legal mechanisms. Later on, the British would shift defaulters and debtors away from the policing channels of the *daroga* and *sipahis* and funnel them through legal procedure and its numerous codes, *vakils* and magistrates. Second, while paper was undoubtedly important as the glue of the Mughal *kaghaz raj*, it seems that revenue administration was equally bound by personal relationships. It was later, under the British, that it would be 'depersonalized' thought standardized paperwork, regulation, agrarian taxonomy, and legal procedure. And by the 1730s the scribes and pensmen who were the intermediaries between courtly authority and the cultivating masses played a significant role in upholding fiscal authority. The following chapter proceeds to examine this looser group of scribes and pensmen, who were not only the administrative mortar of this emerging fiscal edifice but also provided the paper and factual sanction for the early origins of the British empire in India.

Notes

1 I. Habib, *The Agrarian System of Mughal India* (Delhi, 1999).
2 See the recent work by A. Moin, *The Millennial Sovereign* (Berkeley, 2014).
3 M. Alam, 'The pursuit of Persian', *Modern Asian Studies* 32, 2 (1998), pp. 317–49
4 B. Messick, *The Calligraphic State: Textual Domination and History in a Muslim Society* (Berkeley, 1993); P. Rahman, *Islamic Calligraphy in Medieval India* (Dhaka, 1979); A. Siddiqi, *The Story of Islamic Calligraphy* (Delhi, 1990); Habib, *The Agrarian System of Mughal India*; J. Sarkar, *Mughal Administration* (Patna, 1925), pp. 71–162.
5 Rahman, *Islamic Calligraphy*, p. 43; Siddiqi, *The Story of Islamic Calligraphy*; Tritton, *Materials on Muslim Education in the Middle Ages*; Messick, *The Calligraphic State*.
6 A. Ali, *Making of India* (London, 1925), p. 87.
7 Siddiqi, *Islamic Calligraphy*, pp. 81–2.
8 Sarkar, *Mughal Administration*, pp. 71–5.
9 Ibid., p. 8.
10 M. Spears, *The Wasikadars of Awadh: A History of Certain Nineteenth Century Families of Lucknow* (New Delhi, 2008); M. Fisher, 'The imperial court and the province: a social and administrative history of pre-British Awadh, 1775–1856', unpublished PhD dissertation, University of Chicago, 1978; A. Rahit, *Tarikh Badshan Begam*, M.T. Ahmad, trans. (Allahabad, 1938).
11 V. Raghuvanshi, *Indian Society in the Eighteenth Century* (New Delhi, 1969), p. 4.

12 H. Court, trans., *Araish-i-Mahfil* ('The Ornament of the Assembly') (Calcutta, 1882), pp. 71–9; Raghuvanshi, *Indian Society*, p. 4.
13 DrVibhuti Rai, Raj and Naheed Verma, Lucknow, 2004, 2006, 2008, 2009; L. Narayan, *Ruqat-i-Lachmi Narayana* ('Letters by Lakshmi Narayana') (Lucknow, 1880).
14 G. Khan, *History of Islamic Education in India and Nadaut ul-ulama* (Delhi, 2004), p. 40.
15 S. Jafar, *Education in Muslim India* (Peshawar, 1936), pp. 146–7.
16 Raghuvanshi, *Indian Society*, p. 191; R. Martin, *The Indian Empire* (London 1858), Vol. I., p. 185.
17 N. Haider, 'Norms of professional excellence and good conduct in accountancy manuals of the Mughal Empire', *International Review of Social History*, 56, S19 (2011), pp. 263–74; A. Mukhopadhyaya, *Reform and Regeneration in Bengal* (Calcutta, 1968), p. 7.
18 J. Nanavaty, *Educational Thought* (Pune, 1973), Vol. I, p. 207
19 Sri Sampal and Dr Vibhuti Rai, Raj and Naheed Verma, Sri Ram Advani, Lucknow, 2004, 2006, 2008, 2009. Family Mss. of Sampal Rai, 'Sri Ganeshya Nam', 1915, in author's possession.
20 W. Sleeman, *Ramblings and Recollections of an Indian Official*, (London, 1844), Vol. II, pp. 132–3.
21 M. Weber, *Economy and Society: An Outline of Interpretive Sociology*, G. Roth, C. Wittich, trans. (Berkeley, 1978), pp. 1013–38.
22 Rahman, *Islamic Calligraphy*, pp. 16–21.
23 S. Dale, *Indian Merchants and Eurasian Trade, 1600–1750* (Cambridge, 1994), pp. 130–1; also see S. Levi, *The Indian Diaspora in Central Asia and its Trade, 1550–1900* (Leiden, 2002).
24 A. Soteriou, *Gifts of Conquerors. Hand Papermaking in India* (Ahmedabad, 1999), pp. 38–50.
25 Ibid., pp. 146–9.
26 D. Hunter, *Papermaking: The History and Technique of an Ancient Craft* (New York, 1943), p. 76; M. Law, *Promotion of Learning in India during Muhammedan Rule* (London, 1910), pp. 189–90; J. Sarkar, *The India of Aurangzib* (Calcutta, 1901), p. 95.
27 A. Dubois, *Description of the Character, Manner and Customs of the People of India*, (London, 1817), Vol. I, p. 382.
28 V. Podder, *Paper Industry in India* (New Delhi, 1979), p. 4; also see N. Premchand, *Off the Deckle Edge: A Paper-making Journey through India* (Bombay, 1995).
29 Soteriou, *Gifts of Conquerors*, p. 45.
30 W. Carey, 'Remarks on the state of agriculture in the District of Dinajpur', *Asiatic Researches* (London, 1811), pp. 21–2.
31 M. Martin, *The History, Antiquities, Topography and Statistics of Eastern India* (London, 1838), Vol. I, p. 333.
32 Ibid.
33 Soteriou, *Gifts of Conquerors*, p. 60.
34 Martin, *The History, Antiquities, Topography and Statistics of Eastern India*, Vol. I, p. 334.
35 Ibid.
36 Ibid., Vol. I, Appendix 43.
37 Hunter, *Papermaking: The History and Technique of an Ancient Craft*, 80fn.
38 Ibid., p. 73.
39 Rahman, *Islamic Calligraphy*, p. 17.
40 Ibid., pp. 17–19.
41 Q. Craufurd, *Sketches Chiefly Relating to the History, Religion, Learning and Manners of the Hindoos* (London, 1817), pp. 151–2, fn.
42 H. Garnett, ed., trans., *The Punjab One Hundred Years Ago* (Lahore, 1975), p. 69.
43 Ibid.

44 See Chapters 2 and 3.
45 Dubois, *Description of the Character, Manner and Customs of the People of India*, Vol. I., p. 385.
46 Craufurd, *Sketches Chiefly Relating to the History, Religion, Learning and Manners of the Hindoos*, pp. 151–2fn.
47 J. Sen, *History of Elementary Education in India* (Calcutta, 1933), p. 5.
48 Martin, *The History, Antiquities, Topography and Statistics of Eastern India*, Vol. III, p. 707.
49 Habib, *The Agrarian System of Mughal India.*
50 W. Hunter, *Readings in Indian History* (Calcutta, 1891), p. 62.
51 S. Chabra, *Advanced Study in the History of Modern India* (1707–1813) (New Delhi, 1971), Vol. I, p. 228.
52 J. Sarkar, *Bihar and Orissa during the Fall of the Mughal Empire* (Patna, 1932), p. 57.
53 S. Gupta, *Agrarian Relations and Early British Rule in India: A Case Study of the Ceded and Conquered Provinces* (New York, 1963), p. 26.
54 W. Crooke, *The Popular Religion and Folk-Lore of Northern India* (Westminster, 1896), Vol. II, p. 311.
55 R. Barnett, *North India between Empires: Awadh, the Mughals, and the British, 1720–1801* (Berkeley, 1980).
56 Rahit, *Tarikh Badshah Begam*, p. 1.
57 M. Faiq, *Insha-ye-Faiq* (Lucknow, 1880), p. 19.
58 Ibid.
59 C. Elliot, *The Chronicles of Oonao* (Allahabad, 1862), p. 104.
60 Sarkar, *The India of Aurangzeb*, p. 34.
61 'Full statement of the mode of collecting revenue and administering justice, by Shitab Rai and the Qanungos, pursuant to an Order of Council', 24 January 1773, Mss. ADD. 6586, Fol. 4, IOL.
62 OR. 2011, Fol. 111, Chatar Mal, 'Diwan-i-Pasand', n.d., early nineteenth century, Fols. 15–16, IOL.
63 Ibid. Mal called revenue 'gold' (*zar*), perhaps underscoring the importance of revenue to eighteenth-century kingdoms.
64 OR. 2011, Fol. 111, Chatar Mal, 'Diwan-i-Pasand', n.d., early nineteenth century, Fols. 15–16, IOL.
65 J. Richards, *The Mughal Empire* (Cambridge, 1996).
66 Habib, *The Agrarian System of Mughal India*, p. 331.
67 OR. 2011, Fol. 111, Chatar Mal, 'Diwan-i-Pasand', n.d., early nineteenth century, Fols. 15–16, IOL.
69 C.A. Bayly, *Rulers, Townsmen and Bazaars: North Indian Society in the Age of British Expansion, 1780–1870* (Cambridge, 1983).
70 S. Gordon, *Marathas, Marauders and State Formation in Eighteenth Century India* (Delhi, 1994), p. 41.
71 A. Shakespear, *Selections from the Duncan Records*, Vol. I, p. 45.
72 Ibid., pp. 44–6.
73 M. Faiq, *Insha-ye-Faiq* (Lucknow, 1880). This was a reference to traditional forms of Persian statecraft, taken from the writings of Sadi. I am grateful to Nandini Chatterjee for pointing this out.
74 'Full statement of the mode of collecting revenue and administering justice, by Shitab Rai and the Qanungos, pursuant to an Order of Council', 24 Jan 1773, Mss. ADD. 6586, Fol. 56, IOL.
75 'Opinion of some natives, not names, on the rules to be observed for a proper collection of revenue in Bengal, in 24 articles', Mss. ADD. 6586, Fol. 3, IOL.
76 'Full statement of the mode of collecting revenue and administering justice, by Shitab Rai and the Qanungos, pursuant to an Order of Council', 24 Jan 1773, Mss. ADD. 6586, Fol. 69, IOL.

77 Ibid., Fol. 3.
78 N. Baillie, *Muhammadan Laws on Land Tax from the Futawa Alumgeeree* (London 1853), p. 25.
79 The 24 parganas were then bequeathed over in perpetuity to the Company in 1756, worth Rs. 222,958. See Baillie, *Muhammadan Laws on Land Tax from the Futawa Alumgeeree*, p. 47.
80 For more on Dube, see Bayly, *Rulers, Townsmen and Bazaars: North Indian Society in the Age of British Expansion, 1780–1870*, pp. 168–9; B. Cohn, 'The initial British impact on India: a case study of the Benares region', *Journal of Asian Studies*, xix (1960), pp. 418–31.
81 Baillie, *Muhammadan Laws on Land Tax from the Futawa Alumgeeree*, pp. 96–105.
82 B. Johanson, *The Islamic Law on Land Tax and Rent* (London, 1988), p. 83.
84 'Full statement of the mode of collecting revenue and administering justice, by Shitab Rai and the Qanungos, pursuant to an Order of Council', 24 Jan 1773, Mss. ADD. 6586, Fol. 62, IOL.
85 Baillie, *Muhammadan Laws on Land Tax from the Futawa Alumgeeree*, p. 108.
86 Johanson, *The Islamic Law on Land Tax and Rent*, pp. 85–8.
87 'Opinion of some natives, not names, on the rules to be observed for a proper collection of revenue in Bengal, in 24 articles', Mss. ADD. 6586, Fol. 2, IOL.
88 Ibid., Fol. 5.
89 Ibid.
90 Ibid., Fol. 2.
91 Ibid.
92 'Full statement of the mode of collecting revenue and administering justice, by Shitab Rai and the Qanungos, pursuant to an Order of Council', 24 Jan 1773, Mss. ADD. 6586, Fol. 56, IOL.
93 'Opinion of some natives, not names, on the rules to be observed for a proper collection of revenue in Bengal, in 24 articles', Mss. ADD. 6586, Fol. 55, IOL.

2 The pensmen and scribal communities of Hindustan

Introduction

This chapter shifts to explore the longer administrative and cultural histories of various north-Indian Kayastha families up until the late 1700s. It examines their origins and how and why they were attracted to Mughal service. It outlines how they partly became an 'Islamized' Hindu pensmen group through mannerisms, dress, names and shared circles of association. It argues that Kayasthas, whose 'twice-born' (*dvija*) caste status was always contestable, were vaulted into crucial, and sometimes higher administrative, positions under the Mughals. This enhanced the reach and indeed ability of the Mughals and eighteenth-century successor states to tax, assess and document their domains. It looks briefly at some better-known examples, such as Raja Shitab Rai. But it mainly examines a number of smaller, less well-known families, such as the Lal pensmen of Bihar country and the Srivastava Kayasthas of the middle Doab. The chapter further enriches our understanding of late-Mughal revenue traditions in the transition to colonial rule by specifically examining the broader range of Hindu pensmen and scribes across the Doab and Bihar and their cultural, service and spiritual histories. Bhavani Raman has recently suggested a larger role for subordinate writers and paper managers in the transition between empires in south India.[1] In the Doabi north, by contrast, it could be argued that Hindustan's scribes played an even greater role in the emergence of the colonial state and its fiscal tentacles than in the south. The chapter proceeds to examine their broader cultural, service and spiritual experiences in the context of seventeenth- and eighteenth-century north India and injects a social and cultural history into our understanding of the preconditions for British colonial state formation.

Kayastha marriage patterns

Kayasthas are one of the more understudied social groups in South Asia. Kayasthas trace their lineage from the twelve sons of King Chitragupta, the Hindu god and 'recording angel'[2] assigned with maintaining a record of humankind's deeds in life. Chitragupta was seen as the son of Brahma, and his body (*kaya*) was adopted as a collective name for the recording god's progeny. Brahma was overwhelmed with keeping records of humanity's credits and debts, and Chitragupta became the record keeper of humanity. He was seen as the equivalent of a 'secretary who took down the proceedings of the trials'[3] of Rajas and courts. Chitragupta also played an eschatological role. At the end of days, he was to read from the book in which Yama (the lord of hell/purgatory) had recorded all the good deeds and misdeeds of all humans (*agrasandhani*) to determine everyone's fate. It was to be read out loud from a register in Chitragupta's keeping.[4] He was, in a way, the accountant's deity. Kayasthas claim descent from this eschatological figure and, by extension, the skills he possessed. For example, in the *Yajnavalkasmiriti* (c. third to fifth centuries CE) and the *Vishnusmriti*, Kayasthas are described as record keepers and accountants.[5] And a broader correlation of evidence suggests that Kayasthas traditionally have been a looser group of writers, scribes and recorders of accounts, news and affairs of the sovereign.[6] By worshipping Chitragupta as their ancestor, Kayasthas have also maintained one of the few 'ancestor-worshipping' traditions within broader Indian tradition.

Kayasthas, it must be stressed, are not a uniform, cohesive group. They possess marked regional variations and differences. The first group is the Bengali Kayasthas. Largely seen as an offshoot of the main north Indian Kayasthas, they claim lineage from migrations into Bengal from the ancient capital of Kanauj at the request of Hindu kings (900s) to settle the countryside. These Kayasthas took on the more well-known names of Ghosh, Mitra and Dutt. Over time they fashioned themselves as a Gaur subdivision of a broader Kayastha group, who claimed north Indian origins.[7] A second, though smaller, group of Kayasthas are found in Maratha country and parts of the Deccan south. These are the Chandrasenia ('Prabhu') Kayasthas,[8] who claim descent from the great Kshatriya warrior Chandra Sen. In the Deccan, similarly, the Kayastha scribes and clerks who worked for the Nizam's administration after the 1740s were self-styled 'Prabhus'.[9]

But the most numerous group, and indeed the one most relevant to our present study, is that of the great north Indian Kayastha families. They claim the most direct lineage from the sons of Chitragupta (*Chitraguptavansi*) (Figure 2.1). The north Indian Kayasthas are divided into twelve subgroups, reflecting King Chitragupta's marriages to Devi Nandini and Devi Shobavati, which gave the north Indian Kayastha branches their geographic and occupational diversity. The Mathur, Gaur, Bhatnagar, Saxena, Ambhastha, Nigam, Karan and Kulshretha subgroups all claim descent from Devi Shobavati, while the Srivastava, Suryadhvaj, Valmiki and Asthana families all claim descent from Devi Nandani.

More so than their east and west relations, the north Kayasthas were largely employed as scribes, paper managers and lower administrators, from early Hindu kingdoms up to the Muslim conquests of north India. The Prabhus of the west and the Bengali Kayasthas were relatively more prominent in commerce and trade than the north Indian Kayasthas. For example, north India Kayasthas wrote the eulogies of kings (*prasastis*) for Hindu rajas before Turkic rule.[10] But before the 1200s they seem to have been largely outnumbered by Brahmins at the courts of Hindu kings. This was because of the ritual affirmation that Brahmins provided, plus Brahmanical literacy in the arts, philosophy, statecraft and the puranic cosmologies of broader Indian tradition.[11] Over the centuries Kayasthas' occupational histories largely revolved around various forms of paper-oriented service. But this service was not dharmic in orientation. It was more practical and procedural, involving copying, notation and collation. This was largely because Kayasthas were, crucially, not significant landholders. They therefore placed a high value on education as a means to service and livelihoods. One Bhojpuri saying forewarned that 'the education of a Kayastha child is either literate or dead' (*kayastha ke bachha Padha Bhala, ya Mara Bhale*).[12] As a consequence, practical, vocational learning was, figuratively and literally, a means of survival. Employment and service were crucial for Kayasthas and their identity, as they were, to use Edward Blunt's terminology from the 1940s,[13] one of the 'functional castes' of India. Clerical employment over centuries became a fashioned part of Kayastha identity, so much so that other scribal groups who competed with them were seen as 'interlopers'.[14] The world of commerce was therefore seen as an affront to their identity, for 'trade and industry [were] quite foreign to their mind'.[15] The skills and service of the pen, with its remunerative employment and loose association with administration, became a common thread for diverse Kayastha subgroups across the Doab and north India.[16] In many ways they 'lived by the point of [the] pen'.[17] To later observers such as John Malcolm,

Figure 2.1 King Chitragupta (*Sri Chitragupta ki Maharaj*) and his 12 sons, from whom the north Indian Kayastha sub-braches trace their lineage. On the left are the offspring families, Srivastava, Nigam, Kulshretha and Suryadhvaj, while on the right are the offspring of the Mathur, Karan, Saxena, Gaur, Asthana, Ambhastha, Bhatnagar and Valmiki. Reproduced with permission of Gerard Slothouwer.

Kayasthas 'all assert that their origin was coeval with the creation of letters: that they were created to be intelligent, not a laboring class, and they in consequence deem themselves to be devoted to learning'.[18] As Ronald Inden has demonstrated, the combination of ink, pen and paper with human bodily substance defined this *jati* as Kayastha or a writer (*lekha*) by occupation.[19] Pen, paper and service were intimately part of a Kayastha identity, not as a caste category but as a functional group of pensmen and scribes across Bengal, Bihar and the Doab.

Within the traditional caste hierarchies of India, Kayasthas occupied a somewhat unique if not ambiguous position. They ranked with Brahmins in terms of literacy but were considered ritually lower. Most Kayasthas did not wear the sacred thread (*suta*) indicative of ritually clean, or twice-born (*dvija*), status. Only the Srivastava Kayasthas seem to have donned it more regularly.[20] Kayasthas primarily focused on vocational-based literacy, such as accounts, writing and paper-management in the vernacular and court languages. They therefore commanded a great deal of importance in society due to their practical skills, which were vital to any Indian sovereign. For in a society where the literate were few and far between, Kayasthas were noticeable for their fairly cohesive paper-oriented literacy and long histories of scribal service. And while they never commanded similar social worth and standing, Kayasthas were more numerous and visible than the Brahmins of the Doab, especially in courts and in the presence of kings. Kayasthas do appear as a caste category in Abul Fazl's famed *Ain-i-Akbari*, where they are described as managers and record keepers of indispensable quality.[21] But their identity before the late nineteenth century is probably best understood as a *functional* group rather than as a caste based upon descent and *varna*-defined origins. Still, Kayasthas attracted the scorn of some Hindu kings and pre-Muslim rulers for their paper mastery and for what was possible with the power of the pen. Kalhana's twelfth century 'The Rivers of Kings' (*Rajataranagini*) details a whole slew of accusations against Kayasthas by the famed Kashmiri king Uchala. He railed against 'the ungrateful Kayastha [who] when he has become powerful destroys everything', and compared them to 'low-bred horses [and] persons possessed by goblins'.[22] In an echo of some later Muslim and British observers, Kayasthas' paper mastery and skills had already attracted a scorn for the passive–aggressive power exercised through the pen.

Kayastha subgroups tended to reside in certain areas of Hindustan and Bihar (Figure 2.2). Karan Kayasthas, for example, were found mostly in Bihari country, while the Kulshatras were concentrated around Rohilkhand. The Srivastavas were found mainly around the central and east Doab, and the Asthanas around Lucknow and its immediate southern regions. The Bhatnagars were largely found around Delhi, Muzzafarnagar and Haryana and the Punjab regions, and the Mathurs largely around Agra. The Ambastha Kayasthas, meanwhile, were concentrated around Jaunpur and the Awadhi regions. The Gaurs were in lower Bihar and west Bengal country, while the Saxenas were concentrated in regions such as Unao, Etawah and Fatehpur, where they generally held the status of wealthy, though smaller, landowners.[23]

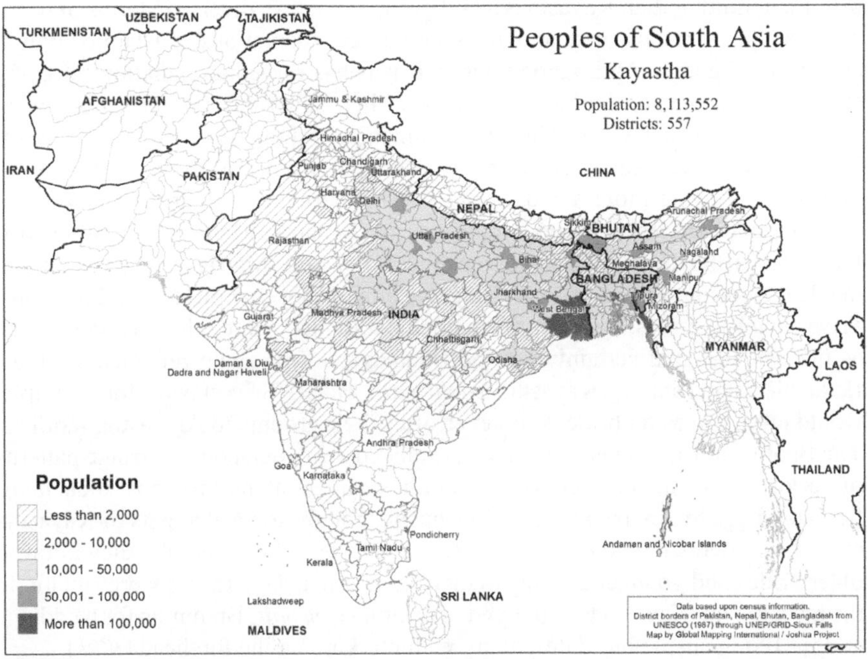

Figure 2.2 Demographic distribution of Kayasthas in South Asia.

Within the 12 Kayastha subgroups there were marked variations in ritual practice, cleanliness and dharmic norms. For example, it seems that only Srivastava families[24] and some Mathurs wore the sacred thread (*suta*) indicative of *dvija* status. And for Kayasthas the thread reflected variations in dietary and ritual habits. Those who wore the *suta*, like the Srivastavas, tended to be vegetarian and largely abstain from alcohol. Kayasthas also practised different mourning rituals. Unlike Brahmins, who traditionally mourned a death for 10 or 13 days, Kayasthas largely undertook a 30-day mourning period, which was more common among various *shudra* castes.[25] But there could still be regional variations in ritual. The Suryadhvajs, for example, were largely 'excessive' in their ritual cleanliness, which some attributed to their claimed mix of Scythian and Brahmin descent.[26] Others such as the Bhatnagars and the Ambasthas, who were called 'fallen' (*brasth*) in Bihari country, were mostly meat eaters and took to alcohol, putting them outside the Brahmanical orbit. The Karan Kayasthas were similar. After the 1200s they adopted the traditions of meat eating from their Turkic rulers. Some Kayasthas subgroups shared food, drink and *hookah*, though it seems to have been practised mostly by the Bhatnagars, Nigams and Ambasthas. The Srivastavas, Mathurs and Saxenas were less likely to break bread with other Kayastha subcastes. This reflected an almost unofficial hierarchy among the 12 Kayastha subgroups, whereby the Srivastavas, Mathurs and Saxenas fashioned themslves as 'higher' in status. A few broader conclusions can be drawn from this. First, north Indian Kayasthas as subgroup were very diverse in terms of occupational status, ritual purity and, to some degree, adaptations of Islamic cultural and spiritual norms. And, second, while Kayasthas earned a reputation for being 'Islamized' in outward culture and speech, their subgroup categorizations were largely distinguishable according to Brahmanical standards of ritual and 'cleanliness'. While Kayasthas' ritual norms were far from uniformly Brahmanical, they still followed more standard marriage patterns according to the *dharmashastra*s and *Mitakshara* legal traditions of Benares. Marriages between different Kayasthas subcastes were, on the whole, rare. Marriage patterns among the 12 Kayastha subgroups were largely, though not completely, endogamous. Srivastava Kayasthas, for example, tended not to marry into other branches, such as the Saxenas, and certainly not the Bhatnagars. This again reflected an unofficial hierarchy among Kayastha subgroups. Bihari Srivastavas, for example, would take Ambastha brides but never offer their grooms to Ambastha families. The Bhatnagar Kayasthas, conversely, followed the exogamous-marriage patterns of various Agarwal and commercial families[27] in an attempt to boost their families' standings by 'marrying up'.[28] Curiously, though, some elements of Kayastha marriage patterns ran counter to the *dharmashastra*s. For example, they allowed older brides and younger grooms to marry.[29] But marriage rituals were ritually in the mainstream. Kayasthas employed officiating (*purohit*) Brahmins for weddings and for fixing auspicious dates, along with marking on the forehead (*tilak*).

These marriage patterns and unofficial hierarchy were largely shaped by occupational status and reputation. The familial occupations of subgroups mattered. Kayastha *qanungo*s and *diwan*s, for example, were considered 'higher' and more respectable than their *patwari* counterparts farther southeast. Descendants of *patwari*s were seen to have the lowest occupational and hence *jati* standing.[30] This meant that Srivastava, Mathur and Saxena Kayasthas tended to look down upon *patwari*s and the Ambasthas, Bhatnagars and Karans of Bihari country. It was sometimes explicit but often subtle. One folk saying noted that 'Ambastha is fallen, Karan is ridged, but brother Srivastava is the best' (*Ambastha Brasth, Karan Kasai, Sabse Upar Srivastava Bhai*).[31] That a subgroup's relative standing depended upon their positions under current and former rulers meant *qanungo* families saw the standing of *patwari*s, generally, as low status at worst and peripheral at best. Kayastha *diwan*s, *qanungo*s and letter writers (*akhbarnavis*) also largely refused connubial relations with *patwari* Kayasthas.[32] Most Srivastava Kayastha families in Awadh, likewise, refused to have connubial or commensal relations with Kayastha *patwari* families.[33] These families included the Srivastava *qanungo* families in Bakhra in Muzzafarur, and Sedisapur in Dinapur, Sirajpur and Arrah. Bhatnagar Kayasthas, found mostly in the Muzzafarnagar regions, were also seen as less 'clean' than other Kayasthas and as 'more addicted to drinking than other Kayasths'.[34] But there were also traditionally *qanungo*s in regions such as Jaunpur, Mathura and Gwalior.[35] Some Kayasthas converted to Islam, but this was very rare.[36] These later Muslim *qanungo*s and *chaudhuri*s were the descendants of initial Kayastha converts to Islam from the 1200s across north India, in *qasbah* townships such as Bilgram, Jaunpur, Kakori, Pratapgarh, Allahabad and Bareli. But they seem to have been, on the whole, less involved in the sinews of paper management and clerical service. Moreover, Kayasthas rarely married into foreign-born Persian and Turkic families.[37] This meant that the transmission of Islamic spiritual and cultural rituals came through occupational experience and not marital bonds and relations. This might explain why Kayasthas maintained close relationships with Muslims but never married into their families.

A few things can be said of Kayasthas' spiritual orientations. While highly Islamized in diet and speech, Kayasthas were still firmly rooted in the cosmological orbit of broader dharmic traditions. While mostly Shaiavite, Chitragupta was worshipped daily by most Kayasthas, as was Ganesh for good fortune and blessings.[38] It is hard to pin down geographic densities regarding Shaivite or Vaishnavite leanings, but it does seem that Bengali Kayasthas were mostly Vaishnavite in orientation with more of a mix between the two upcountry. The Saxenas and Srivastavas were mostly Shaivite and seem to have consumed meat, while some Shakta Kayasthas, such as the Karans of Bihari country, were known for taking to both meat and alcohol. It does seem, though, that Vaishnavite Kayasthas maintained their vegetarian status, at least in private. But even for these families this was qualified, for the meat they took most regularly was goat flesh, but rarely within the domestic sphere.[39]

Muslim rule and the Indo-Islamic cultural world

The rise of Muslim political authority over much of north India from the 1200s started to draw Kayasthas into broader patterns of paper and subordinate service. The rise of Timuri power after the sixteenth century had the effect of opening new, albeit subordinate roles for these pensmen. The expansion of more paper-oriented government went hand-in-hand with an equal, though less than full integration of various Kayasthas into an Indo-Islamic administrative culture. It could best be described as a medial absorption. Their literate vocations benefited from the rise of more paper-oriented forms of governance, and literate non-Brahmin castes such as Kayasthas (and, to some degree, Khattris) were some of the main service beneficiaries of Mughal rule. With the expansion of Mughal power into north, east and central India, Kayasthas were the first groups to learn Persian systematically[40] (some had been more loosely exposed to it under the Delhi Sultanates). The Gaur Kayasthas started to work for the court of Nasiruddin Mahmud in Delhi in the 1200s[41] and seem to have started settling westward towards Budean after parting with Bhatnagars over refusals to share food. In Bulandshahr and the Punjab a variety of evidence suggests that Kayasthas started learning Persian before the formal establishment of Mughal power.[42] In Meerut, which became a Turkic garrison town after the 1200s, Kayasthas were among the very first Hindus to learn the new language of India's conquerors.[43] As one Indian observer put it, they 'were the first to learn Persian, the language of the Muhammedan invaders of India, and to obtain the posts of accountants and revenue collectors'.[44] Many traced their appointments to the era of Akbar and were encouraged by the Court to learn Persian and enter service.[45] The Srivastava *qanungo*s of Allahabad traced their heritage back to Delhi, whence they came in the sixteenth century in Akbar's time to help extend the management of revenue in Allahabad.[46] Kayasthas in Awadh and the middle Doab, such as the Navreens, Vermas, Rais and Narains, were attracted to the literacy-service opportunities under the Mughals,[47] albeit for rulers who bowed westward and spoke the language of the Shahs.

It was really after Emperor Akbar, and perhaps due to the influence of Raja Todar Mal, that Kayasthas became more heavily invested as subordinate stakeholders in the Mughal revenue administration. Since they commanded extant skills of learning and paper service, coupled with the fact they were not an elite group, Kayasthas provided the subordinate bedrock of procedural employment required to harness agrarian wealth. They also possessed local knowledge of agricultural rhythms and crop cycles. Another factor may have been that the number of Persian administrators (*khwaja*s) was too small and expensive for the Timuri system to function as a military-fiscal state. Many Kayasthas learnt the Persian language from their Iranian tutors[48] and under Akbar's and Todar Mal's encouragement.[49] Kayasthas quickly adopted the courtly language of these conquerors, so much so that, as Abdul Sharar noted in nineteenth-century Lucknow, 'sometimes people would laugh at the Kayasthas' speech'.[50] But their greater numbers and locally based knowledge of yields, crop-planting patterns and local procedure around harvest times enabled them to colour the Mughal revenue state to a great extent by the early 1600s.

Kayasthas largely came to dominate the position of the registrar (*qanungo*: 'of the law/custom). The *qanungo* as a repository of local agrarian knowledge seems to have largely been a result of the reforms of Akbar and Raja Todar Mal after the 1560s. In the local village economy Kayastha *qanungo*s became the cultural and customary interpreters for the sprawling Mughal fiscal administration across the Doab. It seems that the first mention of the name *qanungo* was in the records of Sher Shah Suri,[51] who needed them to show what villages had produced in order to complete the rent-roll (*hastobud*). One of the reasons was their local knowledge of custom as it related to agriculture and various castes, hence the title *qanungo*. The *qanungo* was a subordinate officer who possessed 'an intimate acquaintance with the country'[52] and its agricultural aspects, including grain types, seasonal variations and soil qualities. While possessing local roots in townships and *qasbah*s in north India, Kayasthas were also seem by some – namely Brahmins – as intruders and usurpers who lacked firm local roots.[53] This may have been because they represented officialdom and the Turkic conquerors. The increasing scope of Muslim rule also enabled Kayasthas to earn promotion through travel and postings outside their domiciles (*watan*s). The career of one pensmen, Nik Rai, has shown how some could travel across the Indian subcontinent in a career.[54] Muslim rulers seem to have been partial to Kayasthas, mainly for administrative expediency, even if they were looked down upon as 'half believers'. For the new Turkic rulers, Kayasthas were the 'marked recipients of favor from the Mahomaden emperors',[55] and were considered 'the most trusted of the Hindus during the Muhammadan period',[56] especially as learned Brahmins largely shunned service under India's new rulers. Kayasthas also showed some scorn towards Brahmins, sarcastically noting that Brahmin pride got in the way: '[Brahmins] thought themselves debarred from the

State employment as if by heavenly decree'.[57] In many places east of Delhi, the expansion of the Mughal revenue system and its extended cultivation seems to have allowed many Kayasthas to become modest but not substantial landowners. Some of it was due to practical reasons. In areas such as Unao the Dixit Hindu families converted to Islam over generations and immediately were appointed as *chaudhuris*, who had a much smaller hand in daily, detailed revenue matters.[58] This opened up lower subordinate positions for various pensmen from the Saxena Kayastha families, who were numerous in the small township and came to dominate the position of *qanungo* as late as the 1870s.

On the surface, these pensmen might seem part of what scholars have termed a 'secretarial class'.[59] But they were more than that. While subordinate, they were, perhaps equally importantly, participants in various Indo-Islamic cultural forms. Kayasthas became known for adopting Indo-Islamic lifestyles in terms of food, dress, mannerisms and the lexicon of the court. This was done through their integration in, and colouring of, various service positions via patronage. It was also a by-product of the deeper fiscal penetration of the Mughals into the Indian agrarian economy. Kayasthas, often the only literate and 'fiscally intelligent' scribes standing between Timuri revenue demand and cultivators, were in an indispensable position. But it is important to stress, nevertheless, that Kayasthas still faced a degree of prejudice and condescension in spite of their integration into the fabric of revenue administration. The *ulama*, Muslim nobility and Persian poets considered them 'disloyal, cruel, cheats and extortionates [sic]'[60] for their skills exercising power via paper management. It was well known the 'mischief that a qanungo at the *sarkar* level could create'.[61] Hindu munshis and pensmen had sought-after skills. But they were still considered 'lowly' compared to the Muslim nobility and at the court. Mehta Balmukand, the Hindu munshi of Syed Abdullah Khan, whose family held immense sway at the Delhi court in the 1720s and 1730s, wrote in his 'Story of Balmukand' (*Balmukandnama*) that even though the Hindu pensman was indispensable for Muslim sovereigns, he was still considered a 'humble wretch, impossessed of talent… who picks up the corns from the harvest-heaps of the masters of language'.[62]

These humble pensmen were therefore in a rather precarious position. On the one hand, they were essential functionaries of an expanding, paper-patrimonial[63] regime, which rested its fiscal might upon the ability to tax the countryside more intensely than their Sultanate predecessors. On the other hand, most Kayasthas did not convert to Islam. This kept them from integrating into particular circles of Indian Muslim society, even if it did not keep them out of the networks of association based around the Sufi *dargah* and *pir*. Kayasthas were almost condescendingly necessary for Timuri Muslim rule. One Muslim commentator noted that the Hindu pensman who spoke Persian was a 'neo-Muslim, but still retained [sic] the smell of *kufr* [infidelity] and discord in his heart'.[64] Unless it was a fully fledged conversion, which Ayesha Jalal has shown did little to erase regional, class and caste distinctions among Indian Muslims,[65] some Muslims kept these Hindus at a figurative and literal arm's length.

This limited acceptance by the upper scions of Muslim society was compounded by north India's various Brahmins, who largely looked down upon foreign-born

Muslims and the Mughals as 'barbarians' (*mleccha*s). This seems to have been extended to Kayasthas for partaking in certain customary and cultural features of the Indo-Islamic world. Previously it seems that Brahmins held a large number of posts as advisors to Hindu sovereigns. But the establishment of Persian as a language of legitimacy led many Brahmins to lose their posts – not only were these Turks 'barbarians' (*mleccha*s) but they also spoke 'night languages' (*jamini basha*), referring to the Islamic lunar calendar. In parts of the Deccan and Maratha country Prabhu Kayasthas were even considered *shudra*s by various Konkai and Chitpavan Brahmans.[66] Still, the need for Brahmanical ritual affirmation seems to have largely disappeared with the beginning of Muslim rule in north India. This Brahmanical distancing from Kayasthas also transpired over diet. Kayasthas took quickly to meat eating, often boasting among themselves of their carnivorous tendencies.[67] It is hard to ascertain their carnivorous tendencies before Muslim rule, but it does seem that they took to it more regularly as it became an integrated cultural wheel of the Timuri court.[68] Yet, it must be stressed, this was often only in public and outside the domestic sphere. At home, Kayasthas tended to consume vegetarian cuisine. Yet much of this made no difference. To Brahmins and the eyes of the orthodox, meat eating and taking to drink made them ritually impure,[69] which further muddled their caste status.[70] Some officiating (*purohit*) Brahmins also refused to perform rites for these 'Islamized' Kayastha families.[71] Their Persian skills, combined with their carnivorous tendencies, made them doubly suspect in the eyes of the orthodox.

There were further dimensions to Kayasthas' complex and ambiguous caste status. The *Ain-i-Akbari* may have listed Kayasthas as a 'caste',[72] but compared to later colonial ethnologists and taxonomers it left their origins relatively unexplored. Kayastha lifestyles could also vary regionally. Bengali Kayasthas, for example, were far more 'Brahmanical'[73] in their lifestyles and customs with regard to diet. Bihari and Awadhi Kayasthas, by contrast, took on much more of an Indo-Persian lifestyle though dress, mannerisms, speech, the consumption of goat flesh and a shared affinity for wine.[74] And even though 'Kayastha' would not become a caste category until the later nineteenth century,[75] what was more significant before the 1870s was the functionality of a this looser group of pensmen who identified with Chitragupta and paper-oriented service. Though not framed in nineteenth-century debates, Kayasthas' *varna* status was, even in the Mughal period, difficult to define – whether they were twice-born (*dvija*), or whether they were of mixed Kshatriya and *shudra* origin. But Muslim rule, it should be emphasized, did have the net effect of dislodging a great number of Brahmins from service posts to kings and courts, of which Kayasthas were the prime beneficiaries. This semi-rivalry might partially explain Kayasthas' contested status as *shudra*s, since they 'ousted the orthodox Brahmas, quite unintentionally, from… their Government posts… and incurred their wrath and curses'.[76] This was partially because Kayasthas, as their later progeny argued, were 'wise enough to adjust themselves to the new situation'.[77] Caste, competition and *varna* rank were all factors which Turkic rule and administration largely muted in north India until the rise of linguistic and religious revivalisms by the 1870s.

This was all significant for our purposes here. Kayasthas might have been party to the Indo-Islamic world through service, literacy and paper, but they were never fully fledged members of it. They were in close orbit of the Mughal Court culturally but in its outer rings administratively. And unlike various Rajput families, Kayasthas were never significant stakeholders in the workings of Court. But they do seem to have benefited from more indirect patronage at lower administrative ranks.[78] This further underscored the importance Kayasthas attached to service and literacy. For a group which belonged to neither a Hindu nor Muslim religious elite, and who did not engage in military service, survival and adaptability were paramount. Indeed, one reason why Kayasthas appear to have inserted themselves so well into this Indo-Islamic cultural administration had, again, to do with their broader caste positioning. Muslim sovereigns obviously did not need Brahmanical ritual affirmation. This may have been what allowed Kayasthas to affix themselves to Muslim rule so easily. Muzzafar Alam and Sanjay Subrahmanyan have argued that Kayasthas were on the 'fringe of the Mughal state'.[79] But a closer reading of the evidence suggests that they became crucial cogs in the wheels of revenue administration of the emergent state by the mid seventeenth century, and later for the British.

In parts of Awadh some Kayastha branches more readily adopted outward signs of an almost Islamic spiritual orientation. Often known to many as 'half Muslims', many Kayasthas in Muslim employ adopted fasting during Ramadan and other Islamic festivals (*eid*s), such as *Eid ul-Fitr* and *Eid ul-Adha*. Kayasthas regularly participated in the Shia spiritual calendar of Mohurram and Ashura,[80] and some Kayasthas tied strings to their left ankles like some members of the *ulama*.[81] This can also be seen in some of the more theistic tendencies of various Kayastha groups. One group of Kayasthas, called the Sathnami sect, followed the mid-1700s Daryabad District 'monotheist' Jagivan Das. Das received lavish patronage from the Shia Nawabs and specifically Nawab Asaf ud-Daula.[82] The Sathnami sect propagated a more identifiable theism, which resonated with these Kayasthas and, to some degree, diverged from mainstream dharmic traditions. For example, they buried their dead in the earth like their Muslim neighbours.[83] These Sathnami Kayasthas were found mostly in Faizabad, the old seat of Awadh and an Islamic *qasbah*, where they shared circles of association which revolved around the pen, paper and Persian. Many of these pensmen also became remarkably conversant in the lexicon of prophetic lineage, such as those of Isaac, Jesus and Muhammad, invoking their names in Persian treatises and stories.[84] Imagery of angels as divine beings also seeped into their spiritual outlook and cosmologies.[85] But there was always a limit to this engagement. Many Kayasthas outwardly adopted Islamic ritual and court custom, but their inner spiritual orientations is harder to ascertain. It does seem that numerous Kayasthas spoke of an outer spiritual form shaped by Islam; but inwardly we find a spiritual cosmology still in an Indian orbit and largely dharmic. As one Kayastha, Rau Jaswant Singh, admitted: 'in a way we perform idol worship (*bhut parasti*), though outwardly we are Muslim'.[86]

Figure 2.3 A Kayastha scribe, from F.B. Solvyns, *Les Hindoûs* (Paris, 1808).

Kayasthas were further integrated into a shared experience with their Muslim peers through the forms of learning they pursued. They were exposed to the literary sinews of the Indo-Islamic world though primary schools (*maktab*s), which were a key component in their cultural and service histories. Muzzafar Alam and Sanjay Subrahmanyan have outlined how various Hindu munshis went through a course of learning which culminated in the seminary (*madrassa*), but these were largely scribes who pierced the upper echelons of the Mughal court and administrative structures.[87] For the more 'lowly' Kayasthas, who provided the larger and more substantial undercurrent of subordinate paper authority, *maktab*s were the main source of 'remunerative learning'. *Maktab*s were the equivalent of primary schools, usually attached to a mosque. This was where Kayasthas learned the rudiments of basic Persian literacy through an exposure to the great works of

Sadi's *Gulistan* ('Land of Flowers'), Ferdowsi's *Shahnama* ('Book of Kings'), the *Mirzanama* ('Book of the Gentleman') and the *Amundnama* ('Conjugation of Persian Verbs').[88] Some finished with readings of Maulana Yazdi's *Zafarnama* ('Book of Successes'). Often starting at the auspicious age of four years, four months and four days,[89] they were taught by instructors (*akhunds*) to copy and compose *shikasta* and *nastaliq*. Sometimes they learnt informally at the equivalent of a 'bookhouse' (*kitabkhana*). Writing was taught first, and reading and comprehension came later.[90] Various forms of accountancy (*siyaqi*) were also taught,[91] which complemented the basic accounting skills they were taught at home. Kayasthas also seem to have been a majority in *maktabs*, where they learnt the skills of copying and writing, which were necessary for working in various Mughal departments.[92] Consistently reliable statistics are tough to acquire, but data from the late eighteenth and early nineteenth centuries suggest that Kayasthas were a majority in *maktabs* in areas such as Allahabad, Kanpur, Meerut and Jaunpur.[93] Kayasthas from Lucknow's environs, the lower Doab and Bihar, such as the Navreens, Rais, Vermas and Srivastavas,[94] quickly gravitated towards *maktabs* as a means of entering service. The *maktab*, of course, was the only way through which these groups could learn Persian with any degree of regularity and gain any 'pecuniary advantages'.[95] This rudimentary, though broader, Persian tradition seems to have lasted well into the nineteenth century:

> all the Kayasthas here apply to the duties of their profession, and acquire a knowledge of Persian and Hindi writing and accounts [sic]. Some few of them have studied a little Sangskrita [sic] grammar and the usual poetry of the Persians...but in general they confine themselves entirely to accounts and forms of business, and are great adepts in all sort of chicane.[96]

These learning experiences were, however, qualified ones. Unlike many literate Indian Muslims, Kayasthas did not prioritize a literary approach with emphasis on the great works of Sa'di, Hafez and the great Persian *littératures*. The Mathurs, Saxenas and Lals of Bihar, for example, focused on the more vocational ends of *maktab* schooling; and large number of Kayasthas engaged less with the broader Indo-Islamic traditions of the rational sciences (*maqulat*), philosophy (*hikmat*) and logic (*mantiq*), even if they were familiar with this learned lexicon, which was more the curricular mainstay of the *ulama* and the *ashraf* gentry Muslim classes.[97] Kayasthas received some exposure to the great Persian works, but their Persian language experience seems to have been much more pragmatic. They engaged with the Indo-Islamic world of learning on their own, more vocationally oriented, terms, gaining rudimentary skills in accountancy, reading and basic writing[98] to manage paper, copy and collate. Najaf Haider has recently pointed to a tension that existed within the secretarial service between those masters of letter composition and those of accountancy (*siyaqi*).[99] This does seem to be corroborated by the available evidence. Some lesser Muslim gentry families established careers over generations in the late seventeenth and early eighteenth centuries in gentry service, including families from Bilgram, Sandila and Kakori, some of whom were Sayyids. But overall, compared to Kayasthas, they were far less cohesive in terms of their occupational traditions as revenue managers.

Thus, for Kayasthas, Persian acquired a much more utilitarian meaning and less of a literary value. What compounded this was that Indian Muslim nobles and administrators were less likely to specialize in accountancy (*siyaqi*) and revenue-management skills, though a smaller sliver of lesser Muslim gentry service families and Kayastha converts to Islam did establish such traditions as accountants and paper managers. There was a noticeable gap between Mughal officials who could speak Persian and its poetry, and those who could understand it for the purposes of taxes and fiscal management. Kayastha pensmen seem to have largely gravitated towards the latter – a slightly more utilitarian acquisition of Persian and its cultural universe. For example, it was observed that *chaudhuri*s in the middle and lower Doab, who were mostly Muslim, were not 'being bred to the study of accounts as the Canoongoes were'.[100] Kayasthas were a dominant demographic block when it came to the vocational skills of revenue accountancy. They were the vocational mortar of the whole edifice, while the *Ashrafi*, by contrast, seem to have been more invested in the cultural and religious pillars of this Indo-Islamic administrative culture.[101] Indeed, the late Kumkum Chatterjee has demonstrated that scribal families such as Kayasthas were less vested in the arts, such as Persian calligraphy and poetry.[102] The observations of one eighteenth-century Sufi *pir* offers good insight. He noted that while the *ulama* despised Hindu clerks' influence, Islam's learned and landed were unwilling to fill posts of a more 'worldly' nature. This *pir* noted that the *ulama* were only fit to be *qazi*s and *sadr*s, while the Muslim nobility consigned themselves to the *ghazal, mushaira* and the Court.[103] As one Persian observer put it: 'there are very few letter-composers who know accountancy, and fewer among accountants who are letter-composers'.[104] Kayasthas sometimes aspired to and reached the commanding heights of Islam's poetic and powerful. But they could only rise so far in the circles of Muslim power. Most did not convert to Islam.[105] And combined with their lack of landed, military and religious prowess, this naturally limited their 'administrative worth'. Lucknow under the Shia Nawabs, again, might have been the exception. There were thousands of Kayastha calligraphers in 1780s Lucknow who were masters of the great Persian works of Hafez and Sadi.[106]

The Mughal Empire, it would be fair to say, was always uncomfortably dependent upon the employment of numerous Hindu scribes to secure its sources of agrarian revenue. The joust over whether Akbar's eagle-eyed financial reformer, Todar Mal ('that paragon of Hindu vazirs')[107] was either a Kayastha or Khattri[108] does seem to miss the point. The more well-known Chandar Bhan,[109] who rose from a provincial clerkship in seventeenth-century Punjab to become Chief Secretary (*mir munshi*) during the reign of Shahjahan, also seems to have been the tip of a much larger iceberg. The subordinate hands of literate Hindu paper managers assisted in the reach of a revenue system which characterised Mughal India for most of the seventeenth and eighteenth centuries. They served as subordinate, though critical, managers of paper and accounts. Some literate Brahmins, notably the Kashmiri Brahmins of Lucknow, entered into the Indo-Islamic cultural world and service; but Kayasthas and Khattris, considered 'polluted' by orthodox Brahmin society, became some of the most crucial cogs in the Mughal revenue wheel. Kayasthas found service in the wider Mughal system and used their basic Persian literacy skills as subordinate newswriters (*akhbarat*s), informants, surveyors, registrars (*qanungo*s), secret-letter writers (*khufia navi*s), treasurers (*diwan*s) and in accounting (*siyaqi*). Some even became auditors (*musatufi*), a particularly sensitive position with the possibility of exposing the fiscal maleficence of higher-ups. Under Emperors Shahjahan and Aurangzeb Hindu scribes went on to reach artistic heights in poetry and wrote various administrative manuals (*dastur ul-amal*s),[110] and many of them laboured at the lower level of village intermediary in the sinews of Mughal revenue collection,[111] as Najaf Haider has demonstrated.[112] These Hindus, and their skills of paper-management and accountancy, were becoming increasingly important for extending cultivation, documenting revenue receipts and, increasingly, organizing military finance. They dominated the more lowly tiers of the Mughal revenue system, yet they were indispensable for eighteenth-century regional states' fiscal wealth. The treatise 'Advice on the Art of Governance' (*Mauizah-i-Jahangiri*) by the Persian-born Mohammed Baqir Najim-i-Sani (1690s) was perhaps the most direct manifestation of the growing importance of precolonial pensmen. Not only was patronage of learning and educational endowments a prerogative of Muslim sovereigns, but these lowly 'people of the pen' could be more critical to Mughal authority than the sword.[113] To Baqir, these lowly subordinates were 'pillars of the citadel of empire' (*qa'imah-i-qasr-i-saltanat*). The skills they purveyed – rather than the offices they held – would assist the expanding scope of fiscal authority across Hindustan. Their role in upholding fiscal authority and badgering those responsible for producing its wealth was best summarized as follows: 'they are humble with their masters but insolent to their inferiors'.[114]

In spite of being considered more 'lowly' than the Muslim nobility, and rarely reaching the heights of poetic and stylistic mastery, Hindu scribes' participation in broader Indo-Persian cultural forms translated into shared experiences with Muslims. We can track a few of these. For example, the late-eighteenth-century eunuch of Faizabad, Jawahar Ali Khan, possessed a common bond with Munshi Lakshmi Narayan, which according to Khan distinguished them from the *raiyat*, who were 'no better than cattle'.[115] The Karkari Kayasthas of Bihari country were another example of those who had 'seemingly adopted Islam'[116] in their lifestyles as Persian-literate paper managers, while the Ambastha and Srivastava Kayasthas of the middle and lower Doab were known for spending more time with Muslims than Brahmins. Even Jhau Lal, the Saxena Kayastha who was Asaf ud-Daula's favourite deputy (*naib*), was someone about whom people would 'say he is a Muslim though he bares [sic] a Hindu name'.[117] Kayasthas, particularly in Delhi and the upper Doab townships, acquired a reputation for being 'half Muslims',[118] never converting but exhibiting behaviour and mannerisms that indicated they all but had. They adopted the patterns and rhythms of Muslim cultural life – fasting, Ramadan, Islamic celebrations (*eid*s) and particularly *Moharram* and marching in the *taziah* in Shia strongholds such as Lucknow and, farther south, Hyderabad.[119] Some even, as wistful later-nineteenth-century Hindu reformists noted, spent 'their time [under Muslim rule] studying the wishes and predilections of their employers, or in debauchery and Court intrigue'.[120] Hindustan's pensmen were therefore part of a ruling administrative culture, even if they could only rise so high. If such Indian scribes hit the glass ceiling under the later Raj, these Kayasthas sometimes hit a theological one.

Kayasthas also appear to have adopted Persian and Arabic pen names over the centuries. These adoptions of 'Islamicate' pen names were not mere anecdote, for they enabled them to better navigate, and become partially accepted within, an Indo-Islamic circle of service and literacy that rested to some extent on a shared lexicon.[121] Kayasthas adopted Persian and Arabic pen names to help them navigate the circles of the elite, learned and powerful,[122] even if they rarely converted to Islam (Table 2.1).

Other titles Kayasthas adopted included *Malik* ('chief')[123] and *Dastigar*, *Inamdar* and *Bakshi*.[124] Some even adopted names that reflected their professions passed down through generations (Table 2.2).

Many Kayasthas families adopted the name Rai, which came from the Persian 'grandee' (*Rais*). Kayasthas also incorporated an Islamicate lexicon into their prayers. They replaced the words *Pranam* and *Namaskar* with *Dua* (prayer) and *Salam* (greetings), as one put it, 'more freely than others'.[125] When Emperor Aurangzeb banned the wearing of sacred thread (*suta*) at court, many Kayasthas simply left them at home. Other Islamic elements were diffused into Kayasthas' rituals and spiritual fabric. One example is the 'pen and inkpot prayer' (*qalam dauwat puja*). This *puja*, a veneration of the pen, inkpot and Chitragupta, was symbolic not only of their heritage but also of the technologies needed to maintain family honour, standing, status and, most importantly, steady income and support.[126] The *qalam dauwat puja* was also, importantly, symbolic of the skills

Table 2.1 Selection of various Perso-Islamicate names adopted by Kayasthas

Raizada	'Son of a Rais' or 'Boss'
Umid	'Hope'
Khush	'Beautiful' or 'Pleasant'
Gulab	'Rosewater'
Mukhlis	'Sincere'
Mansur	'Victorious'
Daulat	'Wealth' or 'Power'
Fateh	'Victory'
Khushvaqt	'Beautiful Time/Era'
Ajab	'Of interest; intriguing'
Farhad	'Elation', 'Happiness'

Table 2.2 Selection of Perso-Islamicate names and titles adopted by Kayasthas reflecting profession[127]

Daulatzada	'Son of authority'
Qanungo	'Of the law/custom/registrar'
Daftri	'Office-person'

and materials essential for a group which depended upon the patronage and good favour of sovereigns. These were all bound up with Kayasthas' family status, honour and, most importantly, livelihoods. This was especially crucial when income from landholdings or military service was neither significant not guaranteed.

Sufism, though, was perhaps the primary experience which bound together these scribal groups with the Indo-Islamic cultural world. This was also reflected in the spiritual rhythms of Kayastha families. The Rai Kayasthas of Lucknow, for example, maintained a tradition of attending *qawwali*s at the Sufi tombs (*dargah*s) of Allahabad and Lucknow,[128] which fostered circles of association with various Indian Muslims and a concomitant spiritual culture. Kayasthas tended to gravitate mostly towards the Chisti Sufi circles, though in townships such as Kakori they were involved in the Qadiri and Qalandari orders. Shiva Das Lakhnawi, the author of the well-known *Shanama Munawwar Kalam*, was part of Chisti Sufi circles and the shared experiences in *dargah*s.[129] The Verma Kayasthas of Lucknow also participated in *qawwali*s,[130] while the pensmen Nik Rai maintained circles of association with the Chisti Sufis.[131] These Hindus' participation even extended into the sacred. Some pensmen found themselves managing Sufi religious endowments and shrines. Manu Lal was one such example. During the 1820s Lal was appointed by the Mughal emperor Akbar Shah II as the 'Collector of Wishes' (*Nazr-o-Niyaz*) of the Sufi Shrine of Narnul.[132] This seemingly vested the 'power of the pen' of a Sufi shrine in the hands of a Hindu who was at best 'half-Islamized'. Lal recorded donations and expenditures, managed the general accounts and was party to relationships with Sufi devotees, *pir*s and the experience of the *qawwali*.

In the eighteenth century the expansion of taxable cultivation was achieved by Muslim regional states with the help of Kayastha and Khattri pensmen. *Sayyid*s and Muslim zamindars, who expected, and received, preferential treatment for centuries, were alarmed with the rapacity with which *qanungo*s, *amil*s and *patwari*s could push the envelope of fiscal authority.[133] Perhaps it was this reality which prompted the Muslim reformer Shah Wali Ullah to complain that 'all [of India's] accountants and clerks [are] Hindus...they control [sic] the country's wealth'.[134] But this was, after all, nothing new. At the height of Emperor Akbar's reign eight out of twelve provincial (*subah*) finance ministers were non-Brahmin Hindus.[135] Even Lakshmi Narayan had to plead with his Persian-literate Muslim readership that all the Hindu munshis, *diwan*s, *qanungo*s and *khufia navis* did not, as some members of the *ulama* claimed, represent infidelity to Islam.[136] Safdarjung too had to counter the claims of members of the *ulama* that, with his revenue administration packed with Saxena Kayastha pensmen, he was not unhealthily 'pro-Hindu'.[137]

Other reasons why Kayasthas inserted themselves into the Indo-Islamic cultural and service world with such ease had to do with how their own traditions loosely overlapped with Islamic ones, particularly in the realm of eschatology. Kayasthas' patron deity, Chitragupta, was revered as the register and keeper of all deeds, virtuous and evil, who maintained a ledger which would be opened at the end of times.[138] This bore a resemblance, even if only on the surface, to the Islamic concept of Judgment Day (*Yawm al-Qiyamah*). In the eschatology of Islamic tradition every individual would be held accountable for his or her life's actions in God's court. For Kayasthas, someone needed to write the debits and credits down. Chitragupta's ledger and God's omnipotent, all knowing judgment of every soul were not necessarily conceptual opposites, even if their theological and cosmological wrappings were oceans apart. This may have been another smaller, though affective, reason why Kayasthas fitted so easily into the implicit spiritual undertones of an Indo-Islamic culture. These were religious and spiritual perspectives and experiences which enabled Hindustan's *qanungo*s, *patwari*s and *peshkar*s to become partial members of an Indo-Islamic governing culture. But they were never full members, largely due to their reluctance to convert. Nevertheless, such minor cultural adaptations were not mere window-dressing: they enhanced the reach of a Mughal superstructure which had to accommodate itself to a complex and, to some orthodox Muslims, infidel culture.

The cultural and service histories of Hindustan's pensmen

Let us now proceed to examine some examples of Hindu pensmen who not only wrote in the language of the shahs, but whose writings and experiences give us further insight into their cultural and service histories. What we see from various examples is that while some Kayasthas represented the quintessence of political and moral sophistication via letter writing (*insha*), the vast majority served as functionary paper managers in the Mughal fiscal state and its eighteenth-century successors. It is important to emphasize that Kayasthas tended to cover so many positions in the realm of government service, populating the service ranks from 'that of the war minister to the humble calling of a petty copyist'.[139] Muzzafar Alam's and Sanjay Subrahbrahmanyan's portrayal of Nik Rai's career as a pensman, who could travel and advance in a career, seems to represent a broader trend in seventeenth- and indeed eighteenth-century India.

Munshi Daulat Rai Shauk was a prime example of such a pensman. Shauk's work, 'Treasure of writings and the observance of grammar' (*Jawahir-i-Manzouma va Merat al-Sarf*), gives a rough genealogy of his family and its entry into the Indo-Islamic-service world. Shauk's lineage suggests that families such as his drew upon a tradition of Persian literacy and paper service which reached back into India's precolonial past. Shauk's third removed grandfather was Raja Bhakari Das, a Kayastha who had roots in Bihari country from the early 1600s.[140] Over the next few generations the family learnt enough Persian to work as *farmannavis* ('writers of orders') and in general correspondence for Muslim sovereigns and lords. Later, in the early nineteenth century, Shauk benefited from the patronage of Nawab Muhammad Ali Shah (1837–42) in Awadh, where Shauk wrote for the Department of Correspondence (*Beit ul-Insha ye Sultani*), which was where all confidential orders were drafted and received.[141] The Nawab, as Shauk recalled, encouraged him to write Persian well (*khosh-ghat*), and Shauk wrote manuals for conjugating verbs (*amundnama*) and Persian literacy for Lucknow's and Faizabad's learned in the 1830s. His Persian skills were so well known that his Muslim peers commented on his unrivalled skills and suasion of the words which flowed from his pen.[142] Yet Shauk was not just a literary man. He copied manuscripts (*manqulat*) for the Nawab and also wrote secret correspondence for them and for their intriguing, inquisitive guests based in the British Residency.

A more well-known example is Nawal Kishore. Kishore's navigation of the Indo and Islamic worlds was a prime example of the role pensmen played between empires. Most recent attention has focused on his publishing activities out of Lucknow,[143] but his lineage and broader service history have received far less attention from scholars. Kishore ran in the literary and service circles of Faizabad and Lucknow in the 1820s and 1830s. It would be fair to say that Kishore was an 'Islamized' Hindu pensman who found favour and patronage with the Shia Nawabs of Awadh. His 1869 Persian work, *Allah Kudae'i* ('Allah is the God'),[144] offers plentiful insights into the cultural and service worlds of Hindustan's pensmen. Kishore noted that many Hindu scribes in Muslim employ maintained that God was the greatest authority. But adding a Hindu colouring, Kishore claimed that this was so not because he was infinite in power, but because he undertook the same stages of creation (Brahma), preservation (Vishnu) and destruction (Shiva) as understood in the Puranic tradition.[145] Here, Kishore was locating Islamic interpretations in a dharmic context. For Kishore, there was complete symmetry between God's authority over the world (*hakimayat*) and His footprint in nature. Kishore also revealed how Kayasthas adopted themselves to Indo-Islamic spiritual norms. Many Persian literate scribes repeated the names of God (*zikr*) while continuing the Indian custom of covering the ears and eyes to fully absorb the meaning as if it were a traditional *mantra*. Kishore also composed a teaching guide for Indian Persian which circulated in Awadh and north India. It seemingly served as a 'pedagogical guide' for beginners (*mohbtadion*) learning Persian during the early nineteenth century, and it included numerous local taxonomies of oils, spices, health remedies and salts.[146] Culturally, and in terms of writing taxonomy, Kishore was a prime example of the 'Islamized' Hindu scribe.

Shauk and Kishore, though, were only the latest in a series of proto-bureaucrats who supported the Shia Nawabs and other Muslim rulers between Patna and Delhi. At the Mughal-court level various Kayastha pensmen were stitched into the fabric of fiscal administration. Sri Indragan, for example, served as the chief secretary (*mir munsh*) of Emperor Muhammad Shah,[147] and Muhammad Shah's *diwan* was another Kayastha, Tara Chand Saxena.[148] The predominance of Mathur and Saxena Kayasthas in Delhi was so marked that the capital was called 'a rich nursery of the Kayestha, for the supply of able men to the Durbar of Delhi'.[149] Another example is Situl Das. The Mughal emperor Shah Alam (1761–1805) appointed Das as *Diwan*. As a writer and accountant, he was reputed to have advised Shah Alam how to best deal with the Rohilla chief Ghulam Kadir Khan. He seems to have achieved this by manipulating account ledgers to demonstrate that there was sufficient money to raise a force to put his recently established rival to 'instant death'.[150] Das, who had learned his Persian in a *maktab*, went on to serve as an envoy (*vakil*) to the Rohilla chiefs, where his Persian skills proved useful.[151] More generally, the Saxena Kayasthas of Farrukabad learnt Persian, served as *qanungo*s and *diwan*s[152] and helped extend the arm of Mughal revenue-collecting power into regions such as Sikanderapur and Amritpur.

This Kayastha prominence also extended with Mughal authority down the Doab and into the east Bihari regions. Said Rai,[153] for example, helped settle the lush pargana of Sujapur in Bengal country during the 1630s in Shahjahan's reign.[154] Rai seems to have acquired a reputation, which kept him out of more orthodox Hindu circles, as an 'Islamized' clerk, particularly due to his fondness for goat. But it was really in Awadh where these Kayasthas made their mark. The better-known Raja Tikait Rai was a Saxena Kayastha who was Superintendent of Accounts for Nawab Asaf ud-Daula.[155] Rai wielded considerable influence in some Awadh districts (*taluq*s) and with the Nawab himself. Kayasthas also solidified links between Faizullah Khan, Nawab of Rampur, and the Lucknow Court, facilitating into Rampur the movement of cultivators and creditors.[156] Rai's relative, Hulas Rai, even though he was famed for being 'excessively fond of [little] boys',[157] was a cannily shrewd deputy (*naib*) who commanded much influence in Awadh's accountancy paperwork.[158] He was a 'paper-man' (*kaghaz-walla*) who employed his skills in the increasingly paper-dominated environment of eighteenth-century India. Another example is Ratan Singh. A Kayastha who served Nawab Muhammad Ali Shah (1777–1842), Singh's grandfather had been the *diwan* of Asaf ud-Daula (1747–97).[159] Safdarjang (1708–54) relied heavily upon the services of the Saxena Kayastha, Nawab Rai,[160] who helped Safdarjung document military finance and extend cultivation and assessment in his efforts to consolidate his own regional domains. Safdarjang's head *vizir*, Nawal Rai, served as head of military and civil administration. A Saxena Kayastha, he drew upon a long family history of hereditary *qanungo*s in Etawah to lead, as paymaster (*bakshi*), the fiscal organization of the Nawab's armed forces. Marked by a long family history of service to Muslim rulers, Rai's chief fault was his purported propensity for wine (although he 'drank during the night only').[161] Rai founded the town of Nawalganj, 14 miles outside Lucknow, along with Khushalganj, 4 miles east of the Nawabi city. He was someone who had effectively reached the level of 'executive purview' in the Shia Kingdom. Raja Ram Narain was another liminal figure. A Srivastava Kayastha with roots in Shahabad, Narain was deputy-governor of Bihar and drew upon a lineage of gentry and clerical service. His father served as *diwan* of Zainuddin Ahmed Khan, while Narain served initially as secret secretary (*khasnavis*).[162] This trend of raising assessment and taxation, based on paper records, was increasingly being made possible by such officers. Nawab Sa'adat Khan, for example, used the estimates (*daul*s) of various Kayastha *qanungo*s in the Baiswara region to raise the assessment (*jama*) during the 1730s from Rs 70 lakh to Rs 2 crores.[163] Indeed, the ruthlessness with which these humble scribes could upset the fabric of village society in the 1700s was seen in the substantial agitation against tax rates among landholders and *sayyid*s in pre-1750 Awadh.[164] What we see from a broader view of the historical evidence is that most of these Kayasthas possessed substantial local influence within a broader Mughal and especially Nawabi revenue umbrella.

Khattris also picked up gentry-service positions from the mid 1700s. Their expansion into the Indo-Islamic gentry and literate world was no less impressive than the long-standing predominance of Kayastha clerks. Outwardly, Khattris seem to have been the beneficiaries of larger political changes and fortune in northwest Mughal India. After the Sikh Guru Govind Singh (1666–1708) explicitly condemned idol worship, many Khattris fled east from Punjab and settled in the Doab and Bihari regions.[165] Some of these Khattris with literacy skills picked up bureaucratic posts as *qanungo*s and assistants (*muqqadam*s) after establishing relationships with observant Mughal officials who noted their clerical skills.[166] Many of these Khattris did well in the expansive purview of the eighteenth-century regional India states. Some even served as paper managers in Balkh and northwest Punjab. A celebrated example is Sabha Chand, who became *diwan* of Emperor Jahandar Shah's *vizir* Dhulfaqar Khan. Chand commanded a 'strict administration of finances'[167] and was largely in charge of Delhi's finances, however insignificant they had become. This was no small ascent for a middling clerical Hindu whose ancestors at one point were technically refugees.

Munshi Lakshmi Narayan was another good example of a Khattri pensmen who inserted himself into the Indo-Islamic cultural and administrative world. In his brief history we can gain an insight into how and on what terms this Khattri paper manager navigated the cultural and service worlds of Muslim power. Born in Lahore, Narayan's father was Munshi Rai Ram, who had learnt Persian in a *maktab*. Narayan migrated to an area of Delhi known as *vakilpur* and sought out employment in the 1730s. But his stay was cut short by Nadir Shah's invasion (1739), whereupon Narayan fled to Aurangabad in Bihar, where he made acquaintances with the Kayastha Rai Bahadur Singh.[168] He encouraged Narayan to move to Lucknow and then to Faizabad, where in his third year he mastered the prized and remunerative art of *Insha*[169] under the patronage of the eunuch Jawahar Ali Khan. Khan and Narayan's common identity was literacy,[170] which came from their experiences in the *maktab* and their knowledge of the *Shahnama*, *Gulistan*, and the *Terikh Ferishta*.[171] Narayan penetrated Faizabad's poetic and gentlemanly circles by attending *ghazal*s, and he was able to 'write [sic] Persian with a degree of elegance and freedom so great that he was unequalled in his day'.[172] Narayan also worked in Faizabad's revenue offices and benefited from Asaf ud-Daula's patronage, at Rs 100 per month. Yet Narayan's work was also an indication of the types of literacy which were prioritized. Narayan admitted that his poetic skills were scant, and that his written compilation *Ruqat* was simply a compilation of various scattered histories, statements and word-of-mouth gossip (what he called *khutba-rivaj*),[173] but he rose to fairly influential positions. He controlled who entered the *Diwan-i-Khas* of Safdarjang, and he announced the birth of the future Nawab Asaf ud-Daula of Awadh.[174]

One important reason why these Hindu pensmen were so marked in the lower tiers of revenue administration lay in a minute but significant 'training gap'. Hindu Kayasthas and Khattris combined outnumbered Muslims in most north Indian *maktab*s. While statistic on pre-1700s India are hard to come by, it does seem that *maktab*s, because of their local connections with Sufi shrines, were largely availed of by Hindus who were interested in Persian. As an example, if we look at five different districts of Bihar during the 1770s, before the full emergence of colonial rule, the total number of *maktab*s attracted more Hindus than Muslims (2,100 to 1,500).[175] Similar trends were seen in Bengali *maktab*s,[176] and farther upcountry by the mid to late eighteenth century. In fact, in select regions of the lower Doab by 1800, 711 out of 1,486 students (in 291 *maktab*s) were Kayasthas.[177] Many of them went on to become teachers in these very schools and in positions as *qanungo*s, which effectively became inherited positions, passed down over generations.[178] Even as late as the 1830s in a *qasbah* township such as Budaun overwhelmingly more Hindu than Muslim boys were being educated in local *maktab*s.[179] In Bulandshahr as late as the 1830s and 1840s roughly 1,224 out of 1,813 surveyed *maktab* pupils were Hindu.[180] This, in a way, prefigured Hindus' dominance of English education rolls and subordinate clerkships by 1900.

A few conclusions can be drawn from analysis of these scribes' service histories. First, these pensmen's skills of compilation, cataloguing and collection represented a more practical engagement with political authority. These slightly more procedural and regulation-driven forms of administration had also come to define Indian regional politics by the 1740s. Later on they would be prioritized over poetry and *insha* by the more literal-minded British. Second, we see that Hindustan's scribes had indispensably stitched themselves into the fabric of administration across north India by the 1740s. Seemingly humble pensmen, who 'picked up the corns from the masters of language', had, by the eighteenth century, come to command lakhs, lancers and loyalty. Paper and pen had become crucial tools in the exercise of power in India: they connected the courts and chancelleries of power with the larger Indian hinterland. As the British would find later, these scribes were the key to fiscal supremacy in north India.

The emergence of an eighteenth-century fiscal-paper model

The Mughal Empire functioned most effectively when it was rooted in an Indo-Islamic cultural practice which brought Muslim gentry classes and particular Hindu 'writing castes' within a shared cultural and service experience. This 'balance', if we can call it that, lasted until the first three decades of the eighteenth century. It was after the 1720s that Hindustan's scribes increased their influence and ability to mould the character of regional states' administrations. These Hindus, with their skills of paper management and accountancy, were becoming increasingly important for extending cultivation, documenting revenue receipts and, increasingly, organizing military finance. While they dominated the lower tiers of the broader all-India Mughal revenue system, they became indispensable for more fiscally minded, eighteenth-century states. The positions of the *qanungo* and *patwari*, while on the surface merely subordinate, became crucial transit points between regional kingdoms and agrarian economies. These key intermediaries, and the skills and information they held, not only helped facilitate the rise of regional states such as Awadh but also, by the 1820s, the Company state. They became larger than usual cogs in the wheels of eighteenth-century regional fiscalism. Awadh's, Punjab's and Bengal's state finances had become so crucial that they were, in Henry Moreland's words, the second most important aspect of Indian life after the monsoon.[181] Fiscal mastery had become central to eighteenth-century rule and state formation.

As we have seen, these scribes' integration into an Indo-Islamic administrative culture went hand in hand with the extension of the Mughal revenue machine by the 1730s. By the end of Emperor Aurangzeb's reign (1707), Kayasthas had become part of a Mughal governing culture which was bound by literacy, service and Islamic cultural traditions. More specifically, it was the Sufi and cultural traditions of Islam that served as the entry points for Kayasthas. Much of this was made possible by their experiences in the *maktab*. It was not, it must be stressed, a regularized and formal connection between learning and service, but it was the most direct one. Practical skills, such as *siyaqi*, were becoming exponentially important for the Mughal revenue machine and for more-revenue-hungry, eighteenth-century regional states. It made the tabulation of rent rates (*jama*), the audit of accounts (*bhujarut*)[182] and the general wheels of revenue collection move. By the late 1600s various Kayasthas had converted their skills into traditions of clerical service. They had acquired enough proficiency in using the *wasti* pen, shaped like a snake's tongue, and writing *nastaliq* and *shikasta* to gain positions such as registrars (*qanungo*s), secret-letter writers (*khufianavis*), newswriters (*akhbarat*s), revenue reporters (*jamanavis*), budget/number writers (*shomarnavis*), petition-writers, court readers (*peshkar*s), record keepers concerning capital punishment (*almad*s) and as surveyors.[183] Kayasthas excelled particularly in the art of copying manuscripts (*manqualat*), which by the late seventeenth century had become an almost proto-bureaucratic function for duplicating news reports, illustrated manuscripts and secret political intelligence for an increasingly paper-driven administration. Yet, most importantly, these officers and their skills helped the Mughal revenue machine to pincer deeper into the hinterland. Kayasthas eventually became, over the seventeenth and eighteenth centuries, closely tied to the wheel spokes of revenue management and governance.

North Indian Kayasthas held positions which were largely within the fabric of the local village and lowest subdivision of administration (*pargana*). They constituted what Irfan Habib has termed the 'second layer' of revenue management in Mughal India.[184] Habib's characterization, as we will see, largely holds up against the historical evidence. But these second-tier scribes were, upon closer inspection, perhaps more important than Habib envisioned. The most common positions for

Persian-literate Kayasthas were the *qanungo* and the *patwari*. Kayastha *qanungo*s were usually salaried, drawing upon funds through local *malguzar*s, and often received a cess (*suddoi*), equal to 2 per cent of collected revenue.[185] This gave them an incentive to ensure everything was done to yield full collections, though it is difficult to draw any picture as to how regular this was. The *qanungo* dealt more with the rudiments of revenue collection, land records and paper management, where their basic Persian literacy and copying skills were put to use. And it was here that we see Kayasthas' practical approach to Persian learning bear out in their positions. In terms of numbers, the *qanungo*-ship was nearly always 'held by one of the Kaeith class',[186] and they came to nearly monopolize this position.[187] The *qanungo*s' responsibilities made them a centre of local agrarian and, to a degree, fiscal intelligence. For example, they maintained a village registrar of paper records which included:

1. accounts of every village in a pargana
2. demarcations and annexations of all lands
3. crop yields
4. annual revenue returns
5. records of all revenue payments
6. countersigned receipts of payments
7. registration of government documents.

These were valuable sources of agrarian and fiscal intelligence. In total these documents could number in the thousands, which required organization and management. Also, questions of ownership were important. *Qanungo*s usually owned their own papers, which made them public–private actors. They were not 'government property' (it was only later, under the British, that their rent rolls and registrars would be made state documents and part of an archive). This combination made them a powerful repository and arbiter of a village's fiscal affairs and connected them with cultivators, grain merchants and village headmen (*malik*s). When it came to grain tabulations and harvest in the *rabi* and *khurif* months, the *qanungo*'s importance would usually spike. Since they possessed the paper sanction needed to implement broader spending patterns and distributions of grains, they could work at their own pace. This might explain why one early-nineteenth-century French observer noted that they were slow but assiduous in their work.[188] It would also explain why the early colonial state sought them out with such intensity. It is also useful to distinguish between different types of writing skill. Creative writing and letter writing (*insha*) were not required to be a *qanungo*. But copying, collating and accountancy were. The various administrative manuals (*dastur ul-amal*s) written by Hindu scribes suggest they possessed sophisticated skills for calculating in Perso-Arabic numerals.[189]

The other position that Kayasthas dominated was the village accountant (*patwari*). The *qanungo* worked closely with this 'accountant'. Some of the most famous *patwari*s were the Lala families of Bihari country. Unlike the *qanungo*, whose repository included a constellation of fiscal and agrarian information, the *patwari* focused almost solely on accountancy. His statistics were usually collated by the *qanungo* into the broader documents in which sovereigns were interested. *Patwaris* were lower than *qanungos* in 'rank', partially because their occupation required less Persian fluency; it merely required a familiarity with the lexicon and numerology of Persian composition. This also reflected Kayastha subgroups' own hierarchies. Srivastavas were rarely *patwaris*; they mostly served as *qanungos* and *diwans*. But *patwaris*, while 'lower', still exercised considerable power at the local level of administration, for they were often the only 'revenue-learned' in an entire pargana. Bernard Cohn once suggested that Kayastha groups such as patwaris were marginal to precolonial forms of sovereignty and revenue management.[190] Likewise, Muzzafar Alam and Sanjay Subramanyan see the Hindu pensman at the 'fringe' of the Mughal state.[191] Both these approaches, though, are somewhat limited by emphasizing the state, court and landed groups. A closer examination of the historical evidence suggests that from the late 1600s these groups connected agrarian hinterlands with imperial and regional courts through fiscalism. By 1700 they served as the 'village enforcers' of a landed Muslim elite whose authority stemmed from an armed military camp backed up by paper rule (*kaghaz raj*).

Kayasthas, as we have seen, had positioned themselves as indispensable paper managers for the Mughals, most acutely under Emperor Aurangzeb, by 1700. We can discern a few trends in their patterns of employment. For one, Kayasthas' dominance of the *qanungo* position had largely become hereditary by the eighteenth century. Most Kayastha *qanungos* were appointed 'in the time of Akbar',[192] which can be discerned from a broader survey of these families coupled with imperial pronouncements. For example, a *farman* by Emperor Muhammad Shah in 1736 ordered officials to respect the *qanungo* of Chanderi in Malwa country, who was to be given respect 'in the same way as his father, accede to his authority in all matters relating to that office, and rely on whatever he says for the larger income of government and the well being of the peasantry'.[193] Much of this deference was practical. *Qanungos*, as interpreters of local custom as it related to revenue, had more or less a 'monopoly of all [revenue] knowledge' in any district.[194] Another *qanungo*, Jagivan Das, was granted the village of Jagivanpur in Bihari country as *inam*, 'on condition that he would strive daily for the increase of revenue'.[195] In 1682 when Emperor Alamgir ordered that all *qanungos* below the *sarkar* level be abolished[196] this not only reflected the drive towards centralization that he sought to achieve but showed how much Hindustan's pensmen had coloured the Mughal administrative corpus. The *qanungo* may have been subordinate, but when it came to the assessment of any village in the Doab, 'the Qanungo was the permanent repository of information regarding the revenue receipts, area statistic local revenue rates and customs and practices of the parganah'.[197] He was the epicentre of local fiscal knowledge and intelligence and would become even more so under British rule. But he could also cause trouble for authorities. With the command of paper, Kayastha *qanungos* had plenty of opportunities under Muslim and Christian sovereigns 'for cajoling or frightening the villagers'.[198]

The scribal groups of Hindustan were, therefore, indispensable for more revenue-hungry regional states in the eighteenth century. While they rose to great height and breadth in late Mughal administrations, it was with the emergence of the great eighteenth-century regional successor states that these Kayasthas really came into their own. Between Delhi and Dinapur, these pensmen enabled Awadh and Bengal to become fiscally aggressive and penetrating. Not being fully fledged members of the Muslim elite also allowed these pensmen to more easily navigate Hindustan's rural cultural universe and, by extension, make fiscal inroads. Kayastha *qanungo*s and *patwari*s helped regional states tax deeper into the countryside over the course of the eighteenth century. In Bengal, for example, the Kayastha Rai Umid Ram served as a crucial official who negotiated Nawab Mir Qasim's debts with the Jagath Seths.[199] Farther northwest, in Awadh, Kayasthas assessed land yields (*jama*) and taxation rates, and they managed accounts, which enabled the splashing of large cultural patronage (*imambara*s) and, increasingly, large armed forces and soldiers (*sipahi*s). This increasing attention to balance books and revenue shaped the concerns of courts between Delhi and Murshidabad. The British Resident in Lucknow in 1782, Samuel Middleton, immediately saw how significant paper and accounts could be to an Indian sovereign. Nawab Asaf ud-Daula, Middleton observed, was in 'great distraction and hardship [by] examining the papers of...income and expenditure'.[200] He observed that when it came to managing the fiscal affairs of his kingdom, without the 'shrewd Kayastha' the Nawab would be 'at his wit's end'[201] for revenue. These scribes could also serve more overt political machinations with their paper and writing skills. One Kayastha of Piruthana in Shahabad, Jagal Kishore, developed an ink to communicate with the Maratha Sindhia in Gwalior which 'left no apparent traces on the paper'. When discovered, this led to Kishore's disembowelling by an enraged rival, Ismail Beg.[202] So whether as obedient paper managers or intriguing communicators of coded messages with rival kingdoms, those with paper knowledge were pivotal to the dynamics of eighteenth-century Indian regional politics. Already before British rule, paper authority was crucial for political legitimacy in India and the abilities of regional kingdoms to further tax and extract wealth from their domains. These same pensmen would later provide the fiscal information of rolls and records to the British, who would ramp up revenue demands to levels never witnessed in India's history.

Conclusion

This chapter has offered a detailed overview and survey of various Kayastha families in north India, looking at Kayastha origins and the complexities of their caste identity. It has also examined how their learning experiences were integrated within various forms of clerical, though subordinate, service in pen and paper. Outwardly many Kayasthas were 'Islamized scribes'. By virtue of their training in Persian, which afforded them access to positions of service that were subordinate but crucial, Kayasthas established traditions of service which spanned the Mughal Empire and into the eighteenth century. They became the enforcers of fiscal demands on villages and agrarian economies. In the regional politics of eighteenth-century India Kayasthas saw their 'administrative worth' increase markedly. Any regional sovereign – Maratha, Hyderabadi, Sikh or British – had to weld these groups to the emergent state to underpin the fiscal foundations of their kingdom. The skills of paper management and accountancy were becoming exponentially important to Indian politics over the 1700s, likely reaching a peak by the late 1770s. *Qanungo*s, specifically, seemed to represent what the late Kumkum Chatterjee described as a shift towards more rule-bound and procedural systems of governance in the eighteenth century.[203] Ironically, the 'humble wretch' became indispensable in the transition between empires, where the ability to tabulate, document and audit became crucial functions for eighteenth-century regional states, of which the East India Company was one. As the following chapters will demonstrate, these humble pensmen and paper managers would provide physical documentation, 'revenue intelligence' and sanction for the most extractive political regime to which Hindustan's cultivators would yet be subject.

Notes

1 B. Raman, *Document Raj: Writing and Scribes in Early Colonial South India* (Chicago, 2012).
2 P. Carnegy, *Notes on the Races, Tribes and Castes Inhabiting the Province of Avadh* (Lucknow, 1868), p. 58.
3 J. Nesfield, *Brief View of the Caste System of the North-West Provinces and Oudh* (Allahabad, 1885), p. 48.
4 W. Muir *Original Sanskrit Texts* (London, 1858), Vol. V, p. 302.
5 B. Sinha, *Kayasthas in the Making of Modern India* (Patna, 2003), p. 3.
6 See, for example, E. Blunt, *The Caste System of Northern India* (Allahabad, 1931), pp. 54–258; H. Elliot, *Memoirs on the History, Folklore and Distribution of the Races of the North-Western Provinces of India* (London, 1869), Vol. II, pp. 36–180; C. Gupta, *The Kayasthas: A Study in the Formation and Early History of a Caste* (Calcutta, 1996); V. Gupte, *Ethnographic Notes on Prabhu Kayasthas* (Pune, 1904), pp. 2–50; the periodicals *Kayastha* (Agra), the *Kayastha Gazette Press* (Bankipur) and the *Kayastha Samchar*; K. Prasad, *The Kayastha Ethnology* (Lucknow, 1877); L.P. Saxena, *A Short History of Temperance Reform in the Kayastha Community* (Agra, 1911); K.P. Shrivastava, *The Hindu Sociology: Being a Treatise on the Social Position of the Kayastha Community* (Benares, 1913); and W. Sherring, *Hindu Tribes and Castes* (Calcutta, 1872), Vo.. I, pp. 305–11, which all outline the longer histories of Kayasthas' service professions.
7 For the purposes of this book's chronological and thematic focus, Bengali Kayasthas will be treated as 'a distinct class' from those farther upcountry in the Doab. This is mainly because Bengali Kayasthas were far more involved in the mercantile and trading professions than their fellow Kayasthas farther upcountry. Plus, numbers put the demographic orbit of Kayasthas in the Doab and Bihar. As one early 1800s observer noted: 'the number of [Kayasthas] is greater in the interior of the country, especially in the north of Hindoostan'. See S. Lal and S. Varma, *Kayastha Educational Reform*, Series No. 3 (Aligarh, 1901) and F.B. Solvyns, *Les Hindoûs* (Paris, 1808), p. 177.

8 I am grateful to Frank Conlon for pointing this out.
9 A. Steel, *The Law and Custom of Hindoo Castes* (London 1868), p. 94.
10 Sinha, *Kayasthas*, p. 4.
11 Shrivastava, *The Hindu Sociology*, p. 50.
12 R.V. Russell and R.B.H. Lal, *The Tribes and Castes of the Central Provinces of India* (London, 1916), Vol. I., p. 422, for similar insights into the Singh, Lal, Sewak and Prasad Kayasthas of central India. The author is grateful to Aparna Vaidik for noting Russell's original mistranslation.
13 Blunt, *The Caste System*; J. Hutton, *Caste in India: Its Nature, Function and Origins* (Cambridge 1946), p. 148.
14 Sherring, *Hindu Tribes*, p. 305.
15 *Kayastha*, April (Agra, 1896), p. 5; one Bihari folktale noted that employment was as important to a Kayastha's happiness as mangos were to a Brahmin's. See A. Grierson, *Bihar Peasant Life* (Calcutta, 1885), 299fn; over time they became so well known for their literacy that an old folktale notes that 'in a Kayasth's house even a cat learns a letter or two'. See H. Risely, *The People of India* (London, 1915), p. 309.
16 Risley, *The People*, p. 309.
17 Ibid., p. 132.
18 J. Malcolm, *A Memoir of Central India*, (London, 1832), Vol. II., pp. 166–7; V. Raghuvanshi, *Indian Society in the Eighteenth Century* (New Delhi, 1969), p. 184.
19 R. Inden, *Marriage and Rank in Bengali Culture* (Berkeley, 1974), p. 16.
20 Dr Vibhuti Rai and Sri Sampal Rai, Lucknow, 2006, 2007, 2008; Dr Raj and Mrs Naheed Verma, Lucknow, 2006, 2007, 2008; also see *Census of India, 1901* (Calcutta, 1902), Volume 6, Part 1, p. 381; J. Battacharya, *Hindu Castes and Sects*, p. 175; Russell and Lal, *Tribes and Castes of Central India* (London, 1916), p. 33,
21 H. Blochman, trans., *The Ain-i-Akbari* (1873), p. 258.
22 M. Stein, *Kalhana's Rajatarangini: A Chronicle of the Kings of Kashmir* (London, 1900), p. 10.
23 Sherring, *Hindu Tribes*, p. 311; also see Battacharya, *Hindu Castes and Sects*, p. 189.
24 Battacharya, *Hindu Castes*, pp. 175–87.
25 *Census of India, 1901* (Calcutta, 1902), Volume 6, Part 1, p. 381; Battacharya, *Hindu Castes and Sects*, p. 175.
26 Russel and Lal, *Tribes and Castes*, p. 417
27 Sherring, *Hindu Tribes*, Vol. I, p. 305
28 Bayly, *Rulers, Townsmen and Bazaars*, pp. 382–382
29 Dr Vibhuti Rai and Sri Sampal Rai, Lucknow, 2006, 2007, 2008; Dr Raj and Mrs Naheed Verma, Lucknow, 2006, 2007, 2008; Ms Rakhi Reshmi, New Delhi, 2008, 2009, London, 2010, 2012; also see Battacharya, *Hindu Castes and Sects*, p. 187.
30 Battacharya, *Hindu Castes and Sects*, p. 187; also see Russel and Lal, *Tribes and Castes*, pp. 411–12.
31 K.N. Sahay, *Am a ha Ka a ha* (New Delhi, 2001), p. 24.
32 Hutton, *Caste in India*, p. 78.
33 Blunt, *The Caste System*, pp. 222.
34 Elliot, *Memoirs*, Vol. II, p. 36.
35 Ibid.
36 Dr Vibhuti Rai and Sri Sampal Rai, Lucknow, 2006, 2007, 2008; Dr Raj and Mrs Naheed Verma, Lucknow, 2006, 2007, 2008; Ms Rakhi Reshmi, New Delhi, 2008, 2009, London, 2010, 2012.
37 K.N. Sahay, *Am a ha Ka a ha (The Evolution of a Family and Its Socio-Cultural Dimensions)* (New Delhi, 2001), p. 244.
38 Family Mss. of Sampal Rai, 'Sri Ganeshya Nam', 1915, in author's possession; also see K.N. Sahay, *Ambastha Ka a ha*, pp. 200–10.

39 Dr Vibhuti Rai and Sri Sampal Rai, Lucknow, 2006, 2007, 2008; Dr Raj and Mrs Naheed Verma, Lucknow, 2006, 2007, 2008; Ms Rakhi Reshmi, New Delhi, 2008, 2009, London, 2010, 2012.
40 J. Nanavaty, *Educational Thought* (Pune, 1973), p. 107; L. Ballbanlilar *Imperial Identity in Mughal Empire: Memory and Dynastic Politics in Early Modern Central Asia* (London, 2012), p. 59.
41 Blunt, *The Caste System*, pp. 54–5; Elliot, *Memoirs*, Vol. II, p. 103
42 S.D. Lakhnawi, *Shahnama Munawar Kalam*, S.H. Ashair, trans. (Patna, 1980), xii–xiii.
43 Sherring, *Hindu Tribes*, p. 310.
44 Malcolm, *A Memoir*, Vol. II, pp. 165–6; E. Maclagan, *Punjab Census Report*, Vol. XIX (Peshawar, 1891).
45 Sri Sampal Rai (Lucknow, 2006).
46 'Sri Ganeshya Nam', p. 6; Elliot, *Memoirs*, Vol. I, p. 365.
47 Dr Vibhuti Rai and Sri Sampal Rai, Lucknow, 2006, 2007, 2008; Dr Raj and Mrs Naheed Verma, Lucknow, 2006, 2007, 2008; Ms Rakhi Reshmi, New Delhi, 2008, 2009, London, 2010, 2012.
48 'Khulasatu-i-Siyaq', Add. 6588, fol. 64a-65a, IOL.
49 J. Nanavaty, *Educational Thought*, Vol. I, p. 207.
50 A. Sharar, *Lucknow: The Last Phase of an Oriental Culture* (London, 1975), p. 104.
51 W.H. Moreland, *The Agrarian System of Moslem India* (Cambridge, 1929), p. 73.
52 C. Elliot, *The Chronicles of Oonao* (Allahabad, 1862), p. 102.
53 R. O'Hanlon, 'The social worth of scribes: Brahmins, Kayasths and the social order in early modern India', *IESHR* 47, 4 (2010), pp. 563–95.
54 M. Alam and S. Subrahmanyan, 'The making of a munshi', *Comparative Studies of South Asia, Africa and the Middle East* 24, 2 (2004), pp. 61–72.
55 Sherring, *Hindu Tribes*, Vol. I, p. 311.
56 G.S. Verma, *A Peep into the Origin, Status and History of the Kayasthas* (Bareli, 1929), p. 15.
57 *Kayastha*, August (Agra, 1896), p. 24.
58 Elliot, *Chronicles*, pp. 86–8, 112–13.
59 N. Haider, 'Norms of professional excellence and good conduct in accountancy manuals of the Mughal Empire', *International Review of Social History* 56, S19 (2011), pp. 263–74.
60 S. Rizvi, *Shah Wali-Allah and His Times* (Calcutta, 1980), p. 174.
61 *Indian History Congress, Proceedings of the 46th Session, Amritsar, 1985* (Amritsar, 1986), p. 255.
62 M. Balmukand, *Letters of a King-Maker of the Eighteenth Century (Balmakundnama)*, S. Chandra., trans. (Aligarh, 1972), p. 15.
63 This is taken from Max Weber's characterization of the Mughal Empire as a patrimonial-bureaucratic entity.
64 M. Umar, *Islam in Northern India during the Eighteenth Century* (New Delhi, 1993), p. 372.
65 A. Jalal, *Self and Sovereignty: Individual and Community in South Asian Islam since 1850* (London, 2000).
66 A. Steel, *The Law and Custom of Hindoo Castes* (London 1868), p. 74.
67 Dr Vibhuti Rai and Sri Sampal Rai, Lucknow, 2006, 2007, 2008; Dr Raj and Mrs Naheed Verma, Lucknow, 2006, 2007, 2008; Ms Rakhi Reshmi, New Delhi, 2008, 2009, London, 2010, 2012.
68 Ibid.
69 P. Hardy, *The Muslims of British India* (Cambridge, 1972), p. 9.
70 Some later nineteenth-century critics used the diet argument to claim Kayasthas' *shudra* status. See Chapter 5.

71 Battacharya, *Hindu Castes and Sects*, p. 175.
72 H. Blochman, trans., *The Ain-i-Akbari* (London, 1873), p. 258. The Ain-i-Akbari goes into detail regarding Kayasthas and their occupational duties as *qanungos*:

> an officer in each district acquainted with its customs and land tenures and whose appointment is usually hereditary. He receives reports from the patwaris of new cases alluvion, diluvion, sales, leases, gifts of land, & c. which entail a change in the register of mutations. He is a revenue officer and subordinate to the tehsildar.

73 K. Chatterjee, 'Scribal elites in Sultanate and Mughal Bengal', *IESHR*, 47, 2 (2010), pp. 445–72.
74 J. Sarkar, *History of Aurangzeb* (Calcutta, 1924), Vol. V, p 358; Jogendranath Battacharuya noted that 'the Lala [Kayasthas of NWP and Bihar] are very much addicted to drinking… they differ… from the Bengali Kayasthas who are mostly teetotalers'. Bhattacharya, *Hindu Castes and Sects* (Calcutta, 1896), p. 186.
75 See Chapter 6.
76 Shrivastava, *The Hindu Sociology*, p. 51.
77 Sinha, *Kayasthas*, p. 19.
78 M. Yasin, *A Social History of Islamic India* (Lucknow, 1958), p. 48.
79 Alam and Subrahmanyan, 'The making of a munshi', p. 71.
80 I. Qureshi, *The Muslim Community of the Indo-Pakistan Subcontinent (610–1947)* (Karachi, 1977), p. 110; Dr Vibhuti Rai and Sri Sampal Rai, Lucknow, 2006, 2007, 2008; Raj and Naheed Verma, Lucknow, 2006, 2007, 2008; Ms Rakhi Reshmi, New Delhi, 2008, 2009, London, 2010, 2012; also see J. Cole, *Roots of North Indian Shi'i m in Iran and Iraq: Religion and State in Awadh, 1722–1859* (Berkeley, 1989), pp. 116–17.
81 Umar, *Islam in Northern India*, p. 387.
82 B.H. Badley, 'Jagivandas, the Hindu reformer', *Indian Antiquary* viii (Bombay, 1879), p. 289.
83 P. Carnegy, *Notes on the Races, Tribes and Castes Inhabiting the Province of Avadh* (Lucknow, 1868), p. 60; this was also practised by some Prabhu Kayasthas in west Maratha country. See Gupte, *Ethnographic Notes*, p. 39.
84 OR. 1750, Fol. 162, Sanbhu Lal, 'Miftah-i-Khanzain', (1197 AH), 1782, Fols. 7–8, IOL.
85 Dr Vibhuti Rai and Sri Sampal Rai, Lucknow, 2006, 2007, 2008; Raj and Mrs Naheed Verma, Lucknow, 2006, 2007, 2008; Ms Rakhi Reshmi, New Delhi, 2008, 2009, London, 2010, 2012.
86 Umar, *Islam in Northern India*, p. 382.
87 Alam and Subrahmanyan, pp. 61–72.
88 Raghuvanshi, *Indian Society*, p. 191; R. Martin, *The Indian Empire* (London, 1858), Vol. I, p. 185.
89 S. Jafar, *Education in Muslim India*, pp. 151–3; also see the issues of *Kayastha*, September–October (Agra, 1896), which drew out the history of one Kayastha, Ram Saran Das from Faizabad.
90 N. Basak, *History of Vernacular Education in Bengal*, p. 22.
91 A. Mukhopadhyaya, *Reform and Regeneration in Bengal* (Calcutta, 1968), p. 7.
92 Jafar, *Education in Muslim India*, pp. 146–7.
93 Mukhopadhyaya, *Reform and Regeneration*, p. 6; M. Ahmad, *System of Education in Medieval India, 1526 to 1761* AD (New Delhi, 1987), pp. 47–8; M. Law, *Promotion of Learning in India during Muhammedan Rule* (London, 1910), p. 113; S. Nurullah, *A History of Education in India* (Bombay, 1951), p. 37.
94 Dr Vibhuti Rai, Lucknow, 2006, 2007, 2008; Raj and Naheed Verma, Lucknow, 2006, 2007, 2008; Ms Rakhi Reshmi, New Delhi, 2008, 2009, London, 2010, 2012.
95 Jafar, *Education in Muslim India*, p. 86.

96 M. Martin, *The History, Antiquities, Topography and Statistic of Eastern India* (London, 1838), Vol. III, p. 162.

97 The *Dars-i-Nizami* madrassa curricular system was an example. Developed circa the late seventeenth and early eighteenth century by Mullah Nizamuddin, (d. 1748), it contrasted with medieval Muslim traditions, which were less formalized, and was biased in favour of the rational sciences, which tended to outnumber *kalam* (theology) and *fiqh* (jurisprudence). As Francis Robinson has demonstrated, it was only later under the Deobandi *ulama* after the 1870s that the madrassa curricula shifted decidedly in favour of *fiqh*. See Robinson, 'Islamic reform and modernities in South Asia', *MAS*, 42 (2/3) (2008), pp. 259–81.

98 Basak, *History of Vernacular*, p. 22.

99 N. Haider, 'Language, caste and the secretarial class in Mughal India', unpublished Mss. in author's possession; also see Haider, 'Norms of professional excellence', pp. 263–74.

100 Elliot, *Chronicles*, p. 112.

101 Rizvi, *Shah Wali-Allah*, p. 391.

102 K. Chatterjee, 'History as self-representation: the recasting of political tradition in late eighteenth century eastern India', *MAS* 32, 4 (1998), p. 921.

103 Rizvi, *Shah Wali-Allah*, p. 379.

104 C. Barhaman, *Chahar Chaman*, S.M. Yunus, ed. (Delhi, 2007), p. 175.

105 Dr Vibhuti Rai and Sri Sampal Rai, Lucknow, 2006, 2007, 2008; Raj and Naheed Verma, Lucknow, 2006, 2007, 2008; Ms Rakhi Reshmi, New Delhi, 2008, 2009, London, 2010, 2012.

106 H. Snyder, *The Kashmiri Pandits: A Study of Cultural Choice in North India* (Delhi, 1988), p. 57.

107 E. Thomas, *Revenue Resources of the Mughal Empire: from* AD *1593 to* AD *1707* (London, 1871), p. 8.

108 Muzzafar Alam and Sanjay Subrahmanyan take the side that Todar Mal was in fact Khattri. See Alam and Subrahmanyan, 'Making of a munshi', p. 61.

109 R. Kinra, *Writing Self, Writing Empire: Chandar Bhan Brahman and the Cultural World of the Indo-Persian State Secretary* (Berkeley, 2015).

110 Lakhnawi, *Shahnama*, xiii.

111 In some instances, such as the Bijapur Sultanates, forms of Nagri were used in public accounts along with Persian. See R. Eaton, *A Social History of the Deccan, 1300–1761: Eight Indian Lives* (Cambridge, 2005); C. Asher and C. Talbot, *India before Europe* (Cambridge, 2006); Rahman, *Islamic Calligraphy in Medieval India.*

112 Haider, 'Norms of professional excellence', pp. 263–74.

113 *Mauizah-i-Jahangiri* (Advice on the Art of Governance), S.S. Alvi, trans., pp. 17–18.

114 Solvyns, *Les Hindoûs*, p. 177.

115 *Memoirs of Delhi and Faizabad, Being a Translation of he 'Tarikh Farah akh h' of Muhammed Faiz Bakh h*, W. Hoey, trans. (Allahabad, 1888), Vol. II, p. 107. This is Khan's description.

116 F. Buchanan, *An Account of the District of Purnea in 1809–1810* (Patna, 1928), p. 214.

117 P. Basu, *Oudh and the East India Company* (Lucknow, 1943), p. 20.

118 Qureshi, *The Muslim Community*, p. 110.

119 See Cole, *Roo of Nor h Indian Shi'i m* for discussions on Kayastha and Kashmiri Pandits' participation in Shia ceremonies in Lucknow; also see K. Leonard, *Hyderabad and Hyderabadis* (New Delhi, 2014), p. 283–4.

120 *Kayastha*, Oct (Agra, 1895), p. 6.

121 Dr Vibhuti Rai and Sri Sampal Rai, Lucknow, 2006, 2007, 2008; Raj and Naheed Verma, Lucknow, 2006, 2007, 2008; Ms Rakhi Reshmi, New Delhi, 2008, 2009, London, 2010, 2012.

122 Sri Sampal and Dr Vibhuti Rai, Raj and Naheed Verma, Sri Ram Advani, Lucknow, 2004, 2006, 2008, 2009. Family Mss. of Sampal Rai, 'Sri Ganeshya Nam', 1915, in author's possession.
123 Sinha, *Kayasthas*, pp. 19–20; also see Verma, *A Peep into the Origin*, p. 206, which also delineates how various Kayasthas took on names such as Dastigar, Burtaria, Inamdar and Bakshi.
124 Verma, *A Peep into the Origin*, p. 206.
125 Shrivastava, *The Hindu Sociology*, p. 51.
126 Dr Vibhuti Rai and Sri Sampal Rai, Lucknow, 2006, 2007, 2008; Raj and Naheed Verma, Lucknow, 2006, 2007, 2008; Ms Rakhi Reshmi, New Delhi, 2008, 2009, London, 2010, 2012.
127 Ibid.; also see J. Cole, *Roots of North Indian Shi'i m in Iran and Iraq* about Kayastha participation in the *tazieh* and Shia ceremonies of *Morurram*.
128 Lakhnawi, *Shanama*, xvii.
129 Raj and Naheed Verma, Lucknow, 2006, 2007, 2008.
130 Alam and Subrahmanyan, 'The making of a munshi', p. 66.
131 G. Verma, *A Peep into the Origin, Status and History of the Kayasthas* (Bareli, 1929), p. 194.
132 'Akhbarat from Delhi', 8 February 1825, in M. Pernou and Y. Jaffey, eds, *Information and the Public Sphere: Persian Newsletters from Delhi* (Delhi, 2008), pp. 108–9.
133 Srivastava, *The First Two Nawabs*, p. 215.
134 Rizvi, *Shah Wali-Allah*, p. 304.
135 H.K. Mishra, *Bureaucracy under the Mughals 1556* AD *to 1707* AD (Delhi, 1989), p. 28.
136 Narayan, *Ruqat*.
137 Srivastava, *The First Two Nawabs*, p. 256.
138 Sinha, *Kayasthas*, p. 2; Dr Vibhuti Rai, Lucknow, 2006, 2007, 2008; Raj and Naheed Verma, Lucknow, 2006, 2007, 2008; Ms Rakhi Reshmi, New Delhi, 2008, 2009, London, 2010, 2012.
139 Verma, *A Peep into the Origin*, p. 8.
140 D. Shauk, *Jawahir-i-Manzouma va Merat al-Sarf* (Kanpur, 1878).
141 G.D. Bhatnagar, *Awadh under Wajid Ali Shah* (Varanasi, 1968), p. 15.
142 Shauk, *Jawahir-i-Manzouma*.
143 See U. Stark, *Empire of Books*, for an investigation of Kishore's *Awadh Akbar* press.
144 N. Kishore, *Allah Kudae'i* (Lucknow, 1869).
145 Ibid.
146 S.M. Azizuddin Husain, *1857 Revisited* (Delhi, 2007), p. 198; also see Stark, *Empire of Books*, for a further discussion of Nawal Kishore and the fates of various Hindu clerical castes in late-nineteenth-century north India.
147 Shrivastava, *The Hindu Sociology*, p. 73.
148 Ibid.
149 *Kayastha*, August (Agra, 1896), p. 1.
150 W. Franklin, *History of Shah-Aulum, the Present Emperor of Hindostan* (London, 1798), p. 174.
151 Ibid., pp. 174–5.
152 Dr Vibhuti Rai and Sri Sampal Rai, Lucknow, 2006, 2007, 2008; Raj and Naheed Verma, Lucknow, 2006, 2007, 2008; Rakhi Reshmi, New Delhi, 2008, 2009, London, 2010, 2012.
153 Buchanan, *An Account*, pp. 484–5.
154 Ibid.
155 *Memoirs of Delhi*, pp. 26–7.
156 Ibid., p. 30.
157 Ibid., p. 115.
158 Ibid., pp. 107–30.

159 M. Taqiamad, trans., *Tarikh Badshah Begam* (Allahabad, 1938), p. 86fn; S. Khan, *A Translation of the Seir Mutaqherin* (Calcutta, 1902), pp. 105, 147.
160 T. W. Beale, *An Oriental Biographical Dictionary* (London, 1864), p. 299.
161 Srivastava, *The First Two Nawabs*, p. 272.
162 Sinha, *Kayasthas*, p. 23–4.
163 Elliot, *Chronicles*, pp. 73–4; also see S. Gupta, *Agrarian Relations and Early British Rule in India: a Case Study of the Ceded and Conquered Provinces* (New York, 1963), pp. 28–30.
164 Srivastava, *The First Two Nawabs*, p. 215.
165 Rizvi, *Shah Wali-Allah*, pp. 106–7.
166 M. Alam, *Crisis of Empire in Mughal North India* (Delhi, 1986), pp. 169–74; S.F. Dale, *Indian Merchants and Eurasian Trade, 1600–1750* (Cambridge, 1994), pp. 11–12.
167 Rizvi, *Shah Wali-Allah*, pp. 120–1.
168 L. Narayan, *Ruqat-i-Lakhshmi Narayan* (Lucknow, 1880).
169 Ibid.
170 *Memories of Delhi and Faizabad*, Vol. II, p. 107.
171 Ibid., Vol. I, v.
172 Ibid., Vol. II, p. 230; Narayan, *Ruqat*.
173 Narayan, *Ruqat*.
174 Srivastava, *The First Two Nawabs*, p. 163.
175 Mukhopadhyaya, *Reform and Regeneration*, p. 6; also see Ahmad, *System of Education*, pp. 47–8.
176 *Khurshid-Jahan-Numah*, Persian Mss., in Law, *Promotion of Learning*, p. 113.
177 Nurullah, *A History of Education*, p. 37.
178 Ibid.
179 Clarke, 'Report on settlement of Budaun District, 1838', in *Reports on the Revenue Settlement of the North Western Provinces of the Bengal Presidency, under Regulation IX* (Benares, 1863), Vol. II, p. 526.
180 Elliot, *Memoirs*, Vol. I, pp. 434–9.
181 Gupta, *Agrarian Relations*, p. 8.
182 Thomason, 'Collector of Azamgarh', in *Reports on the Revenue Settlement of the North Western Provinces of the Bengal Presidency, under Regulation IX* (Benares, 1863), Vol. I, p. 25.
183 *The Benares Magazine* 8 (Mirzapur, 1852), p. 163.
184 Habib, *The Agrarian System*, p. 331.
185 Elliot, *Chronicles*, p. 112.
186 Ibid.
187 Haider, 'Language, caste'.
188 Solvyns, *Les Hindoûs*, p. 177.
189 Mss. Add. 6599, ff. 1a–185a, 'Dastur ul amal-i-Ilmi-Navisindagi' (Administrative manual and the knowledge of writing), IOL.
190 Cohn, 'Political systems in eighteenth century India', *Journal of the American Oriental Society* 82, 3 (1962), pp. 312–20.
191 Alam and Subrahmanyan, 'The making of a munshi', pp. 61–72,
192 *Indian History Congress, Proceedings of the 46th Session, Amritsar, 1985* (Amritsar, 1986), p. 225; Dr Vibhuti Rai and Sri Sampal Rai, Lucknow, 2006, 2007, 2008; Raj and Naheed Verma, Lucknow, 2006, 2007, 2008; Ms Rakhi Reshmi, New Delhi, 2008, 2009, London, 2010, 2012.
193 *Indian History Congress*, p. 225.
194 G.S. Chabra, *Advanced Study in the History of Modern India* (1813–1920) (Jullundur, 1962), Vol. I, p. 229.
195 *Indian History Congress*, p. 225.

196 Ibid. Aurangzeb's order had little effect, especially after his death in 1707, when it could be argued that the number of *qanungo*s in various parganas increased.
197 Gupta, *Agrarian* Relations, p. 21.
198 Elliot, *Chronicles*, p. 112.
199 A. Khan, *The Transition in Bengal, 1756–1775: a Study of Muhammad Reza Khan* (Cambridge, 1969), pp. 34–6.
200 'Delhi newsletter to Nana Fardis', 19 September 1782, in J.N. Sarkar, *Persian Records of Maratha History* (Bombay, 1953), Vol. I, p. 105.
201 H. Khan, trans., *Tran la ion of Maharajah Kal an Singh' Khulasat-it-Tawarikh* (n.d.), p. 351.
202 S.H. Askari, 'Fragments of a newly discovered Persian manuscript by a Hindu news-writer', *Journal of Bihar Research Society* 36, September–December (Patna, 1950), p. 85.
203 Chatterjee, 'History as self-representation', pp. 936–7.

3 Revenue and state formation in the Doab, c. 1780–1840

Introduction

This chapter shifts from an examination of precolonial India to the late eighteenth and early nineteenth centuries. While the previous chapters have tracked revenue culture and the social history of Hindustan's pensmen, this chapter will look at how the two came together in the early generations of colonial rule in north India. It delineates and analyses the impact of the East India Company's agrarian settlements and revenue administration upon the fabric of governance after the 1750s, and how the broader communities of scribes – and the fiscal knowledge they possessed – shaped the emergence of the early colonial state. It starts by looking at how much the British learned from revenue administration, first in Bengal, then Benares, then farther upcountry along the Doab, and how they worked with extant Kayastha pensmen in enacting the revenue settlements which would, eventually, fund Britain's empire. The Company's obsessive paper-orientation – in its desire to 'know the state of the revenues' – drew upon old officers and their physical records to give sanction to savage revenue demands. Bhavani Raman has recently demonstrated how the British were averse to the Tamil village accountant (*karnam*/*kanakkam*), whose skills often revolved around techniques of memorization. This led the British to insist on the attestation and authentication of documents.[1] Yet north India was a somewhat different story. Kayastha *qanungo*s' records were far more valuable in north India. The British encountered a more pliant corps of subordinate officers who possessed a far greater volume of paper records that, in turn, shaped revenue administration. Kayasthas also were far less mnemonic than their Tamil peers, which made them 'less suspicious' under the early Company's revenue settlements. By the 1820s the Company's agrarian taxation had built upon a network of pensmen and paper managers that reached back into the late Mughal period. The interstices between ruling overlords and the local structures of power and revenue were well established by the 1600s. It was this very nexus between local village society and ruling overlord that the British would control with ruthless, bureaucratic mastery.

Early patterns: Bengal, Benares and Awadh

Upcountry from Bengal, the British by the 1780s knew little about the workings of revenue collection in the lush Gangetic plains, especially in townships such as

Etawah, Kanpur, Allahabad and Farrukabad. They gleaned some knowledge of the working of fiscalism from their experience in Bengal and later in Benares under Jonathan Duncan. But farther upcountry larger zamindari landholders were less characteristic of the Doab's revenue administration, as early Settlement Officers discovered, often with disastrous results. One Settlement Officer in Farrukabad bluntly admitted that 'we are so ignorant of agricultural economy'.[2] Benares was a somewhat intermediary mix. Still, the patterns of revenue collection, and its vagaries tied up with landholding patterns, were far more complicated and complex than that which the British experienced in Bengal. Unlike in Bengal, which saw the ossification of large landed estates after the 1793 Permanent Settlement, one of the main ways the Company worked the revenue machine upcountry was through an extant, looser group of officers and paper managers. They became the 'go-to' scribes and the early Company's fiscal claws in villages. Specifically, they provided the rent-rolls (*hastobuds*), titles (*sanads*) and property registers that allowed the Company to pump out unprecedented amounts of fiscal wealth. With their increasing penetration upcountry from Bengal after the 1780s, the British gradually learned more about how revenue was collected. Real fiscal knowledge and understanding came in fits and spurts, with the British seeking broad patterns and standards in the face of vagaries between parganas and districts. This perhaps explains why the British did not fully grasp the complexities of taxation in the Doab until the 1840s, when they overhauled and standardized under the Thomason generation. But the *ways* in which the Company learned about revenue largely came through the groups of humble accountants and registrars. They provided vital information on rent-rolls, assessment and methods of negotiating rent rates. This also established, by using paper records and sanction, a veneer of legitimacy for the Company in these initial settlements. For any ambitious regional power, be it the Sikhs, Marathas or the British, needed skilled accountants, clerks and paper managers to extend their reach into the subcontinent's hinterlands. These shrewd paper men, between 1780 and 1820, would become the lower pillars of the Company's emergent empire – so what continued into the colonial period was not so much the structures and positions but the demographics, skills and knowledge of the precolonial era. These scribes and pensmen helped extend the revenue and bureaucratic state in the first few generations of Company rule in the Doab and provided the later Raj with its relentless, procedurally based fiscal teeth. The Company's conquest and dominion of north India within two generations had as much to do with its fiscal manipulation as its military prowess or mastery of 'colonial knowledge'.

Bengal and the early trends towards centralization

Questions of proper revenue administration – which eighteenth-century commentators such as Ghulam Hossein Tabatabai and Ghulam Hossein Zaidpuri argued increasingly needed to be guided by good governance[3] – were some of the most immediate and pressing matters facing the Company. The British, straightjacketed by stockholder obligations and their lack of knowledge about Indian taxes and its concomitant moral sensibilities, required 'cheaper and surer modes of collecting the revenue'.[4] Immediately after the acquisition of the 24 parganas after the Battle of Plassey (1757), and after the 1765 acquisition of *diwan*, the Company had to confront fiscalism. This was the first time the Company had been brought into the management of revenue. And while the territories farther upcountry would not come under Company rule until after 1801 (save Benares, which was ceded in 1775), the spectre of Bengal and the 1793 Permanent Settlement hung over the heads of fresh officers posted in the Doab. But we should strike a note of caution. The expansion of the fiscal state in the Doab should not be seen as an 'expansion of governance' or extension from Bengal. As the remaining chapters will demonstrate, the whole fiscal development of the Company's state was markedly different from in east India. Nevertheless, the early Bengal experience did shape the codification of the *bhaiachara* tenures that the British convinced themselves existed. Compared to Bengal, the Doab's estates were much smaller in scale. And because of this, procuring information on rent-rolls and settling the lands quickly after 1801 were of greater importance than farther southeast. They were also far more dicey, difficult and complex. In a way, Cornwallis' 1793 Settlement largely reduced the value of 'fiscal intelligence' in Bengal. In the Doab, though, it was indispensable to state formation. This reality threw the Company into the arms of Hindustan's repository officers: *qanungo*s, *patwari*s and *peshkar*s, who dotted north India's plains and villages.

Let us now examine the dynamics of fiscal sovereignty that the Company encountered in Bengal and would later engage with farther upcountry. Clive appointed the Saxena Kayastha Shitab Rai as *naib diwan* of Bihar, who was also made a member of the Revenue Council of Patna. Managing cordial relationships with Thomas Rumbold (1736–91), the Company's 'supervisor' at Patna, and Harry Verelst (1732–85),[5] Rai provided the Company with reams of fiscal information on the best way to effectively administer revenue. Yet even though Rai was a prime interlocutor, we see early on how the Company began to transform state fiscalism rapidly. For one, we see centralization that cut out the intermediary officers who fortified the countrywide relationships between Nawabs, *peshkar*s and cultivators. British officers, tinged with racial distrust of supposedly 'corrupt' Indian officers, grew increasingly frustrated in dealing with zamindars. This was because they possessed their own forms of judicial authority, which to the British were synonymous with fiscal sovereignty. Moreover, many of the judicial rights zamindars held concerning revenue were accumulated custom and not written down and codified.[6] To the British, fiscal administration needed to be wholly based on paper and procedure, with less flexibility than it had otherwise had. Frustrated by this, Harry Verelst appointed European supervisors to every *diwani* district of Bengal in 1764 and instructed British observers to collect information beyond the simple rent-rolls.[7] Specifically, the Company wanted to know who paid what, what were the historical precedents and, most importantly, who was not paying their proper assessments. From early on in 1760s Bengal we see the beginnings of a relentless drive towards fiscal knowledge which was to be documented on paper.

This centralization was further enhanced after 1765, when Clive established Revenue Councils in Patna and Murshidabad, the two main centres of Company commerce and governance. The Councils further centralized the Company's supervising authority over revenue collection by making historical records a requirement for basing negotiations. Verelst believed fiscal intelligence was crucial, noting that 'the necessary search for, and examination of such old records at Murshidabad... might help the Supervisors in their inquiries', but that they were 'bound to take time'.[8] This again reflected how the British had to 'learn' a broader revenue tradition that was punctuated with paperwork, nuance and, above all, exceptions. Governor Verelst then introduced the policy of Supervision in Bengal in 1769.[9] Based upon experience in Burdwan, Midnapur and Chittagong, where the Company managed revenue officers from above, English supervisors were now given authority to control collections through a combination of advice and 'pressure'. Supervisors could also superintend justice in *diwani* provinces and were given authority to collect information on the pay of lesser officials: *darogah*s, *kotwal*s and *paik*s. Supervisors could also fix what zamindars received from cultivators[10] and summon Collectors (*amil*s, *malguzar*s) to see records and explain them without advance notice. Interrogations of *amil*s and *malguzar*s steadily increased the Company's stream of fiscal intelligence. Yet, ironically for a state that based its legitimacy on law and justice, the whole arrangement had no legal teeth.

The disaster of the 1769 Bengal famine threw this arrangement into the air and accelerated the drive towards fiscal centralization. Controlling Councils of Revenue were established in Bengal and were granted all 'powers of interposition in all matters of importance'. As Robert Travers has demonstrated, this was also shaped by inherent British distrust of Indian officials such as Muhammad Reza Khan and Shitab Rai; their 'corruption' was suspected of having a hand in the famine.[11] The old Supervisor policy of Verelst was therefore given greater teeth by vesting the oversight of these late Mughal-era officers within the Controlling Council. On the spot, British Collectors presided over the revenue courts (*diwani audalat*s) and could use a combination of enforcement and pressure over Indian officers. Shitab Rai and Mohammad Reza Khan, in a marked change, now could not put any seal on any order dealing with revenue without the Controlling Council's permission.[12] Through a legal mechanism, the Company rapidly centralized its revenue authority, took oversight out of Indian hands and concentrated it firmly in British ones.

We also see a trend towards fiscal centralization in Bengal in matters of default and non-payment of revenues. In the 1760s the Company welded law and fiscalism together more firmly than they had been under Bengal's rulers. For the British, justice 'was inseparably linked up with revenue'.[13] They believed that revenue needed to be firmly anchored in law, which would narrow the gap between assessment and revenue paid. This gap, they believed, in a fit of Orientalist sterotyping, was perpetually wide due to the 'despotic' nature of India's 'Moorish' regimes. It was, of course, often a product of British imagination. In the 1760s Harry Verelst helped set up a Court of Judicature to decide cases of default.[14] This was a marked departure from Indian practice, whereby debts and default were not treated, as we have seen, as legal matters but as symbolic and moral ones.

The Court of Judicature had the effect of bypassing the welter of smaller courts that had more specialized mandates. These included courts for suits under Rs 50 (*chota audalat*), over Rs 50 (*bara audalat*), settled charity and rent-free lands (*bazi zamin dastur*), where land rents and revenues were received and where transfers of property confirmed (*sadar kutcheri*), and the appellate court for revenue disputes (*amin dastur*).[15] Compared to the Mayor's Courts of Calcutta, which initially held jurisdiction over British subjects, the Court of Judicature's authority was ill defined. This allowed it to swell in proportion to the Company's fiscal appetite, and it became an orbital convenience for settlements of debts and non-payment. Shitab Rai observed that British efforts to marginalize the *amil*s, by bringing defaulters straight to the Courts, were already generating resistance in Patna. The courts' actions were 'very alarming to the amils of the pergunnahs and inhabitants of the town'.[16] This drew continued agitation from the old advisors Muhammad Reza Khan and Raja Shitab Rai and led to a signed petition of over 200 'respectable residents' of Patna in 1772, protesting the encroachment and centralization of the Company's fiscal legalism.

In Bengal we also start to see the origins of cutting back the costs of Indian personnel. This was a trend that, again, would be replicated with intensity in the Doab. When Henry Vansittart visited Dinajpur in 1765 he replaced all the Indian *amil*s, who had served as intermediaries between zamindars and *diwan*s, with Englishmen.[17] This was likely because *amil*s were accustomed to taking a *dehyek*, or 10 per cent cut from total collections.[18] Verelst, likewise, believed that the multitude of revenue officials – *amil*s, *gumashta*s and *paikar*s – was liable to abuse and was, because of its 'bloat', averse to regulation.[19] This cost-cutting and firing of personnel was officially sanctioned in the 1793 legislation for Bengal, Bihar and Orissa. At Cornwallis' specific request[20] the Permanent Settlement abolished Bengal's *qanungo*s, who he saw, in a Physiocratic fit, as no better than petty middlemen who got in the way of productive landholding estates. This was a preview of the cutting down of intermediate Indian officials in the Doab that would come later, and the privileging of factual knowledge on paper.

The Company's new fiscal ruthlessness made itself felt quickly. This was seen in the rapidly increasing overall revenues it brought in from the Bengal *diwani* (Table 3.1).

Within three years of their ascension to *diwan* in India's most commercially vibrant region the British nearly doubled their annual revenue. They achieved what Siraj ud-Daula and Mir Qasim had attempted for years. From the very beginning the Company possessed an unprecedented fiscal appetite.

Table 3.1 Revenue collected in Bengal, Bihar and Orissa, 1766–9[21]

1766	Rs 200,73,133
1769	Rs 336,64,072
Increase	68%

Another factor which shaped British transformations of revenue administration, in addition to racial mistrust, was language. The British had a tough time learning Persian. Even beyond Bengal, the British never fully mastered the intricacies of letter writing (*insha*). Perhaps this inability to master proper speech, and the political insinuations that went with it, was what was noted by a Swiss engineer who saw that the Mughal Emperor Shah Alam (1723–1806) had been treated with utmost grace by the British, but that it was 'no less true, he had sometimes met with different usage and been much slighted'.[22] In the Murshidabad District, for example, Persian was jettisoned after the transfer of the Crown lands (*khalsa*) to Calcutta in 1772 and was thereafter absent from revenue accounts in select parts of Bengal.[23] Muhammad Reza Khan regularly protested to the British that revenue records should contain 'an exact Persian translation', which may have contributed to his downfall and dismissal. Compared to north India, Persian seems to have died a much quicker administrative death before Macaulay pronounced its corpse in 1835. This quick, though patchy, marginalization of Persian as an administrative language in Bengal had the effect of putting a premium on the physical papers of Hindustan's scribes farther northwest. These developments in Bengal meant that increasingly arrogant young British officers would become doubly dependent upon the *qanungo*s and *patwari*s of Bihar, Benares and the Doab. It was perhaps this increased British drive to utilize the humble officers, who were regarded by some as 'conniving wretches', which led Tabatabai to lament in his *Seir Mutaqherin* that the Company tended to employ those who were not 'noble' and who lacked 'virtue'.[24] The later expansion of the Company's fiscal state, and how it enabled the lowly pensmen to enforce savage revenue demands, was precisely what older observers such as Tabatabai and Mirza Ghalib feared would come with English rule.

Benares: crossroads of the Doab and Bengal

If we can locate the Company's legalization of revenue and its fiscal centralization early in Bengal, both these processes manifested themselves, to a degree, in Benares. Benares after 1775 offers a transition point in understanding the fiscalism that would emerge in the Doab after 1801. The acquisition of the key religious and commercial city of Benares in 1775 pushed the Company deeper into the fiscal management of north Indian agriculture. It also brought the Company closer to the pulse of Awadh's potential revenue; many Lucknow rupees were in circulation in Benares. And the patterns that emerged, particularly under the Residency of Jonathan Duncan, were further amplified in settling the plains of the middle and upper Doab regions after 1800.

Before we proceed to the impact of revenue settlements in Benares, we can examine the role of a key scribe who positioned himself between the late Mughal and early Company empires. The insights of Sanbhu Lal,[25] the munshi of Raja Chait Singh of Benares (1770–81) and later of the British Resident Francis Fowkes, offers crucial insight into the rhythms of revenue administration in this liminal period. Lal noted how for the past generation (from c. 1730s), powerful zamindars had started to jettison the revenue regulations (*zabata*) of Akbar's era. Lal noted that Benares' large zamindars effectively changed the process of revenue collection (*malguzari*) in the blink of an eye (*andak chesh namai*) by substituting guided negotiations between cultivators and *amil*s with armed force. Lal noted that zamindars also started to cultivate direct favour with the Rajas, in what Lal sardonically called 'service' (*kidmat*), mainly by promising higher revenues. The only exception was the Raja of Benares, Chait Singh. Singh largely followed the traditions of Akbar's regulations (*subah khilafeh akbarabad*) and managed to collect Rs 3 crores annually without, on the whole, upsetting cultivators. Lal painted a picture of greedy zamindars who flouted fiscal convention by chasing stories of unlimited wealth in various treasuries (*khazana beshomar-dar Hindustan*). Lal argued that proper, paper-documented regulation (*zabata*) was the only thing that could hold local landlords in check. Of course, this could be seen as a signal to the city's new rulers, but the emphasis on paper regulation did reflect the broader contours of fiscal administration in Hindustan since the 1600s.

Later, under the British Resident of Benares Francis Fowke, Lal offered specific, significant guidance to the district's new rulers. Lal offered a guide to Fowke about the best ways to manage the wealth of the country (*zarhaya-i-Padishahi*). Lal's guide was a refinement and cleaning up (*saf shode*) of regulations and compilations passed down from the munshis of Benares' Department of Composition (*dar ul-Insha*). It was a 'fiscal intelligencer' for the Company. Lal encouraged Fowke to work through the munshis and respected men of letters in Benares' letter-writing house. These munshis, he argued, knew all the regulations and had their fingers on the agrarian and fiscal pulse of the country. Lal noted that munshis possessed the most valuable information regarding taxation and regulations, and that the Rajas of Benares knew far less. Lal also seems to have anticipated the 'paper deluge' that would come after the 1780s, suggesting a symmetry between how munshis worked and the Company's fiscal goals. He noted that the *dar ul-Insha*'s writers knew the proper ordering of revenue documents, what they should consist of and how to order and preserve them to make them accessible for consultation. Lal argued that administration needed procedure and regulation, and the Company also wanted this. There was also the question of trust. Lal claimed that the *dar ul-Insha* was the most trusted source of fiscal information on taxes, land rights and tenures. Unlike the mass of petitions (*urzi*s), which Lal argued created instability, Benares' scribes possessed institutes (*ain*) and consistency. In this way, munshis and scribes served to moderate political temperatures and vagaries. Specifically, Lal invited Fowke to improve the regulations (*zabata*) for governance and taxes and to create a new administrative manual which, unsurprisingly, would be inspected and approved by the city's munshis.[26]

While scribes such as Sanbhu Lal offered their services for Hindustan's new rulers, the early Company did move in rather different directions. In 1770s and 1780s Benares, for example, it was clear early on that the Company's fiscal penetration was unprecedented and had quickly outdone its Indian competitors. For example, some zamindars, who owned lands not yet under Company regulation, seem to have collected revenue (*malguzari*) without *amils*. The benefit was that the Rajas could not seize and coercively regulate these lands, which seems to have been more common in Bengal and Awadh. There was, however, a trade-off. As Sanbhu Lal observed, they were in a precarious position with little protection against corrupted people (*maiyen*), looting, theft and absconders.[27] Lal then went on to compare these zamindaris with Benares lands under Company regulation. What we see is that payments had to be more punctual and there was less flexibility. For example, the first revenue instalments (*qist*) had to be brought to the Company through its *amil*s – that is, through regulated channels. Nothing could be done informally. Lal also noted how the costs of non-payment and default were high. In these holdings (*amil engilisi*) the Company often ruined cultivators for a season because of their insistence on prompt, punctual payment. It was unlike the more flexible, negotiation-driven processes described earlier. The Company's Benares *amil*s were also given authority to search and intrude into personal property and domains, which could upset the honour and standings of 'respectable families'.[28] In addition, the fear of default and its consequences often forced cultivators to flee, unsettling the stability of an agrarian system of taxation that was moored in a tradition that was inherently flexible.

The movement of the Company towards more law-based and regular collection of revenue, coupled with its more 'bureaucratic' administration, was indicative of an early and crucial trend in the Company's early administration. Later in 1780s Benares, under Jonathan Duncan, we see a continuity of trends in Bengal and Benares under Fowke's residency. If the Company had started to shake up the chain of revenue administration, Duncan increased the penetration of Benares' fiscal wealth with double intensity. Duncan, for one, felt the practices described by Sanbh Lal and others – a revenue collection based upon a constellation of officers, private papers and personal interactions – should be more firmly anchored in law. Duncan himself was quickly frustrated in his navigation of the constellation of revenue officers: *qanungo*s, *amil*s and *tehsildar*s. He argued that they lacked legal 'teeth' to enforce standardized procedure. At first he saw hope in the *faujdari* courts, noting that

> the trial of delinquents, opposing the authority of government, in the Foujdaree [military] courts, from its regularity and formality, would contribute more to check this evil than the summary and arbitrary infliction of punishment practiced heretofore by the Zemindars and Amils of Benares.[29]

But he quickly moved away from the *faujdari* courts, as they were too reminiscent of British conceptions of 'oriental despotism'. Duncan therefore was convinced that arrears were best reclaimed though legal mechanisms, which would, compared to armed force, wean people off tax aversion. Duncan believed that 'the most material defect in the general administration of justice in this country was in respect to revenue causes, for which there was properly no Court, the Raja's Moolky Adawlut being principally for the causes of private property'.[30] He claimed, in his Orientalist lexicon, that caste and 'Moorish despotism' prevented the *raiyat* from appealing to higher authorities.[31] He wanted to let the Raja of Benares' *Mulki audalat* expire due to lack of influence/interest[32] and, drawing upon Bengal precedent, wanted *diwani audalat*s to have jurisdiction over revenue matters. There was a dangerous gap in the early Company fiscal state between law and revenue, Duncan perceived. He noted that most criminal officers were

Muslims and knew little of revenue: 'the Officers or Judges [of the Audalat] were Mussalmans, unacquainted with matters of revenue and whose habits and studies bore no affinity to such disquisitions'.[33]

It was here that the pensmen of Hindustan provided valuable fiscal knowledge for the Company. For Duncan, the chasm between law and revenue was the difference between despotism and 'just', regular administration, and the fiscal intelligence of various *qanungo*s and *patwari*s was the link between the two. This desire to 'legalize' revenue administration and the chain of processes therein is what partially propelled these scribes into importance. Their *jamabandi*s and *hastobud*s provided the factual sanction for a legally moored revenue regime. In a way, their Persian documents were 'legalized'. These subordinate Hindu paper managers played a formative role in the Company's north Indian settlements and were crucial to its first skeletal revenue structures. Here, *qanungo*s and *patwari*s moulded the taxation settlements which would eventually fund Britain's Indian empire in its embryonic decades. The *qanungo*s of Saktesgarh, for example, continually frustrated Jonathan Duncan's assessment (*jama*) during negotiations which spanned 1785–6, which kept him, as he put it, 'helpless'. They, not the Company, possessed historical rent rates on paper,[34] which gave them a negotiating hand in hammering out assessment rates and the very basis for such taxes. Without these, the basis for negotiated rent rates could not proceed, for to gain any idea of had been collected previously, the Company's rates needed to be based upon precedent. Outside of Benares in Kolasla, Duncan saw local *qanungo*s as key to legitimizing settlements, as they had been 'far more ready to enter into Cabooliats [revenue-agreements] than in any place I have hitherto been'.[35] Kayastha *qanungo*s commanded significant local loyalty regarding collections of revenue and the storage of accounts, particularly in smaller villages. This would partly explain why they rarely had legal cases brought against them at either the criminal courts (*nizamat audalat*s) or revenue courts (*diwani audalat*s), and why these more humble subordinates have escaped the eyes of historians during the transition to colonialism. Such paper power was seen during Jonathan Duncan's settlement of Shadiabad, after 1785. Here, the local *qanungo*s' mastery over paper forced the *amil* Mehndi Ali Khan to wryly complain: 'this year [Fasli 1196/1786] I am a loser of Rupees 2,640... this loss and penalty have not been incurred by your fixing the rental too high, but from the good will of the Canoongoes and their defeat of understanding'.[36] Couched in sarcastically flowery language, it was nevertheless a pointed finger at a subordinate clerical group who had allowed Muslim officers to establish such a fiscal dominance in north India in the first place. In a society that possessed a far from universal literacy rate, simple record keeping could be as powerful as an imperial order (*farman*).

With Duncan's settlement of Benares in the later 1780s, the role of extant scribes and pensmen increased and became firmly stitched into the fabric of the company's early state. *Qanungo*s were some of the first recognizable officers the British worked with in order to enact legitimate, yet ruthless, rent demands. Paperwork and documentation were needed to legally sanction such extractions of agrarian wealth. They were necessary for putting the Company's assessments on a regularized paper footing. Duncan, for example, sought out *jama* records going back 10 years as a basis for new negotiations,[37] and he noted in the early years of the settlement that Kayastha *qanungo*s

> were so materially useful for carrying on the various details of the collection, as well as in the quality of amicable arbitrations and umpires in many instances that never reached any regular court and in the capacity of witnesses in suits relative Zemindari rights of suitors in the Adawlat, that their assistance in all these departments could not be soon disposed with.[38]

Duncan was all the more likely to move towards paper proof since nearly one fifth of Benares' assessed revenue could not be collected due to property disputes.[39] Paper knowledge eliminated uncertainty and contestations over proprietary rights. Duncan's correspondence with various Collectors in the Benares District reveals a crucial role for these groups. In many parganas he gave *qanungo*s substantial local leeway to enforce regularized settlements. For example, he allowed the *qanungo*s in the parganas outside of Benares to determine and fix the rental rates for new leases for cultivation (*patta*s), drawing upon their local agrarian and historical knowledge. This gave them a hand in shaping the local rates of assessment,[40] since they served as the 'paper intermediaries' between cultivators and the Company. The *jama* of Benares for 1787, which increased 10 per cent from the previous year, was itself based upon a modified base of *qanungo* records which Duncan procured.[41] When it came to disputes over proprietary rights, particularly for smaller zamindari holdings, 'the general rule for deciding such cases was the *daul* or estimate of the Qanoongoe of the pergunnah… nothing could in general be fairer than this rule, and accordingly few of the complainants objected to it'.[42] Even famed revenue farmers such as Sheo Lal Dube of Jaunpur[43] could be frustrated by the 'paper authority' these *qanungo*s could exert. Dube accused the Benares *qanungo*s of forging estimates (*daul*s) which effectively took villages in Rauri out of his legal ownership.[44] Benares' net revenue yield to the Company dropped in 1780–7 by Rs 1 lakh,[45] but the pace of assessment, paper circulation and documentation all doubled in intensity after 1787. From the late 1780s Benares' yield increased annually. With the British seeking the most expedient form of sanction for their revenue demands, these humble officers' cooperation – and the documentation they provided – were essential. And these patterns reverberated farther up the Doab after 1803 and, with more intensity, in Awadh after 1860.

Bureaucratic administration and 'settling the countryside', c. 1780–1830

The mid to late eighteenth and early nineteenth centuries were periods which saw increased scope for Indian kingdoms to document and tabulate authority through taxation. These eighteenth-century state-formation processes, which were noticeable in most regional kingdoms, were vital in vaulting Kayasthas into positions to mould regional politics and state formation. Middling subordinate pensmen quickly found their skills in paper, penmanship and accounting valuable for any aspiring regional power, be they Nawabi, Maratha or British. If anything, the regionalization of Mughal power enhanced the political value of paper, pen and, by extension, those who were masters of such. It turned the 'second layer' of revenue administration, to use Irfan Habib's phrase, into an almost primary one. What is remarkable is that between 1770 and 1830 so many of these Hindus found ready demand for their services, not simply by creating themselves anew but by drawing upon select skills which they had honed for generations. These 'lowly wretches' found their political utility increase markedly in the period of British penetration of north India's agrarian wealth. A close analysis of how the Company gained its grip on north India's agrarian wealth reveals that these pensmen helped extend an agrarian tax base that would eventually fund Britain's Indian empire. It is in the first few decades of the nineteenth century that we can see the early colonial state's revenue tentacles and the formation of the modern colonial state. The origins of a more bureaucratic, procedural administration lay in the working of revenue collection in north India after the 1780s, the patterns of which would last deep into the colonial period. Extant eighteenth-century fiscal trends converged with the paper intensity of India's new rulers to greatly shape the emergence of the colonial state.

Northwest of Bengal country, in the large swathes of Awadhi territory ceded in 1801 and the upper districts of Agra and Meerut, wrested from the Marathas in 1805, the Company followed much of the precedent established in Benares. The territories the Company acquired between 1801 and 1805 were crucial, for they wrapped around the remaining Nawabi domains. This brought them into contact with Kayastha families who had served the Shia Nawabs' fiscal system. In districts such as Kanpur and Etawah Saxena Kayasthas transcended the recent demarcations between Company territory and Nawabi Unao. One of the reasons these scribes' importance was heightened compared to Bengal was that the British knew far less about fiscalism in the lush Gangetic plains, especially in townships such as Etawah, Kanpur, Agra, Allahabad and Farrukabad. The British gleaned some knowledge of the working of revenue, as we have seen, from their experience in Bengal after the 1760s. But upcountry the main way they worked the revenue machine was not through an intermediary zamindari class but through looser, extant groups of officers and paper managers. *Qanungo*s and *patwari*s, as Erik Stokes observed long ago, were the only real sources of information for the British when it came to settling these districts after 1803.[46] Of course, Stokes' generation was not interested in the social and service histories of these pensmen: they largely focused on British debates about proprietary rights and the nature of rent (which Stokes later admitted was no more than 'one clerk talking to another'). But upon closer inspection, the social and service histories of the Kayasthas of the Doab offer new ways of viewing state formation and how the East India Company secured what was, arguably, the most valuable agrarian tax base east of Suez. These provinces were so valuable because, if properly assessed and collected, they stood to double the Company's overall revenue[47] and offset its debts and liabilities to shareholders and from foreign China trade. Settlement Officers after 1801 quickly realized that Kayasthas were subordinate, though useful fiscal officers, for they were

> all taught to read and write Persian...the qualifications which they derive from their education and industrious habits are always in market…in all offices which require a knowledge of writing and accounts, such as secretaries and clerks in the army, and in the country down to the lowest village registers.[48]

These scribes provided the rent-rolls, *jamabandi*s and physicality of paper authority necessary for the Company's voracious fiscal appetite. Kayastha *qanungo*s quickly attached themselves to the Company's sprawling agrarian settlements in the Ceded and Conquered Provinces after the early 1800s (Figure 3.1).

Allahabad's settlement reveals some interesting early patterns that set the tone for the rest of the Doab. Acquired in 1801 from the Nawab of Awadh, Allahabad, aside from its significance as a pilgrimage setting for religious gatherings (*mela*s), was a stepping stone to the agrarian track upcountry and the Grand Trunk Road. It stood poised to offer sizeable revenues to the Company. Initial settlements began after 1803. And it was an area where Hindustan's paper managers shaped the early patterns of revenue administration in the first years of the nineteenth century. Allahabad's *qanungo*s worked with the British Collector, Edward Cuthbert, and provided physical paper records and histories of revenue returns which served as a basis for negotiations with cultivators, *tehsildar*s, zamindars and, particularly, those who held rent-free lands. Cuthbert found them indispensable, noting that 'at present the Qanoongoes… are the only constituted authorities to which to refer in

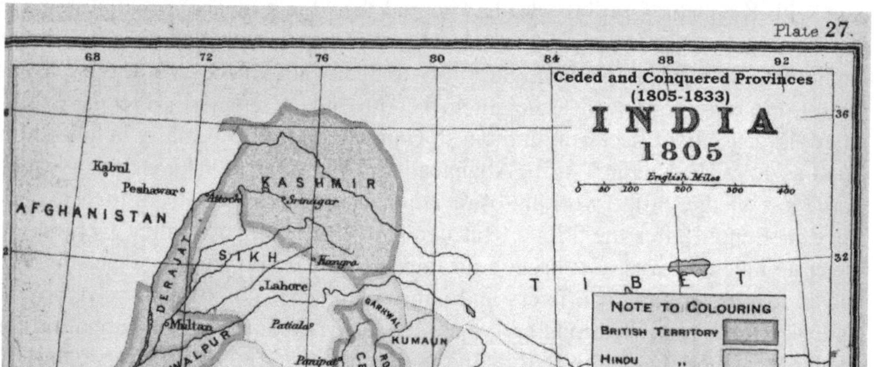

Figure 3.1 The Doab and the 'Ceded and Conquered Provinces' after 1805, modified from original. Reproduced with permission of Oxford University Press, USA.

questions of the Revenue of the Country and the only regular persons who keep the accounts of the receipts for the Pergunnah's [sic] actual produce'.[49] Of course, the British had a keen interest in bringing these officers over to Company governance. In the Allahabad District particularly it was noted that one service *qanungo*s provided to reluctant zamindars was shielding their land from assessment (*inam*) by the Nawabs through outright paper manipulation.[50] It was in Kayasthas' own interests to point out to their new rulers which landholders were engaged in what India's new rulers termed 'tax evasion'.

Similar dynamics were seen farther north. In Kanpur in the 1820s various *qanungo*s worked with British Collectors to identify additional sources of revenue from inherited property. In one case, the *qanungo* of Rasulabad brought to the attention of Henry Valpy lands which had a balance of Rs 2,500. This had been sitting for decades, uncollected by the Nawabs. But the *qanungo* noted that when it was passed from Sunsukh Roy to Musumah Subhodh via adoption it was liable for taxation; technically, it was a taxable estate transfer.[51] Agra District's savage assessments after the 1810s were made possible by the cumulative actions of lesser-known Indian actors. One was Khab Chand, a *qanungo* in Fatehpur Sikri. In 1822 he recovered revenue owed from one deceased Mir Mal Missur, which added Rs 187 to the estate's assessment.[52] This was just one example of Chand's contributions to expanding the Company rent role. Farther northwest, in Bareli, the Collector J. Routledge found it 'necessary to summon them [local *qanungo*s] for the purpose of… obtaining information respecting accounts and statements'.[53] For Routledge, the settlement could not go ahead without the local Kayasthas having the physical rent-rolls, which outlined historical rates. Farther north, in Saharanpur, Edward Thornton ensured that the stream of paperwork continued to go to the village *qanungo*, a position he saw as 'much desired'[54] in light of increasingly burdensome administrative, paper-oriented work. These pensmen, while evading the eyes of historians and kingly anthologies, were some of the most crucial staffers in the entire Company's early administration. It was in the British interest to employ these record holders and managers to help sanction their taxation demands and help navigate what, for them, was a labyrinth of revenue administration.

These dynamics persisted into the first four decades of the nineteenth century and provided the foundation for the emergent colonial state. Allahabad in the 1830s offers another example. This decade saw the Company dig deeper into its potential revenue under the 'Thomas generation' of administrators. Robert Montgomery, the Collector of Allahabad in 1839, found himself dealing with the realities of record keeping, assessment and paper. For Montgomery, the rates of *jama* were nearly impossible to assess without some precedent which could be physically documented. Here, the role of the subordinate record keeper (*peshkar*) and *patwari* proved indispensable. The *peshkar* gathered rent-rolls from neighbouring zamindars and *patwari*s, which allowed Montgomery to see, as he put it, 'the actual sum which had been collected from this village in more prosperous days'.[55] The corralling of these rent-rolls, made possible by *patwari*s and the *peshkar*s, facilitated Montgomery's decision to increase the assessment (*jama*) by nearly 20 per cent within a year.[56] Here, we see the increasingly savage revenue demands made possible by the material documentation scribes provided. For most Collectors and Settlement Officers, the paper rent-rolls were 'the most important part of whole [sic] settlements'.[57] Farther north, in Sardhana, T.C. Plowden's settlement in the late 1830s actually increased the overall number of accountants (*patwari*s and *qanungo*s) in assessing land value and rent rates,[58] which gave increased scope for these scribes. Increasing the personnel of his Collectorships widened the fiscal scope and reach of the colonial state. It also allowed *patwari*s, especially in districts where revenue was paid in grain, to exert substantial local influence. They could adjust the grain estimate (*kankut*) to punish or pamper 'loyal' or 'disloyal' cultivating castes, such as the Koeri in Bihar and the Ahirs of the Doab. Pen and paper, as much as policy, drove the Company's parasitic fiscalism deep into the Indian hinterland.

Enforcing payment and exposing 'fraud'

Another noticeable aspect of the early fiscal state was how it tightened the margins of flexibility and instalments in the payment of taxes. The Doab's pensmen sometimes forcefully assisted the Company in ensuring payment of revenue. Here, the more 'lowly' scribes were increasingly used to expose the rent-free holdings and hidings of various landed families. This was seen early on, in 1780s Benares. Uday Lal, the Kayastha *qanungo* of Singrauli, worked with a large zamindar, Raja Adil Shah, to get the *malguzar*s to enter revenue agreements (*qabooliyat*s) with the Company in the late 1780s. These *malguzar*s refused to recognize British authority. But they ultimately yielded, and paid, after Lal suggested to the British Collector: 'if you despatch a company of sepoys and a gun to punish the aforesaid rebels, the Government money will be realized'.[59] The *qanungo* could sometimes exercise subtle, though razor-like power. The Raja of Benares, Bulwant Singh, went as far as to destroy the *qanungo*s' records that contravened his claims to assessment-free lands.[60] For the Raja, these physical papers were the only things which stood between himself and increased Company taxation and, by extension, British meddling. Farther southeast, Collectors in Bihar followed a similar pattern. *Qanungo* papers were used to confirm *mafi* lands, which, like the Raja's case, was the difference between assessment and none.[61] The differences in this seemingly clerical categorization could be the difference between status via dispensed patronage and something lesser. In so many cases across the Doab and Bihari country the 'lowly' Hindu pensmen assisted the Company in rapidly expanding the reach and might of a new, more fiscally minded sovereign than its predecessors. And because a *qanungo* was a repository of fiscal knowledge, their signature was one of the most important written words in a whole settlement. One Settlement Officer considered the Kayastha's seal 'the most trust-worthy attestation to private deeds and agreements… regarding Landed Property'.[62] Factual, paper sanction was what India's new rulers wanted. And Hindustan's pensmen had plenty of it.

It also seems that the Company, after it started to settle the old Nawabi regions, after 1803, drew heavily upon extant records and pensmen who served the Shia rulers. These were the same *qanungo*s, *mohurir*s and *patwari*s who assisted the Nawabs in ramping up taxation after the 1750s. After 1800 they and their progeny continued to provide paper skills for the British. Here, we can discern two trends. First the early colonial state was a regime in constant 'want of necessary records'[63] from the regions wrapped around the Awadhi heartland. And, second, the possessors of such *kistbandi*s, *jamabandi*s and accounts came largely from older Kayastha lineages that straddled the late Mughal and early British period.

The British encountered numerous Kayasthas who drew upon history from a very early period. What we see is that the Company, in confirming the pedigrees and claims of various *qanungo*s, often encountered titles of recognition (*sanads*) from the Shia Nawabs. In places such as Bareli the early Company drew upon old officers with Nawabi roots. In confirming *qanungo*s and *patwari*s who were poised to work with the Company's new revenue settlements, the Collector Thomas Thornhill drew upon *sanad*s issued by Asaf ud-Daula from 1793.[64] They were then put to work quickly. Thornhill worked with the *qanungo* Mir Chand, who helped determine whether *jagir* lands held by one Ahmed Khan could continue to be cultivated by those who had no permanent interest in the land (*paykasht*). Chand gave an entire history of the land, how various rival claimants tried to obtain the *jagir* and explained to Thornhill how he could declare it taxable.[65] In Aligarh in 1809 the *qanungo*s of Sikander Rao prepared statements of *jama* paid to the Nawab between 1799 and 1803 at the cusp of British power. These statements noted how farmers, *malguzar*s and *tehsildar*s historically tried to prevent *qanungo*s from having too much information on the assets of their Estates. This was done mainly because they feared they would pass it on to the Nawabs, who would raise their assessments.[66] These scribes, perhaps ironically, ended up doing exactly that under the auspices of the early British colonial state.

There were plenty of other examples of the early Company state drawing upon older Nawabi officers to consolidate their gains across north India. Andrew Ford, the Collector of Etawah in the 1810s, hired one particular *peshkar*, Baghchand. Baghchand and his family were long-time residents of Farrukabad, and he had been employed by Nawab Asad ud-Daula for 16 years as a *peshkar*. In 1803, when Farrukabad was handed over to the British, he became a deputy scribe (*naib munshi*) in the Company's collectorate and later was appointed by Francis Ferguson as *peshkar* in Aligarh. Baghchand's family had a broader history of service, during both the Nawabi and early British periods. As Ford noted, 'several of his relations are now in the employment of Government', and his brother Bishen Chand was the *nazir* of the Diwani Court in Aligarh.[67] In Shahabad we see similar examples. Kitcha Ram, who worked in the Nawabi days from the late 1700s, went on to be a munshi for the District's collectorship under British rule and then a writer of local custom/tradition (*rusumnavis*) at the *diwani audalat* in the old *qasbah* of Jaunpur. Ram was later made Alexander Campbell's record keeper,[68] maintaining a handle on Campbell's ballooning paper establishment. A few decades later a newer Collector, Michael Mainwaring, drew upon two *qanungo*s who had service histories that reached into the precolonial past: Sheo Narain and Bhavani Dial. Narain's ancestors were *qanungo*s in the Nizamabad regions and had worked with Robert Barlow in Lucknow in the 1780s British residency, furnishing 'him with all the information and ancient documents required as appears by Mr Barlow's acknowledgement'.[69] Narain later gave Mainwaring 'considerable information by his knowledge of the former possessors of estates, and the history of the landed property in the Pergunnah'.[70] Here was another example of a humble scribe giving the Doab's new masters the fiscal paperwork needed to begin pincering the countryside. Farther west, in the middle Doab in Etawah, the Saxena Kayasthas Amir Singh and Bukhtawar Singh provided documentation in the form of instalment payments (*kist*s), revenue assessments (*jama*s) and collection and balance statements (*wasil bakis*), which, the British Collector observed, demonstrated that their lineages had been bound up with managing paper since the era of Akbar.[71] Nand Kishore was another example. From a prominent Kayastha family with roots in Saharanpur, he drew upon a longer lineage of service under the Mughals and then the British. Kishore's family had been learning Persian since the 1600s, and he became a *tehsildar* upon the district's conquest by the Company. In 1833 he was made a Deputy Collector and then a Deputy Magistrate in 1843, with powers of Covenanted Assistant.[72] He fetched a handsome salary of Rs 250 per month, which was higher than most *qanungo*s and *patwari*s across north India.

It does seem that many continued the service professions through generations, secured through patronage and, in some cases, strategic marriage patterns. The Saxena, Mathur and Srivastava Kayastha *qanungo*s continued to reaffirm occupational status and subcaste standings though endogamous marriages. Many of these scribes married within the same Kayastha subcastes to keep the occupational position within an extended family.[73] This had the effect of reaffirming the distinctions between regional Kayastha subcastes. The Saxenas of Unao and Etawah, for example, largely remained at the higher rungs of subordinate revenue administration. The net effect by the 1820s was that Saxena Kayasthas had greatly coloured the *qanungo*-ship and, eventually, the lower tiers of the Company's bureaucracy that reached into Hindustan's hinterland (*mofussil*). In 1820s Aligarh, again, the machinery of revenue administration drew upon Kayastha families with service roots in the Doab's precolonial past. The *qanungo*s in the Aligarh headquarters – Kaliah Singh, Gulab Singh and Mansur Rai – were all effectively hereditary, later being passed on to their sons, not through official sanction but by maintaining marriage patterns and learning traditions to position themselves as the most viable option for an expanding fiscal colonial state. And since these three were between 25 and 40 years of age,[74] this put their fathers in the service of the Nawabs as *qanungo*s. Across the borders in the Nawabi domains, *qanungo*s continued to confirm the accounts of *patwari*s in Awadh as late as the 1830s.[75] When Awadh was annexed by the Company, in

1856, these *qanungo*s were in a position to heavily tax Awadh and Lucknow's role in the 1857 Great Uprising and Rebellion.[76] It was a convergence of which the British availed themselves after 1858.

Paper records, landholding and the extension of taxable cultivation

Hindustan's *qanungo*s, *patwari*s and *peshkar*s, scattered across the riparian regions of the Doab, were the scribes with whom the Company came into early, frequent contact. From the early 1800s they greatly shaped early Company revenue settlements. And they also enabled the Company to consolidate their holdings more rapidly and efficiently than other regional states by extracting more agrarian wealth. Revenue assessments on the surface may have looked, according to some apologists, like 'more or less crude guesswork'.[77] Even Stokes himself seemed to imply that the British knew very little about fiscal and proprietary matters in the Doab. But a deeper inspection of early settlements shows that Settlement Officers and Collectors knew exactly how to work the dynamics of revenue collection, even if they wistfully whined about its complexity. The Company's fiscal state, in its early formation, drew heavily upon a welter of rent-rolls, paperwork and historical records to sanction their tax demands. And Hindustan's scribes played a crucial role. What the British did better, rather than differently from other kingdoms, was to more aggressively weld paper and scribes to the fiscal machinery of the state. Indeed, we should see the success of the Company state in its hijacking of key elements of eighteenth-century revenue trends, more than its mastery of 'colonial knowledge' or coopting of commercial families in the Doab. This was because the broader sinews of fiscal procedure would last deep into the colonial and independence period.

Much historical literature has focused on British views towards Indian property and rights. Indeed, Ranajit Guha's classic work on the Bengal Permanent Settlement remains the case study.[78] But the papers and rent-rolls possessed by Hindustan's scribes played a far more crucial role in altering proprietary rights and adjudicating land disputes after the 1780s. The British might have brought new legal conceptions of property to India, but they were shaped by the tier of scribes who possessed the paperwork of extant holdings. Benares, again, was a starting point. Jonathan Duncan after the early 1780s gave *qanungo*s the authority to eject zamindars and leasing cultivators (*pattadar*s) who refused to enter revenue engagements (*qabooliyat*s) with the Company.[79] Here, the early state's conception of fiscal sovereignty changed proprietary rights rather than vice-versa. There were other examples later, including in Allahabad in 1808. In that year a dispute broke out between one zamindar, Ganga Parshad, and the British Collector. Parshad claimed his individual *jama* was Rs 50 less than the previous year's. Cuthbert proceeded to consult the *qanungo*, whose papers demonstrated that Parshad had relinquished his zamindari lands, which had previously shielded him from the Rs 50 liability. Parshad tried to conceal this from the new authority but ended up paying when faced with the paper evidence.[80] He had his proprietary rights altered at a pen's stroke. The scribes' paper records also played a role in the legal dimension of landholding. In judicial cases, for example, *qanungo* records often decided the difference between legitimate and spurious land claims.[81] In places such as Kanpur and Allahabad in the first decade of the 1800s *qanungo* papers were used by British magistrates in adjudicating suits over land ownership.[82] In the 1820s a good number of Muhammadabad's *tehsildar*s were ejected from their holdings and their lands put up for auction, on the basis of the lack of documents on which 'they rest[ed] their claims to have the lands free of assessment'.[83] Here, simple paper records were used to alter landholding patterns in order to maximize their taxable value for the Company. In Gorakhpur the local *qanungo*s, Kishen Pershad, Purmesri Pertaub and Mokum Singh, provided Alexander Ross with 'paper proof' that the rent-free *jagir* held by one Mirza Lalun in Rampur was, in fact, liable for assessment (in spite of Lalun's protestations). Lalun went so far as to provide a copy of a *parwanah* from Asaf ud-Daulah and other documents from former Nawabi officials. Ross admitted that the lands were given to Lalun as *jagir* by Nawab Shujah Daulah,[84] and he suspected that the *amil*s had continued to collect revenue between 1794 and 1806. He then proceeded to consult the *qanungo*s of Gorukpur, whose documents indicated that the *jagir* was not rent-free as claimed. It was an allowance given to Lalun, and he had started to pay *jama*s through his *qabooliyat* with Raja Surfraiz Pal in 1806. Lalun's *jagir* was negated and included in Ross' triennial settlement[85] – a telling example of how scribes and pensmen helped push assessment and paper intrusion in the flux between Nawabi and Company rule.

From Saharanpur in the north to Ballia in the east, and the townships which wrapped around Nawabi Awadh, *qanungo*s were quickly attracted to the Company's more paper-intensive forms of accounting and, at times, relentless drive for accuracy. It is important to emphasize this. The procedural, paper-based nature of the early Company's fiscalism resonated with the Doab's scribes, and made their paper essential to British power. It also enhanced their value and that of the documents they possessed. Their Persian records were the foundations for settlement negotiations and tax assessments, which were the building blocks of empire. And there is a wealth of examples. In Etawah after 1803 the Saxena Kayastha *qanungo*s provided William Salmon with records that documented accurate assessments (*jama*s) and instalment agreements (*kistibandi*s) during the last eight years of Nawabi administration. Salmon noted that *qanungo*s could already be considered the Company's first generation of 'native Mofussil officers', who enabled the Company to actually collect revenue.[86] Another *qanungo*, Daulat Rai, provided Salmon documents which attested to the veracity of various written orders (*parwanah*s) *jama*s and *kistibandi*s.[87] Salmon wrote of his desire to 'know the state of the cultivations [in past years]',[88] and since they possessed revenue agreements (*jamabandi*s), balance sheets (*wasil baki*s) and historical rates of revenue paid, it was perhaps unsurprising that he admitted, like may early Settlement Officers, 'the realization of the Revenue depends on the permanence of the office of [the] Qanongoe'.[89] These revenue demands, which were the first real tentacles of the emergent state, accompanied by regulation, procedure and paperwork, were facilitated by the rent-rolls provided by these humble pensmen, who in so many districts were the most important officers for the colonial state.

In some instances, these scribes worked the grey area between custom and law to help cut some zamindars and *taluqdar*s down to size. Here, we see that paper documentation was becoming increasingly important to put teeth into legal adjudication of land disputes. For example, in Farrukabad in 1804 a zamindar from Churlamau named Mahapit Singh held villages in Bhawalpur, Pulia and Jaffarabad. Singh claimed allowances (*nankar*), which brought his assessment down to Rs 500 rather than the Rs 1,600 which the British Collector claimed was due.[90] *Nankar* payments were, on the whole, customary rather than codified and written down. But India's new rulers were impatient with grey, non-codified definitions and rights. The Collector looked at the *qanungo* records, which usually did not detail any payments.[91] *Nankar*s were known to the *qanungo*s but, crucially, were not written down. The local, old *amil* officers claimed the *nankar* was valid, as it was custom. But when the British Collector again checked the *qanungo* records, he concluded that the registers showed that 'any indulgence of this nature is not attested by the Canongoes, nor was his name included in the statement delivered in by the Regent'.[92] Singh's assessment, and the later selling-off of his lands, could be traced to its eventual 220 per cent tax-demand increase. Here, the welding of *qanungo*s to the new fiscal state created new categories of tax and land law by privileging, more than ever, the physicality of paper.

Another crucial development between 1780 and 1820 was the expansion of the state's scope of assessment. The Company brought more land under its scope than any sovereign before by cutting away at various 'exemptions'. *Inam* holdings were audited with *jagir*s, and the authenticity of *sanad*s was interrogated like never before. But the scribes who were able to shape British interpretations of documented Indian agriculture have been overlooked by historians. These pensmen, by providing more and more documentation to the state, helped bring further agrarian tracts under cultivation and assessment. The net effect of this was to increase the overall volume of taxable agrarian wealth and build up the fiscal belly of the early Company state. Indeed, the historical debate on north Indian agriculture in the first half of the nineteenth century has largely revolved around whether extended cultivation actually produced commensurate grain outputs.[93] But the intricate workings of *how* cultivation was extended have largely been ignored. These particulars in the paperwork shed interesting light upon the working of this paper-oriented revenue system and how it changed with the transition to British rule. What we see is that scribes and paper managers provided the British with the paper information necessary to penetrate deeper into Hindustan's agrarian wealth. These included drainable swamp tracts and uncultivated soils. Irfan Habib has pointed to the aggressive colonization of wastelands by the Mughals,[94] but the British outdid the Mughals by every measure, using scribes and paper to sanction these extensions. Again, 1780s Benares is a good example and set a precedent for farther upcountry. Here, *qanungo*s provided Duncan with detailed soil information, gleaned from their rolls, showing that a further 5,000 *bigha*s (roughly 4.8 square miles)[95] of new land could be farmed. Duncan quickly sanctioned this in the pargana of Dhoos Khas,[96] which put pressure on cultivators over the next decade. *Qanungo*s did much the same in Bulea.[97] Within a few years of their acquisition Kayasthas helped identify wells and clearable jungle tracts in Kanpur, Allahabad, Meerut and Shahabad, scouring through instalment documentation (*kistbandi*s), revenue returns and land surveys.[98] Even if some walled (*pukka*) wells cost Rs 300[99] to construct, which was a massive investment for the time, Kayasthas do seem to have been active in identifying sites for their construction with the cooperation of Collectors. But when it came to extending cultivation, Kayastha *qanungo*s were co-partners with their new hat wearers (*topi sahib*s). In Etawah in 1807 Saxena Kayasthas were the main pivot in helping the British Collector to raise the assessment by over 15 per cent.[100] The Saxenas helped identify uncultivated lands, locations for well-digging and, crucially, lands which had previously been un-assessed (*inam*). To the British, *inam* lands might as well have amounted to tax evasion and the 'defrauding' of government. Poor rains nearly ruined Etawah's yield in 1808, but 'the personal exertions of the Cannongoes …encourage[d] the Ryots in the cultivation', with the same assessment being paid as in the previous year.[101] In Etawah in the early 1820s the British Collector, Henry Newnham, worked with the records of two *qanungo*s, Sukh Lal and Nund Lal. Once they had pored through their papers, which stretched back into the late Nawabi era of the 1780s, they identified jungle tracks in Lakna that could be cleared and the soil tilled for cultivation. The whole pargana was brought under cultivation – an additional 231 *bigha*s.[102] Delhi between 1817 and 1837 experienced increased cultivation and taxation, and these pensmen continually provided and managed the assessments, returns and collation of agrarian revenue.[103] Kayastha pensmen helped Captain Lawrence survey Gorakhpur in the late 1830s and gave paper sanction to its increased assessment thereafter.[104] Indeed, the British were so dependent upon these scribes in the colonial state's early formation that officers in the 1830s later remarked how they manipulated British (mis)understanding of proprietary rights and how numerous *qanungo*s managed to get their own zamindari claims approved.[105] In the central Doab, total agricultural – and, by extension, assessable – land increased by roughly 25 per cent by the 1830s. Hindustan's scribes, as we have seen, played a key role in the expanded fiscal reach of the state.

In a good many instances the extension of assessable land came at the expense of older landed Muslim families. In Ghazipur in 1821 *qanungo*s brought un-assessed estates held by female descendants of old Muslim *jagir*s to the attention of the Collector, Robert Barlow.[106] This brought a further 19 villages under taxable cultivation, and the following year's assessment for the district was ramped up by 20 per cent.[107] One *qanungo* of Naharganj in Agra, Deo Shankar, managed to prise 26 *bigha*s of land near the Sikande Rao cantonment from one Turab Ali. Ali's argument was that his ancestors purchased the land, for which he provided a *sanad* from the old Shia Nawabs. But Shankar pointed out in his papers that the lands had been appropriated to the military cantonment before 1803,[108] which provided the precedent the British needed to deny Ali's claim. Ali went landless and destitute. In Bihar in 1816 the *qanungo*s Roshan Lal, Todar Mal and Maiwar Lal came forward with papers that proved a deed of rent-free-land grant (*altamgah sanad*) of one Mokurut Khan was forged. Khan's land were then assessed and brought within the tax roll.[109] In Dehradun in 1820 *qanungo*s played a key role in the settlement, the last section of which was an old Muslim *jagir* of one Erich Khan. This and four other estates were left unsettled by Samuel Middleton in the 1780s, and the Collector, William Money, wanted to bring them under *khas* management. But Khan's inheritors refused. The *qanungo*s then brought to light documentation which questioned the nature of the proprietorship, which made its assessable value skyrocket from nil to Rs 701, or a 77,000 per cent increase.[110] And in the process, again, the *qanungo*s proved their paper mastery: Rup Narain, Rambaksh, Madan Singh and Bikari Lal were all registered in the proprietary roll for ownership based 'upon the report of the Canoongoe'.[111] In the 1830s and 1840s estates in Shahjahanpur, Manikpur, Sukor and Nipsiya fell out of landed Muslim hands, and the prime beneficiaries were the very Kayasthas who managed the pincer paperwork of British revenue demands.[112] These included the Kayasthas Lala Sahay and Bhunipat Rai, the latter's father being the newswriter (*akhbar-navis*) of Nawab Asaf ud-Daula.[113] In some cases, as we can see, the 'Islamized' pensmen were helping undermine the very 'Islamic' undertones of Indian revenue administration.

There were crucial reasons why these more humble officers were so valuable for the early Company state. One was fiscal assessment. Many *qanungo*s, seeing the appetite of the colonial state, saw it in their interest to inflate assessments in areas with poor agricultural prospects. Many officers confirmed this and noted that they were as likely to inflate assessments as zamindars were to conceal them.[114] In many cases, *qanungo*s' estimated assessments looked enticing to early Settlement Officers. Their records' actual measurements 'generally gave [sic] a greater quantity [of assessed lands] than the [original] estimate'.[115] This had the net effect of booting out old families from their holdings. This happened in Agra after the mid 1810s, when Agra's assessment ramped up in three figure percentages. Here in 1815 the Collector Alexander Ross seems to have relied heavily upon the written records of the city's *qanungo*s. He had each *qanungo* survey (*nazarandaz*) the quality of land under current cultivation, and when their estimates were checked against the records of the *mirhad*s Belas Rai, Lalji Mal and Shaikh Ashraf the *qanungo*s' records gave a greater estimate of cultivated land. At a pen's stroke, the tax base was widened by 16,212 *bigha*s (about 6,500 acres),[116] which ramped up revenue demand the following year. And, to boot, Ross assented to the *qanungo*'s estimate that more wasteland could be brought under cultivation and, by extension, assessment.[117] Similar developments took place in Kalpi in the 1820s, where *qanungo*s' estimates (*daul*s) tended to be higher than those of the *tehsildar*s.[118] This trend persisted for another generation. Edward Thornton in early 1841 observed that *qanungo*s tended to provide higher estimates of produce in the presence of European officers than in their own accounts and rolls.[119] Indeed, it had become so marked that even Governor-General Moira noted in his diary written on the Ganges that one of the main blotches of the Company's short 12 years of rule in the Doab was the acquisition of auctioned lands made possible by 'Native Officers'.[120] Moira had the *qanungo*s of Hindustan in mind.

Kayasthas, of course, saw their own interests align with those of the early Company state. Because India's new rulers were voracious in their appetite for paper and fiscal knowledge, Hindustan's scribes stood to benefit from the extension of cultivation. They were the 'mofussil officers' in whom the British placed any vestige of trust regarding paper records and documentation – they would manage the paperwork. Kayasthas possessed the documents that mattered most to the fiscal state. This buoyed their importance to India's new rulers, who constantly had a 'want of necessary records'[121] to tax as they saw fit. Andrew Cockburn, the Collector of Allahabad, noted that *qanungo*s were 'the only Mofussil Officers upon whose accounts any dependence can be places and as they are fully capable of affording such useful information respecting the resources… of the different mehals'.[122] He worked with the *qanungo*s Punjab Rai and Basti Lal, both of whom painstakingly 'detailed accurately the particulars of many places, the Jumma and other particulars'.[123] And, again, there were reverberations from Bengal. Most zamindars who benefited from the Permanent Settlement (1793) in Bihar maintained Kayasthas as *diwan*s,[124] which further enhanced their importance. These *qanungo*s might have been private actors, but they still reflected broader shifts towards more intrusive paper management, regulation and assessment across north India. The importance of this office, and the enforcement capabilities of the new colonial state, were underscored by one crucial regulation. In most parganas between Bareli and Patna all 'summons for payment' (*dastak*s) had to be drawn upon the '*qanungo*'s office' (*qanungo daftar*).[125] These agrarian settlements, the spearheads of modern, emergent forms of government, allowed Kayasthas to reassert their local influence with double intensity under these paper-minded sovereigns from across the seas.

Continuity and change: welding pensmen to the state

Early British agrarian settlements, as we have seen, unleashed new forces of intensity and regularity into Indian governance. The fiscalism of the colonial state by the 1810s clearly suggested this. Yet at the same time this newfound intensity lent weight to forces which encouraged an uneasy, though interconnected, degree of continuity and change. First, there was significant change in the fabric of revenue administration under the early Company. By putting *qanungo*s on a permanent, regular footing, backed by funds paid out of the Benares treasury, the British firmly welded these officers to the emergent state. Their paper skills and their actual paper repositories became stitched into the new state's prerogatives. Anand Yang, in his examination of the Saran District of Bihar under the Permanent Settlement, has argued that *qanungo*s lost out under the British. But if we take a broader look across the Doab, much evidence points to the contrary.[126]

The Company achieved this not just by affixing *qanungo*s to the state, but also by severing their precolonial interconnectedness with other revenue officers.

Take the case of *amils*. *Amils* in the eighteenth century had started compensating *qanungos* via monies and smaller land allowances[127] and served as middlemen between district authorities (*sarkars*) and village economies. This largely replaced the system of direct salaries established under Akbar. British Settlement Officers outdid the *amils* by immediately paying *qanungos* and *patwaris* from the Benares treasury. This bound them to regulation and procedure. In 1780s Benares Duncan achieved this remarkably quickly, by issuing new 'titles of recognition' (*sanads*), salaries and by 'releasing them from any dependence upon the Amils over whom they stood as the natural and constitutional checks'.[128] By simply buying them out, the British immediately linked *qanungos* to the machinery of revenue collection and administration. Similar developments were seen in Bundelkhand after the 1810s with respect to *patwaris*. They were not replaced, but left in place and brought under greater regulation, where their accounts and physical paperwork were duplicated and made state property.[129] British Collectors constantly wrote in the 1810s and 1820s of the need to 'continue the office of the Canoongoe… under a liberal system and appropriate *regulation*'.[130] New regulations for the Ceded and Conquered Provinces in 1803 recognized *patwaris* as established 'revenue officers', while *qanungos* were made similarly official a year earlier.[131] *Patwaris* and *qanungos* could still be retained by zamindars, but the orbital gravity of Company regulation and paper-driven administration – in addition to guaranteed steady salaries – ensured that they rarely were. They mostly gravitated towards work with an expanding colonial administration in which paper enhanced their importance in local society.

Many of the extant pensmen and scribes of the Doab were quickly integrated into the colonial state's fiscal apparatus. Benares, again, was a key city. Duncan moved quickly and refashioned the Benares *qanungos* into 'Native Registrars'[132] as early as the 1780s. He saw them as indispensable in realizing land revenue and managing the Company's paper-oriented dominion. Duncan did trim their numbers to two per pargana,[133] but they clearly helped shape his settlements and set the standards for revenue administration for the next two generations. Kanpur after 1803 was another example. Even though British Collectors were constantly averse to 'inherited' *qanungo*-ships (which they interpreted as a licence for waste and inefficiency), these officials were valuable in providing the physical paper needed to underpin revenue demands. The Collector of Kanpur in 1807 allowed their replacements to come from the same families: 'where the [heir] of any Canungo may be found capable he should be preferable by the Collector in his nomination for the Sanction of Government'.[134] In these early years, the Company entrenched rather than cut down the *qanungo* lineages (*qanungo ka khandan*). And since they regularly taught their offspring the required skills of accountancy and paper management,[135] in addition to their *maktab* schooling, *qanungos* adapted well to the bureaucratic, paper orientation of the Company. By the 1800s the Nigam Kayasthas of Kanpur were already instructing their children how to work under the new Company's regulations and expectations in order to maintain the *qanungo* as an inherited position.[136] And into the mid nineteenth century, much of these extant lineages were projected into the sinews of the colonial state's fiscalism.

Nevertheless, there were still significant changes in how *qanungo*s and Kayasthas worked. The Company's new extractive agrarian settlements enacted major changes in the composition of precolonial positions. Between 1803 and 1806 the regular complaint of British Settlement Officers was about *qanungo*-ships being handed down to brothers, sons and relations on spurious claims.[137] Regulations which revised the office of the *qanungo* were enacted by the Board of Revenue in 1802 and 1822. On the surface, the Board's pronouncements regularly charged Settlement Officers with keeping 'economy' and 'waste' in mind, to avoid simply passing the *qanungo*-ship to one's son. But often the opposite happened. The value these pensmen offered to India's new rulers proved substantial enough to maintain Kayastha families' inherited traditions of paper service and, by extension, subcaste standing. One example was seen in Chakkan Lal. A Kayastha from the village of Aryano in the Allahabad District, Lal came from a tradition of paper management under the Nawabs.[138] Lal was later was employed by Cap Kirkpatrick, Maj Stewart and Maj Palmer as a newswriter (*akhbarnavis*) to communicate messages across various districts.[139] Given how important literacy was to Kayasthas' identity, a Kayastha family's dominance of a position over generations was possible in spite of it being 'de-inherited' by Company regulation. This enabled Kayasthas to turn the office of *qanungo* into a hereditary position, in spite of its inherited nature being officially scrapped in 1808. Michal Mann has pointed out how Regulation IV (1808) got rid of the hereditary nature of *qanungo*s, moving towards a system of merit appointments.[140] But legislation did not simply wish it away. Kayastha *qanungo*s were able to maintain the inherited nature of the post deep into the nineteenth century. Another example was seen in Bareli after 1803. A number of older *qanungo*s, aged 50–60, were recommended for dismissal by local zamindars. But the Collector, Thomas Thornhill, had their younger offspring – Jaswant Rai, Purun Mal, Bhup Singh and Jawahar Singh – appointed for 'rendering the Office of Canongoe… useful and efficient'.[141] In Shahabad in 1816 the officer in charge of court pleas (*sheristadar*) of the collectorship, Shankar Lal, retired after 'long and faithful services and respectful character'. His son, Gopal Chand, was nominated by Andrew Campbell to succeed him and hold a joint appointment as assistant treasurer in Campbell's office.[142] *Qanungo*s between 1800 and 1830 tended to become hereditary and tenured in spite of regulation. In a way, the unofficial 'tenuring' of the position within extended families had been a tradition since the time of Emperor Akbar.[143] And Company regulations seem to have not had that substantial an impact upon this continuity within various lineages.

Of course, over a generation a good number of *qanungo*s were dismissed. But again, if we read closely, it seems to have been particular ones. The *qanungo*s who were not appointed officially by the Company seem to have been those claiming the *suddoi* cess (around 2 per cent of revenue collected).[144] This customary 'cut' riled early Settlement Officers and came under the cost-cutting radar almost immediately after 1803. In the spirit of Emperor Alamgir, the Company reduced the number of official *qanungo*s to two per pargana. But, of course, many remained and refashioned themselves as *peshkar*s, decree writers (*decreenavis*) and more general paper managers. Kayasthas also utilized marriage alliances within endogamous Kayastha subgroups (save the Bhatnagars) to ensure that most large landed proprietors in Bihar had Kayastha treasurers (*diwans*) managing their estates.[145] In these cases the inherited nature of positions was replicated *in spite of* official regulation. What Company rule did was to confirm rather than contort this dynamic.

Still, these scribes did experience significant change. Much of their daily workplace rhythms and aesthetics were changed markedly. As *qanungo*s and *patwari*s, Kayasthas were transformed from Persian-literate gentlemen, who managed revenue and distantly symbolized courtly culture, into clerks who represented the emergent colonial state's bureaucratic and utilitarian authority. They were more bound by regulation than they had been under the Shia Nawabs. Kayasthas became more regularized officers, bound by time sheets, increased paper regulation and, after the 1830s, by a new official language of governance. Increasingly, alongside the *Fasli* calendar they had to account for a new calendar (*taghvim-i-ingilisi*), with seasonal and liturgical rhythms markedly different from those of both the Persian and *Fasli* versions.

Cutting down the old administrative apparatus

As we have seen thus far, *qanungo*s were indispensable to early agrarian settlements. They helped shape the contours of the early colonial state's fiscalism. But this came at the expense of other 'old officers'. It was a zero-sum scenario. This can be seen in what happened to various *amil*s. *Amil*s, who were the equivalent of a Collector before Company rule, initially worked well with British settlements. In Awadh before 1801 *amil*s had acquired extensive local authority in bringing the *raiyat* to heel under the Nawabs and in enforcing payment.[146] They held considerable powers under the Nawabs[147] by extending the Shias' tax reach deeper into the middle Doab's countryside. They therefore played a crucial role in helping the Nawabs ratchet up their revenue collections after the 1730s. Part of the reason had to do with their non-official status and the extra-judicial ability to use force to ensure payments, commanding smaller detachments of soldiers (*sipahi*s).

But under the Company *amil*s lost out quickly. The British, obsessed with procedure and 'extra-juridical authority', believed they wielded too much authority. They fell foul of a procedural state that disliked 'violent collections'. It was too reminiscent of stereotypes of 'Oriental despotism'. In the eyes of the British, though, *qanungo*s were paper repositories with little executive purview. They were far more malleable. The British Collector theoretically negated the *amil*'s very administrative existence, as in Bengal after 1772. But by paying and regulating pay, the Company made *qanungo*s dependent upon the state and not upon *amil*s. The latter were made irrelevant to the new working of revenue collection overnight, for *amil*s neither possessed records nor issued salaries to those who did. Between Bareli and Benares British Collectors severed these links by issuing the *qanungo*s' salaries and making them take oaths to bear honest, impartial accounts. They held the axe of dharmic judgment over these clerks' necks, codifying a penalty of 'loss of dharma' (*adharma*)[148] for fraud and perjury. Aware of

Kayasthas' reputation for paper chicanery, the Company, perhaps crucially, forbade the use of Kaithi in rent-rolls under its jurisdiction.[149]

Various other cogs in the pre-British revenue wheels also lost out quickly. *Chaudhuri*s and 'headmen' (*mirhad*s) are perfect examples. In the settlements of Etawah after 1803, for example, it became clear that *chaudhuri*s and *mirhad*s were some of the first 'native officers' to be axed under the Company's new, more paper-intense and economically minded revenue demands.[150] They received no salaries and most were either fired or pensioned off. *Chaudhuri*s themselves were often large zamindars and had little management over the revenue papers that mattered most to the British. But because they either possessed or were made to work with 'any paper relative to the public revenue',[151] *qanungo*s' skills and training were exactly what was required to harness India's vast agrarian wealth. There was also the bolstering of the *tehsildar* at the expense of older officers such as *amil*s, *chaudhuri*s and *mirhad*s. *Tehsildar*s were put under direct state control and pay. They became the enforcers of revenue patterns and law in villages across the Gangetic plain.[152] In the northwest, in Rohilkhand, *tehsildar*s were estimated to have become as powerful as *amil*s were in Nawabi Awadh.[153] So much so that one British Collector admitted that 'the Cutcherry of the Tahsildar is a tribunal at the door of every man'.[154] While the *tehsildar* mattered less for revenue, his enhanced political position was a by-product, rather than a cause, of these broader ruptures in the fabric of revenue administration.

Yet Hindustan's observant pensmen, navigating these broader changes, also played a role in shaking up the character of revenue administration. For example, they often gave regular encouragement to the British to strike the various *malguzar*s and *amil*s out of the chain of revenue administration. Sanbhu Lal, as early as the 1780s, called on the Company to cut out *malguzar*s and *amil*s, claiming they fleeced farmers, siphoned off revenue (*namakhari*) and 'ate the wealth of people' (*mal mardom khori*) as intermediaries. Lal accused these officers of selling the company's grain revenue for profit on private markets[155] to *bania*s and merchants. *Malguzar*s and *amil*s, as we have seen, were in an ominous position when faced with such accusations and lost out rapidly. Hindustan's scribes set themselves up to become the enforcers of a purportedly more 'neutral', procedural and paper-based revenue administration. This eliminated the need for *malguzar*s, *amil*s and extant revenue officers, who, to the British, were too mired in personal relationships, irregular procedure and the prospect of 'graft'. Lal, like so many other *qanungo*s across the middle and lower Doab, encouraged the British to maintain a 'lean' fiscal administration by positioning scribes as the real repositories of fiscal and agrarian intelligence.

The scribe Chatar Mal, again, offers us another example of how Hindustan's scribes adjusted between empires. In the early nineteenth century one of the most rankling issues for these new pensmen was that the Company used the *Fasli* and Persian lexicon of revenue but their dates were often side noted using the Gregorian calendar. Mal observed that this could cause irregularities in documenting harvests and collection dates.[156] He noted that while the *Fasli* calendar was well suited to the rhythms of the monsoon cycle and India's agricultural seasons,

English seasons were disjointed from its agricultural rhythms. Some months covered different lunar and solar periods. Mal therefore constructed a codex for future pensmen to calculate which *Fasli* months corresponded with English months (*ingilisi ma*s) (Figure 3.2). He wrote that in the Company's calendar, based on age of Jesus (*Hazrat Isa*), the months were set and inflexible. But the Persian (*taghvim-i-farsi*) and *Fasli* calendars (*taghvim padishahi*) were calibrated with the actual changes in seasons. Specifically, he wrote that while months in these calendars normally had either 30 or 31 days, the Gregorian calendar (*taghvim-i-ingilisi*) had the odd month of February, with only 28 days.[157] This caused confusion, Mal noted, for anyone who wanted to know the rhythms of the Collectors' movements. The confusion demanded a codex, which he constructed to help estimate the duration of *rabi* and *khurif* seasons and harvests, and to show how revenue agreements (*bandobast*s) done according to the *Fasli* season corresponded with the English calendar. In a way, Mal's *diwan* kept the pulse of revenue administration consistent, and served to facilitate the transition between Indian and British rulers, which boiled down to keeping the pulse of paperwork and revenue consistent. Mal was just one example of a scribe who adjusted minute yet crucial paperwork during the colonial transition.

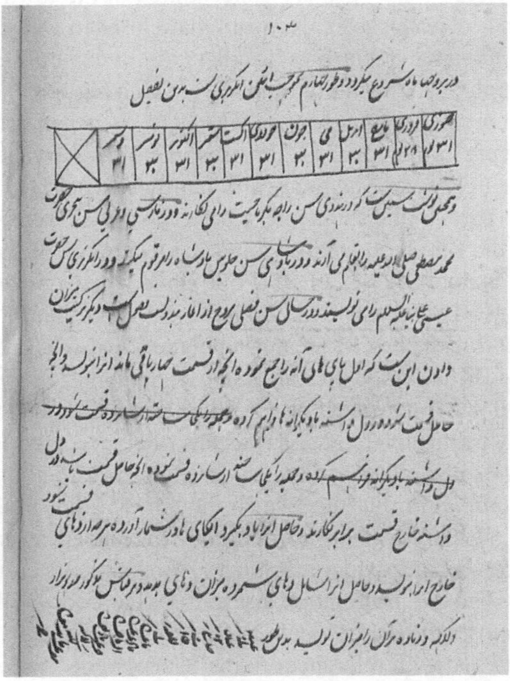

Figure 3.2 Codex used to correlate the Fasli calendar (*taghvim padishahi*) with the Gregorian calendar (*taghvim-i-ingilisi*), from 'Diwan-i-Pasand', Chatar Mal, c. early nineteenth century. Reproduced with permission of the British Library.

At the local level the Kayastha *qanungo* was often the only lettered person in a village, which gave them some degree of flexibility to temper local tax demands. Under the Company, though, this flexibility was largely eliminated by the Company's patterns of procedural revenue administration and, in theory, rendered illegal. Previously, as we have seen, these scribes worked within a morally interdependent concept of taxation based upon good persons and character. Long seen by cultivators and the *raiyat* as 'the refuge of the husbandman',[158] the emergence of a more rational bureaucratic form was apparent. Kayastha scribes were 'depersonalized' into utilitarian enforcers of procedural, bureaucratic authority. Their orientation also changed. The early colonial state shifted the *qanungo*'s horizon and interactions away from the cultivator and towards the trail of accountable paper authority which emanated from far southeast, in Calcutta.

Geographic variations: between Dinapur and Delhi

There were, though, important geographic variations in agrarian settlements. The salaries *qanungo*s commanded, and the degree to which they became stitched within the fabric of governance, often reflected regional demographics. Kayastha *qanungo*s and *patwari*s were far less common the farther the British travelled north from Benares. These scribes were far more concentrated in the townships and villages of the middle and lower Doab. This meant that closer to Delhi they often fetched higher salaries. *Qanungo* records in Rohilkhand, for example, seem to have been in far shorter supply than the middle and lower Doab regions.[159] This put a premium on paper documentation – and those who held it – when officers needed to complete assessments in the upper Doab. Around Delhi, Haryana and the upper Doab *qasbah* townships lesser Muslim gentry families do seem to have fared better than their counterparts to the southeast, where Kayasthas were more concentrated. Astonishingly, the Bareli *qanungo*s Gulab Rai, Nathwud Misra Lal and Munna Lal commanded annual salaries of Rs 1,500 under the Company.[160] Some could earn as much as Rs 4,800 each year.[161] Closer to Benares and Patna, the dynamics of labour markets kicked in. The greater supply of Kayasthas brought down average salaries, for the British could pick and choose; here most *qanungos* commanded in the mid Rs 600–800 range annually.[162] While the British paid them less than they earned under Muslim sovereigns, Kayasthas often accepted lower salaries than Muslim *qanungo*s, *chaudhuri*s and *tehsildar*s. *Qazi*s not only had a smaller fiscal purview than *qanungo*s, but the British thought Muslim munshis and scribes were 'exorbitant in [their] demands for fees'.[163] This made Kayasthas, who knew enough Persian to work the actual machinery of revenue, even more attractive to the British. They had the information and cost less to boot. Still, the effects could be uneven. The closer the British got to Delhi, the less frequently revenue proceedings were punctuated with references to the 'Canoongoe's records'. A close reading of the Company's revenue proceedings reveals a marked regularity of references to the 'Canoongoes' and their appointments in the early decades of Company rule in the lower Doab and especially around the Benares district. Yet this still made Kayasthas as valuable as their counterparts farther down the Doab to a sprawling regime which based its sovereignty on the right to collect revenue.

Fiscalism's effect upon the Indian countryside

The effects of this new fiscal Company state upon the countryside, townships and cultivating communities were substantial. The Doab provided a massive pool of fiscal resources to help fund the Company's increasingly regular border wars, bloating bureaucratic personnel and, to a degree, patterns of trade. If the *diwan* of Bengal initially made the company a proto 'fiscal state', then the revenues of the Doab and Bihar made the Company an Indian-invested empire. The slippery slope of the Company's military fiscalism – accentuated by Wellesley's expansionism, the border wars with Nepal, Burma and the Northwest Frontier and the rash of expansionism after the 1830s – all hit the Doab's peasants hard. Early British rule not only brought these peripheral regions of India more into the orbit of the north Indian plains, it brought the Indian cultivator more into the orbit of the Company's balance book. Paper and pensmen, as we will see, helped the Company's fiscalism bear down upon the Indian cultivator and peasant.

One of the most immediate effects of the new Company rule in the Doab was axiomatic: higher taxes and assessment. But there were a number of reasons for significantly higher taxation which reveal crucial trends in the early patterns of British governance, not least British stereotypes. As Robert Travers has demonstrated, it was the conviction that Indians could not be trusted as impartial administrators which largely led to Muhammad Reza Khan's quick downfall in Bengal.[164] This racially infused suspicion also made itself manifest in the broader effects and working of the early Company's fiscal state across the Doab, and punctuated the Doab's revenue administration after 1800. Early British Collectors were highly distrustful of the mostly Muslim *amil*s, *malguzar*s and *chaudhuri*s. The more paper-oriented, yet officially subordinate Kayastha *qanungo*s and *patwari*s, by contrast, had much less to lose. The British saw them as far more pliant. The Collector of Muzzafarnagar, Stephen Martin, found *qanungo*s far more cooperative, unlike Muslim officers, Rajputs and Jats, whom he called 'all disorderly classes'.[165] Maybe this is because these scribes were already somewhat procedural, having become so over the eighteenth century.. To Settlement Officers, Kayasthas' value lay in the factual repositories and fiscal intelligence they possessed. The higher Muslim *amil*s, *malguzar*s and other officials, as we have seen, oiled the revenue system by maintaining relationships across a constellation of stakeholders. They were less invested in the paperwork of fiscalism. The British, though, had no patience for navigating their complex social intricacies and etiquette (*tehzeeb*), which they loosely associated with the edifice of 'Moorish despotism'.

Another development that emerges from the first decade of the 1800s is the forcible binding of the Doab's agricultural economy into the web of the Company's fiscal liabilities as a joint-stock entity. The very organization of India's new empire subjected the rhythms of cultivation seed procurement to distant balance books in Calcutta and, ultimately, Leadenhall Street. The the vagaries of the Company's balance book took a toll on cultivators. For example, when the Company's deficits skyrocketed in 1797–1805 (largely as a result of wars with the Marathas and Mysore) Settlement Officers in the lush tracks of the middle and upper Doab were under significant pressure to maximize revenue. In 1802 the Company ran a surplus of Rs 9,635,832. But within three years, after it acquired the Ceded and Conquered Provinces, it accumulated a deficit of Rs 26,969,509.[166] Initially, the acquisition of these provinces in 1803 did little to attenuate the Company's bleeding finances. Much of this was due to the fiscal–military state of expansion and conquest under Wellesley.

Another trend we see early on, and in a break from eighteenth-century trends, has to do with the punctuality and procedure of collections. The Company was far more inflexible when it came to enforcing payment. British officials decried Indian rulers for using *sipahi*s to coerce cultivators and zamindars to cough up, which they associated with 'oriental despotism'. But the early Company taxed the countryside with an intensity that, in practice, wholly discounted a concern for the welfare of north Indian cultivators. As we have seen, this was a pillar of legitimate kingship for both Hindu and Muslim sovereigns. In the Jumna regions near Bhangipur the Collector Alexander Rose noted that, due to British tax demands, even if they were not all collected, 'all the profits which the poor people had had for years accumulated were forced into the government treasury'.[167] Etawah's poor rains in 1808 did not stop the Collector from getting the same overall revenue as the previous year,[168] at great cost to cultivators' livelihoods. Even in times of what the Company termed 'drought of extreme intensity' cultivators in Turi were still liable for at least 35 per cent of their assessed taxes.[169] Numerous other precolonial practices were jettisoned. The practice of instalment payments (*qistibandi*s) to alleviate scarcity was largely disregarded by the early Company. In a clear departure from the late Mughal revenue tradition, which allowed the perpetual delay of payments if not the cancellation of assessments, the Company had little patience. The British may have claimed that 'the country was never more prosperous',[170] but they were, at the end of the day, unrelenting and inflexible in their tax demands. This was exacerbated by the British inability to fully comprehend the nature of proprietary rights across the Doab, which ensured that they never yielded enough revenue to cover their commitments. Thus a zero-sum scenario emerged: the early Company state neither fully worked with nor understood the whole system of taxation and landholding rights, which invariably put pressure on Indian cultivators in the form of higher assessments. In a way, the ratcheted-up rents that punished the Indian peasant were broadly a failure in British 'colonial knowledge'.

Of course, it is important to draw out the variation in taxation's impact across north India. The new fiscal state did not affect all regions equally. What is revealed is that the Conquered Districts – mainly Agra, Aligarh, Bundelkhand and Saharanpur – received the brunt of Company revenue demands. These were some of the most savage revenue demands in early colonial history. For example, the areas of Bundelkhand and upwards from Agra saw their assessments ramped up to astronomical heights (Table 3.2).

Table 3.2 Changes in assessment in north India, 1805–18[171]

	1805 Assessment	1818 Assessment	% increase
Delhi	Rs 7 lakhs	Rs 7 lakhs	142
Bundelkhand	Rs 36 lakhs	Rs 118 lakhs	222
Saharanpur	–	–	325
Farukabad	–	–	173
Conquered Provinces[172]	Rs 4 lakhs	Rs 12 lakhs	225

Delhi, in spite of the British claim to be 'protecting' the Mughal emperor from the Marathas and Rohilla Afghans, saw its overall assessment rise over 142 per cent within a decade and a half. But it was the old Pathan and Rajput contested township of Bundelkhand that got the worst of it. Its overall *jama* climbed 417 per cent within 15 years. In so many cases, 'rebellious' countrysides and townships were 'pacified' through savage, unattainable revenue demands. Districts north-west of Agra regularly fell into deficits after the 1810s because parganas could not meet British revenue demands. This had crucial spillover effects upon early patterns of colonial governance. It engendered more regular litigation and civil suits over regulation and rights. Since Bundelkhand was not formally wrested from the Peshwa's authority until 1817, it does seem that fiscalism was used as a tool to slowly prise the region from the Marathas' grip, partly by creating crises of fiscalism.. It also did not help that the Bundelkhand's settlements were made in Lucknow rupees. The Nawabs' rupees were more valuable than the Srinagar rupees previously in circulation. In a monetary twist, this made the costs of paying the Company 40 per cent greater than they would have been otherwise.[173] This potent combination of fiscal inflexibility and emergent state formation is what frightened cultivators and tenants the most – precisely what Henry Tucker in the 1820s called the 'deadly hand of the tax gatherer'.[174] Cultivators saw a direct relationship between the two certain things in life: death and taxes. And the effects compounded themselves over generations. The Company's high revenue demands, combined with falling prices for *jowar* and other grains, often forced peasants to switch over to cash-crops. Faced with the encroachment of cash-crop farming with *bania* money, cultivators were doubly hit. It should be no surprise that one of the highest taxed regions of the Doab – Agra District – saw 78 per cent of cultivators in debt by the 1870s.[175] Instructively, a close reading of fiscal procedure reveals that famine and dearth were never officially listed as legal reasons for altering a village's *jama*.[176] The British Collector, backed up by a staff of subordinate, paper-wielding scribes, was often seen as an ominous sign, an affirmation that humanity was living in the dark era (*kaliyuga*).

The Ceded Provinces of the middle and lower Doab seem to have been taxed less heavily (Table 3.3). But they still saw their assessments rise quickly. Between 1803 and 1818 the overall *jama* of the Ceded Provinces jumped a mere 5.6 per cent, whereas that of the Conquered Districts skyrocketed 225 per cent.[177]

Table 3.3 Changes in assessment in north India, 1805–18[178]

	1805	1818	% rise
Ceded Provinces[179]	Rs 14 lakhs	Rs 17 lakhs	6

But the net effect of Company administration upon the Doab on the whole was still marked and felt across the fabric of village society. Across numerous collectorships in the lower Doab after the early 1800s the *jama* was raised 44 per cent within five years.[180] After the 1830s and the effects of the Thomason generation the Doab accumulated enough agrarian discontent that it should be no surprise that these regions ended up at the epicentre of the Indian Mutiny and Great Uprising of 1857. And all these cases aside, the cumulative effect of new British settlements enabled the Company, perhaps aside from the famines of 1833–8 in the Baiswara region, to pump out significant portions of Hindustan's agrarian wealth between 1770 and 1840. Even by the mid 1810s the Company had managed to extract an additional Rs 14 million[181] from the provinces it had acquired through conquest. If the Mughals attempted for generations to crack what John Richards called the 'hard cyst' of village autonomy,[182] the British were far more successful. They achieved it by surreptitiously piercing it with procedure, paper, fiscal sovereignty and an army of scribal groups, whose papers' weight was felt in the smallest pargana.

Broader effects upon the countryside: demographics and discontent

The broader effects of the Company's new 'fiscal state' upon the countryside of the Doab and Bihar were substantial. The Company's fiscalism penetrated deep into the Indian agrarian economy and the fabric of villages. Mike Davis has famously argued for the role of colonial policy in the emergence of several 'late Victorian holocausts' in India, mainly the famines of 1876 and 1896 in north India.[183] While British aloofness contributed towards later nineteenth-century famines, the famines of the early nineteenth century seem to have received less attention. A careful examination of the early fiscal regime of the Doab does suggest that the Company's taxation arrangements were as crucial as the commercialization of agriculture in the impoverishment of Indian cultivators and peasants. The tax demands of the Company state exacerbated the fits of drought and flooding that punctuated the 1830s.

One can gauge the impact of new Company revenue arrangements by looking at the levels of agrarian discontent in the first half of the nineteenth century. Michal Mann has demonstrated how these regions were subject to constant, low-level revolts against British tax demands[184] and, as we have seen here, new regulations. The effects were felt immediately after 1803. There were repeated uprisings in Etawah District after 1803,[185] and the disturbances in 1824, well documented by the 'rebel bureaucrat' Frederick Shore[186], seem to have largely been the result of Regulation VII (1822).[187] Specifically, this legislation pushed for more intense scrutiny and projection of anticipated yields and sought to discount the long-standing *khusrah* surveying method. Company directors convinced themselves that the *khusrah* was not only inaccurate but that it did not reveal what was actually there. Again, this was the perennial British distrust of Indians and precolonial fiscal methods. Yet the aspect of paperwork was perhaps the most crucial. Settlement Officers demanded so much historical precedent because of the way in which the Company's fiscal procedure worked. They had to project future yields by looking at historical rates of return. They naïvely believed they could anticipate yields in five to ten years' time. This approach – drawing heavily upon Smithian, Physiocratic and Ricardian economic theories – dangerously presumed lineal improvement and economic development. It was a major misconception that would have disruptive and deadly effects for the Indian peasantry. The way instalment payments (*qist*s) were remitted was also changed. *Kist*s were crucial, for they were the 'mortgaging' instalment plans which, when flexible enough, allowed cultivators to meet Mughal revenue demands within a reasonable degree. Previously, under the Nawabs, there were about eight or nine per year. The NWP government in 1841 reduced this to four, with two *khurif* crop *kists* (November to December and then around January) and two *rabi kist*s after 1 May.[188] This meant that the lien on expected produce, a staple of Mughal and Awadh administration, was entirely discarded. This might have disempowered many pensmen and *qanungo* registrars, but the net effect was to harden demands on cultivators, which in itself generated further paperwork to cover default and, eventually, legal procedure. Cost-cutting and efficiency raised the stakes for cultivators to meet the less regular, though higher, levels of taxation.

Yet there were serious flaws to this sanguine approach. 'Anticipated' yield ended up as a convenient cover for higher assessments. This kicked the can down the road, hoping that higher yields would eventually balance out the initial assessments. This was compounded by an early generation of Company officers in the Doab between 1803 and 1820 who were still 'learning off the cuff'. This made them unduly dependent upon the papers of pensmen and bound them to the Company's expected returns. It also ensured that the most expedient settlements, which themselves were subject to inflexible procedure and deadlines, were based upon *expected and anticipated* agrarian output. This had the net effect of generating regular over-assessment. Other local fiscal traditions were also done away with. *Taqavi* loans, which were used as advances to cultivators for growing crops and usually paid out of the local treasury (*khazana*), were replaced with private merchant money. In the 1830s many pre-1830s *taqavi* loans were called back, which further impoverished a peasantry already under heavy assessment and falling agricultural prices. Discontent was simmering. The disturbances in Rohilkhand – reeling under the pressure of tax demands which were then exacerbated by *bania* lending practices – were so frequent by the 1840s that one piece of advice given to British Collectors was 'take your gun in your hand, and go among the people'.[189] In so many cases the British created a myth that they had 'settled' the north Indian planes with 'just' administration. In reality, they had merely 'papered' over cracks their fiscalism had created in the first place.

The fiscal trends of the early Company also had a major impact upon the Doab's demographics and migration patterns. For example, the tendency to 'average' revenue assessments for an entire district had significant demographic effects.

Assessment rates could vary considerably between parganas within a single district. Cultivators who could migrate therefore did so, and it seems increasingly so after the 1810s. In a bid to escape the heavy Company tax hand, previously settled cultivators migrated to neighbouring districts to pay lower rates. For example, this was seen in smaller parganas in Kanpur after the 1810s. In Bithur overall assessment in one year was Rs 260,497, but farther north along the Ganges in other districts it was only Rs 11,264.[190] New methods of assessment also became more invasive after the 1810s. Officers from the Great Trigonometric Survey saw their machinery smashed,[191] symbolizing resentment against this new fiscal invasiveness. Francis Fowkes' munshi Subhan Lal, having witnessed Benares' transition from Raja to Company supremacy, wistfully noted in the 1780s that India had never faced the disaster of such interrogations and questions about agrarian wealth (*hindutsan aslan ru mostofi na dide va motlaga mosibat baz pours va baz khaste ne keshida ast*).[192] Sometimes this resentment towards the state's prying eyes translated into smaller-scale migrations, especially during the scarcity and dearth of the 1830s. Agra in 1838 saw tens of thousands emigrant cultivators from throughout the Doab arrive, hoping that the large administrative and cantonment presence would offer better chance of relief.[193] In the cases where it was feasible, many simply ran from the Company taxman and his army of scribes.

The reverberations of these fiscal patterns, and their spillover into demographic change, also had a commercial and financial aspect. To begin with, paper procedure did not always 'settle' the countryside. In many instances it seems to have unsettled the countryside through migration and agrarian discontent. This, in turn, froze credit from bankers and *mahajan*s, who were less willing to lend for seed, ploughs and cattle in unsettled districts. In Agra *bania*s stopped lending seed in lieu of ceased *taqavi* loans from the Company.[194] Much of this converged, it must be stressed, due to the toxic combination of increased assessment and surveying. Indeed, the 1837 famines in Agra and the upper Doab, representative of the 1830s' 'scarcity cycles',[195] were largely set in motion by punishing revenue assessments. When the *khurif* crop failed in 1837, and tax demands were not waived, the areas most affected had some of the highest revenue assessments in the Doab: Mathura, Agra, Etah, Farrukabad, Kanpur, Kalpi, Etawah and Mainpuri.[196] The Commissioner of Farrukabad, lamenting the passing of Holt Mackenzie's Resolution VII (1822), which mandated greater regularity in reporting averages, condescendingly quipped that 'men… so improvident as [those] of India, do not live by averages'.[197] The middle and upper Doab of the 1830s was a tragic example of cultivators' ruination on the altar of mathematical averages.

The Company's military positioning across the north India plains also had an important effect. In districts with a large British military presence, such as Kanpur, Allahabad, Bareli and Agra, assessments were regularly higher than in neighbouring districts. This was due to the larger demand for agricultural produce and regular rations for *sipahi*s, British soldiers and officialdom.[198] Cultivators in Agra district were particularly hit. Soldiers' higher purchasing power, which, in turn, brought merchant credit and demand for agricultural produce into the district, eventually helped ramp up assessment rates. Combined with the dearth of the 1830s, cantonments became targets for discontent. In the autumn of 1837 in Rohilkhand, Allahabad, Aligarh, Agra and Bulandshahr, armed men roamed about 'in quest of plunder', seeking relief from Company granaries.[199] Most of these cities had a substantial cantonment presence, which had higher overall assessments than neighbouring districts.

The early Company state exacerbated these broader demographic and fiscal changes through its ruthless efficiency in collections. Raising assessments was one thing; collection was entirely another matter. John Richards once noted that the Mughal state was plagued by the large number of *jagir*s that collected their own revenue.[200] Moving to the eighteenth century, Muzzaffar Alam has demonstrated how the Nawabi and Sikh kingdoms were hamstrung by gaps between calculated assessment and what was actually collected as revenue.[201] The British between 1780 and 1820 eliminated this disparity through a newfound bureaucratic ruthlessness, regardless of its impact upon agrarian markets, landholding patterns and the literal stomachs of India's cultivators. What was assessed was to be paid. And the Company became frightfully efficient at this. In the North-Western Provinces in 1818, for example, the Company drafted a net assessment of Rs 2,793,546 and managed to collect Rs 2,777,912, or 99.4 per cent of overall assessment.[202] Later revenue collections in Aligarh managed to collect 99 per cent of assessed revenue by the mid nineteenth century.[203] In places such as Azamgarh and Jaunpur, Collectors even managed to collect more than their assessed amounts.[204] It was perhaps this obsessive belief that not all assessments were being realized which explains why British officials claimed that the Wajid Ali Shah in Awadh passed up an unrealized Rs 14–20 lakhs every year.[205] While claiming to work the Mughal system, part of British success was that this unprecedented fiscal mentality was wrecking it from within.

And even if the Company could not collect all that had been assessed, its demands still initiated broader movements and changes in the fabric of village society. Many cultivation leases (*patta*s) found their leasing rights were usurped through the *lambardar* system of the upper Doab. The British saw *lambardar*s as the 'community representatives' of the Doab's *bhaiachara* land systems. With high revenue assessments that villages could not meet, Regulation VII (1822) authorized a Settlement Officer – if the village was in default – to hold the entire *mahal* to account and initiate legal proceedings against each individual leaseholder (*pattadar*).[206] In parganas where the Company quickly welded *qanungo*s and *patwari*s to the state these scribes and pensmen could exercise almost tyrant-like power in local villages. Agra in 1837 offers a great example. James Thomason found that because *qanungo*s and *patwari*s were the repository of land records, they could thrown their weight around and adjudicate local disputes: 'the power which the *putwarre* possesses of formatting these records [of payment and land] is great'.[207] Anchored to the taxonomical needs of the Company's fiscal state, the *patwari* in some cases could exercise almost passive–aggressive powers over peasants, cultivators and cattle herders. These masters of paper management, rent-rolls and land records were able to create categories of loyal and disloyal. With a simple strike in *nastaliq* – and later in Roman characters – these scribes, backed up by the colonial state, could exercise a 'paper tyranny' over cultivators and peasants.

Kayasthas and land acquisition

The broader fiscal effects of Company taxation and procedural, paper administration had another unintended effect. Kayastha pensmen, who were crucial in these developments, put their paper authority to use in acquiring lands after the 1780s. This seems to have built upon a pattern that emerged in the mid eighteenth century. Munshi Ratan Chand, agent of Syed Abdullah at the Delhi Court in the 1710s, noted early on that 'by fraud and force [Hindu scribes] had acquired rank beyond their deserts, and accumulated in their hands all the most profitable *jagirs*... after this the Hindus put every obstacle in the *diwan*'s [treasurer's] way'.[208] This might have been an overstatement, but Kayasthas were already translating their skills and vocations into consolidated landholdings, which was made possible by the ascendency of more paper-oriented administrations after the 1750s.

Far less land transferred hands in the first few generations of Company rule in the Doab than in Bengal. For example, in the middle and lower Doab only one tenth of cultivated area (around 95,000 acres) had changed hands by the 1840s.[209] This was in marked contrast to Bengal, where historians have estimated that more than half of zamindari estates changed hands via auction after 1793. But farther northwest, the paper intensity of the Company's fiscal administration served to enable Kayasthas to work the system and acquire significant landholdings in spite of the absence of zamindari legislation. In districts with large concentrations of Kayastha *qanungo*s the effects were substantial. In places such as Unao it was lopsided,[210] with almost one third of the district's lands falling into Saxena Kayastha hands. These acquisitions took on a newfound intensity under the Company's new fiscal regime. Historians have paid attention to the commercial *bania*s who gobbled up lands put up for auction by the Company's courts. But Hindustan's scribes, a looser group that historically had never been significant landowners,[211] gobbled up a substantial amount of land too. They were, after all, in a position to work the paper repositories that mattered most to British magistrates who adjudicated such suits.

In many districts across the Doab Kayasthas usurped the original owners in some parganas, which they accomplished by codifying their deeds and rights in the *qanungo*'s registrar of records.[212] They then moved quickly to consolidate their village power bases through their adjudicating paperwork. For example, in negotiations with the British Settlement Officer in Mainpuri in the 1830s Kayasthas were allowed to select their own managers and record keepers (*almad*s), along the lines of *jati* affiliation and marriage alliances.[213] As well as this, Edmonstone, the Settlement Officer, allowed these *qanungo*s to pay all *patwari* and *chaukidar* wages.[214] This underscored Kayasthas' ability to enforce local loyalty through paper.

Sometimes these transfers via paperwork could even acquire a 'communal' dimension. Again going back to Edmonstone's settlement of Mainpuri, Kayasthas persuaded him to keep the hereditary Muslim collector (*sadr malguzar*) shut out from this process. This effectively 'debarred [him] from interference of every description'.[215] *Malguzar*s often were modest landowners and in Mainpuri attempted to shield their lands from assessment. The more service-dependent, paper-wielding Kayasthas were in a prime position to point out to the British those who were not 'paying their share', imagined or not. Edmonston also described how *qanungo*s used their paper skills and outright shrewdness to reclassify land records as inheritance of a member of the extended family, thereby codifying such rights and registering them with the land registry.[216] Henry Elliot, who settled Meerut in 1836, observed that by the time he arrived 'many families of Syeds, who possessed influence under former Governments *had* their residences here'.[217] This was especially so in the 1844 auctions which saw Muslim landholders lose substantial holdings, some of which went to Kayastha paper managers. In Azimgarh District Kayastha *qanungos* during the 1830s and 1840s gained substantial lands as zamindaris on default of revenue payments by both old Muslim families[218] and newer *banias* who could not meet British revenue demands. Many Muslim landlords who fell into arrears under the heavy British demands had to sell and mortgage their lands to Kayasthas *qanungos*, who possessed the paper know-how.[219] In Aligarh by 1810 many Syed families had been booted out, because, as the Collector noted, *qanungos* could manipulate the land records to put forth their own zamindari claims.[220] In Mainpuri, again, George Edmonston noted that

> Kayasthas'skill, perseverance and good manners are the more remarkable, when the condition of and appearance of the villages which they hold are viewed in juxtaposition, and compared with those coterminous and held by other proprietors.[221]

In the early days of state formation, as Hindustan's scribes knew very well, the pen was often mightier than the sword.

There are numerous examples of scribes acquiring landholdings through paperwork. In Suryapur in the Shahabad District it was noted that Kayasthas practically 'owned' the city through their dominance of the office of *qanungo* and ability to register lands in their families' names.[222] In the 1840s estates in the parganas of Sukor, Shahjahanpur, Manikpur and Nipsayeh seem to have ended up into Saxena Kayastha hands across Etawah.[223] Much of this intensified as the century wore on, and as British fiscal administration pierced deeper into Richards' 'village unit'. Farther to the northwest, in Bundelkhand, which had been hammered by Company assessments and collections, Kayasthas became the second largest group of landholders by the 1870s.[224]

These scribes also contributed to the broader changes in landholding pattern though liquidation. In many cases, their rolls provided Settlement Officers with justifications for selling off lands as a means of increasing revenues. One example was in 1804, involving the *tehsildar* of Kanpur, Akbar Ali. Ali noted that the *malguzars* had yet to pay up and that incarcerated debtors could not cultivate if they possessed little property. He cited a precedent of using force to compel payment. Punishment, after all, in the eighteenth-century Indo-Islamic tradition was partially symbolic. For Ali, the best solution was to liquidate the *malguzars*' land and personal property via auction:

> I am in hopes that from the sale of the villages, the said Sums in arrears may be caused to be paid – or that the amount may be returned to me by Government, or that in the Kist of 1212 F.S. the same may be credited to me.[225]

Various other Kanpur *tehsildar*s, such as Sheikh Rostam Ali from Musingnagar, pushed the Collector, John Richardson, to auction off the *malguzar*s' lands.[226] Their proprietary rights were to be verified, crucially, by the Kayastha *qanungo*s: Shitab Rai, Padam Singh, Mohan Singh, Surup Singh, Achuru Singh and Chatta Lal.[227] In Kengawon, the *patwari*, Omid Rai, played a crucial role in identifying lands to be liquidated, declaring to the Collector, Alexander Ross, that Phundun Lal had held 50 *bigha*s of rent-free lands since 1806, which missed by the Company's early settlements. Rai had been *patwari* since 1797 and had papers which indicated that Lal's lands were not registered under the 1803 Regulations. Rai also brought up paperwork that indicated a further 150 *bigha*s owned by one Bakshiram, who claimed them as inherited from one (lesser-known) Shitab Rai. Omid Rai checked against paper records and found that this was based on a false claim. Shitab Rai, the *patwari* pointed out, had been dead for four years. Ross then ordered that Phundun Lal's 50 *bigha*s, and the rest of Bakrishnan's 150 *bigha*s, also be put up for sale.[228] 1820s Jaunpur saw a massive sell off of lands to meet insatiable revenue demands, many of which were made possible through the consultations of rent-rolls held by the pensmen of Hindustan. In so many cases across the Doab, Indian scribal intermediaries actively assisted the Company in the liquidation of landed assets via auctioneering.

Magistrates and measures: legalizing India's fiscal administration

The paper repositories possessed by Hindustan's pensmen also helped channel fiscal administration into more legal channels. The whole revenue administration under the early Company was 'legalized'. The processes of, and failure to meet, payment were made hard legal obligations. Precolonial traditions, as we have seen, allowed for the threat of violence to be held as a means of compelling payment. Earlier Indian rulers tended to negotiate and, ultimately, use armed force to coerce payment and force cultivators and revenue farmers to cough up. This was particularly the case after the 1730s in places such as Bihar, Awadh and upper Bengal, where the regular display of cavalry was meant to induce reluctant debtors to pay. For example, Muhammad Faiq in Sultanpur suggested, in a borrowing from Sadi, that the arrival of 50 armed horsemen would be enough to persuade any debtor to pay up.[229] And early on the Company played this pattern. One Collector, William Leicester, called a regiment into Moradabad in order to 'secure fair payment from the assets of the country'.[230] But, on the whole, the violence of collections informed British stereotypes of a turbulent, declining Mughal empire. The remedy was procedural, legally backed revenue administration.

This 'legalization' of revenue procedure was where Hindustan's pensmen played a crucial role. Their papers were used regularly for adjudicating suits over land tenure, the status of proprietary holdings and, increasingly, disputes over rent-free lands. The legalism which underpinned British revenue procedure, and which privileged written, recorded and stored knowledge, stitched scribes into the fabric of India's new fiscal–legal regime. Their rent-rolls, balance sheets and *sanad*s acquired a new, legal value based on paper materiality and procedure. Examples abounded. In Etawah in 1810 the *qanungo* Suhar Sahay's papers were some of the most valuable documents in settling the wave of legal disputes over land ownership after 1803. His papers were used to settle Court disputes over ownership and, ultimately, tax liability.[231] Regulation tended to deepen this. *Qanungo*s were required to keep deposited copies of all petitions (*urzi*s). In Jaunpur *qanungo* papers and testimony helped decide a case brought by three parties claiming an estate. The victor, Hunsbakim Singh, was awarded the claim as zamindar based entirely upon the 'statement[s] of the Canoongoes'.[232] This legalization of revenue collection went hand in hand with removing physical force from the whole process. Debtors were no longer being met with armed *sipahi*s but were summoned by lawyers (*vakil*s) sent through legal procedure. Gone were the 'turbulent' days of intimidating debtors with armed cavalry. By the 1830s NWP Revenue Officers noted how rare it was to imprison defaulters who owned property.[233] Instead, they were hauled in front of British magistrates, who themselves drew upon the rent-rolls and fiscal documentation of Hindustan's pensmen, speaking in a language few Indians understood.

A few conclusions can be drawn from these developments. Since *qanungo*s held the paper repositories upon which all revenue, assessment and land holdings were made, they stood to benefit from the deepening fiscal state of the Company. They were in the best position to shield and adjust these records to their advantage. This was done either via patronage or outright manipulation. And the records mattered. Their *qistibandi*s and *jamabandi*s could make or break a village. This may explain why *qanungo*s were rarely involved in suits in both the revenue courts (*diwani audalat*s) and criminal courts (*nizami audalat*s). *Qanungo*s, after all, provided the stamp of officialdom on all public documents related to revenue. Few were in a position to question such authenticity.

Romanticizing: the source of problem

One of the origins of the detrimental effects of Company taxation upon the Indian countryside lay in British attitudes and stereotypes. The British tended to romanticize India's agricultural past, its potential and, by extension, its future. They saw India as 'a country of husbandmen and small farmers',[234] which created the conditions for a revenue administration that, while claiming to be just, restricted peasants' and cultivators' mobility with paperwork. It was part of the broader 'peasantization' that Chris Bayly documented.[235] This can be seen particularly in how Settlement Officers sanguinely forecasted *in extremis*. They were optimistic, often to the point of delusion. Collectors' reports were regularly punctuated with phrases such as 'former health', 'former agricultural glory', 'potential of this district' and 'unequal assessment' of Moorish predecessors. This was significant, for the drive towards standardization and uniformity produced a welter of glib, roughshod assessment throughout the Doab region after 1803. The British convinced themselves that the *riayat* of the Doab were now 'released from the yoke of a Sovereign [Nawab] whose oppression and tyranny were notorious'.[236]

In so many cases Settlement Officers were convinced that India possessed almost unlimited agricultural wealth. One British Collector, who surveyed Delhi in 1825, estimated that half of the surveyed area was waste which could be cultivated if only proper effort and inducements were made.[237] This really meant proper documentation, procedure and regularity on official paper.

Settlement Officers' future agricultural projections tended not only to be more sanguine but more long-term than Mughal revenue estimations, which, as we have seen, were largely based on immediate projections of yields closer to the harvest. At most, projections rarely stretched beyond a few years, as in some cases in Awadh. In this sense, the system set up by Akbar and Todar Mal lasted well into the eighteenth century.[238] But the Company started to project decades ahead. Planning based upon statistical averages became the mainstay of fiscal administration. Assessment officers sought out patterns and averages over longer periods of time, and sought to project these into the future through what one observer called a 'prophetic vision into the misty future'.[239] Settlement Officers and observers often sanctioned higher rates of *jama* based on upon over-estimations on the condition of the *raiyat* and *bhaichara* village communities, believing that the more 'corporatist' nature of *bhaichara* holdings would incentivize everyone towards further agricultural productivity. Settlement Officers also hoped for extended cultivation and increased yields, which would offset the higher overall demands. 'Careerism' was also a factor. Many Settlement Officers, aiming for promotion, saw and framed raised *jama*s as reflective of agricultural prosperity. Henry Tucker wistfully noted that Collectors were 'too prone to exact the utmost farthing, because their credit depends upon the amount of their collections… our lightest assessment is, perhaps, too heavy'.[240] But the trade-off was that this prevented many officers from overlooking the actual abilities of cultivators to pay. Gorakhpur, which was hammered by the Company's assessments after the 1810s, was romanticized into a paradigm of unlimited agricultural growth:

> pergunnahs, which now pay a revenue of about [several] lakhs of Rupee, are known to have yielded at no great distance of time upwards of 50 lakhs… there can be no doubt that every progress in the increase of population would tend rapidly to restore the jumma.[241]

In this case, Mathusian population theories were turned on their head. By convincing itself that the lands of the Doab could yield more, the fiscal state set the countryside on a course for over-assessment. Coupled with an increasingly ossified aloofness, rushed expediency, paper procedure and obligations to overseas creditors, the Company's tax demands were bound to reverberate through the north Indian agrarian economy. British views of Indian agriculture were disturbingly Whiggish. Indeed, the British created many of the shortfalls in agricultural output through their presumptions that Indian cultivators *could produce more*, if prodded and backed up with regulation, paperwork and procedure. Robert Montgomery's 1839 settlement in Allahabad, for example, increased the assessment (*jama*) by over 20 per cent based upon what he *anticipated* the districts would pay in the future, which, of course, was due to the 'benevolence' of British administration: extended cultivation of higher-priced cash crops, well-digging and an unshakeable belief in future agricultural growth.[242] It was a toxic combination of British romanticism and to-the-point paperwork and scribes, which helped spearhead the most intense levels of taxation in the Doab's history.

This romanticizing of Indian agriculture, informed by Orientalist stereotypes, also had the effect of gutting the Hanfi-Islamic aspects of revenue administration. Even though the British employed its residual lexicon, their suspicion of 'Moorish jurisdiction'[243] rapidly dismantled the Islamic legal edifice of Mughal revenue administration. Company officers were quick to criticize the theoretical abstracts of Muslim rule, in which they saw no constitutional or theoretical limits to the amount of revenue the sovereign could demand from India's cultivators. For the British, only paper procedure could temper the whims of an 'unchecked sovereign'. The British also clearly broke with Hanafi *mulki* law when it came to default. Hanafi jurisprudence largely held that defaulters, even those who fled to avoid payment, could not be deprived of their proprietary holdings. The guidance for the sovereign (*nizam*) was to lease the land out to maintain its agricultural productivity, usually for the public good.[244] But the British brought a much more exclusive conception of property to bear in north India. And the traditional Hanafi stance on land's inherent nature was also largely discarded. Revenue farming across north India (*ijara*) had largely been sanctioned by Hanafi jurists, but it was only through *ijara* that land's productive nature could be classified as a commodity.[245] The Company dispensed with this nuance and saw all land as a commodity to be bought and sold for the highest profit. The British also broke with Hanafi *mulki* practice by legalizing the material proceedings of revenue collection – by giving the revenue agreement (*jamabandi*) the 'weight of Judicial Authority'.[246] In prior generations they were referenced in courts, but they were not adjudicating documents. This meant that many Collectors and Settlement Officers were 'frequently called upon to exercise functions essentially judicial'.[247] This further enhanced the legal characteristic of an inherently fiscal officer, who had to work not only as a Collector but also a magistrate, registrar and accountant, all wrapped into one. And these officers were overworked, overstretched and overburdened with a morass of regulation and paperwork. This led later-nineteenth-century wistful, powerless observers such as Charles Elliot to note how the indiscriminate nature of debt enforcement ruptured older traditions:

> under the British government, a village once lost is always lost. The Nuwabee principle was to drive no one to desperation. The English mete out to every one the same inexorable justice.[248]

The old traditions of tax collection, calibrated according to social status, caste and rank, above all with a concern to maintain stability, contrasted with the ecumenicalism of English justice and fiscal legalism, which came to define the new and rupturing nature of the colonial state by the 1780s.

Conclusion

This chapter has examined how broader patterns and methods of taxation changed between empires in north India. It has argued that a crucial component of the British conquest of India was its fiscal intensity, regularity and welding of extant scribal groups to the colonial state. This allowed it to tax more effectively than its rivals (and predecessors) and to bind these old officers to the machinery of the colonial state. The Company did this with more ruthlessness and intensity than their Indian predecessors and contemporaries. Its revenue administration affected landholding patterns but hit cultivators the hardest. These were unprecedented changes that made the Indian cultivator look at the District Collector and his scribal staff (*qanungo*s, *peshkar*s and *patwari*s) as the 'unpopular character of tax-gatherers'.[249] The British worked this whole constellation of revenue scribes to extract more agrarian wealth out of India than any ruler in the country's history. Already by the mid 1810s the Company was able to extract a further Rs 14 million from its new agrarian tracks northwest of Bengal.[250] But the ways in which the Company achieved this were more significant than the end results. With a pen's stroke reverberating through the Doabi countryside, the British shook up the fabric of revenue administration and the broader agrarian economy. Procedural bureaucracy also solved the perceived 'irregularities' of Indian administration. But, as we have seen, the Company largely used this regularity to 'paper' over their increased revenue demands by championing its apparent predictability and 'justice'. Here, Anand Yang's 'limited Raj'[251] looks much more intrusive and disruptive. The Indian peasant, through this complex, ruthless fiscal regime, punishingly paid for the wider British Empire. This is best testified by the regular levels of agrarian agitation from 1803 until the situation exploded in 1857.

Yet at the same time there were some aspects of continuity with the late Mughal patterns of taxation. If anything, the fiscal expansion of Company power northwest into India was a sub-imperialism of extant, looser groups of scribes that had sustained the Mughals and now sustained the British colonial state. These Hindu scribes and pensmen by the mid eighteenth century had found themselves in positions with direct power over financial records and management. This portfolio, it has been stressed, was crucial for the success of the early Company, but a more regularized and paper-driven administration did not necessarily mean that change was completely transformative. Though the new colonial taxation apparatus took on a rather different complexion in its forms, procedure and language of government, many of the veins underneath its skin remained. *Qanungo*s and *patwari*s might have lost much of their 'village purview', but the centrality of procedure and paper to the Company state ensured they remained crucial intermediaries between courts (now committees) and cultivators. Their skills in paper management, such as copying, verification, collating and managing, which provided livelihoods and honour, remained remarkably unaffected. But the fact that they became more firmly anchored to the state was still a remarkable change. They were transformed from hybrid public–private officers to strictly public ones. This reflected the Company's insistence on a monopoly of sovereignty, of which fiscal affairs were paramount. They were not a new type of lower administrator but a refashioned one. Much of this applied to Awadh as well. In the Nawabi domains, as in the Company's Doab territories, Hindu pensmen increasingly punctuated the state's fiscal-administrative manpower. Awadh's fiscal wealth would be coopted by the Raj after 1858. Between 1780 and 1830 Hindustan's scribes helped push the colonial state towards further regulation and procedure, building upon an eighteenth-century trend. These scribes were in some ways no less important, if not more so, than the commercial intermediaries who helped bankroll the company and their operations in north India.[6] The dissenter James Connell may have called them 'mere hack clerks',[252] but these scribes became the bureaucratic mortar of the colonial state and its early authority. Agrarian settlements created new legal, bureaucratic and fiscal categories, but they also employed old officers and their extant papers. It was a curious, almost uneasy mix of change and continuity. This symbiosis between the lowly paper manager and British bureaucratic authority – all backed up by legal sanction – had greatly shaped the emergent colonial state by the 1820s.

If we step back, we can ascertain a number of important early developments between 1780 and 1820. First, it does seem that the Company knew much more about the working of revenue administration than their contemporary critics, and later scholars, gave them credit for. British Settlement Officers picked the right types of 'native officer' for their early fiscal arrangements, mainly Kayasthas. They bypassed a whole mass of middlemen and older Mughal officers such as *chaudhuri*s, *mirhad*s, *amil*s and *malguzar*s. This enabled them to pump out significant amounts of agrarian wealth. The second important pattern that emerges is the overall level of taxation. It does seem that the Company, with its more intense commitment to statistical veracity, used this to justify higher rates of assessment, simply because they had the papers which enabled them to demand such. Company levels of taxation were, early on, heavier than under the Mughals. They tossed out the tempering influence of Hanfi *mulki* law which, we have seen, engendered a revenue administration that was often less legal and more customary, predicated upon a looser concern for the *raiyat*.

There is also the question of how much more broadly the British worked precolonial dynamics to their advantage, and how much change the early colonial state enacted. Much of British success lay in the workings of particular elements of statecraft in eighteenth-century India. And law and fiscalism were two of the most important. A generation ago, Bernard Cohn described a broader 'system' that operated in precolonial north India,[253] mainly at what he termed the revenue and legal levels. As we have seen, the British specifically manipulated an eighteenth-century 'system', fusing legal and fiscal domains into one aspect of governance. Making revenue agreements (*jamabandi*s) legal documents was a perfect example. Cohn, like many of his later students, saw disruptive change and an appropriation of Indian knowledge as crucial to the conquest.[254] The late Chris Bayly famously argued for a great deal of continuity, arguing that British expansion was largely a 'sub-imperialism' of commercial groups based out of Benares.[255] For Bayly, Indian religious and commercial groups greatly moulded the emergent colonial state. This book, thus far, has seen evidence for both conclusions. One the one hand, Hindustan's scribes and their papers continued to populate the many tiers of revenue administration, whether it was for Muslim or Christian sovereigns. Or, as one observer put it, 'the collection of revenue… [has always been] in the hands of the Hindoos'.[256] On the other hand, the Company affected significant change. The Company ended up substituting an 'oriental despotism' for a 'bureaucratic despotism'. The latter was based upon the inviolability of procedure and matter-of-fact paperwork that probed more intensely than its predecessors. The Company's fiscal state might have made Indian agricultural more intelligible to fresh British Collectors and assessment officials, but it had the effect of stunting the flexibility and human-relationship nature of an eighteenth-century revenue administration. The continuity and change in north Indian fiscal administration after the 1780s were, curiously, interdependent, with tragic consequences across the plains of Hindustan.

Notes

1 B. Raman, *Document Raj: Writing and Scribes in Early Colonial South India* (Chicago, 2012).
2 District Commissioner of Farrukabad, 1816, in *Selections from the Revenue Records of the North-West Provinces 1818–1820* (Calcutta, 1866), p. 26. Hereafter *SRRNWP*.
3 K. Chatterjee, 'History as self-representation: the recasting of political tradition in late eighteenth century eastern India', *MAS* 32, 4 (1998), pp. 913–48,
4 W. Hunter, *Readings in Indian History* (Calcutta, 1899), p. 62.
5 Shitab Rai entertained Europeans in his huge residence in Patna, and possessed a particular liking for game fowl. M. Fisher, *The Travels of Dean Mahomet* (Berkeley, 1997), p. 36.
6 B. Misra, *Judicial Administration of the East India Company in Bengal, 1765–1782* (Delhi, 1961), pp. 76–7.
7 N. Chatterjee, *Vereslt's Rule in India* (Allahabad, 1939), pp. 237, 246. *Hastobud* comes from the Persian *hast* ('is') joined with *bud* ('was'), meaning a collection of 'what was and is'. It generally refers to historical rent-rolls, usually with a specified timeframe.
8 Ibid., p. 252.
9 The policy of Supervision lasted until the 1772 passage of North's India Act. B. Misra, *Judicial Administration of the East India Company in Bengal, 1765–1782*, p. 30.
10 Ibid., p. 35.
11 R. Travers, *Ideology and Empire in Eighteenth-Century India: The British Bengal* (Cambridge, 2007).
12 Misra, *Judicial Administration*, p. 43.
13 Ibid., p. 39.
14 'Translation of a Persian petition from the native inhabitants of the Subah of Azeemabad to the King', 17 July 1772, Mss. Eur F218/30, IOL, for the Kayastha Shitab Rai's petition to Harry Verelst about the 'evils' of the newfound Court of Judicature and how it settled cases of default.
15 Chatterjee, *Vereslt's Rule*, p. 269.
16 'Translation of a Persian petition', Fol. 220, IOL.

17 K. Bahadur Safaraz Husain Khan, trans., *Translation of Maharajah Kalyan Singh's Khulasat-et-Tawarikh*, p. 426.
18 G. Saletore, ed., *Banaras Affairs (1788–1810)* (Allahabad, 1955), pp. 206, 237.
19 Chatterjee, *Vereslt's Rule*, p. 232.
20 A. Yang, *Limited Raj: Agrarian Relations in Colonial India, Saran District, 1793–1920* (Berkeley, 1989), p. 99.
21 Chatterjee, *Vereslt's Rule*, p. 225.
22 J. Sarkar, *Fall of the Mughal Empire* (Calcutta, 1964), Vol. II, p. 394.
23 A. Khan, *The Transition in Bengal, 1756–1775: a Study of Muhammad Reza Khan* (Cambridge, 1969), p. 267f.
24 G.H. Tabatabai, *Seir Mutaqherin*, Vol. III, pp. 158–213.
25 Sanbhu Lal noted the large volume of foreign wine (*farangi sharab*) in Benares in the 1770s and 1780s, and how many Benares scribes in the Resident's employ employed couriers in bringing bottles of *farangi sharab* from the bottle house (*botekhana*). OR. 1750, Fol. 162, Sanbhu Lal, 'Miftah-i-Khanzain', Fols. 6–7, IOL.
26 OR. 1750, Fol. 162, Sanbhu Lal, 'Miftah-i-Khanzain', (1197 AH), 1782, Fols. 22–3.
27 Ibid., Fol. 16.
28 Ibid.
29 A. Shakespear, *Selections from the Duncan Records* (Benares, 1873), Vol. II, p. 52.
30 Ibid., pp. 41–2.
31 Ibid., p. 43.
32 Ibid.
33 Ibid.
34 Duncan to Cornwallis, 25 February 1788, in Ibid., p. 44.
35 Ibid., Vol. II, p. xcix.
36 Mehndi Ali Khan to Jonathan Duncan, 1786, in Ibid., Vol. I, pp. xxxv–vi.
37 Ibid., p. lvii. It does seem that Duncan drew upon Akbar's standard of decennial settlements for a precedent, which also ran as a thread through the *diwan* of Chattar Mal.
38 Ibid., p. 18.
39 F. Hamilton, Col of Benares, to BOR, 24 August 1816, P/111/60, IOL.
40 Ibid., p. 130.
41 Ibid., pp. 66–116.
42 Ibid., pp. 98–9.
43 For more on Dube, see C. Bayly, *Rulers, Townsmen and Bazars: North Indian Soicety in the Age of British Expansion, 1780–1870* (Cambridge, 1983), pp. 168–9; B. Cohn, 'The initial British impact on India: a case study of the Benares region', *Journal of Asian Studies* xix (1960), pp. 418–31.
44 Shakespear, *Duncan Records*, Vol. I., pp. 102–6.
45 Ibid., p. 22.
46 E. Stokes, *The English Utilitarians and India* (Oxford, 1959), p. 85.
47 In the late 1810s the *jama* of Bengal was Rs 33,310,827, and in the CCP it was Rs 28,065,161. *SRRNWP*, 71fn.
48 J. Malcolm, *Memoir of Central India, including Malwa, and Adjoining Provinces* (London, 1832), Vol. II, pp. 166–7; V. Raghuvanshi, *Indian Society in the Eighteenth Century* (New Delhi, 1969), p. 184.
49 E. Cuthbert, Allahabad, 20 Oct 1806, Ceded & Conquered Provinces Revenue Proceedings, P/91/20, IOL. Hereafter CCPRP.
50 Ibid.
51 H. Valpy, Col of Kanpur to BOR, 2 Feb 1822, P/94/36, IOL.
52 H. Boulderson, Col of Agra, to BOR, 6 Feb 1822, P/94/36, IOL.
53 J. Routledge, 30 Dec 1806, CCPRP, P/90/55, IOL.
54 E. Thornton, 1 February 1839, *Reports on the Revenue Settlement of the North Western Provinces of the Bengal Presidency, under Regulation IX* (Benares, 1862), p. 117. Hereafter *RRSNWPBP*.

55 R. Montgomery to R. Louther, 1 October 1839, in *RRSNWPBP*, Vol. II, pp. 433–47.
56 Ibid.
57 Ibid.
58 T.C. Plowden to G.F. Frances, 16 March 1840, in *RRSNWPBP*, Vol. II, p. 245.
59 Shakespear, *Duncan Records*, Vol. I, p. xlvii.
60 M. Salmon, Benares, 16 September 1809, Bengal Revenue Proceedings (BRP), P/112/46, IOL.
61 Sec of BOR, Nesbit, to Middleton Bihar, 29 February 1816, P/111/54, IOL.
62 *Directions for Revenue Officers in the North-Western Provinces of the Bengal Presidency* (Calcutta, 1858), p. 230.
63 C. Russell, Allahabad, 24 September 1803, CCPRP, P/91/20, IOL.
64 T. Thornhill, Col of Bareli, to BOR, 30 April 1804, P/90/42, IOL.
65 Ibid.
66 C. Elliott, Col of Aligarh, to BOR, August 1809, P/91/40, IOL.
67 A. Ford, Col of Etawah, to BOR, 3 May 1821, P/94/23, IOL.
68 A. Campbell, Col of Shahabad, to P. Nisbet, Sec to B&B Commissioner, 14 June 1816, P/111/58, IOL.
69 M. Mainwaring, Col of Jaunpur, to BOR, 15 July 1820, P/112/35, IOL.
70 Bayly, *Rulers, Townsmen and Bazaars*, p. 146.
71 W. Salmon, Etawah, 29 April 1806, and 26 February 1807, CCPRP, P/91/20, IOL.
72 W. Muir to Sec Sadr BOR, 7 March 1856, P/220/76, IOL.
73 Dr Vibhuti Rai and Sri Sampal Rai, Lucknow, 2006, 2007, 2008; Dr Raj and Mrs Naheed Verma, Lucknow, 2006, 2007, 2008; Ms Rakhi Reshmi, New Delhi, 2008, 2009, London, 2010, 2012.
74 G. Harding, Col of Aligarh, to Sec of BOR, 1 April 1822, P/94/38, IOL.
75 C. Elliot, *The Chronicles of Oonao* (Allahabad, 1862), pp. 138–9.
76 V. Oldenberg, *The Making of Colonial Lucknow, 1856–77* (Princeton, 1984), chapter 5. Oldenburg notes that Lucknow was one of the most heavily taxed cities in India after the 1860s, likely for its support for the 1857 Uprising and Rebellion.
77 M. Mann, 'A permanent settlement for the Ceded and Conquered Provinces: revenue administration in north India, 1801–1833', *Indian Economic and Social History Review* 32, 2 (1995), p. 257.
78 R. Guha, *A Rule of Property for Bengal: An Essay on the Idea of Permanent Settlement* (Chapel Hill, 1996).
79 Shakespear, *Duncan Recrods*, Vol. I, p. xii.
80 E. Cuthbert, Allahabad, 5 March 1808, BRP, P/91/19, IOL.
81 Judicial Dept, 1 October 1808, CCPRP, P/91/24, IOL.
82 J. Richardson, Kanpur, 6 October 1804, CCPRP, P/91/20, IOL. Dirk Kolff has recently hinted at this. D. Kolff, *Grass in Their Mouths: The Upper Doab of India Under the Company's Magna Charta, 1793–1830* (Leiden, 2010), pp. 508–9.
83 R. Barlow, Mahomedabad, 12 April 1821, BRP, P/112/46, IOL.
84 A. Ross, Col of Gorukpur, to BOR, 24 July 1804, P/90/43, IOL.
85 Translation of Report of Qanungos, in A. Ross, Col of Gorukpur, to BOR, 24 July 1804, P/90/43, IOL.
86 W. Salmon, Etawah, 26 February 1807, CCPRP, P/91/20, IOL.
87 Ibid., 29 April 1806.
88 Ibid.
89 Ibid.
90 C. Russell, Agent to Gov. in Farrukabad, to Sec BOR, 18 July 1804, P/90/43, IOL.
91 Minute by Earl Moira, Gov-Gen, on River Ganges, 21 September 1815, in *SRRNWP*, pp. 338–9.
92 C. Russell, Agent to Gov. in Farrukabad, to Sec BOR, 18 July 1804, P/90/43, IOL.
93 See, for example, M. Mann, *British Rule on Indian Soil* (New Delhi, 1999), chapters 3–5; A. Siddiqi, *Agrarian Change in a Northern Indian State: Uttar Pradesh 1819–1833* (Oxford, 1973).

94 I. Habib, 'The social distribution of landed property in pre-British India', in R. Sharma and V. Jha, eds. *Indian Society: Historical Probings in Memory of D.D. Kosambi*, (New Delhi, 1974).
95 Based on the usage in Uttar Pradesh, with 1 *bigha* equalling 0.25 hectares.
96 Shakespear, *Duncan Records*, Vol. II, pp. 64–5, 136.
97 Ibid., pp. 179–80.
98 E. Cuthbert, Allahabad, 29 October 1806, CCPRP, P/91/20, IOL.
99 H. Evans, *Report on the Settlement of District of Agra* (Allahabad, 1880), p. 13.
100 H. Elliot, *Memoirs on the History, Folklore and Distribution of the Races of the North Western Provinces of India* (London, 1869), Vol. I, pp. 337–45.
101 R. Ahmuty, Allahabad, 15 May 1808, CCPRP, P/91/20, IOL.
102 H. Newnham, Col of Etawah, to BOR, 1 May 1821, CCPRP, P/94/23, IOL.
103 S. Brown, Delhi, NWPRP 13 August 1837, P/217/60, IOL.
104 J. Thomason, 19 September 1837, NWPRP, P/217/60, IOL.
105 *SRRNWP*, p. 91.
106 R. Barlow, Ghazipur, 25 March 1821, BRP, P/112/46, IOL.
107 N. Martin, Ghazipur, 28 March 1821, BRP, P/112/46, IOL.
108 R. Martin, Col of Agra, to BOR, 10 January 1810, P/91/40, IOL.
109 M. Money, Col of Bihar, to BOR, 31 July 1816, P/111/60, IOL.
110 W. Money, Col of Bihar, to BOR, 24 July 1820, P/112/36, IOL.
111 Ibid.
112 M. Gubbins, *Report on the Settlement of Zillah Etawah* (Agra, 1844), pp. 5–7.
113 Ibid.
114 E. Dawes, District Commissioner of Farrukabad, 1816, in *SRRNWP*, p. 33.
115 C. Lloyd, Shahabad, 5 March 1808, CCPRP, P/91/19, IOL; Siddiqi, *Agrarian Change*, p. 72.
116 Using the custom in the upper Doab and closer to Delhi, where 1 *bigha* normally amounts to 0.4 acres.
117 A. Ross, Col of Agra, to J. Sherer, Sec to Board of Commissioners, 29 August 1815, in *SRRNWP*, p. 164.
118 H. Valpy. Col of Kalpi, to BOR, 15 December 1820, P/40/18, IOL.
119 'Settlement report and statements of the District of Moozuffernugger for the year 1866', F. Williams, Commissioner, in *Settlement Report of the District of Moozuffernugger* (Allahabad, 1873), p. 4.
120 Minute by Earl Moira, Gov-Gen., on River Ganges, 21 September 1815, in *SRRNWP*, p 329.
121 C. Russell, Allahabad, 24 September 1803, CCPRP, P/91/20, IOL.
122 A. Cockburn, 13 October 1803, CCPRP, P/91/20, IOL.
123 E. Cuthbert, Allahabad, 29 October 1806, CCPRP, P/91/20, IOL.
124 C. Oldman, *Journal of Francis Buchanan Kept during the Survey of the District of Shahabad in 1812–1813* (Patna, 1926), p. 28.
125 W. Salmon, Etawah, 29 April 1806, PCCPR, P/91/20, IOL.
126 Yang, *Limited Raj*.
127 R. Ahmuty, Allahabad, 17 May 1808, CCPRP, P/91/20, IOR; Habib, pp. 333–5.
128 Shakespear, *Duncan Records*, Vol. II., p. 52
129 Consultations, 2 Sept 1814 No. 15, in *SRRNWP*, p. 132
130 E. Cuthbert, Allahabad, 29 Oct 1806, CCPRP, P/91/20, IOR.
131 Hussein, *Land Revenue Policy in North India, the Ceded & Conquered Provinces* (New Delhi, 1967), p. 22.
132 Shakespear, *Duncan Records*, Vol. II, pp. 236–7; it is tough to ascertain whether Duncan took Akbar's policy in the 1580s as a precedent, which established two salaried *qanungos* per pargana. Habib, *Agrarian System*, pp. 331–5.
133 Shakespear, *Duncan Records*, Vol. II, pp. 236–7.
134 C. Dumbleton, Kanpur, 10 July 1807, CCPRP, P/91/20, IOR.

135 Ibid.; Dr Vibhuti Rai and Sri Sampal Rai, Lucknow, 2006, 2007, 2008; Dr Raj and Mrs Naheed Verma, Lucknow, 2006, 2007, 2008; Ms Rakhi Reshmi, New Delhi, 2008, 2009, London, 2010, 2012.
136 Ibid.
137 J. Stracey to J. Fombelle, Sec to Gov., 8 November 1803, P/91/2, CCPRP, IOR; J. Stracey, 8 November 1803, CCPRP, P/91/2, IOR; C. Dumbleton, Col of Kanpur, 4 November 1806, CCPRP, P/90/55, IOR; A. Ross, Col of Agra, 26 December 1806, CCPRP, P/90/55, IOR.
138 S.H. Askari, 'Fragments of a newly discovered Persian manuscript by a Hindu news-writer', *Journal of Bihar Research Society*, 36, September–December (Patna, 1950), p. 84. Lal famously claimed that the Taj Mahal cost 9 crores, 9 lakhs, 9,000,900, 9 Rs, 9 fulus and 9 kharmorahs, and that this is secretly inscribed on the outer wall of the Taj. Much doubt is cast upon this claim.
139 Askari, 'Fragments', p. 84.
140 Mann, 'A permanent settlement', p. 253.
141 Col of Bareli, T. Thornhill, to Board of Revenue Proceedings Bengal, 16 March 1804, P/90/43, IOR. Hereafter BORPB.
142 Co. of Shahabad, A. Campbell, to Sec of B&B Commissioner, 1 May 1816, P/111/57, IOR.
143 Elliot, *The Chronicles*, p. 106.
144 Ibid.
145 Oldman, ed. *Journal of Francis Buchanan*, p. 28.
146 P. Basu, *Oudh and the East India Company* (Lucknow, 1943), pp. 145–8.
147 Hussein, *Land Revenue Policy*, p. 13; Saletore, ed. *Henry Wellesley's Correspondence*, p. 267.
148 T. Thornhill, Bareli, 15 March 1804, CCPRP, P/91/20, IOR; Shakespear, Vol. I, pp. li–liv.
149 J. Nesfield, *Brief View of the Caste System of the North-West Provinces and Oudh* (Allahabad, 1885), p. 46. But in Bihar Kaithi continued to be used, albeit less frequently.
150 J. Richardson, Kanpur, 20 September 1803, CCPRP, P/91/20, IOR.
151 C. Dumbelton, Kanpur, 10 Jul 1807, CCPRP, P/91/20, IOR.
152 *SRRNWP*, pp. 322–3.
153 E. Brodkin, 'British India and the abuses of power: Rohilkhand under early company rule', *IESHR* 10 (10), 1973, pp. 147–8.
154 J. Thomason, *Report of the Collector of Azimgurh on the Settlement of the Ceded Portion of the District* (Agra, 1837), p. 25.
155 OR. 1750, Fol. 162, Sanbhu Lal, 'Miftah-i-Khanzain', (1197 AH), 1782, Fol. 10.
156 OR. 2011, Fol. 111, Chatar Mal, 'Diwan-i-Pasand', n.d., early nineteenth century, fols. 55–6.
157 Ibid.
158 P. Saran, *Provincial Government of the Mughals* (Allahabad, 1941), p. 294.
159 Seton to Mercer, 28 February 1803, Board of Commissioners Proceedings, 12 April 1803, IOR.
160 J. Routledge, Bareli, 30 December 1806, CCPRP, P/90/55, IOR.
161 Ibid; E. Cuthbert, Allahabad, 29 October 1806, CCPRP, P/91/20, IOR for the cases of Munu Lal, who as *qanungo* of Cuttah earned an astonishing Rs 4,800 annually.
162 J. Routledge, Bareli, 30 December 1806, CCPRP, P/90/55, IOR.
163 M. Bane, Tirhut, 18 February 1820, BORPB, P/112/46, IOR.
164 Travers, *Ideology and Empire*.
165 'Settlement report and statements of the District of Moozuffernugger for the tear 1866', in Williams, *Settlement Report*, p. 4.
166 H. Tucker, *A Review of the Financial Situation of the East India Company, in 1824* (London 1825), p. 13.

167 C. Girdlestone, *e ort on ast a ines in the orth-Western ro in es* (Allahabad, 1868), p. 41.
168 R. Ahmuty, Allahabad, 15 May 1808, CCPRP, P/91/20, IOL.
169 Girdlestone, *Report on Past Famines*, p. 105.
170 Girdlestone, *Report on Past Famines*, p. 37.
171 Authors' calculations, taken from 'Appendix A – 'Statement of the Jumma or Demand on Account of Land Revenue of the Ceded and Conquered Provinces and Delhi for the Revenue or Fuslee Years, from 1209 to 1225 F.S.', in *Selections from the Revenue Records of the North-West Provinces 1818–1820* (Calcutta, 1866), especially pp. 156–7, hereafter *SRRNWP*; E. Stokes, *The Peasant and Raj* (Cambridge, 1979), p. 89.
172 Agra, Aligarh, Bundelkhand, Saharanpur.
173 S. Sinha, *The Revolt of 1857 in Bundelkhand* (Lucknow, 1982), p. 52.
174 Tucker, *A Review*, p. 103.
175 Evans, *Report*, p. 24.
176 *Directions for Revenue Officers*, pp. 253–4.
177 Author's calculation, taken from *SRRNWP*, p. 156–7.
178 Authors' calculations, taken from 'Appendix A – 'Statement of the Jumma or Demand on Account of Land Revenue of the Ceded and Conquered Provinces and Delhi for the Revenue or Fuslee Years, from 1209 to 1225 F.S.', in *SRRNWP*, especially pp. 156–7, Stokes, *The Peasant and Raj*, pp. 89, 325.
179 Allahabad, Bareily, Kanpur, Etawah, Farukabad, Gorukpur, Moradabad, Shajahanapur.
180 J. Deeds, Sec to Sadr BOR to J. Macsween, Sec to Gov. Revenue, 11 November 1835, P/217/40, IOL.
181 Author's calculations, Board of Customs, Farukabad, to Gov. Gen., 21 March 1815, in *SRRNWP*, pp. 362–9.
182 J. Richards, *The Mughal Empire* (Cambridge, 1996), pp. 86–93.
183 M. Davis, *Late Victorian Holocausts: El Niño Famines and the Making of the Third World* (London, 2002).
184 M. Mann, *Britischen Herrschaft auf Indischem boden: Landwirtsschaftliche Transformation und ökologische Destruktion des 'Central Doab' 1801–1854* (Stuttgart, 1992); also see Mann, 'A permanent settlement', pp. 256–7.
185 Mann, *Britischen Herrschaft*, p. 192.
186 Ibid.
187 P. Penner and R. Maclean, *The ebel Bureau rat: rederi k John Shore as Criti of Willia Benti k's India* (Delhi, 1983), p. 82.
188 *Directions for Revenue Officers*, p. 185.
189 J. Thornton, 'The Settlement of the N.W. Provinces', *The Calcutta Review* XII (July–December, 1849), p. 429.
190 G. Ravenscroft, Col of Furukabad, to E. Colebrook and J. Dean, 1 January 1816, in *SRRNWP*, p. 275.
191 M. Edney, *Mapping an Empire. The Geographical Construction of British India, 1765–1843* (Chicago, 1999).
192 OR. 1750, Fol. 162, Sanbhu Lal, 'Miftah-i-Khanzain', Fo. 18.
193 Girdlestone, *Report on Past Famines*, p. 58.
194 Ibid., pp. 51–3.
195 Bayly, *Rulers*, pp. 292–8.
196 For various interpretations of the causes and run-up to the famine, see S. Sharma, 'The 1837–38 famine in U.P.: some dimensions of popular action', *Indian Economic and Social History Review* 30, 3: 337–72; Siddiqi, *Agrarian Change*, p. 222, Bayly, *Rulers*, p. 530; and Girdlestone, *Report on Past Famines*, iv, p. 110.
197 *SRRNWP*, p. 80.

198 H. Rose, *Report on the Settlement of the District of Cawnpore* (Agra, 1842), pp. 18–20.
199 Girdlestone, *Report on Past Famines*, p. 43.
200 Richard, *Mughal Empire*, pp. 66–78.
201 M. Alam, *The Crisis of Empire in Mughal North India: Awadh and the Punjab, 1707–1748* (Delhi, 1986), p. 315.
202 Report of the Board of Commissioners to Governor-General in Council 27 October 1818, in *SRRNWP*, p. 4.
203 *Annual Report on the Operations under Act II of 1878* (Allahabad, 1884), p. 5.
204 In Janupur in the early 1880s, for example, Rs 17,000 were assessed and Rs 17,106 were collected. See *Annual Report on the Operations under Act II of 1878* (Allahabad, 1884), p. 18.
205 Foreign Department, Political Consultations, 30 December 1848, No. 427, Table 5, NAI.
206 *Directions for Revenue Officers*, pp. 70–9. This also, incidentally, stimulated an exponential degree of procedural paperwork in initiating cases against individual leaseholders (*pattahdar*s).
207 J. Thomason, *Report of the Collector*, p. 20.
208 W. Irvine, *Later Mughals* (New Delhi, 1971), pp. 334–5.
209 Hussein, *Land Revenue Policy*, pp. 49–60; E. Stokes, *The Peasant and Raj* (Cambridge, 1979), p. 103.
210 Elliot, *The Chronicles*, p. 112.
211 See Chapter 2.
212 *Reports on the Revenue Settlement of the North Western Provinces of the Bengal Presidency*, p. 165.
213 Ibid., p. 166.
214 Ibid., pp. 165–6.
215 Ibid., p. 166.
216 G.F. Edmonston, 16 Nov 1840, *RRSNWPBP*, Vol. II, p. 165.
217 H. Elliot, 27 October 1836, in *RRSNWPBP*, p. 205. Emphasis is author's own.
218 Thomason, *Report of the Collector*, pp. 10–11.
219 C.J. Connell, *Land Revenue Policy – Northern India* (Calcutta, 1876), 180fn.
220 Collector of Aligarh, 21 August 1810, in *SRRNWP*, p. 104.
221 G.F. Edmonston, 16 Nov 1840, *RRSNWPBP*, Vol. II, p. 143.
222 Oldman, *Journal of Francis Buchanan*, p. 28.
223 Gubbins, *Report*, p. 5.
224 *Bareilly Settlement Report*, pp. 360–1.
225 Petition from Tehsildar of Kanpur, Akbar Ali, 11 September 1804, P/90/44, IOL.
226 J. Richardson, Col of Kanpur, to BOR, 15 September 1804, P/90/44, IOL.
227 Ibid.
228 A. Ross, Col of Bareli, to BOR, 8 May 1821, P/94/23, IOL.
229 I am grateful to Nandini Chatterjee for pointing this out.
230 W. Leicester, Col of Moradabad, to J. Fombelle, Sec of Gov., 24 March 1804, P/90/42, IOL.
231 W. Laing, Col of Etawah, to BOR, 24 January 1810, P/91/40, IOL.
232 Collector of Jaunpur, 7 March 1820, P/112/32, IOL.
233 Circular Order Sadr Board of Revenue, No. 11, Append. No. VII, Par. 68, *Directions for Revenue Officers*, p 354.
234 G. Ravenscroft, Col of Furukabad, to E. Colebrook and J. Dean, 1 January 1816, in *SRRNWP*, p. 266.
235 C. Bayly, *Indian Society and the Making of the British Empire* (Cambridge, 1988).
236 Girdlestone, *Report on Past Famines*, p. 13.
237 Report by T. Metcalfe, in *Selected Reports, on the Revision of Settlement under Regulation IX* (Agra, 1846), p. 8.

238 Full statement of the mode of collecting revenue and administering justice, by Shitab Rai and the Qanungos, pursuant to an Order of Council', Mss. Orn. Add. 6586, 24 January 1773, fol. 53.
239 Connell, *Land Revenue*, p. 46.
240 J. Kaye, *Memorials on Indian Government; Being a Selection from the Paper of Henry St George Tucker* (London, 1853), p. 115.
241 Court of Directors to Sec Gov of Bengal (NWP), 6 September 1815, *SRRNWP*, p. 13.
242 R. Montgomery, Vol. II, pp. 433–7.
243 Khan, *Transition in Bengal*, p. 269.
244 B. Johanson, *The Islamic Law on Land Tax and Rent* (London, 1988), p. 83. This largely animated the interactions between Shitab Rai and Harry Verelst in Bengal in the 1760s, in which Rai criticized the methods of the Company's Court of Judicature, and how they hauled debtors in front of court with disregard to rank, status and character. Bellenoit, Chatterjee, 'Judges and taxmen in early colonial India, *c.*1765–1793', unpublished Mss. in author's possession; also see 'Full statement of the mode of collecting revenue and administering justice', by Shitab Rai and the Qanungos, pursuant to an Order of Council', 24 January 1773, Mss. ADD. 6586, Fol. 53, IOL.
245 C. Mallat, *Islam and Public Law: Classical and Contemporary Studies* (London, 1993), p. 37.
246 *Directions for Revenue Officers* (Calcutta, 1858), p. 79.
247 Ibid., p. 174.
248 Elliot, *The Chronicles*, p. 129.
249 Kaye, *Memorials*, p. 123.
250 Board of Customs, Farukabad, to Gov. Gen., 21 March 1815, in *SRRNWP*, pp. 362–9.
251 Yang, *Limited Raj*.
252 Connell, *Land Revenue*, p. 136.
253 B. Cohn, 'Political systems in eighteenth century India: the Benares region', *Journal of Asian Studies* 19, 4 (1962), pp. 418–31.
254 B. Cohn, *Colonialism and Its Forms of Knowledge: The British in India* (Princeton, 1996).
255 Bayly, *Rulers*.
256 G. Valentine, *Voyages and Travels to India* (London, 1809), Vol. I, p. 99.

4 'Accounting for every grain'

The origins of the colonial archive in north India

Introduction

This chapter shifts focus away from examining the broader fiscal consolidation of the Company's early state to looking at one of the most crucial by-products of this whole process of fiscal consolidation: the accumulative and organized repository of agrarian and fiscal knowledge from the time of Clive. This chapter engages with the development of what scholars have termed the 'colonial archive'. Historians and anthropologists have broadly framed the development of the archive as a result of either the taxonomic tendencies of caste and social categories or as part of a systematized effort to exert power through 'colonial knowledge'. Chris Bayly, for example, saw the colonial archive as a result of a shift away from mastering affective knowledge in Indian social communities towards abstract, statistical knowledge which crystalized in the archive.[1] Arjun Appadurai has argued that such repositories were largely the result of an unprecedented 'quantification' of aspects of Indian society. Here, the Company's tendency to organize, classify and number everything led to the formation of the colonial archive.[2] Nicholas Dirks has made a similar, though more forceful, argument. He maintains that the colonial archive was intimately related to knowledge production and the construction of working caste identities, in which Indian intermediaries were quickly marginalized and 'written out'.[3] And Matthew Edney has argued that the cartographic needs of the Company state led to a sophisticated, accumulative body of knowledge located around the need to 'know the land'.[4]

This chapter, however, takes a slightly different approach to the colonial accumulation of knowledge. While India's agrarian history has largely been interpreted through the prism of understanding the shifting fortunes of cultivating communities, broader economic history and landholding patterns, little attention has been paid to the role fiscal consolidation played in the formation of the early state's accumulative knowledge. As we have seen thus far, the paperwork and fiscal knowledge the company obtained after the 1780s from Benares, made possible by Hindustan's scribes, meant the Company state's knowledge of India's agrarian potential was more intense than its predecessors'. Its records of *bandobasts* and *jamabandis* – combined with inviolable paper-based procedure – steadily built up over the late eighteenth and early nineteenth centuries to produce an indexed, organized and accessible corpus of knowledge. It became one of the most pronounced accumulative facets of the early colonial state. This chapter therefore argues that the origins of this knowledge – the paper depth of the colonial state – lay more in the desire to harness India's agrarian wealth than in caste taxonomy, cartography or quantification. The Company's fiscal motives were no different from its Indian predecessors'. But the means it employed to pursue such ends, as we have seen, were unprecedented in India's history, taking levels of state power to new, more intrusive heights.

'Accounting for every grain': the orgins of the agrarian archive

As we have seen, the Company's sprawling fiscal-paper state rapidly exploded in breadth and depth across the Doab after 1800. Drawing upon an extant network of pensmen across Hinudustan, the Company was able to fiscally conslidate its holdings more quickly and ruthlessley than any other regional Indian kingdom. The British quickly outdid the Marathas, and the Nawabs of Bengal and, to a lesser degree, Awadh. This was done mainly by welding fiscal regulation to the arm of law. By the 1820s the Company had already asserted its fiscal discipline and mastery aross the former Mughal and Nawabi trerritories. This was a crucial development, having taken place within the sinews and rhythms of the early fiscal state. Harnessing the agrarian wealth of India, in a way that met the demands of the Company's external obligations required a level of paperwork, attestation and documentation unseen in India's history – and the colonial archive was a by-product of this broader fiscal consolidation. In the first decade of the nineteenth century the regularity, standardization and intensity of revenue collection skyrocketed. And in this management and extraction of India's agrarian revenue we can see the beginnings of modern Indian bureaucratic organization and the statistical depth of the state. The emergence of colonial rule and its state apparatus in the Doab was not so much 'about the production of an archive of (and for) colonial rule'[5] as it was the confluence of the remnants of the Mughal and Awadhi traditions and its ratcheting up by the British, all, of course, with the assistance of the scribes of the Doab.

Agrarian settlements and the rythyms of taxation precipitated the need for a vast 'knowledge state' when it came to India. Officials in the new Doabi territories required surveys to know the volume of houses, villages, gender ratios, population densities and infanticides. The colonal fiscal state, from a very early period, was a 'financial system resting on the solid basis of minute local inquiry'.[6] This regularized, local inquiry – attuned to the rhythms of the monsoon and agricultural cycle – inflated the paper depth and knowledge of the colonial state. And while metropolitan forces[7] from above – namely the Court of Directors – helped shape the emergent archive through regulation, much of the drive towards paperwork and procedure came from the encounter between the Company's fiscal needs and the residual officers and traditions they encountered in Hindustan. It was the minutiae of agrarian affairs and the accumulation of local fiscal knowledge that served as the impetus to the early archival tendencies of the colonial state. It is important to stress that the depth and regularity of fiscal materiality changed with the early Company state. Because the British could understand only so much of the revenue administration, they felt India's eighteenth-century revenue traditions lacked the proper amount of paperwork to 'see how it was'.[8] The Company's fiscal needs required – and generated – volumes of paperwork. There were also British stereotypes. Antipathy towards 'mendacious' Indians, coupled with 'Oriental despotism', meant that the interconnected web of relationships that drove the workings of fiscalism would be replaced with paper-based procedure. What also stimulated this unprecedented paper management was the British obsession with physical proof. Only when Settlement Officers had information on all soils, crops, stocks, agricultural castes and detailed historical assessments could the fledging Company state get close to any sort of pattern it considered accurate. Indeed, many settlement officers saw it as 'scientific'. And it was this pattern upon which the Company would base its savage revenue demands. Specifically, historical returns, such as *jamabandi*s, which *qanungo*s and *patwari*s generally possessed, carried the most weight. Because the fiscal state established its tax claims on the basis of accurate, detailed and historically based trends, rent-rolls (*hastobud*s) were the most significant documents for Doabi Settlement Officers. They were the first documents to be regularized and made official. And it was these regularized, taxonomic papers which spawned the beginning of the massive, deep and detailed referencing which became the colonial archive.

This merging of legalism and fiscalism further deepened the emergence of a registered archive. It reinforced the 'bookishness' of India's new rulers. And it was driven by British stereotypes about 'Moorish' despotism, which saw Indian rulers as less bound by paper, procedure and law than their own ambitions. John Stuart Mill argued that revenue administration, unlike the late Mughal traditions outlined previously, needed the 'force of a judicial decision'.[9] This was seen early in Bengal, after the 1760s, and set a pattern that would later reverberate northwestward through the Doabi territories. When it came to settling debts and non-payment in 1770s Bengal, for example, the Company decided to litigate against debtors and use juridical levers to obtain payment. When Shitab Rai and residents of Patna filed a petition (*urzi*) with Governor-General Verelst in 1772, they complained how the Company's actions against debtors were 'contrary to the customs, mode, usages and institutions of this country' and that the legal cases were becoming too bookish and expensive, for they 'required [sic] innumerable books and volumes without end'.[10] Under the Company, 'violence was not tolerated'[11] when it came to fiscal matters, so the Company from the late 1780s started to channel defaulters into legal channels, whose procedural rhythms required standardized paperwork, documentation and the officers who were purveyors of such information. The *qanungo*s' papers regularly punctuated the courts of Benares after 1775, and those of the Doab after the early 1800s, and filled the libraries of *vakils* and magistrates across Hindustan.

Classifying soils, sands and grains

Some of the first movements towards agrarian taxonomy were seen in understanding the composition of the soils of Hindustan. The agricultural rhythms and ecology of north and east India were remarkably different from the reference point of many Settlement Officers: the British Isles.[12] Since the Company's fiscal solvency and administration largely rested upon the regenerative quality of the north Indian plains, soils were crucial. They needed to be comprehended in order to better understand the diversity of plants, pulses and, eventually, cash crops that could be harvested. In terms of soil types, alkaline and acidity levels, India possessed an ecological system that was far more diverse than northern Europe's. Learning the ecology of various soils – from the red soils of Tamil country to the black soils of the Garhwal regions – was itself an exercise in taxonomy. Coupled with the guiding patterns of the monsoon season and rainfall patterns, north India presented a challenge to the Company's fiscal permanence. But this was also because of the ecological and agrarian diversity *within* the Doab. Soils in some areas of Kanpur tended to be more sandy, while in Unao and Bareli soils and acidity levels tended to be claylike (*domut*). Different soils determined which crops were suited to particular regions, which, in turn, determined which cultivating communities would work them, which itself had a bearing upon the overall yields, revenue and solvency of the Company. Paper knowledge, documentation and procedure were combined to make sense of this ecological diversity.

Previously, under the Nawabs and the Mughals, knowledge of soil quality and differentiation seems to have been largely limited to agriculturalists, cultivators and the scribes who managed the paperwork within parganas. It was not state knowledge but a localized form of it, upon which sovereigns drew through a vast corpus of officials: *amil*s and *malguzar*s. *Qanungo*s and *patwari*s had this information on their various rent-rolls and paperwork, which partly explains why the office of the *qanungo* became so important to the Mughal's revenue administration.[13] But the degree of soil gradation and taxonomy was not as detailed as it would become under the British. That was because *qanungo*s and local cultivators already possessed an 'ecological intelligence' which precluded the need for large taxonomies. Pre-Company patterns tended to defer to these localized forms of knowledge and its officers. What the Company started to do was bring such ecological knowledge within the purview of the state and its paper tendrils. After 1800 it expanded the depth and detail of its agricultural intelligence and documented the hitherto largely unwritten knowledge of the Doab's ecological diversity.

Starting from the early 1800s, Settlement Officers began classifying various soil types, which regularly punctuated the proceedings and correspondence of the early fiscal state. Unlike south India and the red soils of Tamil country, and the laterite soils of central India, the largely alluvial soils types of north India possessed greater variation in mineral composition and acidity. This informed how settlement officers assessed the potential for agricultural output. They regularly wrote that alluvial soils held a greater potential for agricultural yields, and the Doab was well suited for the irrigation and cultivation of rice, wheat, maize, sugar cane, tobacco, jute and oilseeds. Within these broader alluvial soils were various subsets, which the Company sought to document. After the early 1800s dark, rich, loom (*dakur*), light, mouldy (*rouslee*), sandy (*bhoor*, usually 60–70 per cent sand), clay (*kupsa-doruss*) and claylike (*domut*) became part of the agrarian-settlement handbook.[14] The soil taxonomy also included micro-specifics. Reports began to distinguish soil that was fertile, light and sandy in colour (*khaddar*) from soils made oily from neighbouring well waters in areas where extended cultivation was undertaken (*bangar*).

Early Settlement Officers and the Board of Revenue presumed that knowledge of soil types would better enable the Company to tax fairly and effectively. But such taxonomy was also shaped by British stereotypes. The state's agricultural and ecological intelligence, buttressed by the steady accumulation of knowledge, would also, importantly, prevent fraud. Thus if the state and its fiscal operatives possessed the required knowledge on soil qualities, then decent rains and procedural fiscal administration would almost guarantee regular, anticipated agricultural returns – only evasion and Indian 'mendacity' could explain lower assessments. So early settlements in the middle and lower Doab immediately plunged into categorizing various types of soil quality. The Company sought to document as much soil taxonomy as it could in order to maximize assessments according to 'scientific principles', eliminate uncertainty and prevent Indian evaders from concealing agricultural wealth from the state.

Another by-product of this taxonomy of soil was a cataloguing of the broader universe of agricultural produce in north India. The regional variations in soil also affected the various types of agricultural output, which was ultimately to be taxed to fund the Company's state. Avoiding mismatches between soil types, grains and pulses was crucial to the fiscal heartbeat of the state. The whole cornucopia and nutritional diversity of Indian agriculture was now being brought within the scope of the paper-driven, taxonomic administration: pulses (*urud, moong, masoor*, peas), vegetables (*tori, pyaz, gajar*), grains (*gehun, jowar, bajra*) and various flours (*grams*). This lexicon started to punctuate the early proceedings of Settlement Officers.[15] Settlement manuals also sought to establish trends in production and pricing over decades, again reflecting the Company's historically based archival drive for knowledge based upon precedent. This started in the 1810s as a result of a British obsession with price levels and meeting revenue demands, and most districts in the Doab by the 1840s had established pricing trends. By the 1840s the settlement of Muzzafarnagar had established grain and produce prices covering two generations. Crucially, again, they were collated from information from *chaudhuri*s of the bazaar and *qanungo*s in the wider district.[16] Such statistical compendiums required documentation and organization on a previously unseen scale.

This taxonomy of grains and, crucially, prices also fed into the broader 'commercialization' of Indian agriculture. The establishment of prices and historical patterns not only gave certainty and a degree of forecasting to settlement offices but also provided a entry point for the higher-priced cash crops such as jute, cotton, indigo and opium. In a good many cases, Settlement Officers examined the taxonomically organized patterns of low agricultural prices as a basis to encourage higher-priced cash crops – and, by extension, the lending of *bania* money to cultivators. George Ravenscroft, who had experience in the middle and upper Doab from the early 1800s, like many of his generation held views about agriculture which were moored in both laissez-faire economics and an aversion to rent racking by Irish and Scottish landlords. Ravenscroft thought the dire situation of the Indian cultivator was due to low prices, which made, he reasoned, the farmer a 'family bondsman to the landlord for life'.[17] Regularly referencing Adam Smith and historical price patterns, he argued that the growing of commercial crops such as tobacco and indigo would bolster the peasant against supposedly 'rapacious' landlords. Ravenscroft invoked this in looking at Kanpur and its well-documented sandier soils, suited to pulses and grains. Here, his inquiries with *lumbardar*s suggested that if normal agrarian revenues yielded Rs 27–28 lakhs, cotton would yield upwards of Rs 81 lakhs, and sugarcane and tobacco up to Rs 140 lakhs.[18] Ravenscroft noted the history of low grain prices and saw this not only as the root cause of the cultivator's poverty but also as a possible solution to a Company increasingly on the brink of insolvency. The comparison of agricultural and cash-crop prices, based upon the archive of agarian knowledge, gave powerful weight to the argument for opening Indian agriculture to commerce.

There were numerous other categorizations of aspects of the agricultural cycle. For example, we can see that from a very early period water supplies and sources increasingly punctuated settlement reports. In the constant search for sanguine agricultural forecasts, Settlement Officers, seeking 'scientific' trends, started to measure the proportion of 'pukka and kutcha wells' to revenue-bearing (*malguzari*) lands. The proportions of wells was also measured relative to overall cultivation and to overall cultivation averages.[19] Such tables and calculations generated volumes of paperwork and statistics.[20] And in so many cases, again, the information on wells and land came from the papers of various *qanungo*s and *patwari*s. Indeed, it seems the archival depth of early agrarian taxonomy drew heavily upon the numbers and categories of *jamabandi*s, *hastobud*s and *wasilbaki*s. For example, Kayastha *qanungo*s helped identify wells and clearable jungle tracts in Kanpur, Allahabad, Meerut and Shahabad in the early 1800s, drawing upon (*kistbandi*s), revenue returns and land surveys.[21] In Agra *qanungo*s helped identify and document sites for walled (*pukka*) wells.[22] In Etawah in 1807 Saxena Kayasthas identified and documented locations for well-digging.[23] And in early 1820s Etawah two *qanungo*s, Nand Lal and Sukh Lal, pored over their papers, which went back to the 1780s, and identified further sites for well construction.[24] The steady accumulation of water knowledge, supplementary to that of the annual monsoon rains, proceeded rapidly and drew upon extant paperwork from the late eighteenth century– and it would itself populate the early colonial archive.

The agrarian archive was also pervaded by statistical averaging. These averages encompassed grains, prices, types of land and their relationships to each other. Averaging was meant to render Indian agriculture and its vagaries of rainfall, produce and output intelligible and, hopefully, predictable. This was crucial for the Company. By the 1830s most settlement reports included categories on averages. Indeed, they were a favourite statistical 'show off' tool used by Settlement Officers to impress upon the Company how much of the agrarian world had been understood. For example, reports even listed prices of sugar cane and thefts (*chori*) per acre of land.[25] Sometimes the semantics were overly microscopic. Auckland Colvin, who settled Muzzafarnagar in the 1870s, reprimanded his subordinate officers for failing to distinguish between 'cultivable' and 'recently abandoned' land. Seemingly trivial, these minute distinctions were used to apply different 'soil rates' of assessment to each village, using a more statistically driven method to practise price discrimination.[26] Here, the colonial archive was not only a by-product of increased assessment and taxation but a precondition of the very process.

Another by-product of this taxonomical development was the emergence of measurements of rainfalls. Eighteenth-century Indian traditions of agricultural planning largely lacked elements of projection. But the early Company state injected meteorological forecasting into their fiscal administration. The vagaries of the monsoon seasons over numerous years frustrated early Settlement Officers, whose only reference points were the relatively more predictable rainfalls of the British Isles. The Company's external obligations required as much consistency as possible in the rhythms of agricultural production and, ultimately, taxation. This was seen in how rainfall measurements started to punctuate agrarian proceedings. After the 1820s Commissioners of Revenue were required to have two rain gauges constructed, one in every police district (*thana*) and another in the *tehsildar*'s office. This required further documentation and attestation in annual settlement reports. By the 1840s rainfall reports were to be supplied annually to Settlement Officers,[28] following the devastating famines in Agra in 1837–8. Each district's annual rainfall was to be measured and recorded. Measures even had to be taken to ensure that buckets were not fraudulently filled. This required further attestation by *qanungo*s and generated even more paperwork, statistics and attestations. But much of this was, again, driven by British prejudices. Concerned with accurate assessment, Collectors started to record on paper the monthly returns of rain, as a way of preventing fraud and tax evasion.[29] This had not been done under the Mughals or the Nawabs, where the Emperor's favour with God and His will explained the monsoon's ups and downs and the vagaries of harvests. Traditionally, *pir*s and *pandit*s offered their own explanations for the monsoon's ways, invoking dharmic forces or divine mysteries. The British, though, believed man could understand the weather's vagaries through statistical and procedural documentation. More accurate knowledge of everything that came from the clouds would ensure minimal fluctuations in agriculture output and, by extension, revenue to the colonial state.

The state's agrarian taxonomy spilled over into numerous other ancillary aspects of the agricultural cycle. From the 1830s onwards settlement manuals read like taxonomies of village ecology and soil science. This expanded and deepened anything that existed before the British. Mughal and eighteenth-century era administrative manuals (*dastur ul-amal*s) rarely mentioned these terms, the knowledge of which remained with India's cultivators, grain traders and, to a degree, its scribes. Yet under the British the ecology and science of agriculture was increasingly coopted by the state, rendering its usage 'public'. The intelligence appetite of the Company sought to classify, document and organize this knowledge so that it could be searched and broader patterns drawn from it. To do so, and to manage the fiscal state's taxonomical tendencies,[30] required volumes of paper, record keeping and a commensurate level of staff.

This early agrarian taxonomy and documentation also seems to have been the inspiration for the larger taxonomies of Indian flora that emerged by the 1860s and 1870s. These later compendiums included Jonathan Hooker's *The Flora of British*

India, which was an impressive agricultural taxonomy of India's various wheat (*angiosperms*) and pulses (*phaseolus*).[31] Horace Wilson's *Glossary of Judicial and Revenue Terms*, published in 1855, is, on the surface, a book of broad, encompassing legal lexicon. But it is even more striking for how much ecological taxonomy punctuates its entries, such as moist soil (*ab khez*), soil freshness (*ahal*), rocky soil (*chatan*) and barren soil (*kalar*).[32] In a way, the whole taxonomy of Indian flora was a by-product of agrarian fiscalism, where the taxonomy of the agricultural economy generated statistical averages, which, while attempting to account for vagaries, could not help but reduce such meterological and agricultural complexities to manageable, predictable simplicities.

Deepening taxonomy: fiscal procedure

Agricultural taxonomy was also reflected in the procedural paperwork which managed the entire fiscal edifice. The Company's fiscal needs led Settlement Officers, under Company regulation, to add taxonomical details to the Persian proceedings beyond what would normally be included. The rent-roll (*hastobud*) was perhaps the biggest impetus for archivzation in the early colonial period. Usually held by *qanungo*s, it contained a wealth of agrarian and fiscal information, from cultivators' names and historical rates to assessments, counts of alluvium and diluvium soils.[33] The *hastobud*'s content and detail rapidly expanded under early settlements. Table 4.1 is a sample of what would be included in a *hastobud*.

It was not just grains and the vegetative powers of the soil that were to be accounted for. All financial transactions that fell within the expanding fiscal-agrarian umbrella were to be tabulated, even the profits derived from mango trees.[34] There was also a cross-fertilization of the early archive. The fact that Settlement Officers had Persian proceedings written into their reports in addition to their own taxonomical details[35] doubled the depth of the archive and paperwork required. And while Persian was jettisoned after the 1830s, later generations found the forces of archival accumulation hard to reverse. If anything, it grew with resentment and despair, but always exponentially and relentlessly.

Company policies and regulations also played a crucial role in shaping the early colonial archive. H.V. Bowen's argument that the business of imperial regulation generated paperwork in the colony certainly applies here.[36] The Board of Directors in London demanded a steady stream of information about Indian fiscal affairs. Regulation, paper and taxonomy made the dynamics and vagaries of Indian agriculture intelligible. For example, Regulations I and VII (1822), which drew inspiration from Thomas Munroe's *raiyatwari* settlements of south India, pushed this archivization deeper into the fabric of administration and circulation. It created a new way of seeing predominant landholding patterns, setting aside the concept of large propriety landholding rights. In theory, this anti-zamindari reactionary regulation empowered cultivators.[37] But, more importantly, this empowering of so-called corporately held lands (*bhaiachara*) meant a greater volume of paperwork than for larger estates. The Regulations also introduced the concept of 'net produce' criterion, or, as Eric Stokes put it, 'what total will the lands yield?'.[38] This was a fairly

Table 4.1 Rent-roll (*hastobud*) – required statistics, c. 1850s[39]

1	Names and numbers of villages divided into original ownership (*asuli*) and land taken possession of (*dukholi*)
2	Names and numbers of co-partners
3	Total comprised lands with a village boundary (*rukba*), divided into those written down (*ketabi*) and those not documented, where any ascertainment of the latter description may have been made, with distinct specification of the size of the *bigha*
4	Cultivable land that is not cultivated
5	Land occupied by houses, tanks, etc.
6	Waste lands
7	Rent free (*lakhiraj*) lands, with the descriptions in columns
8	Revenue land in cultivation
9	Number of *bighas* respectively cultivated, with the chief articles of husbandry under separate columns, with the highest and lowest rates of each quality of land
10	Numbers of *bighas* cultivated by hereditary ownership (*khudkasht*) and tenant-at-will cultivators (*paykasht raiyats*) respectively
11	Profits from pasturage, water usage (*julkur*), fruit-bearing trees (*phulkur*) and other miscellaneous sources of revenue
12	Average gross produce
13	Average net produce
14	Number of houses
15	Number of ploughs
16	*Jama* of expired settlement
17	Proposed *jama*

new category in India's fiscal-administrative history. Regulation IX (1833) went deeper still. It mandated that assessments had to be based upon 20 years' worth of records and documentation. Again, this was the concept of precedence. It opened up the *qanungo*s' and *patwari*s' papers to the historical reach of the colonial state in order to correct what the Board of Revenue called the 'enlightened guesses'[40] of early Settlement Officers in north India. By the 1810s the Company's agrarian intelligence and knowledge was already voluminous. The more assessments were formed and enforced annually, the exponentially deeper the archive became. We can see the early, almost numbing archival procedure being built up in the world of the District Collector. In the Doabi districts these officers were required to file both weekly and monthly returns for the items in Table 4.2. On a quarterly and annual basis, Collectors had to file further, detailed statements, which drew upon, and often reproduced, the thousands of weekly and monthly returns (Table 4.3).

The whole fiscal system became so documented – even to an absurd degree – that Collectors were even required to formulate a section on 'The Preparation of

Table 4.2 'Weekly and monthly returns' for Settlement Officers, c. 1840s[41]

1	Quantity of silver coin
2	List of Supply Bills drawn
3	Register of subscriptions to Government loans
4	Cash balance report
5	Estimate of probably receipts and disbursements
6	Treasury account
7	Monthly account of demands, collections and balances (*hal tauzi*)
8	Abstract of summons for default of payment (*tulubnama*)
9	Fines statement
10	Extracts of register of receipts and repayments of deposits
11	Extracts of register of interest paid on government loans
12	Monthly account of demands, collections and balances (*hal tauzi*), prepared and transmitted 12th of each month, prepared in the Sadr Office, drawn out specifically on 'foolscap paper')
13	Instalments plans for the entire pargana (*pargana kistibandi*) – drawn out on foolscap paper, to be dispatched 15th every month

Table 4.3 'Weekly and monthly returns' for Settlement Officers, c. 1840s[42]

1	Inefficient balance report
2	General treasury account
3	Pargana installments plans (*pargana kistibandi*)
4	Assessment current balance sheet (*jama wasil baqi*)
5	Annual comparative statements on assessment totals (*jama*)
6	Account of estimates of crop without measuring fields (*buqia tauji*)
7	Annual statement on *taqavi* loans (advances for seed and cattle)
8	Anticipated revenue from liquor duties (*akbari jama wasil baki*)
9	Report on the progress in decisions of civil suits
10	Particulars of pensions
11	Balance of deposits

Records'.[43] This sought to document economy in the materiality of colonial archive. Regulation itself, and the constant search for a verifiably true state of agricultural wealth and how it was to be managed, ensured that the archive ballooned exponentially from the early 1800s. Its depth and breadth far surpassed anything the Mughals and their eighteenth-century avatars achieved.

Deepening fiscal proceduralism and Hindustan's scribes

While much of the colonial state's archival depth was driven by regulation and the British penchant for accurate, detailed information, it was also dependent upon the information and papers of Hindustan's scribal communities. This ensured that they played a role in shaping the broader process of fiscal consolidation and expansion. It ensured, too, that they coloured the contours of the colonial archive. It was in the small district collectorships across the regions villages and townships where we saw how north Indian scribes helped deepen the state's repository knowledge. British revenue settlements – whose ultimate aim was to extract as much agrarian wealth as possible under the semblance of 'justice' – generated a voluminous amount of paperwork. But it also drew upon the papers of these extant officers. Combined with the fiscal state's prerogatives, they together pushed regulation, procedure and archival depth into the most remote *mofussil*s in the Doab. They achieved a penetrating intensity and an ability to tax, document and enforce, about which the Mughals could only have dreamed.

The agrarian archive emerged from two directions: the fiscal prerogatives of north India's new ruler and the scribes who had provided the Company with so much fiscal information in the first place. Unlike in Bengal after 1793, the Company's Doabi territories lacked a large zamindari establishment. In the Doabi territories the distinction between land rights and collection was far more clearly defined, which created the need for a massive subordinate staff to document and manage the whole fiscal edifice. The revenue system by the 1840s was, as a consequence, far more corporatist, involving numerous officers and middlemen. These complex arrangements between cultivators and landholders, and the burdens of taxation which were borne more broadly by cultivating communities, partly explains why the uprisings of 1857–8 acquired such wide levels of participation. When the Company's tax demands were made, all the village communities in the Doab were likely to have shared the feeling of 'fiscal injustice'. And here, British conceptions and debates over the nature of landholding and rights mattered. Holt Mackenzie's influence made itself felt in his constant insistence that proprietary rights to the soil were held in village communities (*bhaiachara*). Larger *taluqdar*s were quietly being undermined, save for, perhaps, the Nawabi domains before 1857. Romanticizing the Indian peasant and cultivator as the 'sole hope of Indian agriculture' meant that the fiscal machinery of north India generated a greater volume of paperwork, regularity and procedure than in Bengal.

Hindustan's scribes shaped the recruitment and staffing of the revenue department in the Doab and, later, Awadh, and they built up a body of bureaucratic protocols, organization and an ethos which revolved around paper, cataloguing and documentation. The *qanungo* became the effective 'communicator of fact' to the Collector, and these extant officers were required to maintain a ready, easily consultable repository of agrarian knowledge. *Qanungo*s owned their own records and had deposited copies (albeit inconsistently) under the Nawabs. But later, under the British, their *jamabandi*s, *hastobud*s and *sanad*s became property of the state; they became regularized. This had the important effect up building up the archival state. For example, if we look at the requirements for Settlement Officers' staff, we see a voluminous personnel and paperwork. Each Settlement Officer required 31 Indian officers, including 21 Collectors and 10 Assistants.[44] These numbers only grew over time, and these staff generated thousands of volumes of paperwork. Regulations passed in 1803 and 1810 mandated that all *patwaris* and *malguzars* deposit copies of their papers with the pargana's *qanungos*.[45] *Qanungos* also maintained deposits of all petitions (*urzis*),[46] which flooded the Company's offices after the 1770s in Benares and in the middle and lower Doab after 1803. And the regulations for managing *qanungos*' paperwork drove the archive to an unprecedented depth. For settlement officers, these included, as early as 1804, the items in Table 4.4. In Bareli, for example, 23 separate regulations managed *qanungo* paperwork and documentation. Aside from the usual register of *rubikaris*, *jamabandis* and attestation certificates (*sanads*), *qanungos* were now expected to add further detail and granular statistics to their reports. Via regulation and taxonomy, the British quickly welded these subordinate officers to the fiscal machinery of the colonial state.

Numerous other aspects of the broader revenue process were documented, stored and deposited, including *qabooliyats* with *malguzars* for cultivating leases

Table 4.4 'Weekly and monthly returns' for Settlement Officers, c. 1840s[47]

1	Detailed accounts of all villages ploughs, cattle, the inhabitants and caste
2	A regular, legible *jamabandi* every year and for all proprietors – with abstract and then details
3	A report of the extent of cultivation of valuation of crops in *tehsils*, in order to prevent *tehsildars* from undervaluing the crops
4	*Dauls* (estimates) in the anticipated settlement, including every type of grain and every particular produce of the soil
5	Reports on the 'character and responsibility of the renters'
6	The annual *jama* of each place settled by the Collector, and to ensure they corresponded with copies in Collector's Sadr Office and *katcheri*, and those of the *tehsildar*'s accounts
7	Report on any security tendered by former and current *malguzars*
8	Daily accounts of receipts of revenue
9	Daily accounts of *jama wasil bakis* and *kistibandis*
10	Recorded measurements taken during ploughing, indicating where extra wells can be dug to extend cultivation
11	Duplicate copies of *sanads* for *mafi* and *lakhraj* villages
12	Countersignatures for all *dastaks* in a pargana
13	Reports of any cases of *abwab* (levy) or *bhaint* monies which had to be reported immediately to the Collector
14	Register of all *patwaris* in the pargana

(*pattas*). They not only needed to be written on standardized and bound (what British settlement officers condescendingly called 'English paper'), but one copy needed to be deposited at the Office of the Revenue Accountant in the District. Another had to be deposited at the Record Office at the Bengal Presidency in Calcutta,[48] entailing long-distance travel and transport of paperwork. The *tahsildari* establishment, which the early colonial state did so much to bolster, was increasingly regulated by paperwork and the procedure of revenue. For example, *tahsildars* were required to file with the District Collector an account of sent petitions (*urz irsal*), which had to be written by village intermediaries (*lambardars*). These contained a standardized account of monies sent and accounts to be credited (the object, it seems, was to protect the *lambardar* against fraud by officials and moneylenders). *Tehsildars* were also required to file a separate 'book of occupancy' (*dakhila bahi*), which identified specific creditors in the filed *urz irsals*.[49] And here, again, the 'reforming' era of the 1830 had an impact and pushed the archivization of agriculture and fiscalism deeper. Under Regulation IX (1833), Sections 12 and 13 required that *patwaris* submit the items in Table 4.5 to every Collector's Record Office.

Hindustan's scribes helped European surveyors unlock the taxonomy of Indian agriculture. The fiscal prerogatives of the colonial state penetrated deep into the agrarian hinterland. And Hindustan's pensmen played a crucial role in creating the taxonomies of soil, grain and rents, which were used to sanction higher assessments. For example, Kayastha *qanungos* in Bareli were required to notate various qualities of soil, the crops being sowed and historical rents. The *jamas* in one pargana in Bareli immediately felt the imapct of how taxonomy and archival depth pushed up rents. In 1812 this pargana's assessment was Rs 43,136. But within five years, after the taxonomy of soils, crops and more specific details, its *jama* was raised 44 per cent to Rs 62,847.[50] The formation of the archive went hand in hand with greater assessment, a more intrusive fiscal state and a hammering of agrarian livelihoods.

By the mid 1850, at the cusp of the Uprising and Great Rebellion, the *qanungos*' and *patwaris*' records were already deeply integrated into the fabric of fiscal administration and revenue procedure. This gave the Raj an archival

Table 4.5 'Rules for Tehsildar's Accounts'[51]

1	Assessment agreements (*jamabandis*)
2	Supplements to the assessment agreements (*melan khusreh*)
3	Abstract of accounts (*teerji*)
4	Statement of realized revenue (*jamawasil baki*)
5	Statement of realized revenue in the tehsil (*jamawasil baki tehsili*)
6	Assessment expenses (*jama khurch*)
7	Register of all property mutations

depth that largely orbited around grains and 'granular' detail, all bound up and ordered by procedure and consultation. *Qanungo*s maintained in their offices a formidable volume of reports, lists and registers, which were used as indisputable fact (Table 4.6).

Hindustan's pensmen were integral to the expansive power of the Company's taxonomy, which itself greatly assisted the emergence of the Company's fiscal state. It expanded vertically in the sense that the British penetrated deeper into the countryside than any of its predecessors. But it also expanded horizontally in its formation of a broad, ecumenical repository of papers, surveys and statistics, which began to constitute the colonial archive.

Taxonomy of the 'professional' and *khusrah* surveys

The colonial archive was deepened not only by ecological and procedural taxonomy but by the increasing surveying and measuring of lands. Before the British, eighteenth-century north Indian agriculture was *normatively* surveyed, and it seems to have been guided by *Hanafi* jurisprudence. This included a map of villages, households and revenue produced, as best exemplified in the *khusrah* survey, which was largely the standard measure for the old Nawabi domains

Table 4.6 'Circular order for the Sadr Board of Revenue'[52]

1	Old village papers (*mauzinah*) or village registers under former Nawabi and Company governments
2	Register of villages (*mauzah*s) for every pargana
3	All rules and orders of practice for guidance, printed or in manuscript
4	List of rent
5	List of free estates
6	List of parcels
7	Histories of past estates furnished to settlement officers
8	All money agreements (*rukabandi*s) compiled for the pargana
9	Transfers to and from another pargana
10	Register of wells, shallow waters (*jheel*s), and rents paid on them (*taut*s)
11	Register of all inherited (*nuzul*) buildings
12	List of villages (*mauzah*s) on margin of rivers
13	Census papers
14	Register of proprietary mutations and alterations
15	*Patwari* List No. VII
16	Registers of classified proprietary tenures settlement statements IV, V and VI area
17	All annual assessments (*jama*s) going back to the Nawabi era
18	Registers and details on names, salaries and castes of rural police

and east India. But already by the 1780s in Benares, and in the Doab after 1803, the colonial state and its fiscal needs insisted on even more specific detail. As Ian Barrow has argued, surveying was partially about appropriating lands in the image of possession and rule.[53] But, although it is often taken as axiomatic to the point of not requiring explanation, surveying was ultimately anchored to the Company's fiscal priorities. Surveying was a method of realizing the fiscal prerogatives of the new Company state. As one Settlement Officer put it bluntly, 'the survey is for Revenue purposes'.[54] And after the 1810s surveys shifted away from the normative aspects of assessment towards a *positive* approach based upon the Great Trigonemetric Survey of India, backed up by a vast, accumulative corpus of agrarian knowledge and by Hindustan's scribes. Again reflecting changes in regulation, ecological knowledge shifted towards an ideal of what the lands *could* yield at the expense of what they did yield. This broadly echoed the framework that Settlement Officers brought to bear when assessing Doabi districts. And it was this major conceptual shift that helped deepen the agrarian archive even further and enhance the Company's *kaghaz raj* by the 1840s.

Hindustan's pensmen and surveying before the 1820s

The Company's early surveys utilized the normative aspects of the *khusrah* surveying method in the first generation of rule in the Doab. Here, paperwork shaped and enhanced the statistical and taxonomical imperatives of the colonial state. These early methods, used by *qanungo*s to maximize land's taxable value, gained currency in the first generation of Company rule. For example, Richard Ahmuty, the Collector of Allahabad in the early 1800s, worked closely with two *qanungo*s, Udai Rai and Khudai Lal. Ahmuty found their surveys and methods 'absolutely necessary'[55] in enforcing the measurement of land holdings via rods and ropes (*jarib*s). Ahmuty argued that the *qanungo*s' paperwork prevented 'sundry abuses and irregularities in the system of measuring the lands'.[56] Likewise, in various Bihari districts – for example, in villages such as Mundun – the process of taking new measurements was usually conducted by one general scribe (*mohurir*) 'in the presence of the Canoongoes'.[57] These scribes then checked the measurement against their own paper records. On the whole, British Collectors between Bhagalpur and Bareli regularly noted that the 'qanoongoe papers' were crucial in their standardized measurements and early surveys. In Tirhut, for example, the Collector Michael Pane noted that when it came to surveying lands, the paper records held by *qanungo*s helped him shape settlements and rates of assessment. And Pane noted the contributions of his late *qanungo*, Bhawani Sahay:

> in some cases a correct judgment cannot be formed from the documents produced… I request that you will do me the favour to forward to me such information regarding the former state of these villages, as may be contained in books prepared by Mr. Chamberlain from the old Canoongoe Records of this District.[58]

As in so many cases across Hindustan, when the statistically minded Company fell short of its own self-imposed standards for assessment, *qanungo* rent-rolls plugged the gaps in the state's statistical mastery. These examples, in turn, helped to standardize the early workings and rhythms of revenue collection. Some of the earliest verifications that the colonial state used for surveying were, crucially, checked with and informed by the paper repositories of Hindustan's scribes.

In Awadh after the 1850s Kayastha pensmen assisted the Raj in surveying and assessing. They did much the same as their caste fellows did elsewhere in the Doabi regions. Matthew Edney has argued that the Great Trigonometric Survey introduced new categories of measuring, namely the novel shift towards the counting of people.[59] Yet this overlooks the actual scribes and tools that were part of this transition. When we scratch beneath the surface, we see that a good deal of Nawabi-era rolls found their way into the Raj's fiscal toolkit after the 1850s. One example would be 1840s Kanpur. At the high point of the Thomason generation, fully two thirds of the old Kanpur *khusreh* surveys were directly incorporated into the officially sanctioned Professional Survey.[60] The *khusrah* worked by showing a map of a village, with sections numbered. The numbers had a corresponding key that listed the owner, crops grown and the rent of the field. The *khusrah* did not use mathematical triangulation, the triumphal ribbon of the Great Trigonometric Survey. Instead it worked on a village-by-village (*mauzawar*) process that drew from the precolonial past. Table 4.7 shows the basic categories that were included on the standardized form.

In order to penetrate more deeply into the *mofussil* of the countryside the *khusrah* survey – and the officers who worked it – were indispensable. In the Doabi territories the *khusrah* survived deep into the late nineteenth century as part of the fabric of revenue administration, along with the officers who maintained the records. *Patwari*s and Kayathas assisted a stern and vengeful North-Western Provinces (NWP) administration in deepening the archival depth of the state in post-1858 Awadh. For example, *patwari*s kept copies of the *khusrah* survey in Hindi, used in regular assessments after the 1860s.[61] The old Saxena Kayastha *moonserim*s and *qanungo*s were responsible for surveys of contiguous villages (*halka*), and Kayastha *qanungo*s fanned out from Lucknow and inspected thousands of estates to make surveys (*nazarandaz*) of the quality of land in cultivation. They seem to have won favour with numerous British Collectors for their drive towards 'statistical consistency and accuracy', especially for an administration that wanted to tax Lucknow as punishment for being a centre of the Uprising and Great Rebellion of 1857.[62] Jonathan Perkins, a Settlement Officer in recently pacified

Table 4.7 Overview of the *khusrah* survey[63]

1	The nature of soil
2	The types of crop planted
3	A complete record of cultivators' separate fields
4	The specific terms on which they are held

Sutlanpur, instituted the formation of regular 'Weekly Progress Reports' to trace the progress of *khusrah* surveys. This inflated the paperwork and archival depth of the state in Awadh from the mid 1850s. The cultivator might have dreaded the arrival of the measurement rod, but it was his extant paper superiors – the *qanungo* and *patwari* – who bolstered the actual mechanisms of British revenue demands.

The materiality of 'bureaucracy' in early colonial India

The East India Company, as we have seen, stepped into an extant paper-intensive and paper-driven revenue and fiscal tradition. We have seen how the employment of substantial numbers of subordinate Hindu pensmen helped generate a depth of paper that was organized, indexed, referential and taxonomic. The increasing presence of Company Settlement Officers and soldiers, with their pay bonuses (*batta*s), audits of accounts (*bhujarut*s) and assessments, all stimulated a wider culture of pen and paper that connected townships, tax ledgers and Persian literate *qanungo*s. Indo-Islamic North India, it seems, witnessed not so much a decline in what Brinkley Messick has called the 'calligraphic state'[64] as much as it experienced a refashioning. For one, the transition between the late Mughal and early British periods saw a revenue administration draw heavily upon scribes who straddled the later Mughal and early British empires. Indeed, as this book has argued, the very concept of a 'calligraphic' decline might be too simplistic, the paper upon which such writing was done possessing value under both Mughal and British rule. The persistence of paper-infused fiscal administration made changes in script and writing less important than in other Islamic lands. And if we look at the materiality of the bureaucratic processes that emerged, we see the true rise of a 'paper state'.

There was a profound materiality to the new Company's state that, while it drew upon the materiality of eighteenth-century revenue administration, the British pushed to new heights. It permeated the rolls, registers and bound volumes that increasingly came to define the regular rhythms of Company administration. The next section turns to the key aspects of this materiality: paper and ink. As we have seen, these 'administrative ingredients' had dynamics that were profoundly precolonial in their trade, production and usage. There was what we could call a 'writing economy' of ink, paper and pens, which stretched across the north Indian plains and connected Bengal with Kashmir. Let us now see how this changed under the Company's more paper-driven fiscal state.

Benares origins and paper

The Company was far more paper-intensive than previous Indian rulers. And this was seen from a very early period, especially, in 1780s Benares. Benares was a key transit point in the transition from Bengal upcountry to the Doab, particularly under Jonathan Duncan's residency. Duncan received hundreds of petitions (*urzi*s) in his first year as Resident, but what struck him was the particular nature of some of them. In 1788 he noted to Governor-General Cornwallis that many of them concerned commercial benefits for pen and paper merchants. He noted various petitions from the 'merchants of Multan, Kabul and Punjab' requesting a 5 per cent tariff be cancelled on ink and paper being brought into Benares.[65] Here, the demand for paper in British Bengal may have been at the forefront of the minds of these merchants, who commanded the trade sinews between Benares and the ink and paper production of Punjab and Kashmir. The Company's voracious appetite for paper was already well known by the late 1700s within the paper and ink trade. Duncan, who had to learn much about the fabric and traditions of revenue machinery from *qanungos*, used paper and ledgers far more than the Raja of Benares. In 1790, for example, the Raja's annual stationery costs amounted to Rs 528, while Duncan nearly doubled this volume and spent Rs 813.[66] The Company's reputation for paper and the work it entailed quickly became known. It was noted in the 1780s that Bengalis farther southeast had already started to do more secretarial and home-based work to adjust to India's new rulers. The scribe Sanbhu Lal called this work 'within the home' (*khaneghi*),[67] implying that the British preferred the more 'settled' aspects and materiality of paper and ink to coercing collections with swords and cavalry.

The ascendency of more paper-bound forms of administration also had the effect of altering the more human and personal elements upon which Indian revenue administration rested. Francis Fawke's munshi in Benares, Sanbhu Lal, again provides a fascinating insight. Lal noted how in the Company's offices (*kacharis*) the Indian newswriters (*akhbarnavisis*) were required to write about defaulters and report them to Calcutta and the Board of Revenue. But, as Lal noted, there was a break from established practice. The reports were dry and abstract, stripped of the human dimensions that led to default, including drought and dearth. Previously, such hardships were reported to *malguzars* and *amils* in person. But the materiality of British paper procedure eliminated this. These paper reports, Lal noted, did not describe the situations (*halat*) of the poor. Lal lamented that abstract, routine and voluminous paper information meant the plight of the downtrodden (*mazloom*) was never reported to consulates, only the state of default. Here, the materiality of paper depersonalized taxation's real and unavoidably human dimensions. What was more, since the newswriters had no human, face-to-face connection their superiors in Calcutta,[68] the voices of the *raiyat* were silenced. It was the only effect a procedural, paper-driven administration could hope to achieve. Paper procedure made India's fiscal world intelligible to the British. But the human element, which defined the Mughal and eighteenth-century traditions, was cut out rapidly, with drastic consequences across the north Indian plains after the early 1800s. The Indian cultivator was reduced to a decimal and statistic in a larger, complex fiscal-agrarian equation.

A ballooning paper administration

The Company was particularly quick and aggressive in formulating settlements of the Conquered and Ceded districts after 1803, and the emerging tendrils of its fiscal apparatus stimulated a pre-existing culture of paper and pen. Naturally, this had a direct impact upon the paper and ink economy and trading networks. What we see is that Indian paper and ink production did not decline in the first few generations of British rule. In a good many instances the British were dependent upon local procurers and supplies to codify their new agrarian settlements. These, after all, enabled them to enforce new regulations. The settlement of Azamgarh after 1803 is an example. Here, the British Collector attempted to set up a revamped police post (*kotwal*), and in defining the 'hereditary kanungos' he had to allocate Rs 4 per month for procuring the paper on which to keep records. Company supplies had yet to reach him. As such, this ingredient of authority in South Asia had to be procured from the local *tehsildar*,[69] who was bound up with long-distance trades and production of Indian-made paper from Bihar and upper Bengal.[70] The paper seems to have come from the 'paper township' of Arwal, known for its voluminous production. A similar situation transpired in Kanpur that same year. The Magistrate, John Stracey, ran out of stationery in the cool and productive month of November. Stracey had to spend his own Rs 17 and 12 *anna*s to procure it from a local trader.[71] In collectorships across the Doab early revenue settlements tapped into the Nepali paper trade. This was seen in Kanpur in 1806, too, when the Collector, Charles Dumbleton, spent his own Rs 25 for country stationery from Nepal 'owing to the delay in sending up the supplies for the year'.[72] That same year farther east the Collector of Agra had to spend Rs 144 at the Agra bazaar to purchase 600 quills, two penknives, one eraser and five black-lead pencils, which were 'immediately wanted for the use of the Office'.[73] In so many instances the Company's voracious paper appetite stimulated extant networks of trade, production and transport. In the 1830s Robert Montgomery Martin surveyed the ink and paper markets in lower Bihari country with a view to securing supplies for the Company's offices. He tapped into the over 240 families who produced paper to an annual value of over Rs 30,000.[74] Here, the Company's sprawling agrarian enterprise had to reach into the local 'paper economy', which, in turn, had been essential for legitimate government in the subcontinent since the seventeenth century.

The rhythms and procedure of revenue settlements stimulated an extant culture of paper to unseen degrees. This reflected a paper materiality and obsession with veracity and the accummulation of statistical knowledge. The settlement of a single village involved thousands of pages of paperwork, including even the individual names of cultivators, their caste, occupation and how much rent they paid in cash and in kind. Most new revenue regulations, guided by British frugality, made paper volume balloon, and this benefited Kayastha pensmens' ability to position themselves as crucial fiscal intermediaries in the process of state formation. In Farrukabad from 1803 onwards Collectors had to keep duplicate copies of all rent-tolls (*jamabandi*s), which instantly doubled the circulation of a district's paperwork.[75] In the regions bordering Nawabi Awadh, British Collectors insisted on 10 years' worth of *qanungo* records for the 'country settlement' (*mofussil bandobast*).[76] This was to give historical precedent for the base minimum of Company revenue demands and succour to the British obsession with averages. In 1806 Edward Cuthbert, the Collector of Allahabad, increased the number of 'Persian and Hindoostanee writers'[77] in his employment in order to grapple with the volume of land records needed for assessing land rates and historical yields. According to Cuthbert, paper and documentation on a previously unseen scale were needed for the British to fully realize their revenue demands. The Company's fiscal prerogatives required historical precedent, which would allow it to ascertain patterns and, according to its Physiocratic mindset, increase agricultural output over time along with tax revenue. In Bundelkhand, large landholding estates were required to deposit duplicate copies of their paperwork and land records with the local *qanungos*.[78] All of this meant that the volume of paper as a symbol of authority easily increased eight to tenfold within a generation. Moreover, the tendency to run annual assessments in the Doab territories early on had the effect of multiplying the overall number of subordinate officers required to comb through statistics and make inquires, all of which needed to be written down in an exponentially exploding volume of paper.

The overall volume of government paper in circulation reached almost absurd heights. By the 1830s, as William Sleeman observed, the *qanungo*-ship had become infused with volumes of paperwork in which 'records of great bulk are annually prepared which give the most minute details about every holding and each field'.[79] The Settlement Officer was generally considered 'the most busily occupied Officer of the district',[80] a precursor to the sun dried and roasted bureaucrats' of the later Raj.[81] The Meerut Collectorship in the 1830s offers a good example. Its staff and paperwork exploded after the early 1830s. Its Collector, Nathaniel Hamilton, begged Calcutta for more writers, paper managers and writers of assessments (*jamanavis*). He specifically requested one Bihari Kayastha, Heera Lal.[82] In his bloated establishment the collectorship's costs actually reached one third of the total assessment in his District.[83] Writers of decrees (*decreenavis*) were even created by the Company to ensure the production of standardized, documented decrees.[84] By the time the Mutiny and Great Uprising broke out in the Doab there were even procedural, official forms for registering complaints against parties who stole manure.[85] It was no surprise that Collectors regularly complained about 'the trouble and labour that the preparation of such [Revenue] Indexes necessarily imposes'.[86]

Officers in charge of treasuries in NWP might have had the worst of it. They had to comply with a mind-numbing set of regulations and standardizations regarding paperwork and accounting, most of which emanated from Calcutta and London. Table 4.8 shows what they had to enter in their weekly and monthly returns.

Treasury paperwork increased hugely after the 1830s economic depression hit the Company's finances. And the paperwork and materiality of regulation often prevented regular, long-term settlements (and fiscal certainty) from taking root. Smaller

Table 4.8 Weekly and monthly returns required to be filed by treasuries[87]

1	Memorandum of silver coin
2	List of Supply Bills drawn
3	Register of subscriptions to Government loans
4	Cash balance report
5	Estimate of probably receipts and disbursements
6	Treasury account
7	*Hal tauzee* (monthly account of demands, collections and balances)
8	Abstract summons for default of payment (*tulubnama*),
9	Extracts of register of receipts and repayments of deposits
10	Extracts of register of interest paid on government loans

pargangas such as Lalitpur and Jalone, which the Company acquired in 1803, did not have regular consistent settlements until 1869,[88] largely because Settlement Officers could not keep abreast of the constantly snowballing regulations. In every sense, Collectors and magistrates were buried in paperwork. The British instituted, to borrow from Radika Singha, a 'despotism of paperwork' to rule India.[89]

Various regulations which aimed to check 'corruption' and 'improve efficiency' had two effects: they transformed paper's innate value from private to state property and increased the regular volume of paperwork circulating through the colonial state's veins. The first decade of the nineteenth century saw the volume of paperwork used by *qanungo*s and *patwari*s almost triple. Copies were needed for British officials. But the state also welded these Indians scribes and their paperwork to regulation by having them cross-deposit their papers, often in multiple copies. For example, as early as 1808 *qanungo*s had to

1 Keep a duplicate set of accounts regarding the *tehsildari*
2 Were responsible for countersigning all accounts of all revenue officers in a pargana, mainly *patwaris*, *tehsildars*, *malguzars* and *amils*
3 Were responsible for countersigning all receipts for land revenue furnished to the parties.

The *qanungo* had to receive, arrange and examine the *patwari*'s papers and bring any inconsistencies to the notice of the *tehsildar*.[90] Since they possessed written records guided by the state's regulatory procedures, the *qanungo* became the fact checker and unofficial auditor of a village. By the 1860s it was admitted that 'the chief value of the Qanoongoe's Office consists in the check which it afford over the Pergunnah's Accounts and Returns'.[91] These scribes therefore played a crucial role in the emergence of the 'attestive state'[92] by the 1820s. The *qanungo* became the statistical pillar of British rule in the agrarian countryside.

Similarly to the seemingly humble *qanungo*, the *patwari*'s paper volume was also enhanced under the early colonial state. *Patwari*s, for example, were required to attest all written engagements between proprietors and cultivators, and to record all arrangements of land between coparceners in joint estates. Previously, they simply had their own personal, non-standardized records of cultivators, which included crops sown, returns of agricultural yields and rents paid.[93] By regulating their records, the fiscal state again transformed the papers from private to state property. This changed the inherent value and materiality of the records. After each *rabi* and *khurif* harvest, *qanungo*s and *patwari*s had to countersign all *jamabandis*.[94] Regulation stimulated an absurd degree of paperwork. Under Regulation III (1803), copies of all revenue-paying lands' decrees needed to be registered with the Collector.[95] The District Collector became, quickly, an orbital nexus of rent information, paperwork, tenures and litigation, surrounded by chests and rolls of overflowing paper. In some cases it was so managerial and intrusive that one Company official wistfully observed: 'what prevents this natural progression [of agriculture]? The officers of government'.[96]

The British obsession with exposing and preventing fraud generated additional paperwork and regulation. One of the effects of the early fiscal state was to transform the nature of official paper. Under the Mughals and eighteenth-century states, paper was not taxed. Its production was seen as a meritorious process in the service of the even more meritorious art of writing. Learned Muslims and Kayasthas possessed a long appreciation for the culture of ink and paper as a refinement and art form, one enhanced (and made possible by) by proper behaviour (*akhlaq*). There were degrees of formatting for various administrative manuals, employed by munshis and scribes, but the consistency was patchy across north India. The British, on the other hand, viewed paper as possessing a more fiscal-utilitarian function. This made it subject to regulation and hence management by the state. This was seen in how the numerous regulations after 1803 transformed the value of paper and repository knowledge. Regulation X (1829), for example, introduced for the first time stamp taxes and 'legal' paper dimensions. Older *jamabandi*s and *hastobud*s, even if their information carried over, had their details integrated into stamped, regulated paper. Over the next decade a whole market of stamped paper emerged under the first generation of Collectors in the Doab. It was observed that 'paper becomes valuable according to the amount of stamp which it bears… as though it were paper money'.[97] By making revenue paperwork state property, the British, at a pen stroke, altered the inherent value of paper and created categories of 'legitimate' and 'illegitimate' paper.

But theses attempts at attestation and verification were, on closer inspection, not wholly transformational. The Company state needed to compete with a still vibrant paper economy. A welter of Indian paper merchants, who procured their various papers from old *kaghazi* families, competed with the Company to supply paper to the *qanungos*, *patwari*s and Company officials across the Doab. This perseverance is seen in how local officials had to respond to market forces in the paper trade, and how they had to compete with Indian suppliers. For example, the NWP Revenue Department, in order to keep prices stable, kept a surplus stock of paper, which could be shipped from the Superintendent in Calcutta. This was a reserve mechanism in order to counter the proliferation of Indian paper sources and what officials called 'fraudulent' paper. What they really meant was unregulated paper. Revenue Officers had to maintain 'trusted' paper vendors in areas where they had competing interests. If they colluded, revenue officers undersold them by selling stamped paper directly from the Treasury at a discount equal to the previous year's average cost of collections.[98] Much of this had to do with an obsessive concern with forgery and attestation. Magistrates, for example, often claimed they encountered fraudulent paper in Indian affidavits (*razinama*s) in legal proceedings. Here, the materiality and value of paper changed. The NWP government used particular watermark technologies to check fraudulent *razinama*s and initiated fictitious legal suits to compel the value of the stamp. Observations read like detective sleuths undertaking intelligence work:

> native ink does not act chemically on the paper, and hence a common fraud is to wash out the old writing and to use the paper a second time. Sometimes also it has been the practice in the Civil Courts to allow two papers of small value to be filed instead of one of larger value; only one of these two pieces is written upon, the other is filed blank, and at some future period is withdrawn from record, and sold for use a second time.[99]

One of the reasons paper became more regulated by the state was the sources upon which extant officers drew. *Patwari* and *qanungo* papers were often Indian 'hill paper' (*baus ka kaghaz*), produced and distributed by networks that stretched between Arwal and Sialkot. Even after revenue departments standardized official papers' size and dimensions in order to legitimize their value,[100] the flood of Indian paper often countered (and fulfilled) the voracious paper appetite of the British.

There was a great irony in the materiality of the Company's early paper administration. While the British chided Indian governance for its despotism, corruption and bloated administrations, the reality was that the early revenue settlements had the effect of inflating the number of officers on Company pay. The fiscal drive of the Company state drew more and more people into government employment, which enhanced the power and reach of the state. As British obsession with fraud expanded, so too did its bureaucratic and paper depth and its centrality as a local employer. It was a contradiction that was never resolved under colonial rule. To increasingly manage and administer 'just' governance, the archival state had to grow increasingly larger and employ more and more subordinate Indian staff. This toxic and parasitic duality, with its origins in managing agrarian revenue, saw the genesis of the dreaded 'Home Charges' that Dadabhai Naoroji later criticized so eloquently. The emergent taxonomical fiscal state, because it was so regulatory, created the very need for its own inflated staff and expense. Board of Revenue regulations mandated complete and accurately detailed information. Yet this meant paper needed to be copied, which required numerous Indian copyists and indexers. They were also cheaper than European copyists. This had spillover economic effects that reverberated into the north Indian paper economy. The Company legally made all revenue documents available to the public, which stimulated a broader market for copyists and forgers. It also led to a tax in NWP of 1 *anna* on the annual *jama* plus two fifths of non-assessed lands' produce to maintain the public Record Office.[101] Henry Tucker sarcastically noted that the whole revenue arm of the Company was

> a system requiring a multiplicity of instructors, surveyors, and inspectors; assessors, ordinary and extraordinary; potails, curnums, tehsildars and cutcherry servants… a flight of locusts, devouring in their course the fruits of the earth.[102]

In a way, the Company's own regulations were the very means by which assessments became even more savage. In other words, the Indian cultivator was forced to pay for the very paper records and management which documented his produce, down to every single grain.

Shifts: away from people and to paper

As we have seen, the value of paper changed markedly under the early Company. But the proliferation of paper also served to alter one crucial aspect of precolonial revenue administration: the British ate away at the constellation of officials bound by human interaction. After the early 1800s paper became the Company's substitute for human interaction. No longer did tax collectors meet face to face with cultivators: they connected with the *raiyat* through paper forms and an exponentially increasing subordinate Indian staff. The rise of paper, because it was impersonal and required less human interaction, reflected an increasingly imperial British hubris. It was no coincidence that the 'age of reform/hiatus' also became the age of bureaucracy, which itself was a coded form of racism. The British not only bypassed a constellation of intermediate officers who, as we have seen, interacted with each other, but they reduced the ones they did employ – including *qanungos* and *patwaris* – to mere functionary enforcers of a paper empire (*kaghaz raj*). The advice given by largely older Muslim officers who either had substantial land rights or some administrative purview, such as *chaudhuris* and *amils*, was quickly dispensed with by a colonial state that had little patience for the human-interactive aspects of revenue administration. Paper also proliferated to make India's agrarian universe intelligible. For example, it was noted in the mid-1850s manual for Settlement Officers and Revenue Officials in NWP why paper was crucial for company governance: 'difference of religion and of social system necessarily separates him [the British Collector] from them, and prevents his forming that accurate estimate of character, which is only to be acquired in confidence of private intercourse'.[103] This reflected not just a more removed, racial aloofness but, more importantly, just how different Britain's revenue administration was from its predecessors'. Administration was depersonalized and replaced with paper, procedure and taxonomic depth. In a way, it became 'Weberian' from a very early stage.

Broader materiality of the archive and economic markets

As well as the general fabric of village society and landholding patterns, the emergent fiscal state affected particular economic sectors. Paper production and procurement were just a few examples. The Company's fiscal state stimulated extant networks of paper production. *Kaghazi* families in regions such as Bihar, Delhi and Kashmir benefited from the unprecedented paper intensity of their new rulers. Even as late as the 1850s the Company was somewhat dependent upon Indian networks of paper supply, refiners and ink dyers to secure the physical sanction for their revenue demands. The large-scale importation of pulped paper into India seems to have only taken off substantially after the 1850s. Indian paper commerce worked with the colonial state in the first half century of British rule in north India. For example, the Dinajpur District and Serampur, with their abundant coniferous trees, supplied the paper-producing (*kaghazi*) families of Bihar and the lower Doab.[104] Another example can be seen in the regulations issued for District Collectors in NWP by the late 1840s. Written by Charles Allan, an accountant with the Bengal Civil Service, it gave a detailed guide for using paper and adhering to the standards for Company documentation and archiving. It suggested that Serampur or 'good country paper' should be used when none is available.[105] This happened more often than not. Serampur seems to have been a major supply centre for the Company's paper needs, supplying Collectors hundreds of miles upcountry. Also, the Sadr Office offered guidelines which demonstrated that the fiscal state reached deep into local production networks. For example, monthly accounts of demands, collections and balances (*hal tauzi*) needed to be prepared and transmitted on the 12th of each calendar month. They were to be drawn out on 'foolscap paper', a mixture of local fabrics and cloths which were bleached then dyed. Foolscrap paper was also regulated for usage in the NWP's instalment payments (*pargana kistibandi*), of which there were tens of thousands of sheets for the tens of thousands of Doabi parganas. These had to be dispatched on the 15th of every month,[106] which easily equated to hundreds of thousands of individual pieces of paper, all circulating across the countryside. As late as the 1860s various types and varieties of Indian paper were used by the colonial state to document, assess and prosecute the prerogatives of the fiscal state.

North Indian and particularly Nepali merchant families seem to have benefited from the expansion of the Company's fiscal outlook after 1800. One of the reasons Nepali trade made inroads into the north Indian paper economy was its abundance of forested and mountain tracks, which provided plentiful amounts of timber and coniferous trees for pulped paper. Nepali supplies also seem to have benefited from the extensive deforestation in north India since the 1600s.[107] It was observed at the Court of Nepal in the 1860s that making paper was a laborious, interconnected process, which bound townships, producers and refiners across north India and Nepal. Specifically, demand largely drew upon the Nepali Daphne plant (*daphne cannabina*), known in India as *mahadeva*:

> the daphne is a small evergreen perennial shrub, somewhat like a laurel, which bears poisonous berries. There are several species of it in Nepal, from which, I am told, that paper is made. In some kinds the flowers are pure white in others dirty white, tinged with pink or purple; and in my rambles last spring, at the back of a high mountain, north of the residency, I found two or three varieties of it, the flowers of which were bright yellow, much like the large yellow jessemine, for which, at a little distance, I mistook it. These shrubs grow to a height of ten or twelve feet. I believe the Nepaul paper has been sent to England in quantities, in all stages of preparation; but no notice has been taken of it… of the prepared pulp I sent two manuds to Messrs. Mackey & Co., of Calcutta, in November 1855. It cost 22 Rs 2a per manudm delivered at Dinapore, and was intended for some fibre company in England. But as I have not had a line from those gentlemen since regarding it, I presume it was not found to answer. There is an impression in the Plains that the Nepaul paper is prepared with arsenic. This is quite a mistake, for arsenic is not allowed to be sold here… under a heavy penalty.[108]

Existing Indian networks of production seem to have lasted into the 1840s, and the fiscal state drove demand for paper production, refinement and distribution. For example, Rangpur supplied many offices (*daftar*s) and ledgers of the Company across Bengal and into the lower Doab and Benares. Its paper was not as starched and firm as that from the other 'paper city' farther west, Arwal.[109] The proceedings of British Collectors seem to have been interspersed with Arwal's paper. Even in the 1830s Robert Montgomery Martin surveyed the ink and paper markets in west Bengal and lower Bihar with a view to procuring supplies for the Company's sprawling fiscal state – and Arwal was the centre of it. It possessed over 70 houses and employed over 240 men who produced paper to the annual value of Rs 32,000.[110] Arwal's links to the Indo-Islamic world of paper were well known. Arwal's paper was 'commonly used by Persian writers all over Bengal [and Bihar]',[111] and the trade was so profitable that as late as the 1830s many Muslim paper (*kaghazi*) families 'live[ed] in easy circumstances'.[112] The trade was largely export-driven across north India. A bit farther north, Patna probably exported close to Rs 5,550 of paper annually.[113] This perserverance of a broader, extant paper economy can also be seen in the limited inroads industrially produced paper made in north India by the late nineteenth century. By 1900 the India Paper Mill Company in Lucknow was the only one in north India. Its secretary was Ram Saran Das Verma, a Srivastava Kayastha,[114] who had a near monopoly on mill-produced paper.[115] Bombay and Bengal, meanwhile, each possessed three paper mills that were rapidly attracting Indian and British capital.

The early-nineteenth-century fiscal state also tapped into the Company's increasing 'criminalization' of *thagi* and defaulters. Here, legal adjudication and paper production were bound up with the materiality of the Company's fiscalism. After the 1820s, for example, at major jailing stations, such as the Central Jails in Meerut and Agra, prison labour was used to produce what were called 'rag papers', made from old ropes and gunny bags.[116] In Meerut paper was made out of hemp. But it was more cheaply produced in Agra, where the jail's old bags and ropes were boiled, broken down and bleached with a mixture of lime and carbonate soda, at roughly Rs 5–10 per ream.[117] Foreshadowing the evolution of the practice of 'incarceration labour' by modern states, the Company was already using the legally adjudicated to produce the pulped sinews of its own fiscal and legal authority.

Even some of the first Company officials and Collectors in the newly acquired 1803 territories were involved in the paper economy of north Indian revenue administration. Richard Ahmuty, who helped form settlements with Kayastha *qanungo*s in Allahabad in the first decade of the nineteenth century, grew to know the local paper production. He had pored over *jamabandi*s and *hastobud*s in places such Allahabad in 1803–4, when he worked with the *qanungo*s Udai Rai and Khudai Lal. He helped found Ahmuty & Co., which six decades' later was given an award at the 1862 London Illustrated Exhibition for fibre paper prepared from Dhaincha (*aeschynomene cannabina*).[118] More often used as a fertilizer, it was commonplace in parts of the lower Doab and Bihari country, and some of its cultivation seems to have shifted away from agricultural production towards mechanized paper production. But the venture to mass-produce and mechanize paper production did not get off the ground quickly. This was largely due to an acute lack of demand for expensive stationery, coupled with the Company's reliance upon local networks in regions which were outside Calcutta and larger cantonment townships.[119] Some British companies such as Stephens & Hay did manage to secure contracts to supply the paper for the master ledgers of proceedings.[120]

But, even here, the supposed change was not as great as it seemed. Indian traditions of paper production, procurement and long-distance trade survived as late as the 1840s. When steam power came to Indian paper production after the 1840s, local *kaghazi* families assisted in its adoption for operating the beaters which pressed the pulped paper.[121]

Broader effects of the 'archivization' of the agrarian economy

The depth of the agrarian archive was striking. First, the relentless drive to document, accurately assess and – perhaps most importantly – check fraud and 'native corruption' spawned a whole set of forms, regulations and procedure. Compared to the description by Muhammad Faiq in 1820s Sultanpur, the Company state was far more paper-intensive, detailed and intrusive. Faiq described, if we recall, a revenue administration in Awadh that was more of a constellation of interconnected middlemen and individuals, in which accurate records were needed but were not procedurally adjudicating in and of themselves. There was always flexibility in terms of payment and instalments. The volume of overall paperwork could be substantial. But paper's role was to temper, more than to drive, fiscal proceedings. Moreover, grain types, prices and rainfall amounts were not included in his description of what papers should contain.[122] These were details that remained in private hands in the repositories of those with localized, agrarian and fiscal knowledge: *qanungo*s and *patwari*s. *Sarkar*s, *malguzar*s and *mukhtarkar*s possessed paper information that detailed who paid what, their names, when payments were made and who defaulted, along with more general descriptions of the pargana.[123] But they did not possess the same degree of fiscal depth and historical information as later British revenue officials. This is probably why Faiq admitted that *qanungo*s and *patwari*s, because of their position as 'fiscal intelligenciers', could get away with fraud and tax evasion. But unlike the later Company state, he never held them accountable to oaths and centralized regulation. The *qanungo* and *patwari* were often mini paper-rajas in their villages.

The 'Colonial Register'

An important by-product of this increasing fiscal regulation and procedure was archival apparatus. Agricultural taxonomy and the Company's insistence on posessing fiscal and agrarian information led to the emergence of an exemplar document: the 'Colonial Register'. The Register seems to have been formed through the accumulation of various papers from *qanungo*s, *patwari*s and *malguzar*s, beginning in the middle and upper Doab – again, in Duncan's tenure in Benares. Regulations XLVIII (1793) and XIX (1795) created a *malguzari* register, which later, under Regulation VIII (1800), made mandatory a complete listing of estates in every pargana.[124] The listing also had to detail all tariffs on substantial commerce coming in and going out of Benares. The link between the fiscal security of the state and fiscal intelligence was crucial from the very beginning:

> it is essential for the security of the Government Revenue, as well as for the maintenance of private rights of property in the land, that a complete system of registration be devised, and that the registers be maintained with accuracy.[125]

After the acquisition of the middle and upper Doabi territories in 1803, Benares' regulations were extended through a requirement for a Register of Landed Property. The details required by the new Registers were more extensive than those required by any documents that preceded the Company (Table 4.9).

The later revenue demands of the Company stimulated further demand for statistical accuracy and information which deepened the Register as a function of colonial archiving. Regulations VII (1822) and IX (1833) made Registers of property a standard point of reference in property and, by extension, fiscal disputes. They became a complete record of what the British felt were agrarian truths. The archival depth, and officials' and (in theory) subjects' access to it, was to be guaranteed. It was, after all, what the British claimed made their procedural, documented paper administration an improvement on Muslim rule. It was noted that an effective Register, and a larger record office in the District, should only require a few minutes to furnish requested documents on any village.

The Register was to become the fiscal officer's handbook for readily accessible, truthful information, upon which the entire edifice of 'justice' rested. But it was also to serve as a forecasting guide. The Register had became a 'Meteorological Register in which the fiscal prospects of the Faslee year are exhibited',[126] and was to showcase, as accurately as possible, British mastery over the vagaries of the monsoon. But the connections between revenue and the archive were put most clearly by one official:

> in India the Government has a direct interest in the preservation of these records [parnaga and malguzri registers], because the greatest part of its revenues is drawn from the rents of land, or from a tax on those rents.[127]

Table 4.9 Requirement for 'Register of Landed Property' in CCP, c. 1810s

1	Union of all estates, through marriage
2	Divisions of all estates (*butwaras*). If co-parcenres cannot agree on who owns what, then they have to settle in Court via arbitration. If no agreement, then Collector can go ahead and divide up the estates in question
3	Changes of proprietors (*kharij dakhil* cases)
4	*Mouzahs* brought on to the rent-roll (*hastobud*)
5	Villages (*mouzahs*) removed from the rent-roll (*hastobud*)
6	All alterations, in detail, of the villages' assessments (*jamas*)

This was a direct, telling example of the connections between the colonial archive and agriculture which were forged after the early 1800s. And it played itself out in how revenue administration unfolded in north India: in embryonic form in Benares, grown to utmost intensity across the Doab and then projected deeper into Awadh after the 1850s.

Legal factors and procedure also made the Register more 'archival'. For the early Company state, like the later Raj, 'justice was inseparably linked up with revenue'.[128] This was seen in how the fiscal-agrarian intelligence in scribes' papers, and later in bound form in the Register, became the fulcrums upon which legal cases were decided. For example, the procedure for legal cases in revenue courts (*diwani audalat*s) was based on the regulations governing the *patwari*'s papers and accounts. Papers and the Colonial Register became points of reference for settling legal disputes and cases of default and non-payment. They were often noted by British magistrates when adjudicating cases. The same held for *qanungo*s. Their *hastobud*s, *jamabandi*s and various other revenue documents were used early on to adjudicate land disputes and cultivation tenures, and to determine levels of taxation. In Benares, where disputes over proprietary rights and assessments proliferated in the 1780s, Jonathan Duncan quickly realized that 'the general rule for deciding such cases was the *doul* or estimate of the Qanoongoe of the pergunnah… nothing could in general be fairer than this rule, and accordingly few of the complainants objected to it'.[129] These legal disputes, which ultimately were settled to enforce payment, orbited around the Register. It formed the archival basis for authenticating land titles and transfers of lands and deeds, and it was bound up with the *qanungo*, *patwari* and their papers.

The fiscal archive, reflecting the tendency of Settlement Officers to produce statistical compendiums and averages, reached absurd depths. Settlement Officers had a fetish for the statistical and granular, as a way of glorifying their rule. The workings of revenue collection taxonomized even the costs of surveying itself. Indeed, settlement manuals encouraged officers to adhere to 'the strictest economy in all branches connected with [the] preparation of records'.[130] For example, the costs of surveying per unit of land in Sitapur were laboriously calculated – including personnel staff, travelling expenses and stationery costs – to be Rs 63 per acre.[131] This appeared in many settlement reports after the 1830s, reflecting the obsession with statistical averages. The agrarian taxonomy of the fiscal state became a joke for later colonial administrators and scholars. William Crooke noted that while

> Akbar was a master of detail… [ours] is pushed to the extreme... it is everywhere assumed that the control of business depends on the compilation of appropriate registers, which is one of the besetting delusions of the native official of our days.[132]

This was, perhaps, a wistful acknowledgement that the steady accumulation of knowledge did not make India more intelligible.[133] The cadre of John Stuart Mill and the Thomason generation in NWP might have felt that only paper could justly administer India.[134] But some scions of officialdom saw the expansion of bureaucratic staffing as 'the source of a growing and intolerable charge upon the revenues of India'.[135] It was a dangerously circular logic: the fiscal needs of the colonial state created its own bloated paper and personnel costs, which were paid for by the Indian peasantry and cultivating classes on top of inflated assessments (*jamas*). These were the origins of the fiscal critique of the British Raj and its 'Home Charges' that would later be given their most articulate voice by Dadabhai Naorji's *Poverty and un-British Rule in India.*[136]

Conclusion

This chapter has examined how the early, rapid formation of the Company's fiscal state unleashed unprecedented volumes of paperwork, regulation and procedure. The British devoured far more paperwork than their Timuri and Muslim predecessors. In this massive fiscal-agrarian administration the intrusiveness of assessment, no matter how much paperwork it required, generated an accumulative depth of knowledge which was recorded, organized, indexed and made procedural. This was the beginning of the colonial archive. Bernard Cohn and, to a degree, Nicholas Dirks have argued that 'investigative modalities' of caste and language drove the taxonomizing colonial.[137] But this privileging of cast and language seems less convincing when viewing the sinews of revenue administration and fiscal management. For one, what we see is that there was little concern with categorizing caste and language. If anything, soil classification, well tracking and unlocking the mystery of proprietary rights were more immediate and paramount. In other words, the pulse of daily administration was important; it more regularly affected the lives of cultivators and intermediaries than abstract racial or caste taxonomies. And soil, grains and prices fed into the master calculus of maximizing agrarian revenue, which had been the mainstay of Indian sovereigns for centuries. The origins of the colonial archive, in the Company's early period in the Doab, lay more in its desire to harness the wealth of grain than to classify caste and religion as a means of comprehending Indian society. The categories of caste and religious 'community', which some have seen as the origins of the taxonomic state, were more by-products of this whole process of fiscal 'archivization' than preconditions of it.

Of course, all this paperwork and procedure were not without a point. In fact, its purpose was twofold. First, it was to render the complexities and vagaries of agrarian wealth manageable and accessible to the British, including welding the rhythms of Indian agriculture to British interests, as much as they could. In doing so, the Company state also depersonalized the broader fiscal system by placing law, rule and procedure above personal relationships. As we have seen, interconnected relationships, tempered by paper, were characteristic of the eighteenth-century tradition into which the Company stepped. By creating standardized forms, procedure and regulation, the British very quickly made tax collection about procedure at the expense of personalities and human interaction. The increased accumulation of fiscal knowledge was also seen in a broader anxiety among eighteenth-century Indian observers about paper depersonalizing administration.

Tabatabai, for example, noted how the English were largely indifferent to their Indian subjects.[138] Paper and procedure served to cut the human dimension out of precolonial fiscal administration.

Second, paper and procedure reflected an increasing imperial hubris. One could interpret the emergence of various strands of colonial racism by seeing their early origins in the routine of bureaucratic-fiscal administration from the 1780s and 1790s. Indeed, it was not just in personal relationships and matters of gender and sexual propriety[139] that early colonial racism made itself apparent. Often it was more subtle, buried deep in the procedural lexicon. It was also paternalistic. The Indian cultivator could only be protected from the 'rapacious' nature of Indian rulers through 'just' British administration backed up by the juggernaut of procedural paperwork. In a way, the colonial archive was very much a site where social and cultural assumptions were fashioned.[140]

Was this system of paperwork and regularity productive? Did it eliminate the 'inconsistencies' and 'corruptions' that punctuated British writing on Indian rulers? It is hard to say. For one, British judgments on Indian fiscal regimes' moral bearings were themselves extremely biased. But it does seem that the procedural nature of British revenue administration lent itself to a few crucial developments. It regularized the rhythms of assessment, attestation and filing more effectively than under the Mughals and their successor kingdoms. It also, crucially, eliminated the flexibility that was characteristic of the eighteenth-century traditions. Discounts for cultivators in times of dearth were not only scaled back: they dotted the paperwork of the new state less frequently.

It is hard to assess how well the British managed to work the paper-driven bureaucratic nature of the very beast they created. The British seem to have mastered some degrees of the agrarian and fiscal worlds, and their regularity and procedure made this possible. If we narrowly define 'success' based on overall yields, then the Company was a marked victor. As we saw in the previous chapter,[141] the whole development of agrarian taxonomy allowed the Company to extract more wealth than the Mughals and their eighteenth-century avatars. They collected more per assessment (and per cultivator) than any ruler in India's history. And the sheer breadth and depth of agrarian knowledge accumulated into procedure and paperwork was astounding. The archive of the early Company was accumulated quickly and penetrated deeply. It was an impressive, almost staggering marshalling of agrarian knowledge and information. And while the Company Raj drew upon information from extant scribes and officers, India's new masters injected a mind-numbing specificity and relentlessness when it came to knowing the agrarian countryside and preventing 'corruption'. They also transformed the value of paper and its materiality. For example, the specificities of previously localized forms of agrarian knowledge – such as estimates (*dauls*), historical returns (*hastobuds*) and assessment balances (*jama wasil bakis*) – were brought into the orbit of central fiscal authority like never before. The information was transformed into state property through standardization, organization and indexing. The hundreds of thousands of rent rolls, historically deep archives and sheer materiality all reflected a real mastery of agrarian knowledge. Settlement

Officers' obsession with averages, though, perhaps did more than anything to drive the archival depth to absurd levels.

But this seeming mastery of agrarian knowledge was largely pyrrhic. It looked impressive, but beneath the surface there were crucial shortcomings. For one, it does seem that the Company never had a full hand on, or an understanding of, the complexity and flexibility of Indian revenue traditions. Many parts of the Doab did not have regular settlements until the 1860s. The fact that even as late as the 1870s the British did not fully understand the 'fictitious *bhaiachara* system' of land tenure in the Doab is a perfect example. Paperwork, documented data and procedure gave the British a misleading, though soothing, sense of mastery. The East India Company had become a real paper empire (*kaghaz raj*). But the whole accumulated morass of paperwork and procedure also reflected an abject British failure. The agrarian agitations that simmered through the first three decades of the 1800s across the Doab were reflective not only of the Company's self-interests but of how the vast accumulation of knowledge did little to 'settle' the countryside. In a way, the Great Uprising and Rebellion of 1857 was a blood-soaked affirmation of this failure and 'blinding by paper'.

Of course, this is not to say that revenue was the sole generator of paperwork in early colonial India. The Company's army and military paperwork – which started registering everything from caste to religion – was the other major early source of the colonial archive. The growth of the Company's mercenary force between 1750 and the early 1800s rose from 10,000 to almost 200,000 paid soldiers. The recruitment and retention of such as large standing army required vast, unimaginable amounts of paperwork to account for bonuses (*bhatta*s), dietary restrictions, uniform orders and caste observances. The army's overall archival depth and breadth might have emerged first and most voluminously, but the archival-fiscal state served as the army's lifeline of funding.[142]

The effects of this archival and paper depth of administration had crucial reverberations beyond the Doab. The *kaghaz raj* of the Doab affected later generations of administrators and the patterns of governance farther northwest. The development of such a routinized, procedural approach to harnessing agrarian wealth seems to have generated a reaction in the generation of Punjab administrators after the 1850s. After the Great Rebellion and Uprising of 1857 the Punjab saw an administration, namely that of the Lawrence brothers, which centred around the 'strong will and personality' of one man. This could be seen as a reaction to the mind-numbing paperwork in the Doab, where procedural filings could quickly humble even the most strong-willed administrator. By romanticizing the Sikhs as 'martial', the Lawrence brothers eliminated the need for a cumbersome and procedural fiscal state in the first place. They and their progeny were lauded for the ways in which they governed *without* recourse to bureaucracy.[143] And, of course, the British had a love–hate relationship with their bureaucracy. The Raj greatly relied upon it for the state's fiscal needs. But, as the evidence has demonstrated, it was regularly detested. Northwest of the lush Gangetic plain, the 'strong collector', by sheer force of will, voice and word, moved the Punjab's grains to the Raj's treasuries in a manner far less convoluted than that back in Hindustan.

Notes

1 C. Bayly, *Empire and Information: Intelligence Gathering and Social Communication in India, 1780–1870* (Cambridge, 1996).
2 A. Appadurai, 'Number in the colonial imagination', in C.A. Breckenridge and P. van der Veer, eds. *Orientalism and the Post-Colonial Predicament* (Philadelphia, 1993).
3 N. Dirks, *Castes of Mind* (Princeton, 2001).
4 M. Edney, *Mapping an Empire: the Geographical Construction of British India* (Chicago, 1997).
5 Dirks, *Castes*, p. 107.
6 Holt Mackenzie, 1 July 1819, to Sec Board of Governors, in *Selections from the Revenue Records of the North-West Provinces 1818–1820* (Calcutta, 1866), p. 74. Hereafter *SRRNWP*.
7 T. Richards, *The Imperial Archive: Knowledge and the Fantasy of Empire* (London, 1993). Also see H. Bowen, *The Business of Empire: The East India Company and Imperial Britain, 1756–1833* (Cambridge, 2006).
8 B. Misra, *Judicial Administration of the East India Company in Bengal, 1765–1782* (Delhi, 1961), p. 34.
9 J.S. Mill, *Memorandum of the Improvements in the Administration of India during the last Thirty Years and the Petition of the East India Company to Parliament* (London, 1858), p. 4.
10 'Translations of correspondence and documents relating to various persons including 2 letters from Mr Jaffar… a petition from the native inhabitants of Azimabad (Patna) complaining of conditions in their district', Verelst Papers – Mss. Eur F218/29, IOL.
11 C.J. Connell, *Land Revenue Policy – Northern India* (Calcutta, 1876), 81fn.
12 See B. Avery, *Soils of the British Isles* (Wallingford, 1990); R. Simonsen, *Historical Aspects of Soil Survey and Soil* (Madison, 1987).
13 H. Bellenoit, 'Between *qanungo*s and clerks: the cultural and service worlds of Hindustan's pensmen, 1750–1900', *Modern Asian Studies* 48, 4 (2014), pp. 872–910.
14 *Selected Reports, on the Revision of Settlement under Regulation IX. of 1833, in the Delhie Territory* (Agra, 1846), p. 6.
15 'Report on the Permanent Settlement of the Western Pergunnahs of the Moozuffernugger District', Alan Cadell, in *Settlement Report of the District of Moozuffernugger* (Allahabad, 1873), p. 113.
16 'Ibid.
17 G. Ravenscroft, Col of Furukabad, to E. Colebrook and J. Dean, 1 January 1816, in *SRRNWP*, p. 268.
18 Author's calculations, from G. Ravenscroft, Col of Furukabad, to E. Colebrook and J. Dean, 1 January 1816, in *SRRNWP*, pp. 271–4.
19 'Settlement Report and Statements of the District of Moozuffernugger for the Year 1866', F. Williams, Commissioner, in *Settlement Report of the District of Moozuffernugger* (Allahabad, 1873), p. 123.
20 See, particularly, *SRRNWP*.
21 E. Cuthbert, Allahabad, 29 October 1806, Ceded & Conquered Provinces Revenue Proceedings, P/91/20, IOL. Hereafter CCPRP.
22 H. Evans, *Report on the Settlement of District of Agra* (Allahabad, 1880), p. 13.
23 H. Elliot, *Memoirs on the History, Folklore and Distribution of the Races of the North Western Provinces of India* (London, 1869), Vol. I, pp. 337–45.
24 H. Newnham, Col of Etawah, to BOR, 1 May 1821, CCPRP, P/94/23, IOL.
25 Appendix III, in *Settlement Report of the District of Moozuffernugger* (Allahabad, 1873), p. 132.
26 A. Colvin, Settlement Officer, Muffazarnagar, 8 January 1864, in *Settlement Report of the District of Moozuffernugger* (Allahabad, 1873), p. 133.

28 *Review of the Revenue Administration of the Province of Oudh* (Allahabad, 1886), pp. 1–14.
29 Appendix No. IV, Para. 43: Circular Order Sadr Board of Revenue No. IV, in *Directions for Revenue Officers in the North-Western Provinces of the Bengal Presidency* (Calcutta, 1858), p. 325. Hereafter *DRONWP*.
30 Maj M. Reid, Sec to Chief Commissioner, to Settlement Commissioner, Awadh, 18 July 1864, in *Papers related to Land Tenures and Revenue Settlements in Oude* (Calcutta, 1865), p. 464–99.
31 See, variously, J. Hooker, *The Flora of British India* (London, 1871), 2 Vols., and M. Vicziany, 'Imperialism, botany and statistics in early nineteenth century India: the surveys of Francis Buchanan (1762–1829)', *MAS* 20, 4 (1986), pp. 625–60.
32 H. Wilson, *Glossary of Judicial and Revenue Terms* (London, 1855), pp. 1, 12, 104, 581.
33 *DRONWP*, pp. 253–4.
34 Ibid.
35 Consultations, 2 September 1814, No. 15, in *SRRNWP*, p. 141.
36 Bowen, *Business of Empire*.
37 *DRONWP*.
38 E. Stokes, *The English Utilitarians and India* (Oxford, 1959), p 92.
39 From *Directions for Revenue Officers in the North-Western Provinces of the Bengal Presidency* (Calcutta, 1858), pp. 253–4, hereafter *DRONWP*.
40 Ibid., p. 103.
41 C. Allen, *Accountant's Manual for Collectors and Other Officers in Charge of Treasuries in the North-Western Provinces* (Agra, 1847), pp. 5, 10, 13.
42 Allen, *Accountant's Manual*, p. 5.
43 C. Lindsay, Settlement Officer, Hurduri, to C. Currie, Settlement Commissioner, Awadh, No. 138, 12 May 1864, in *Papers related to Land Tenures and Revenue Settlements in Oude* (Calcutta, 1865), p. 508.
44 Consultations, 2 September 1814, No. 15, in *SRRNWP*, p. 138.
45 M. Money, Col of Bihar, to BOR, 7 Aug 1816, P/111/60, IOL.
46 *Translation of a Proceeding Regarding the Settlement of a Village According to the System Pursued in the North-Western Provinces* (Agra, 1847), p. 214.
47 Col. of Bareli, T. Thornhill, to BOR, 16 March 1804, P/90/43, IOL.
48 Consultations, 2 September 1814, No. 15, in *SRRNWP*, p. 146.
49 Appendix No. XXVIII – Para. 311: Rules for Tehsildar's Accounts, *DRONWP*, p. 511.
50 J. Deeds, Sec to Sadr BOR, to J. Macsween, Sec to Gov, Revenue, 11 November 1835, P/217/40, IOL.
51 Appendix No XVII, Para. 147: Circular Order Sadr Board of Revenue No. III, *DRONWP*, p. 424.
52 Circular Order for the Sadr Board of Revenue, No. 4, Appendix No. 7, 4 Mar 1856, P/220/76, IOL.
53 I. Barrow, *Making History, Drawing Territory: British Mapping in India, c. 1756–1905* (New Delhi, 2003).
54 J. Thomason, *Direction for Settlement Officers and Collectors of Land Revenue* (Agra, 1849), p. 7.
55 R. Ahmuty, Allahabad, 17 May 1808, CCPRP, P/91/20, IOL.
56 Ibid.
57 C. Buller, Col of Bihar, to Gov-Gen of India, 6 April 1820, P/112/32, IOL.
58 M. Pane, Col of Tirhut, to Sec Board of Commissioners, 18 April 1820, P/112/33, IOL.
59 Edney, *Mapping an Empire*.
60 H. Rose, *Report on the Settlement of the District of Cawnpore* (Agra, 1842), p. 12.
61 J. Perkins, Deputy Commissioner and Settlement Officer, Sultanpur, 18 July 1864, in *Papers related to Land Tenures and Revenue Settlements in Oude* (Calcutta, 1865), p. 460.

62 Mr Ross, Col of Agra, to J. Sherer, Sec to Board of Commissioners, 29 August 1815, in *SRRNWP*, p. 144.
63 H. Rose, *Report on the Settlement of the District of Cawnpore* (Agra, 1842), p. 13.
64 B. Messick, *The Calligraphic State: Textual Domination and History in a Muslim Society* (Berkeley, 1992), p. 249.
65 A. Shakespear, *Selections from the Duncan Records*, (Benares, 1873), Vol. II, p. cxxiv.
66 G. Saletore, ed., *Banaras Affairs (1788–1810)* (Allahabad, 1955), p. 240.
67 OR. 1750, Fol. 162, Sanbhu Lal, 'Miftah-i-Khanzain', (1197 AH), 1782, Fol. 15.
68 Ibid., Fols. 16–17.
69 'Statement exhibiting the police establishments kept up by the Tehsildars of Zillah Goruckpore in their capacities of Police Darogahs', 8 November 1803, Z/P/794, BRP (Ceded & Conquered Provinces), IOL.
70 J. Stracey to J. Fombelle, Sec to Gov, 8 November 1803, P/91/2, BRP (Ceded & Conquered Provinces), IOL; also see M. Martin, *The History, Antiquities, Topography and Statistic of Eastern India*, (London, 1838), Vol. I, pp. 333–5 for details of the paper trade that spanned the Ganges river valley.
71 J. Stracey, 8 November 1803, P/91/2, BRP (Ceded & Conquered Provinces), IOL.
72 C. Dumbleton, Col of Kanpur, 4 November 1806, P/90/55, BRP (Ceded & Conquered Provinces), IOL.
73 A. Ross, Col of Agra, 26 December 1806, P/90/55, BRP (Ceded & Conquered Provinces), IOL.
74 Martin, *The History*, Vol. I, p. 333.
75 Farrukabad, 6 March 1808, CCPRP, P/91/19, IOL.
76 G. Johnstone, Lucknow, 14 November 1789, in Shakespear, *Duncan Records*, Vol. I, p. lvii.
77 E. Cuthbert, 25 November 1806, CCPRP, P/90/55, IOL.
78 *SRRNWP*, p. 337.
79 W. Sleeman, *Rambles and Recollections of an Indian Official* (London, 1844), Vol. I, 78fn.
80 *Papers related to Land Tenures and Revenue Settlements in Oude* (Calcutta, 1865), p. 548.
81 D.C. Potter, *India's Political Administrators: from ICS to IAS* (Delhi, 1996).
82 N. Hamilton, Col of Meerut, to Sadr BOR, 14 April 1835, P/217/40, IOL.
83 R.H. Bulloch, Col of Meerut, to BOR, 2 February 1822, P/94/37, IOL.
84 J. Hutchinson, Commissioner of Meerut Division, to Sec to Agra Gov, 15 April 1835.
85 Circular order of 1836, resent 4 January 1856, P/220/73, IOL.
86 H. Valpy, Col of Kanpur, to BOR, 19 January 1822, P/94/36, IOL.
87 Allen, *Accountant's Manual*, p. 5.
88 Connell, *Land Revenue*, p. 68.
89 R. Singha, *A Despotism of Law: Crime and Justice in Early Colonial India* (Oxford, 1998).
90 *DRONWP*, p. 230.
91 Ibid.
92 The phrase is taken from B. Raman, *Document Raj*.
93 Dr Vibhuti Rai, Sri Sampal Rai and Mr Ram Advani, Lucknow, 2006, 2007, 2008; Dr Raj and Mrs Naheed Verma, Lucknow, 2006, 2007, 2008.
94 *Directions for Revenue Officers*, p. 513.
95 Ibid., p. 287.
96 H. Tucker, *A Review of the Financial Situation of the East India Company, in 1824* (London, 1825), p. 134. Emphasis is Tucker's.
97 *DRONWP*, p. 221.
98 Ibid.
99 Ibid.
100 Ibid., p. 133.
101 Ibid., p. 225.

102 Tucker, *A Review*, p. 134.
103 W. Hammond, Sec Sadr Board of Revenue, Appendix XX, 'Instructions by the Sudder Board Revenue concerning the revision of settlement in the Sahaunpore District', n.d., in *DRONWP*, p. 181.
104 W. Carey, 'Remarks on the state of agriculture in the District of Dinajpur', *Asiatic Researches* (London, 1811), pp. 21–2.
105 C. Allen, *Accountant's Manual for Collectors and Other Officers in Charge of Treasuries in the North-Western Provinces* (Agra, 1847), p. 4.
106 Ibid., p. 13.
107 D.D. Dangwal, *Colonial Forestry and Deforestation in the U.P. Hills, 1815–1947* (New Delhi, 1998); D. Peers, *India under Colonial Rule, 1700–1885* (London, 2013), pp. 13–14; M. Rangarajan, 'Imperial agendas and India's forests: the early history of Indian forestry, 1800–1878', *IESHR* 31 (June 1994), pp. 147–67.
108 J.F. Watson, *The London Illustrated Exhibition of 1862, Vol. III: Colonial and Foreign Division* (London, 1862), p. 247.
109 Martin, *The History*, Vol. I, p. 333.
110 Ibid.
111 Ibid., p. 334.
112 Ibid.
113 Ibid., Vol. I, Appendix 43.
114 See Chapter 5.
115 P.M. Bose, *A History of Hindu Civilisation during British Rule* (Calcutta, 1894), p. 292.
116 N. Premchand, *Off the Deckle Edge: A Paper-making Journey through India* (Bombay, 1995), pp. 24, 83.
117 Watson, *The London Illustrated*, pp. 246–7.
118 Ibid., p. 279.
119 V. Podder, *Paper Industry in India: a Study* (New Delhi, 1979), p. 5.
120 See the Revenue Proceedings in Bengal and Bihar, after 1810, IOL.
121 Podder, *Paper Industry*, p. 5.
122 M. Faiq, *Insha-ye-Faiq* (Lucknow, 1880), p. 19.
123 Ibid.
124 *DRONWP*, p. 233
125 Ibid.
126 Extract Paragraphs 2 & 3 of Revenue Report, R. Gibbins, Col. of Agra, 18 October 1852, P/220/73, IOL.
127 W. Hammond, Sec Sadr Board of Revenue, Appendix XX, 'Instructions by the Sudder Board Revenue concerning the revision of Settlement in the Sahaunpore District', n.d., in *DRONWP*, p. 263.
128 Misra, *Judicial Administration*, p. 39.
129 A. Shakespear, *Selections from the Duncan Records* (Allahabad: Medical Press, 1873), Vol. I, pp. 98–9.
130 J. Perkins, Deputy Commissioner and Settlement Officer, Sultanpur, 18 July 1864, in *Papers related to Land Tenures and Revenue Settlements in Oude* (Calcutta, 1865), p. 463.
131 Capt E. Thompson, Settlement Officer, Sitapur, to Settlement Commissioner, Awadh, 4 June 1864, in *Papers related to Land Tenures and Revenue Settlements in Oude* (Calcutta, 1865), p. 549.
132 W. Crooke, *The North-Western Provinces of India: Their History, Ethnology, and Administration* (London, 1897), p. 101.
133 See Bayly, *Empire and Information* on the decline of 'affective knowledge' after the 1820s.
134 M. Moir, 'Kaghazi Raj: notes on the documentary basis of Company rule, 1783–1858', *Indo-British Review* 21, 2 (1993): 185–93.

135 J. Kaye, *Memorials on Indian Government; Being a Selection from the Paper of Henry St George Tucker* (London, 1853), p. 84.
136 D. Naoroji, *Poverty and un-British Rule in India* (London, 1901).
137 B. Cohn, *Colonialism and Its Forms of Knowledge: The British in India* (Princeton, 1996), p. 5; N. Dirks, *Castes*.
138 K. Chatterjee, 'History as self-representation: the recasting of political tradition in late eighteenth century eastern India', *MAS* 32, 4 (1998), p. 940.
139 D. Ghosh, *Sex and the Family in Colonial India: the Making of Empire* (Cambridge, 2006).
140 J. Shwartz and T. Cook, 'Archives, records and power: the making of modern memory', *Archival Science* 2, pp. 1–19.
141 See Chapter 3.
142 The Military Proceedings held at the National Archives of India and the British Library are both testaments to this. They require further exploration by historians as we wish to better understand the emergence of the 'colonial archive'.
143 See P. Mason, *The Men Who Ruled India* (London, 1985), pp. 196, 215, 229.

5 Kayasthas, 'caste' and administration under the Raj, c. 1860–1900

Introduction

Allan Octavian Hume, a founder of the Indian National Congress, had relatively gentle words for moderate, 'loyalist', educated Indians. But when it came to a few particular groups, he did not mince his words. In the 1880s he called for the colonial government to

> tax the… Kayasths… who, while growing rich by the pen, oust their betters from their ancestral holdings, and then are too great cowards to wield a sword either to protect their own acquisitions or to aid the Government which has fostered their success'.[1]

Addressed to such a loose group of scribes and pensmen, who crucially assisted the rise of British fiscal power from the 1780s, Hume's comments might seem surprising. But perhaps Hume touched upon a hard reality of late-nineteenth-century colonial governance. The Raj's fiscal might, which itself was the pillar upon which colonial power was based, was largely dependent upon a broader class of Kayastha scribes and clerks. And while these Bhatnagar, Ambastha, Srivastava and Saxena families were important for the colonial state by the 1860s, they were also beneficiaries of British success and power in India. They shaped the materiality of administration and populated the ranks of the Raj's intermediary enforcement. The particular trajectories of state formation, which, as we have seen, privileged paper-based fiscal knowledge backed up by legal procedure, enabled these scribes to amplify their dominance within the fabric of administration in the Doab. However loose a group, they become the most dominant scribal families in Hindustan's plains. By 1900 they were broadly considered by various Indian, British and missionary observers to be the most educated and influential of the 'service castes'. As we will see, most of the Raj's future subordinate clerks in Hindi-speaking North India came from the old traditions of paper, Persian and a looser lineage from Chitragupta.

The previous four chapters have largely focused on how early state formation – in taxation, paperwork and colonial archiving – was shaped by the scribes of Hindustan and the papers they possessed. This chapter shifts gear into the latter half of the nineteenth century. It moves away from the fiscal and archival history of north India towards a more detailed social and cultural history of these pensmen. It argues that Hindustan's scribes' importance for early state formation enabled them to colour later-nineteenth-century patterns of governance. This chapter therefore examines the prominence of Kayastha pensmen in the lower and middle tiers of the colonial state, particularly the service and cultural worlds of Kayastha families after the 1840s. It explores in detail how various families made the adjustment from serving as *qanungo*s to clerks in the first hundred years of Company rule, examining the nature of their work, how they shifted from gentlemanly paper managers to utilitarian clerks with time cards and from learning Persian to English. It argues that rather than being transformed into 'new administrators', these pensmen served as refashioned links between a late Mughal period of bureaucratic administration and the new paper, procedural administration of the British. And because Kayasthas experienced refashioned cultural and service worlds, they were also shaped by later-nineteenth-century debates on caste. This chapter will examine how their disproportionate influence in colonial administration subjected Kayasthas to hotly contested debates over caste origins, ethnology and ritual, and how various families responded. By establishing links between the 'transitionary' period of 1780–1830 and the Indian pensmen who came to dominate the lower tiers of the Raj's administration, we can gain a better appreciation of the nature of change and continuity in modern India.

The literature on Kayasthas and how they fit within caste debates and norms has only lightly been engaged with by historians. Karen Leonard's well-known study of the Mathur Kayasthas who served the Nizam of Hyderabad argues that questions of occupation, more than varna status, defined Kayasthas as a group. She has made the point that it was their occupation and cultural bearings, rather than agreement over their varna origins, that gave them cohesion.[2] This chapter aims to shed more light upon their fortunes in north India, how they fashioned a caste identity and the justifications they used to make their arguments. Indeed, by 1900 the question of Kayasthas' varna status was inescapable for jurists and reformers, who increasingly had to justify their respectability in a more caste-conscious public sphere.

Hindustan's pensmen colour the colonial state

The predominance of Kayasthas as paper managers, clerks and functionary enforcers of colonial administration and regulation was apparent by the 1830s across north India. Indeed, many of these families, as we have seen, drew upon old records and traditions of service under the Shia Nawabs. In a sense, the Company built upon the scribal edifice of the old Nawabi administration to bolster, regularize and deepen British fiscalism across the middle and upper Doab between 1803 and 1856.

When one turns to Awadh in the aftermath of the Great Rebellion and Uprising, one sees markedly similar trends. Indeed, one is struck by just how much these scribal groups would come to predominate Awadh's fiscal administration after the 1850s. Some logistical dynamics need to be established first. For one, the period between Awadh's annexation in 1856 and the outbreak of violence some 13 months later left little time to adequately integrate the territory into the fiscal rhythms and administration of NWP. With the Uprising and subsequent counter-insurgency and suppression, the former Nawabi territories were not fully settled until the 1860s. Also, many old Nawabi records were destroyed in the fighting in Lucknow and to a lesser degree in Faizabad. In places such as Muzzafarnagar most extant Nawabi revenue documents, from both the *daftar-i-diwani* and the *beit ul-Insha-ye-Sultani*, went up in flames.[3] Thus when the dust settled much of the paper knowledge that greased the fiscal wheels of the Shia kingdom was gone. But scribes' and *qanungo*s' accumulative skills, traditions and papers, which documented local villages, traditions of collections and how disputes were arbitrated, were still held by the large number of Kayastha pensmen who had bolstered the Nawabi state since the 1740s. By welding these pensmen and scribes to the machinery of colonial rule, the British fiscal state in post-1860 Awadh was able to rapidly tax, assess, settle and integrate the region into north Indian administration.

After 1860 the real agrarian economic settlement began in the Awadhi tracks of Faizabad, Lucknow and Etawah. This represented, in a way, the last thrust of fiscal state consolidation in north India. The region's Settlement Officers after 1860 required and demanded volumes of paper work to entertain claims and to check against extant *qanungo* records. And, again, as in the Doab regions that wrapped around Awadh, Kayastha pensmen would play a significant role in the region's post-1860 fiscal consolidation. Saxena Kayastha *qanungo*s, already predominant in the Shia Nawab's reign, were crucial in providing precise details and accurate statistics on land. To the new generation of Settlement Officers who rapidly fanned out across Awadh,[4] the Saxenas provided agrarian information on what was cultivated, wasteland and wasteland that could be cultivated. And as in the other Doabi regions, the *qanungo* records were used to adjudicate land disputes and contested proprietary rights. For the Raj, then, Awadhi Kayasthas were a valuable class of paper managers and a real source of 'fiscal intelligence'. Of course, it could work the other way for Settlement Officers. In Daryabad, Frederick Chalmers, when settling disputes with the 'notoriously quarrelsome Kidwaiee family', was quite peeved with the old Srivastava Allahabad *qanungo*s, whose 'unreliability' in testimony he claimed was 'the chief difficulty in deciding dispute claims in the pergunnah'.[5] As in so many landed and fiscal settlements, the *qanungo* was the fulcrum of local fiscalism, and, as in the rest of the Doab, he quickly became the linkage between agrarian settlements and procedural fiscal and legal administration.

Immediately before the 1857 Uprising and Great Rebellion important changes were rapidly enacted which suggest that the British quickly understood the valuable role that Kayastha scribes served in consolidating the Company's fiscal state. Having learned how crucial and effective their knowledge and paper repositories were in the rest of the Doab, the Company quickly moved to weld these scribes to regulation, procedure and salaries paid out of the Allahabad treasury. For example, in 1856 it decided to standardize the workings of the *qanungo*s and *patwari*s by confirming the *qanungo* as a repository of factual, paper knowledge in a pargana. It was noted that 'the Kanoongoe's Office is properly that of a Register of Statistical information, and Custodian and Scrutineer of village papers for the portion of the District under his charge'.[6] From the start, the British envisioned *qanungo*s as an archival register, whose papers would be consulted to adjudicate legal and land disputes. One can also see this in how the NWP provincial government rapidly widened its fiscal umbrella. In 1861 it sold all wastelands in perpetuity to redeem revenue lost after the events of 1857–8.[7] This expanded the scope for well-placed pensmen and writers to assist in extending the fiscal state's bureaucratic tendrils even deeper into the Doab. Many of these settlements of newly sold wastelands required staffing, paperwork and managers of the now overflowing 'colonial-fiscal archive'. And much of the revenue management and paperwork needed to attempt to convert wastelands into cultivated, taxable land were managed by various Saxena, Ambastha and Srivastava families. Even if these wastelands produced little agricultural output, the bureaucratic staff were still present – a regular reminder of British administration.

After the 1860s various elements of pre-British revenue administration continued into that of north India. The nature of surveying is one example, not least an instructive 1851 surveying manual for Settlement Officers in north India. While it saw the *khusrah* as complementary to the new Professional Survey, a closer reading of its language reveals a constructive, useful lexicon for the *khusrah*'s accuracy. One reason why they were still useful had to do with scale. The Professional Surveys were grand and ambitious, attempting to capture all of India. But many smaller *mofussil* villages, particularly in Awadh after 1856, remained untouched by colonial triangulation, and a good number of *khusrah*s existed for smaller, remote villages the Company did not touch until the 1860s. One Collector noted that 'it is surprising with what accuracy these Khusruhs can be prepared'.[8] When it came to penetrating deeper into villages and the *mofussil* in unsettled districts, the Professional Survey was sometimes less useful than extant forms of assessing and measuring. A lot of this was due to the fact that the *amil*s in Awadh had not yet been cut down to size by British administration, surviving until the 1850s. It was noted that the *amil*s were 'well acquainted with the nature of the tenures, the general capabilities of the soil, and the current dialect language'.[9] In many places in the Faizabad and Lucknow districts *amil*s provided ready information on soil types, crops and uncultivated lands. And as many Settlement Officers regularly noted after the 1860s and deep into the 1880s, in many parts of Awadh only the *khusrah* did this with such granularity. As late as the 1870s the *khusrah* survey was still in use in large parts of NWP,[10] which projected Kayasthas' skills into the early twentieth century. In the middle and upper Doab about 15–20 per cent of lands used the *khusrah*. And the accuracy impressed revenue officers: it usually came within a 2–4 per cent[12] margin of the professional surveys that were a supposed glorification of the scientific advancement of European rule.

The perseverance of the old surveying methods in Awadh after the 1850s ensured that their scribes came to colour the contours of fiscal administration into the late nineteenth century. It was here that Kayasthas made their mark on the later-nineteenth-century colonial state. And the perseverance of the *khusrah* extended the Doab's scribes' importance into the Awadhi countryside. They assisted the fiscal state's surveying and taxonomy, which enabled the later Raj to tax even more efficiently and savagely in one of the most heavily assessed regions of India.[13] Kayastha *amin*s and *qanungo*s carried much weight in the villages for the surveying of post-1860 Awadh. Fiscalism in Awadh was, of course, part of a post-Mutiny strategic policy of punishment. And in this sense, Kayasthas came to be well known among officialdom for the suasion they carried into the *mofussil*:

> Hindoos of the Kyut [Kayastha] caste are always to be preferred for this duty...generally speaking [they] are respectable, well-dressed and intelligent, and carry much weight with them on entering a village, assuming great consequence, and summoning the village authorities to attend with a great deal of parade and show…he never appears without a bearer holding a *chattah* (umbrella) over his head.[14]

Kayasthas such as Rattan Narain and Kish Narain,[15] for example, helped the Raj assess and survey the extensive agricultural tracks around Sultanpur and the Baiswara region after 1860, leading to a further expansion of the taxonomical-colonial state. And the repository procedures also amplified these scribes' importance. District surveys composing both the professional and *khusrah* forms were deposited with Kayastha *qanungo*s who managed them. This deepened the colonial archive, noticeably in old Awadhi regions such as Lucknow, Faizabad and Sitapur. Here, the *khusrah* surveys were still utilized by various *patwari* and *qanungo* families in the 1890s in the rhythms of collation, documentation and assessment.[16] There was a mixed encounter: the scribes of Hindustan were able to colour the surveying taxonomic state, working with the new outer shell of administration while maintaining many precolonial inner linings.

There are various examples of Kayastha scribes using paper information and records to further leverage the post-Mutiny fiscal state in Awadh and the wider Doab. In many cases higher assessments were used to punish former centres of the uprising and insurgency. In Muzzafarnagar, a hotbed of violence in 1857–8, the Collector Henry Keen saw his estimated assessment (*jama*) encounter an objection from his *qanungo*, Rai Nanak Chand. Chand's objection was not because it was too high, but because it was too low.[17] In the fiscal punishment of Meerut after 1857, the *qanungo*s' old grain estimations (*kankut*s) were still being used. Here, the Assistant Collector Charles Grant consulted the *qanungo*s' broader array of documentation, and he seems to have been swayed by the *qanungo* estimates (*daul*s) to 'which [he] gave special preference'.[18] After consulting the documentation, Grant raised the assessment by 18 per cent the following year.[19] Decades later, *qanungo*s' signatures had become the guarantor of legitimacy in procedural paperwork. By the 1880s summons for payment (*dastak*s) needed *qanungo* signatures to be legally valid. In 1884, as an example, *qanungo*s issued 646 of them in Lucknow, 426 in Meerut and 231 in Moradabad.[20] Agra was another area where Kayastha *qanungo*s shaped later administration. In the 1880s Agra drew heavily upon the *patwari*s to provide crucial information to help Settlement Officers determine tax rates. Henry Evans noted how crucial they were at the village level, and that while 'mathematical accuracy is out of the question… an approximation to the truth may fairly be claimed'.[21] In fact, Kayasthas were so crucial and embedded in the fabric of revenue administration that they managed to pay the lowest tax rates in the entire District, save the village of Farah.[22] And in the central northern district of Basti in the 1890s the Collector William Hooper was still using the instalment registers (*kistibandi*) which the district's *qanungo*s had held since the late 1700s.[23] This near dominance of fiscal administration was reflected broadly across the Doab. *Patwari*s and *qanungo*s managed the papers of revenue administration, procedure and attestation in Lucknow, Rai Bareli, Faizabad and Sitapur.[24] In so many districts the *qanungo* was the visual representation and enforcer of the Raj's might and, most significantly, fiscal inflexibility.

The rhythms established by the Company in the Doab in the early 1800s continued to shape the Raj later in the century. In this expanded and bloated bureaucracy fiscalism was arguably the most important function of the colonial state. For example, by the late 1880s the NWP revenue service recruited the same number of staff as the education service and more than any other branch of administration.[25] Nearly half of all recruitment from government schools in NWP and Awadh was oriented towards manning the lower tiers of revenue administration, working as *patwari*s, *qanungo*s and, more generally, clerks and copyists.[26] As late as the 1920s *qanungo*s, now refashioned as 'Native Registrars' (*mohafiz daftar*s),[27] were still integral cogs in the revenue administration of the United Provinces. Indeed, they were so valuable for the later colonial state that the official manual for NWP Settlement Officers noted that 'the Canoongoes are [sic] on a different principle from the other native officers'.[28] And their importance had built up so much that they were able to skirt official regulation. In spite of the 100-year-old ban on inherited *qanungo*-ships, passed in the 1822 Regulations, many *qanungo*-ships were still hereditary. In Ghazipur the *qanungo*-ship held by Lala familes seems to have been passed down through ten generations from the time of Akbar.[29] These families managed to pass along the position not through patronage and direct appointment, as in older times, but through education and its cultivation within extended family networks. After 1909 the School Leaving Certificate (SLC), a requirement to be considered eligible for provincial government employment as a clerk or scribe,[30] was gobbled up by Kayasthas. The *qanungo* records and information were so valuable that they survived in an integrated form in the workings of late-nineteenth-century colonial governance. One direction for revenue officials observed that 'the old Canoongoe Records are very valuable, especially those of a date prior to British rule. They should be preserved with great care'.[31] Here, paper and material record bolstered not just their information and fiscalism but the officers who possessed them. It should be no surprise that one Settlement Officer quipped, perhaps indignantly, that 'the day to day administration of revenue policy [is] in the hands of these officers'.[32]

Kayasthas in the ICS and subordinate administration

Whether as Deputy Inspectors, ICS officers or Native Registrars, Hindustan's scribes greatly coloured the late colonial state's administration. A survey of the larger composition of north Indian administration shows that Kayasthas were to be found in nearly all its branches. While rarely reaching the heights of executive purview, they provided the mortar for the administrative state of the Raj into the early twentieth century. The centrality of Kayastha pensmen to the revenue settlements between Patna and Patiala reverberated upon the broader fabric of colonial governance. Considering that Kayasthas were not a 'caste category' that benefited from the taxonomies of colonial governance, it is remarkable that they dominated areas of subordinate service that were open to literate Indian groups. Indeed, they were noted as the 'clerks and men of the pen all over India'.[33] And nowhere was this better seen than in the Doabi territories.

Kayasthas made their mark on both the appearance and function of NWP governance. As late as the 1880s they were still functioning as *qanungo*s and paper managers in the local fabric of administration in Mathura, Jaunpur and Chhapra in Bihari country.[34] One famous Gaur Kayastha, Brij Bhukhan Lal, became the first Indian to hold the post of Registrar Judicial in Awadh.[35] Kayasthas' general reputation for paper acumen continued through late-colonial officialdom's proceedings, treatises and folktale compilations. Henry Elliot noted these pensmen's shrewd paper skills and that 'some of the cleverest natives have sprung from their number'.[36] They were regularly cited by taxonomers such as Robert Vane Russell and Matthew Sherring as the single largest caste group in government employment. Ethnographers, who would have been familiar with the wider varieties of community and social diversity across north India, regularly attested to Kayasthas' reputation. William Crooke, for example, remarked that 'among castes, the best educated are naturally the Kayastha[s]... it supplies writers and accountant to all classes of the community, official and non-official... as revenue officers... [and] keepers of registry of property'.[37] In the Districts of north Madhya Pradesh, where the Bhatnagar and Saxena Kayasthas were dominant, it was observed that 'Kayastha gentlemen hold the most important positions in the administrative, judicial and public works departments'.[38] Jonathan Nesfield, likewise, observed that by the 1880s 'there [was] no caste in Upper India so largely represented in the revenue offices, the courts of justice and in the literary professions, such as pleader or barrister'.[39] Below the radar of publishers, barristers and ICS officers, for many of these Kayasthas, their work as a humble *patwari* was 'much the same [under Muslim rule] even at the present day'.[40]

But it was the position of the *qanungo* that was truly indispensable to the latter Raj. Its paper-based 'matter-of-factness', as we have seen throughout this book, was amplified by British fiscal interests. In so many cases British ethnographers and officialdom noted the importance of the *qanungo* to the rhythms of local, fiscal administration. Robert Baden-Powell noted that 'the Kanungo has long existed; indeed, in the "watan" districts, there are… officers as under the Muhammadan government surviving to this day'.[41] Baden-Powell was not conjuring up fiction. For example, an Etawah-based Kayastha, Ganga Prasad, was even reputed to hold the same village property his family obtained from Turkic sultans from the 1300s[42] by serving as paper managers and copyists. And while their numbers may have been reduced from eighteenth-century times, there was still one *qanungo* posted in each *tehsil* who served as the registrar of landed property and records. In north India's revenue administration, it was observed, the *qanungo*'s 'signature will be found in all the proceedings'.[43] Kayastha families and their skills, by the 1850s, had become indispensable to the Raj and the daily rhythms of its administration.

But the British, in creating such a time-consuming, paper-based, procedural administration, also created a system that generated a backlash among some scions of officialdom. We see the dominance of these Kayasthas scribes bringing out more critical observations and reactions from colonial ethnologists and administrators. British perceptions of Kayasthas often swung like a pendulum between admiration and scorn. Colonial officials in the Doab acknowledged the Kayasthas as 'subtle, clever [and] intellectual' but also derided them as 'wily and treacherous'.[44] Their dominance of subordinate civil service in NWP was so marked that the Commissioner of Benares issued orders to the District Magistrate in 1900 that the number of Kayasthas in his office should be severely reduced.[45] He was fearful of what he called 'caste collusion'. Here, we see echoes of British anxiety and a 'babu-phobia' that had parallels in Bengal country. In the writings of Allan Octavian Hume, William Crooke and Herbert Risely we also can discern a resentment towards the clerks who, at the end of the day, made British revenue mastery possible. Crooke called the Kayasthas a 'most intelligent and *pushing* people'[46] and took regular swipes at what he called the Bihari Lal Kayasthas (village Lalas, or Kayastha *patwari*s, often Bhatnagars),[47] including some of his crudest criticisms: 'the higher members of the caste rank high... [but] the village Lala, who is very often an accountant, is in evil repute for his astuteness and chicanery'.[48] These scribes' passive aggression had become well known, illustrating the power of the pen. Crooke, for example, cited a north Indian folk tale that 'the pen is the Kayasth's weapon [and] where there are no tigers the Kayasth will become a hunter (*shikari*)'.[49] Some British officials echoed the older sentiments of eighteenth-century Muslim munshis. Montgomery Martin noted the 'chicane' of the 'Hindoo clerk' and would have found himself in warm company with the older Muslim gentryfolk who saw the Kayastha clerks as 'cruel cheats'.[50] Kayasthas had become such a marked feature of the late Raj's bureaucracy, and it caused some concern to have subordinate power concentrated in such hands.[51]

The comments above reflected a few broader developments. The sheer dependency of north India's fiscal administration empowered Indians as indispensable, though subordinate, elements. They were needed to maintain the procedure and rhythms of regular governance. The ballooning of the size, specialization and depth of colonial administration drew on increasing numbers of Indians, who, inevitably, had to be managed by the British themselves. The very expansion of public instruction in north India in a way reflected these broader patterns of government employment and penetration.[52] But the derisions of 'shrewd' Kayasthas also reflected a broader unease towards educated Indians, mostly famously in Bengal. The chorus of contempt in the Anglo-Indian press against educated *babu*s had become marked by 1900 and seems to have made its way into public discourse in north India.

In spite of this Janus-faced attitude, some of north India's Kayasthas did manage to pierce the highest levels of colonial administration that were technically (though rarely in practice) open to Indians. Kayasthas, like other Indians, largely hit the glass ceiling of racial discrimination. Their administrative indispensability could never overcome deeply ingrained British racial attitudes. But they did much better than caste groups such as Brahmins, their main competitors for government posts. We can see this if we examine government legal professions. In 1919, at the cusp of Congress's launch of Civil Disobedience, Kayasthas accounted for two thirds of all Indian Government law members across north India, with most of them in the United Provinces.[53] This was because so many Kayasthas worked as government-paid barristers (*vakil*s) and not as private practitioners, which again reflected their gravitation towards government employment. In the India Civil Service (ICS), too, their predominance was marked for such a smaller-sized caste group. In 1913 Kayasthas held 24 out of 41 ICS posts reserved for Hindus.[54] And with the widening of the nationalist base after the 1920s, Kayasthas did exceedingly well. They outdid Brahmins in ICS posts and examinations after 1930 with the rise of a more populist nationalism, and in 1941 they accounted for four out of eight successful Indian ICS candidates.[55] Romesh Chunder Dutt argued that the number of Kayasthas in service in north India and Bihar was perhaps greater than all other castes combined.[56] Dutt did not offer any statistics to back up his claims. But in a way that missed the point. By the time Congress's mass mobilizations took hold, Kayasthas were, ironically, already major stakeholders in the very state apparatus that Gandhi and other nationalists wished to shake to the core.

The refashioned worlds of Hindustan's Kayasthas

The British were able to hold onto their Indian empire after the Mutiny and Great Uprising of 1857 because they controlled the armed forces and were able to buttress the state with a massive amount of bureaucrats in the Raj's subordinate administration. Nowhere was this more clear than in revenue collection. As we have seen, the formation of the early colonial state orbited largely around revenue, and it was much was the same after the 1850s. Many of these scribes and pensmen – who straddled the late Mughal and early Company periods – extended their positions as paper managers and subordinate staff deep into the colonial period. They made inroads into the subordinate levels of the NWP's and United Provinces' administrations, serving as educational inspectors, barristers and Deputy Collectors. As we have seen, some even pierced the upper echelons of the ICS. Colonial administration in north India by 1900 had been greatly coloured by Kayasthas and their skills, traits and, indeed their broad stereotypes. And it was from among these more lowly, clerical classes that many of India's future nationalist leaders would emerge. Rajendra Prasad, Jayaprakash Narayan, Har Dayal and Lal Bahadur Shastri were all Kayasthas who were manifestations of an inherited culture that drew upon histories of literacy and service, which were also used to organize Working Committee reports, correspond with fellow Congressmen and, ultimately, mobilize them against British rule.

Straddling the Indo-Islamic and British colonial worlds

In previous chapters we tracked various Kayastha scribes in the late Mughal and early British periods. This section proceeds to track various individuals and their progeny to see how they adjusted to the later colonial period. It is often forgotten that the famed Hindi poet Premchand came from a Kayastha heritage. His family had a history serving as *patwaris* in the Allahabad regions. Before he became a known poet, he was made Sub-Deputy Inspector of Schools in Allahabad District, drawing upon the traditional of clerical service performed by postmaster father, Ajab Lal.[57] There are numerous other examples of old scribal families who bridged the early Company and the late era of the Raj, ranging from the Bhatnagars to the Saxenas to the Sahays.

A number of Kayasthas stretched across the late Mughal and British period and projected their skills and lineages deep into the Raj era. A good example is Lala Sita Ram (1861–1936). A Sahay Kayastha with roots in the Allahabad region, Ram's family migrated to the city with Sher Shah Suri in the 1500s. His family became an archetypical Islamized Kayastha, frequenting Sufi shrines (*dargahs*) and adopting the title *Raizada* ('son of a magnate'). Ram's grandfather Raja Raghunath Sahay migrated to Delhi in the 1710s, while his other grandfather, Raja Amrit Lal, served in the Awadhi court of Ghaziuddin Haider (1814–27). His family papers were destroyed at some point, but Ram's son Krishna Kishore compiled a book on his family lineage (*khandan*). Ram also adopted the Indo-Islamic tradition of taking a pen-name (*takhallus*), in his case *Azam* ('Great').[58] Ram maintained associations with another famed Kayastha, Munshi Kali Prasad. He also continued his education in Persian and then English. It was only later, in 1883, after meeting the Hindu revivalist Bharatendu Harishchandra, when posted to Benares, that he started to develop an interest in Sanskrit and Hindi. Ram was elected a Fellow of Allahabad University under the patronage of the then Director of Public Instruction, James Nesfield,[59] and was later appointed a Deputy Collector at Kanpur.

Srivastava families, it seems, did particularly well under the new fiscal colonial state and later under the Raj. Their service histories dotted the townships of Allahabad, Faizabad and Lucknow and largely reaffirmed their 'higher' standing within the twelve family sub-branches. Ram Saran Das Verma (b. 1859) was one example. Born in the *qasbah* of Faizabad, he began learning Persian at the auspicious age of four years, four months and four days. He also obtained an English-language education and headed the list of candidates in 1874 for NWP and Awadh. Verma branched out, too, receiving an MA in Sanskrit in 1879,[60] which he used to weave himself into public service. The following year he became an Assistant Professor at Canning College in Lucknow, with its large Saxena and Srivastava contingents.[61] Perhaps because it was culturally and occupationally fitting, Verma moved into the paper business and was made Secretary of the Upper India Paper Mill Company in Lucknow. This was not quite the '*vaishya* movement' that some Bengali Kayasthas drifted towards after the 1870s (it seems to have been more of a managerial position). Verma then went on to manage the Oude Commercial

Bank,[62] which became the largest Indian bank in Hindustan. Verma's career as an administrator also drew him into other professional circles. In 1879 he was elected to the Asiatic Society of Bengal. He was the only Kayastha elected, most Indian members being Bengali Brahmins. Yet Verma also manoeuvred himself back into public employment. He was made Municipal Commissioner in the newly constituted Board for Faizabad, and in 1887 he was one of the first Indians appointed as a Fellow to Allahabad University.[63] Like Lala Sita Ram, Verma helped edit Munshi Kali Prasad's 1877 defence of the *dvija* status of his community, the *Kayastha Ethnology*.[64] He later became editor of the *Kayastha Samachar* and shaped the *Kayastha Pathshala* in its early years in Allahabad. Verma was the type of Kayastha whose lineages, traditions and work helped maintain Allahabad as a centre of Kayastha public prominence in the city's municipal and educational developments.

Another illustrative example is Rai Janti Prasad. Born in Mainpuri in 1849, Prasad came from a prominent Mathur Kayastha family. His grandfather Raghunath was a *vazir* in Shahjahan's court and authored a Persian work, 'Path of the Prophets' (*Masir ul-Umara*). After the 1739 sack of Delhi by Nadir Shah, Prasad's ancestors migrated from Delhi to Mainpuri. Growing up, he was educated in the local *maktab* and then went to a missionary high school in Agra, Victoria College.[65] Janti then became a clerk in Mainpuri's Settlement Office in 1866, head clerk in the Muttra Collectorship in 1872 and at Moradabad in 1879. Janti undertook land surveys using both the professional and *khusrah* surveys, which helped the Indian Army acquire lands for railway expansion across the Doab. He finally ended up as a Gazetted Deputy Collector in Muttra, earning a handsome Rs 600/month,[66] making him one of the highest-salaried Kayastha officials in NWP and Awadh.

Munshi Kali Prasad, though, was a more popular example. Born in Jaunpur (1840) to a Srivastava Kayastha family, he drew upon a longer history of service – it was said that it was from Prasad's family that 'diwans were usually selected',[67] which again reflected the 'higher' standings that Srivastavas held. His ancestors served as *qanungo*s from Akbar's time, and his father worked under the early Company, corralling records of *jama*, property and *kistibandis*. Prasad was trained in Persian, Sanskrit and English, and after completing his course at Queens College, Benares, he went on to become a Sub-Deputy Inspector of Schools in Allahabad District at the age of eighteen.[68] Prasad gave institutional weight to a newly forming sense of community and association among Kayasthas, whose prominence in north Indian administration was almost impossible to ignore. Prasad founded the *Kayastha Pathshala* in Allahabad in 1872, which became one of the most reputable educational institutions in the provincial capital. He also worked with other Kayastha organizations, such as the Kayastha Institute of Lucknow and the Kayastha Sadar Sabha.[69] Prasad then went on to found the *Kayastha Samachar* periodical in 1872, which ran as an Urdu publication until 1900, when it converted over to English. Prasad perhaps did more than anyone to contribute to a greater sense of commonality and cohesion among Kayastha families. These organizations and associations corralled skills of pen and paper and solidified Kayasthas' reputation as the 'service classes' of Hindustan.[70] Prasad also seems to have tiptoed into the business world. He helped found the Upper India Paper Mill Company[71] and would later have his friend and fellow Kayastha, Saran Das Verma, appointed as acting Secretary.

Some Kayasthas also entered the academy and sought to redefine the old Nawabi era and defend it from pervasive British stereotypes of Oriental despotism. One such example is A.L. Srivastava. Srivastava traced his roots back to the Sitapur Distract, where Kayasthas established a reputation as elite paper managers to the Nawabs and then the British. In his collegiate years Srivastava was a pupil of Jandunath Sarkar and ended up at Lucknow University, where he did his PhD. The old Canning College, in particular, was known for its marked predominance of Saxena Kayasthas after the 1860s.[72] Srivastava published his *The First Two Nawabs of Oudh* in 1933, which offered a pointed reappraisal of British stereotypes about the Nawabs. Srivastava argued for a more sympathetic reflection of the Nawabs and their administration.[73] He characterized the Nawab's pre-1850s revenue administration as 'chaotic', sometimes irregular and occasionally abusive. But the Nawabs' assessments were not nearly as ruthless and inflexible as British ones of the time. He called the Nawabs' fiscalism a 'much abused revenue administration', but it 'appear[ed] to have been mild and the government demand equitable'.[74] There were other aspects to Srivastava's work that reflected the contemporary pulse of 1930s Indian politics. We glean a hint of the emergent communal tensions that had started to characterize provincial Indian politics. Srivastava levelled some criticism towards his former Muslim colleagues and rulers, noting that the broadsides some members of the *ulama* gave Kayasthas for being infidel (*kufr*) 'half-Muslims' was unfounded. Srivastava observed that 'in spite of their simple and definite creed, [Indian Muslims] worshipped relics, revered tombs, and adored saints and illiterate religious mendicants'.[75] Here, we can sense communal sentiment being percolated across the Kayasthas' preferred platform: the written page.

While the prominence of the Saxena, Srivastva and Mathur families was perhaps expected, some Bhatnagar families also did well. Harsukh Rai (1816–89) was born in Sikanderabad; his ancestors had close relations with the Mughals, and his family had fled to Lahore after the Marathas conquered Delhi in the 1750s. Harsukh underwent a fairly 'traditional' Kayastha experience, learning Persian and parts of Arabic, the rational sciences (*hikmat*) and how to compose in the scripts of *nastaliq* and *shikasta*. Starting out as a journalist, Harsukh started the first school of modern journalism in the Punjab with the *Koh-i-Noor* Urdu newspaper. He was also a personal friend of the Maharaja of Kashmir, Pratap Singh, and was a tutor and mentor to another famous Kayastha, Nawal Kishore.[76] Harsukh went on to serve as a Municipal Commissioner in Lahore, and he was one of the first to propose a University for Punjab,[77] which was finally achieved in 1882. He also acted as Secretary for the *Anjuman-i-Punjab*. But, curiously, in spite of Harsukh's connections with Kashmiri Maharaja, Singh possessed a noticeable anti-royalist streak and on many occasions criticized the ostentatiousness of the

Kashmiri Maharaja. In this, he saw the Urdu press as complicit. He advised that the vernacular press should not flatter Rajas and Nizams with falsehood, 'as some of the perverse papers do'.[78]

The Rai Kayastha family of Lucknow provide an example of both the change and continuity that many of Hindustan's pensmen experienced from the late eighteenth century. The history of this family, gleaned from interviews and private family papers, largely mirrors the broader patterns of change experienced by so many scribal families in Hindustan. Originally from Allahabad, the Rai family were an Ambastha subcaste. Since the 1600s they had assisted with revenue management as *qanungo*s. Prior to 1803 they served as paper managers in Nawabi Awadh, and then under the British after its annexation. In the first few generations of Company rule the Rai forefathers continued their work as managers of paper, mainly as *qanungo*s.[79] Later, in the tumultuous events of 1857, Paramasukh Rai was an eyewitness (*ceshmadid*) to the power of the mob and cumulative grievances in the Doab against the Company and its fiscalism. Paramasukh, interestingly, observed that Muslim authority had disppeared long before the Uprising (*qaum mussalman mevati aya karte the*), and he foretold that the *ashrafi* Muslim classes' worldview would forever be changed by these events, with the loss of lakhs and lands with the violent reassertion of British authority. He was also critical of Muslim rule, noting that Muslim sovereigns did little to check the rise of British power. For Rai, their claim to leadership of Indian had gone long before 1857 (*aur unko sarkar ne hidayat hua*).[80] Paramasukh cited a degree of complacency and unwillingness to adapt to new political realities. The Rais weathered the events of 1857–8 well, mainly because they were neither substantially landed nor economically elite. The family continued to offer prayers to Lakshmi (*lakhsmi ji ki puja hoti thi*) and Ganesh, and the inkpot and pen prayer (*dawat kalam puja*) was regularly offered for their continued good fortune. The Rai family also offered prayers that British-ruled Delhi (*farangdilli*) would look upon them with favour.[81] The fact that they saw Delhi and not Calcutta as the true centre of Indian politics and administration perhaps reflected their broader exposure to the Indo-Islamic cultural and political world. After the mid 1860s the Rai family moved west to Lucknow, where they quickly filled the void left after the city's Muslim and *ashrafi* elites had been spiritually (and in some instances literally) banished from Lucknow's neighbourhoods. Paramasukh Rai by 1864 had become a well-known (*maroof*) clerk and poet, drawing upon a longer history of Persian literacy and paper-management. His family seems to have made the adjustment to the English language rather quickly. Paramuskh's grandson Sampal Rai argued that they had to adjust to the new realities of power, mainly because they were not significant landowners.[82] They continued with a looser, albeit diminished, tradition of Persian literacy, which seems to have tapered off after the 1890s.

In all, the Rai family and Paramasukh's descendants seem to have made the transition to English rule, with its diaries, ledgers and new language, fairly easily. They refashioned themselves from Persianite clerks versed in paper management and etiquette to clock-keeping enforcers of the new fiscal state. Paramasukh's descendants, munshis Jagpath Rai and Shivapat Rai, were the second generation educated in English knowledge (*angrezi jyotifi*). But they also continued with elements of their precolonial, Persianite learning. They were taught art (*hunar*), and traditional Persian knowledge of the rational sciences (*hikmat*), for which they still used the Arabic phrase for 'knowledge' (*ilm*).[83] They worked as Native Registrars in the NWP provincial government. And the Rai family seems to have established bonds of patronage under Captain William Hamilton of the 9th Lancers in Lucknow, whose connection was secured by one Rai family member, Ittehfaq Rai, who served as a personal secretary and record keeper to Hamilton. After Independence, the Rai family produced professors for Lucknow University and members of the IAS in Uttar Pradesh.[84] The family history of the Rais in its printed form is in itself interesting. Written in Nagri, the family manuscript is copiously laced with Persian phraseology and grammar, as opposed to just vocabulary. Some examples include 'humble' (*kamtarin*), 'notes' (*yaddasht*), 'books of work' (*karnama*) and the Persian 'and' (*va*).[85] The Rai family were undoubtedly changed into English-literate clerks. But in many ways they continued to fashion older, Persian cultural elements deep into the colonial period. This was a residual marker, at a broader level, of Kayasthas' cultural stakeholding in the Indo-Islamic administrative and spiritual world. In addition, like so many other Kayastha families, the Rais maintained a tradition of paper-based, government employment that traced it origins from the seventeenth century and stretched into the twenty-first.

Vocational crossroads: language, scripts and commerce

In characterizing the adjustments Kayastha scribes made, we can trace a noticeable degree of flexibility. But even though Kayasthas adapted well to a new language of authority and procedure, they still held on to various elements of their Indo-Islamic heritage. Much of Kayasthas' various successes, and their ability to colour the later colonial administration, had to do with education and its sources. A broader reading of the evidence suggests that Kayasthas adapted to English-language education fairly quickly. Their liminal position perhaps made this easier. Many of them adapted to English as they did to Persian and Muslim rule centuries back.[86] Some Kayasthas were even sarcastically called Christians (*kristans*) by Brahmins and north Indian Muslims for learning English so quickly.[87] Kayasthas took to and indeed appropriated English-language instruction in the same way had Persian pedagogy. For many Kayastha families, language was a tool, be it Persian or English, to secure government employment, upon which their livelihoods and family honour were dependent.[88] Surveying, in which they played a substantial role, was similar to the practical paper-based services they had offered to Muslim sovereigns, whether it was rent rolls or new surveys buttressed by the Great Trigonometric Survey. It was because of this adaptability to a new language of administration–partly a result of where they were placed in the precolonial administrative pecking order – that Kayasthas became the single largest clerical group in employment in the United Provinces by 1900. It was no surprise therefore that the proceedings of the 1893 Allahabad Kayastha Conference referred to Kayasthas' 'natural pliancy and versatility'.[89] And they took pride in this adaptability. But being far less moneyed and landed than other caste groups, Kayasthas' versatile literacy and paper-based service were less of an honour and more of a necessity.

The residual cultural world of Kayasthas, coupled with their long associations with Indo-Islamic and then colonial governance, thrust these scribes in the crosshairs of late-nineteenth-century language debates. The emergent Hindi–Urdu debates in north India made Kayasthas a target for various Hindu reformist and revivalist associations. As Ayesha Jalal has pointed out, Hindi and Hindu revivalists often saw Kayasthas as part of a Muslim–Kayastha alliance that sought to hold back the champions of 'pure Hindi' speech.[90] Kayasthas in north India and Bihar tenaciously hung on to many of their distinguishing language markers: Persian, Urdu and the cultural world with which it was associated. Kayasthas were lambasted by various Hindu reformist movements, such as the Arya Samaj, who considered many Kayasthas to be 'half-Muslim'.[91] By 1900 these scribes had acquired a reputation among Hindi proponents for severely complicating efforts to champion more 'pure' forms of Hindi speech.[92] And many Kayasthas, even those such as Lala Sita Ram, who took an increasing interest in Sanskrit, were weary of the Hindi movement.[93] This made itself manifest in 1900 with Antony Macdonnell's Nagri resolution. Many Kayasthas found themselves joining hands with Indian Muslims in opposing the measure.[94] They stubbornly clung to a heavily Persianized Urdu. A story was noted in the *Sitara-i-Hind* weekly of a spurned Kayastha boy throwing himself into a well. A 'Hindi Basha' advocate suggested that his demise was due to an unhealthy overdose of Urdu and Persian love stories. The weekly argued that Kayasthas should 'first teach their sons Sanskrit, and not Persian, in order to save their morals from being spoilt'.[95] Revivalists such as Bharatendu Harishchandra regularly criticized Kayasthas for hanging on to their 'Islamized' lifestyles and heavily Persianized Urdu.[96] For Harishchandra, Kayasthas were a cultural residue, and indeed barometer, of Muslim rule and its courtly culture. One Kayastha from Balramput, Babu Brijmohan Lal, as late as 1900 was writing widely circulated collections of Persian couplets called 'Wisdom of the Minarct' (*Guldustul-Marfat*).[97] The perseverance of the Indo-Persian cultural world among Kayasthas can also be gauged from their attempts to reach a broader population via print media. In the 1890s, with the readership of the Urdu *Kayastha Samachar* limited, Kayastha Sabhas attempted to introduce a Hindi publication, the *Kayastha Conference Prakash*. After a mere five years, it was observed that the attempted Hindi publication was more or less 'doomed'.[98] Of course, it also did not help that the numerous smaller Kayastha sabhas had short lifespans.[99] The readership was even more limited than the Urdu *Kayastha Samachar*. Its attempts to reach the Doab's villages, away from the urban areas of Persian and Urdu circles, proved problematic. But sometimes the pressure got to Kayastha families. In the Aminabad neighbourhood of Lucknow, for example, some Kayastha families tried to pass themselves off as Kashmiri Brahmins to avoid attention from

Hindi proponents.[100] They did this because, even though Kashmiri Brahmins learned Persian and served as scribes, being Brahmin made them less suspicious in the eyes of Hindi and Hindu revivalists. Indeed, their reputation for being 'Islamized' was so well known that as late as the 1900s Kayastha clerks were disparagingly called 'Turks'.[101]

But there were regional variations in the cultural and service fates of north and east Indian Kayastha families. Farther southeast, in Bengali country, some Kayasthas turned their backs on the service professions and reoriented towards the commercial and emergent industrial worlds. A number of Bengali Kayastha families became 'new Vaishyas' by establishing profitable businesses in jute, paper manufacturing and moneylending.[102] This sometimes attracted the scorn of their caste fellows farther northwest in Bihar and the Doab, who criticized them for selling out to 'more profitable, though less reputable, occupations other than writing'.[103] The 1893 Kayastha Sabha meeting in Allahabad ruled that it was 'considered a disgrace to follow any occupation unconnected with letters'.[104] But on the whole those in these occupations were probably only a sliver of Bengali Kayasthas and an even smaller number farther northwest, in the Doab.[105] Farther upcountry, Kayasthas largely maintained their roles as the 'service classes' of Hindustan, serving as functional intermediaries between political authority and the people through the mediums of taxation and administration.

Kayasthas, competition and 'public instruction'

Another major change that Kayastha families experienced had to do with the emergence of public instruction. In north India the by-products of a more competitive system, compared to that of the localized patronage around the *maktab*,[106] reached a far larger slice of the population. This heightened demographic dimension put some strain upon Kayasthas' reputation as the 'educated caste' of India. The eventual drawing into public domain of what were previously private, localized forms of instruction had the effect of widening the scope for competition for enrolment spots. This, in theory and often in practice, whittled away at the near dominance that Kayasthas had exercised from the seventeenth century up through the 1860s. In north India specifically Kayasthas competed more intensely with Brahmins for service posts. They were still the predominant block in north Indian administration, but they felt the squeeze. Curzon's 1904 Universities Act[107] was one such example. The Act restricted the overall number of university spots across India, which was acutely felt in places of Kayastha concentration, such as Lucknow and Allahabad, and the 'monetization' of instruction, through raised fees, squeezed these families further. A close reading of the short-lived periodical *Kayastha*, published out of Agra from 1894, shows it was regularly punctuated with anxiety about the loss of Kayastha dominance of administration because of Brahmins. It noted that 'the system of liberal education has given a death blow to their natural calling'.[108] As fees were a source of revenue for 'public instruction', *bania*s and Brahmins were more likely to be able to afford those charged by private and Grant-in-Aid institutions. Kayasthas' incomes and livelihood were, reformers understood, a by-product of clerical service and not a precondition of it. This reflected a real, marked shift from learning to public education in South Asia, from patronage and hereditary positions to institutional competition.[109] Kayasthas had started to feel the pinch by the 1890s. Departments of Public Instruction reduced spending and increasingly contracted out the privatization of schooling to missionary societies across the Doab. Set fees came to finance public instruction; money came to define access to instruction at the expense of patronage.[110] Kayastha publishers, barristers and scholars were all on the defensive by the 1880s, attempting to paint their caste as legitimately twice-born (*dvija*) in light of such pressures.

The competition engendered a sense of unease among Kayasthas, which was echoed in the types of reform which Kayastha associations advocated. Numerous Kayastha families felt the pinch of competition not only from Brahmins but from higher tuition fees.[111] This generated vibrant debates over domestic economy and household finances and was seen in various efforts to reform marriage rituals and expenses. A reading of the proceedings of various Kayastha associations suggests that there was a direct correlation between rising tuition fees and calls to reduce marriage expenses. The annual Kayastha Association meetings after 1893 regularly issued the call for 'marriage reform', drawing a direct relationship between marriage expenses and expenses for education.[112] The long-standing link between Kayastha livelihoods and learning as a means to government employment was re-invoked with increased regularity after the 1890s. One issue of the *Kayastha* periodical claimed that 'it is clear that either the Kayasthas must educate themselves or die of starvation'.[113] The same issue noted that 'the system of liberal education has given a death blow to their [Kayasthas'] natural calling'.[114] Reform societies noted that Kayasthas were losing out to *bania*s and Brahmins in education, because these groups were more able to afford the increase tuition fees that started to be implemented in the United Provinces after 1904.[115]

Caste, competition and consumption, 1860–1900

As we have seen, Kayasthas' professional service, adaptability and skills greatly coloured the later colonial state's administration. But the very prominence and visibility of these scribal families increasingly brought them into the contemporary social, cultural and language debates of late-nineteenth-century north India. Kayasthas, who had helped extend the fiscal reach of Indian states from the Mughals to the British, now had to confront questions which hitherto they had been able to avoid: debates over varna status, colonial ethnography, vegetarianism, temperance and language. These all shaped an emergent sense of Kayastha caste identity, which started to shift their identity from occupation to origins, lineage and ritual. This section therefore extends our previous analysis of various Kayastha families by seeing how they fared in light of these lively debates. It argues that by tracing various Kayastha scribal families into the later colonial period we gain a better appreciation of how they fashioned themselves in light of very real social changes by 1900.

Emergent debates over caste status

The one major debate with which Kayasthas increasingly had to engage was the question of their caste status. Because the Raj largely administered on the basis of caste taxonomy, these scribes, with their disproportionate dominance of lower administration, saw their caste status fall under increasing scrutiny after the 1870s. Part of this process of caste fashioning involved a newfound drive among Kayasthas and others to write their histories, which were invariably bound up with fashioned lineages. Before the 1870s, it must be stressed, their varna status had been largely ambiguous, if not irrelevant. Kayasthas easily ranked with Brahmins in terms of literacy and educational achievements. But some of their mourning and marriage customs belied those held by castes of twice-born status. Their gravitation into the Indo-Islamic cultural and culinary world over centuries only deepened this ambiguity. Specifically, it accentuated their reputations for non-vegetarianism and alcohol. But by the 1870s, with the rise of larger, more pronounced debates on caste through British and Indian colonial ethnographies, Kayasthas now had to respond to various attempts to classify their *dvija* status. For a looser group of families who were literate and served the sinews of political power, the prospect of being relegated to *shudra* status was a terrifying one.

Ethnography and law: contesting *dvija* status

These debates over Kayasthas' caste status emerged as a result of the confluence of legal debates and colonial ethnography. The usage of caste as a legal category, which has received great attention from historians, was a broader development which affected the nature and practice of caste in colonial India.[116] What we start to see after the 1870s is a 'redefining' of a Kayastha caste category, shifting from occupational definitions to origins and varna debates.

Questions of legal inheritance, coupled with a colonial legal system that employed caste as a means of determining legitimate claims, drew Kayasthas into this debate; in a way, they could not escape them. It seems to have begun with a legal suit in 1860s Jaunpur. A dispute filed earlier in the decade claimed a share in the property of a Kayastha family as an inheritor. The problem was that the plaintiff was considered an 'illegitimate' child by the defendant family. This opened up a whole corpus and literature revolving around ethnography, custom and ritual practice. Jaunpur's Sub Judge, Maulvi Muhammad Habibullah, ruled that among Kayasthas an illegitimate child was not entitled to share in property. While we are not concerned with how the 'illegitimacy' of the child was determined, we are concerned with the debate this suit opened up. The reasoning Habibullah offered was crucial: it opened up the floodgates to both legal and ethnographic contestation of Kayasthas' varna status. Habibullah observed that the custom of granting inheritance to a defined 'illegitimate' child was practised among *shudra*s, who were not twice-born. It was not, he observed, a custom followed by India's *dvija* castes. Habibullah pored over ethnographies and testimony, observing that Kayasthas did not follow this pattern. Habibullah ruled that Kayasthas were, for the purpose of legal caste categorization, of twice-born status.[117]

The effects of this ruling reverberated across the Doab, and a decade later and some 70 miles west Habibullah's ruling popped up as precedent in another adoption suit. A property dispute over inheritance in NWP led to the case being sent up to the Allahabad High Court in 1875 (*Tulsi Ram v. Behari Lal*). The Court had to determine the caste status of a widowed Kayastha, Mussamat Larei.[118] In doing so, it made a regional distinction. It considered the practices of the Bengali Kayasthas as separate and distinct from the 12 Chitraguptavansi sub-branches across Hindustan.[119] This, again, reflected the regional variations of India's wider Kayastha community. The issue at hand for the Court was to establish whether Larei, as a widow, could adopt a male heir without her deceased husband's expressed permission, in line with the *Mitakshara* school of law of Benares.[120] The standing magistrate examined an array of *shudra* practices regarding adoption and inheritance. The Court ruled that Larei, as a Kayastha, could not legally adopt an heir without her husband's living, explicitly stated permission. To do so was not recognized as a *dvija* cultural practice. Justice Mahmud expressed reservations and 'entertain[ed] considerable doubts… as to the view that… the literary caste of Kayasthas… fall under the category of *shudra*'.[121] Even though it was not central to the Allahabad case, the Court's ruling gave further legal succour to the claim that Kayasthas were of *dvija* status.[122]

This string of seeming affirmations of Kayasthas' twice-born status, though, was frayed by a case brought to the Calcutta High Court in 1884. Originating in Bihar, it involved Raj Kumar Lal, four other sons and Bisesur Dial (*Raj Coomar Lall v. Bissessur Dyal*). The question of an adoption's validity and Lal's caste status were intricately interwoven into this debate. As the defendant, Lal argued that the adoptive father of Dial (a Kayastha) could not adopt a sister's son for it was the prerogative of a twice-born husband's sister to adopt her brother's son.[123] In discerning their status, the case drew heavily upon the vast corpus of colonial ethnography. Here, we can see the latter's influence upon caste fashionings. For example, the proceedings involved references to

> a vast mass of authorities... Padma, Purana, Yajnavalkya, Mr. Mandlik's work on Hindu Law, Mitakshara, Viramitrodaya, Wilson's Glossary, Ward on Hindu Law, Steele on Castes, Vivada Chintamoni, Sherring on Caste, Mr. Sarradhicare's work on Hindu Law, being the Tagore Law Lectures of 1880, some census reports, and reports of local officers contained therein, Elliot's Races of British India, the Gazetteers of N.W. Provinces and Oudh; Professor Jolly's Institutes of Narada, Max Muller's Sacred Books of the East, and the Dattaka Mimansa.[124]

Here, we see a direct relationship between the proliferation of ethnography, public scholarly lectures and translations on caste and identity. They punctuated legal debates over Kayasthas' caste origins and varna rank, even if they were secondary to the case at hand. The Court was also taken in by a 'semantic-historicist' argument: that Kayasthas across Bengal, the Doab and Bihar were all originally Kshatriyas. It was argued that Bengali Kayasthas over centuries had intermarried with *shudra*s and slaves (*dasa*s), which explained the common Bengali Kayastha surname of Das.[125] The Court's ruling had a significant effect: it regionalized Kayasthas as a larger community according to varna debates and norms, affirming that Bihari Kayasthas were of *dvija* origin. The adoption of Dial was therefore ruled invalid, with the implication that Bengali Kayasthas were not of twice-born status.

Another 1916 legal case in Bengal engaged with the question of Kayasthas' twice-born status. This case at the Calcutta High Court considered a property dispute over a zamindari estate claimed by Asita Mohan Ghosh, whose father Radha Mohan was a Bengali Kayastha (*Asita Mohan Ghosh v. Nirod Mohan Ghosh Maulik*). What is interesting about the case is that at no time was the issue raised over Bengali Kayasthas' *shudra* status. It was established that 'Radha Mohan's family is a family of Bengal Kayasthas, who are Sudra'.[126] Here, the Court presumed that Bengali Kayasthas were of non-twice-born status, largely basing it on the 1884 precedent. The 1916 ruling was immediately appealed by Bengali Kayasthas, through 'considerable research and ingenuity of argument'.[127] It was eventually brought to the Privy Council in London in 1918.[128] And while it dismissed the appeal, the Council seems to have been sympathetic to the argument that Bengali Kayasthas were *shudra*s. The Council also referred to the regional variations of Kayasthas and in its proceedings noted that Bihari Kayasthas performed rites common with other *dvija* castes,[129] which had been affirmed by the courts in Jaunpur and Allahabad. But the Privy Council demurred from making a final ruling on the matter.

This 'regionalizing' of north and east Indian Kayasthas through legal sinews can also be seen in a case filed with the Patna High Court in 1926. It involved a suit over a mismanaged property inheritance (*Ishwari Prasad v. Rai Hari Prasad Lal*). The Indian magistrate overseeing the case, Jwala Prasad, was himself a Kayastha. Perhaps unsurprisingly, Prasad characterized the Calcutta High Court's 1884 and 1916 rulings as 'inconclusive', noting that the customs and rituals of Bengali Kayasthas were markedly different from those of Bihar and the Doab. He noted that Kayasthas upcountry were joint Hindu families, according to the *Mitakshara* school of law of Benares, while in Bengal Kayasthas largely followed the *Dayabhaga* school of law, which held different view on the 'joint-ness' of the Hindu family.[130] Over a 47-page judgment citing every *smriti* and puranic tale he could muster,[131] Prasad argued that north Indian Kayasthas had Kshatriya origins on the paternal side. Prasad also cited numerous colonial ethnologists, such as Herbert Risley and William Crooke, using their qualified endorsements of Kayasthas' *dvija* origins. Prasad ultimately ruled that Kayasthas were of Kshatriya origin and hence of twice-born status. The Patna ruling, like in Allahabad, seems to have reflected the broader demographics and influence of Kayastha *patwari*s, *qanungo*s and barristers in the colonial administration. This gave Kayasthas an ability to muster louder and more numerous voices of their 'respectable' status. A careful look at the variety and regional dimension of these cases seems to indicate that in the suits originating in the Bihari and Doabi heartlands rulings that Kayasthas were of twice-born status were more likely. Closer to Bengal country, though, the legal rulings tended to assign a *shudra* status. This largely reflected demographic concentration, in addition to how much Kayasthas had permeated and coloured the rhythms of colonial administration upcountry from Bengal. Bengali Kayasthas encountered different dynamics and an atmosphere which was much more suspicious of claims to twice-born status.

These might have seemed like abstract legal rulings. But their cumulative effects between Calcutta and Allahabad seem to have had knock-on effects farther upcountry. The rulings, and the interpretations of them, rippled through the social fabric of Bihar and the Doab. They seemed to have somewhat affected Kayastha families' social standings and how other twice-born castes interacted with them. For example, newly moneyed *vaishya*s across north India and Bihar, who often resented the official status these families had monopolized over generations, started to fashion themselves as superior to Kayasthas as a result of the Calcutta High Court's ruling.[132] Moneyed merchant communities also bolstered their claims to twice-born status, serving as patrons of religious pilgrimages and festivals, whereas Kayasthas rarely served as patrons of temples (*mandir*s) and reenactments of the life of Ram (*ramlila*).[133] To some, Kayasthas' lack of religious patronage, coupled with their residual Islamic cultural bearings, made their claims to twice-born status doubly suspect. Kayasthas in Lucknow, for example, sought to bolster their claims to *dvija* status after various Brahmins attracted to service positions in Lucknow openly started to contest Kayasthas 'respectable caste' claims.[134] This sensitivity perhaps explains why annual Kayastha Association gatherings would read out the names of members who had violated 'twice-born custom' (*dvija dharma*), such as allowing their widows to remarry as a way of enforcing customary cohesion.[135] Annual Kayastha gathering became increasingly sensitive to such infractions and sought to police such behaviour. For Kayasthas, with their broad traditions of the pen, paper and service, challenges from commercial men, coupled with a barrage of suspicion being thrown on them, the Calcutta High Court's rulings were the ultimate occupational insult.

We can also see the incremental heightening of caste sensitivity among Kayasthas in the way disputes between families were increasingly settled. Perhaps cognizant of the ways in which their varna status would be subject to microscopic inspection through legal procedure, Kayasthas in some cases started to take disputes over property and inheritance outside the legal channels. For example, from the 1890s in Jaunpur, Philbit, Etawah and Tanda intra-Kayastha disputes were increasingly settled by local Kayastha assemblies (*kayastha sabha*s). Perhaps this was one way of avoiding the uncomfortable question of varna status, to which the Courts regularly referred. Out-of-court arbitration, avoiding official colonial legal channels, was a reform specifically called for at the Kayastha Conference in Allahabad in 1893, and such resolutions picked up in frequency after 1900.[136] It does seem that the reverberating effects of legal rulings put Kayasthas on the defensive. For example, the annual Kayastha Conference, which kicked off in Lucknow in 1887, does seem to have largely had the purpose of closing ranks and positioning the broader community as *dvija*.[137] This had the effect, ironically, of channeling Kayasthas' legal disputes outside the very sinews of legal administration and procedure, which they had coloured since the 1780s.

The broader swathe of European taxonomies on caste and origins also tended to be ambiguous, if not outright dismissive, about Kayasthas' claims to twice-born status. Here, we are less interested in the veracity of European ethnographic studies. What matters more for our analysis here is how they set the contours of debate on caste origins. What we see is that Kayasthas actively contested colonial ethnography. Let us start with Matthew Sherring's taxonomy of the castes of Benares. Sherring argued that Kayasthas' varna status was at best ambiguous, occupying a liminal position between *shudra* and *vaishya*.[138] The Reverend argued that Kayasthas, based upon traditional varna norms, did not deserve to wear the sacred thread (*suta*), noting that only the Srivastava Kayasthas regularly donned it. Horace Wilson, by contrast, was less dismissive of Kayasthas' claims. In his taxonomy of India's agrarian economy and revenue administration Wilson argued that Kayasthas, who he saw having a longer history bound up with Mughal rule, were of mixed Kshratriya and Vaishya origin.[139] He saw this as rooted in the *functionality* of Kayasthas, more than anything. In a way, Wilson skirted the whole varna-origins debate, arguing that occupational tradition and lineage explained and indeed defined Kayasthas' 'respectable' origins. Herbert Risely's influential *The People of India*, though, took a fairly ambiguous stance on Kayasthas' varna status. While Risely, like Wilson, saw Kayasthas as a highly placed 'functional caste',[140] he argued that their varna origins were murky and difficulty to justify on the basis of a claimed Rajput lineage. Henry Colebrooke's earlier writings are another example. Colebrooke had argued that the names 'Kayastha' and 'Karana' were interchangeable.[141] In his reading of the 'Treatise on Caste' (*Jatimala*) writings, 'karana' referred to the offspring of a *shudra* mother. Colebrooke also argued that Bengali Kayasthas had largely married into *shudra* families, noting the prominence among Bengali Kayasthas of the surname Das, which he interpreted as a modification of the term for slave (*dasa*).[142] So, via a semantic argument, Kayasthas could not be of twice-born status. Like Risely, William Crooke largely saw anthropometry as the scientific way of determining racial as opposed to the varna origins of caste groups. And Crooke seems to have privileged occupation in determining origins, even if he did not take a definitive stance: 'the case of the Kayasths of Bengal is not so clear'.[143] Crooke, though, noted how touchy the topic was for Kayasthas, observing that they were 'particularly sensitive as to any imputations on the purity of their descent'.[144]

Various Kayastha writers directly engaged with, and indeed contested, the broader landscape of colonial ethnography. A prime example is Munshi Kali Prasad. Prasad bolstered a broader articulation of twice-born Kayasthas in his 1877 *The Kayastha Ethnology*. Published by the American Mission Press in Lucknow, his piece was a pointed attempt to fashion a Kayastha identity that was not only flexible and pliant with political power but firmly moored in India's varna norms. A close reading of Prasad's work, though, strongly suggests he was on the defensive. Indeed, it seems punctuated with anxiety. Prasad uneasily juggled two approaches throughout his defence of Kayasthas: occupation and origins. Prasad spent seven pages refuting 'erroneous statements' about Kayasthas,[145] and cited over 626 pandits who argued that the ancestors of Chitragupta were *dvija*, and that they possessed Rajput lineage. This made Kayasthas a 'pure caste'.[146] Prasad directly refuted Matthew Sherring's characterization of a mixed *shudra-vaishya* origin. Over six pages in a 'Refutation of Erroneous Statements', Prasad contested Sherring's conclusion that Kayasthas did not deserve to wear the *suta*. Prasad proceeded to take on another titan of colonial ethnography, Henry Colebrooke, arguing that Colebrooke based his whole argument on the semantic misstep of conflating slave (*dasa*) with the Bengali surname Das. He noted that Colebrooke relied heavily upon the *Jatimala* writings, which possessed far less weight than the *dharmashastras*. Prasad noted, somewhat dismissingly, that 'the compiler of the Jatimala does not appear to be a writer of great authority'.[147] Prasad accused Colebrooke of relying upon far-from-reliable evidence. Throughout, Prasad regularly invoked the crucial trope of 'respectable occupation' to demonstrate that even if the varna origins of Kayasthas were murky, their occupational reputation achieved over centuries made them a 'respectable' caste. Kayasthas' literacy and clerical service history under the Mughals and then the British had put them in the same category as Brahmins in terms of literacy and learning. While ethnography and the translations of Western Orientalist scholars could make the Kayasthas' case, these scribes' cumulative service and occupation histories did the most to define their respectable status. It was an uneasy argument but a powerful one.

Gopinath Sinha Verma was another Kayastha who contributed to this public debate over Kayastha origins. His 1929 work *A Peep into the Origin, Status and History of the Kayasthas* took a different approach from Kali Prasad. Verma vested much of his argument in what he saw as Prasad's fallible argument that Kayasthas had Rajput lineage. For Verma, the argument that Kayasthas had Rajput lineage was an argument that Kayasthas could not win, given the sheer weight of Indian and British ethnography: 'no species of arguments will ever transform the quill driving caste of the Kayasths into a Rajput clan'.[148] So what Verma did was to locate Kayasthas within an occupational framework, whose respectability translated into a corresponding twice-born status. Verma fashioned an argument which drew upon history. Kayasthas, he argued, had been indispensable to Indian rulers 'since time immemorial'.[149] The contributions of Kayasthas as scribes, *qanungo*s and *diwan*s in India's history – under Muslim rulers then the British – vaulted them into the same ranks of Rajputs and Brahmins as at the 'top' of Indian society. In a way, Verma sought to redefine how Indian society should constitute rank and 'respectability'. To Verma, the rulers may have changed throughout the eras, but Kayasthas were the scribal mortar of sovereigns in India. Kayasthas had 'always, irrespective of the nationality of the rulers, supplied the administrative body of India'.[150] This, rather than origins, constituted their high status. Yet his writings too were punctuated with anxiety. He noted that much of the ill will towards Kayasthas came from Brahmins who had lost out economically under the late Mughal era and early British administration. He noted that jealousy motivated much of the Hindu reformist movements: Kayasthas were 'a caste that was ever obnoxious to the priests and… Brahman superiority'.[151] Verma observed how this punctuated debates among Bengali Kayasthas. Noting just how dominant the Bengali Brahmins were in service posts, Verma argued this had accentuated

Bengali Kayasthas' sensitivity to their caste status, and partially reflected the 1916 Calcutta High Court ruling. Again, for Verma, Bengali Kayasthas could not win the origins debate, so they sought to deflect it by adopting more 'Brahmanical' norms of vegetarianism and abstention from alcohol.

A survey of Indian writers and commentators further suggests that many of Kayasthas' neighbours, confidants and co-workers saw them as twice-born. For example, Abdul Sharar, intimately familiar with how Kayasthas coloured the Nawabs' administrations and prominence in Lucknow, argued that Kayasthas were of *dvija* status, claiming that they had Kshatriya and Vaishya origins.[152] For Sharar, this could be explained by their high level of prominence as learned, Persian-literate *diwans*, administrators and *qanungo*s, and it was inexplicable that such a prominent literate service group of non-Muslims could have *shudra* origins. They were literate, learned and were crucial for Muslim then Christian sovereigns. Rabindranath Tagore is another example. Even though he had Bengal specifically in mind, he argued that the Dutts, Ghoshs and Guhas were of Kshatriya origin, again citing their 'respectability and prominence in administration and overall rates of literacy'.[153]

However, not all Indian observers threw their support behind Kayastha claims. Given the broader influence of Kayasthas in colonial administration, coupled with more vocal and forceful publications that asserted their *dvija* origins, the most spirited rejection of Kayastha claims tended to come from Brahmins. The best-known refutation came from the Bengali Brahmin Jogendra Nath Bhattacharya. His 1896 *Hindu Castes and Sects* clearly had Munshi Kali Prasad's *Ethnology* in mind, even if it was never made explicit. To unlock the coding of Kayasthas' varna status, Bhattacharya focused not on claims of lineage but on lived rituals and customs. He specifically looked at mourning. He argued that since Kayasthas between Dinapur and Delhi mourned for 30 days, like *shudra*s, they logically had to be *shudra* in origin.[154] This was very much a 'ritualist method' of ascertaining Kayasthas' origins. Nothing else, Bhattacharya argued, could explain why a supposed twice-born caste would adopt such a custom. Even if he placed them in the 'upper layer' of Indian society in terms of their literacy and 'respectability', the way they grieved the deaths of loved ones suggested a strong *shudra* lineage and influence. Bhattacharya also noted that the majority of Kayasthas did not wear the *suta*,[155] save the Srivastavas. To Bhattacharya, this explained why Bengali Kayasthas, who tended not to wear it, were so sensitive to their *shudra* status. Bhattacharya smugly noted that this sensitivity was a positive influence. It made Bengali Kayasthas sober, moderate *shakta*s who 'follow[ed] the discipline imposed upon them by their Brahmin gurus'.[156] In this sense, Bhattacharya broadly reaffirmed the regional differences of Kayasthas' rituals. Bengali Kayasthas, he noted, were far more Brahmanical in ritual than Kayasthas farther upcountry, who had a reputation for consuming flesh and drink.[157] In fact, Dutt bluntly called the Bhatnagar Kayasthas drunkards. It was no surprise therefore that the Brahmin editors of the Allahabad daily *The Pioneer* claimed that Kayasthas' regular claims to Kshatriya status were 'tiresome and pointless'.[158]

Reverberating effects of caste origins: temperance reform

Of all the evidence that was drawn upon to legally advocate Kayasthas' *dvija* status, perhaps the most important aspect was the question of 'moral consumption'. Subject to increasing scrutiny of their varna origins and rituals, Kayasthas' consumption habits increasingly came under the radar of debate. Debates over *dharmashastra* and Brahmanical-squared ritual and custom, as we have seen, punctuated legal proceedings between Allahabad and Calcutta and the ethnographies of the late nineteenth century. The issue of 'moral consumption' therefore started to be drawn into the orbit of this debate. Kayastha societies and writings began to address these questions, encouraging temperance and vegetarianism as moral alternatives. After the 1870s debates over moral consumption started to punctuate Kayastha debates, publications and annual association gatherings.

The issue of drink was interwoven with debates about twice-born status and dharmic behaviour. This was, it must be stressed, a vexing issue for reformers. Kayasthas had acquired a not always deserved reputation for their 'partiality for wine'.[159] Indeed, north Indian folk tales bordered on the crude (one claimed that 'drinking comes to a Kayasth with his mother's milk').[160] Kayastha associations, conscious of high-caste norms that privileged abstinence, and the role of temperance among various strands of Hindu reformers,[161] took up the cause of temperance with increased vigour after the 1890s. They saw their claims to twice-born status bound up with teetotalism and, if not, temperance. In this sense, it does seem that Kayasthas groups were responding to reformist advocacy. There were, of course, regional variations among Kayasthas when it came to drink. Bengali Kayasthas, as we have seen, tended to be more abstemious than Bihari Kayasthas. The Bengali Brahmin Jogendra Nath Bhattacharya observed that 'the Lala [Kayasthas of NWP and Bihar] are very much addicted to drinking, they differ from the Bengali Kayasthas who are mostly teetotalers'.[162] Spirituous liquors therefore became a part of the wider debate on Kayasthas' caste identity. The other effect of Bhattacharya's work was to raise the stakes of Kayastha respectability. But whether Kayasthas really were partial to drink was beside the point. What mattered more was that Kayasthas were forced to respond to a broader literature of ethnographic and anecdotal stereotypes, which were both accentuated by high court rulings.

At the 1887 Annual Kayastha conference in Lucknow, for example, reform-minded Kayasthas resolved to confront 'the evil of drink', which during the proceedings 'came in for a large share of its active and acute attention'.[163] Munshi Kali Prasad led most of the discussion. He wanted Kayasthas to abstain from drink, even though, he claimed, the reputation was inflated. Prasad noted that this reputation had stuck because Kayasthas openly drank at festivals such as Holi.[164] And this was not lost on observers. The Urdu newspaper *Mehra-Nimroz* observed that it was a touch ironic that Kayasthas were leading such a sustained temperance movement, given that 'wine drinking, [was] most prevalent among the Kayesthas'.[165] Even Kayastha editors themselves acknowledged the hurdle. The *Koh-i-Noor* Urdu weekly, whose founder was another Kayastha from

Sikanderabad, Harsukh Rai,[166] noted that it was quite the task for Munshi Kali Prasad to lead this effort among his caste fellows. Rai expressed little envy for Prasad and his efforts to maintain what he called a 'wall of sand'.[167]

On the whole, though, there were broader movements towards temperance. Abstinence was seen as too difficult a standard to maintain. And it does seem that larger numbers of Kayasthas took temperance pledges after the 1870s. The Bengali paleontologist Pramatha Nath Bose, for example, noted that Kayasthas were fast giving up alcohol consumption and the giving of alcoholic gifts for marriage celebrations.[168] Some Kayastha efforts were even semantically zealous. In Agra local Kayasthas founded the 'Kayastha Drink Destroyer Society'.[169] It is tough to gauge how successful it was. But it does seem that the Bhatnagars, perhaps because they were considered a 'lower' Kayastha subgroup, gave up on drink in larger numbers much earlier than the higher Mathurs, Saxenas and Srivastavas. These temperance societies also made connections with the famed Mathur Kayasthas of Hyderabad.[170] Networking and building connections of association through all-India Kayastha societies, Hyderabad's Kayasthas in 1895 made the Muslim Nizam of Hyderabad an honorary patron of the all-India Kayastha Temperance Society.[171] Temperance, honour and caste status all seem to have converged by the 1890s and shaped the contours of debate over Kayasthas' origins and caste status.

While the temperance-reform movement gained a strong currency among Kayastha organizations, debates over vegetarianism did not make as much headway. Vegetarianism was seen as less crucial than confronting the stereotype of wine drinking. But by the early 1900s, particularly when debates over Kayasthas origins reached a new pitch, some Kayasthas organizations were advocating vegetarianism as a moral alternative. The *Kayastha Samachar* series after 1900 was studded with calls for vegetarianism, encouraging barristers, *vakil*s and inspectors to give up flesh in their diets.[172] Various letters recommending abstinence from meat (*goshti chittis*) in Bihar and the Doab after the 1890s were handed out in villages by organizations such as the Kayastha Temperance Reform Association out of Kanpur.[173] Temperance movements often worked hand in hand with calls for vegetarianism, arguing that the combination of meat and drink sullied Kayasthas' hard-earned reputation as a highly placed 'service caste'. It also, it was argued, precluded them from winning any debates over varna origins. Here, these groups tried to persuade Kayasthas that the consumption of flesh, which they had shared with their Muslim neighbours for centuries, should be scaled back and that vegetarianism was more easily squared with dharmic norms. Munshi Kali Prasad relentlessly published tracts and gave speeches to encourage Kayasthas to abstain from flesh. But, again, the effects were uneven and largely regionally based. The Chandraseniya ('Prabhu') Kayasthas of west India seem to have adopted vegetarianism in greater numbers much earlier.[174] Back in the Doab others made compromises. Some purged the domestic home of flesh consumption, only to consume it in restaurants, eateries and at Sufi shrines.[175] They were 'domestic vegetarians' but 'public meat eaters'.[176] And many Lucknawi Kayasthas continued to consume meat, regardless of current debates, in the carnivorous city's various *dasturkhan*s.[177]

Conclusion

This chapter has argued that the ways in which Hindustan's pensmen and scribes shaped the early rhythms of the colonial-fiscal state had a real impact upon the Raj's lower tiers of administration by 1900. The expansion of a more paper-oriented and obsessed Company government after the early 1800s, and its accumulative effects in revenue administration, the colonial archive and broader patterns of paper-patterned governance, all reverberated into the later nineteenth century. In terms of personnel, the continuance of Hindustan's pensmen were the manifestations of these churning dynamics. By the turn of the twentieth century Hindustan's pensmen were providing the mortar for the Raj's lower tiers of authority, maintaining their roles as India's service classes, even if their administrative superiors went from being Muslim to British. They were often the 'go to' classes for Settlement Officers, which enabled these more 'middling' scribes to extend their numbers and reputations deep into the colonial period. And because of their own dominance in north Indian administration, combined with broader Hindu and Hindi reformist movements, Kayasthas' caste status was contested, articulated and refashioned in new and unprecedented ways. So while Kayasthas undoubtedly did well and came to colour the Raj in north India by 1920, they still could not escape emergent debates over scripts, drink, varna and languages, which came to dominate so much of Indian public discourse. While remaining the dominant functional group in the Doab and Bihar, they also felt the pinch from the emergence of public instruction, competition and rising tuition fees.

This brings us to debates over the colonial state and caste as a category and identity. Nicholas Dirks' controversial work *Castes of Mind* has argued that the colonial state played a significant role in the invention of new caste categories for the purposes of colonial governance.[178] Dirks has pointed mainly to ethnography and taxonomy, seeing them as shaping not only how caste was administered, but how it was understood and practised. Rashmi Pant, meanwhile, has argued that bureaucratic routine had the effect of standardizing and creating caste categories out of multifarious and contested identities.[179] This present study sees another, more opportune angle from which to gauge the role the colonial state played in constructing and shaping caste categories. By examining a longer history of this scribal group – how they coloured the colonial state, and how their 'caste' was refashioned by 1900 – we see a picture of caste as less defined through taxonomy and more through occupation. The term 'Kayastha' – and its earlier iterations of 'Kaith', 'Kyait' and Kyut' – had some usage in the early periods of British rule in the Doab. Duncan's and other Settlement Officers' references to 'Canoongoes of the Kaith caste' were common in late-eighteenth-century records. In this sense, this work finds common ground with Pant's argument. But it also sees differences, for the success of creating a Kayastha caste category was an incomplete process. Indeed, the rhythms of fiscal and archival administration were markedly bereft of categories when describing castes and ensured that in many parts of Hindustan by the 1840s the terms '*qanungo*' and 'Kayastha' were almost synonymous. 'Kayastha' seems to have largely maintained its occupational interpretation. It was only with the spurt of legal suits after the 1880s that Kayasthas started to be defined by non-Kayasthas according to varna norms and origins. When caste debates, in which the colonial state played a minimal role, were coupled with these legal rulings, 'Kayastha' as a term started to be seen more as a caste category based upon varna origins rather than occupation. Kayasthas had been challenged and had to respond via print media, associations and the encouragement of ritual and customary cohesion. Their status needed to be defended according to the parameters established by legal procedure and ethnographic evidence. But Kayastha publicists did so on the back foot. The passionate defences of Kayasthas' twice-born status by Munshi Kali Prasad and Gopinath Verma were punctuated with anxiety, as were the *Kayastha Samachar* and the *Kayastha* series published out of Agra.

Of course, colonial ethnography played a role. But not in the way we might think. A close reading of Herbert Risely's and William Crooke's ethnographies largely speak of 'Kayastha' in terms of occupational status, which was a reputation well established before the full onslaught of colonial ethnography by 1900. Crooke, for example, stressed the occupational characteristics that bound Kayasthas, noting that the differences in custom and Brahmanical ritual between Bengali and Doabi Kayasthas. Indeed, while Crooke may have labelled them a caste, he argued that their origins were muddled.[180] Risley, similarly, emphasized that what bound Kayasthas was their 'clerky' functionality, not their ethnic origins.[181] In so many aspects of colonial ethnography, 'Kayastha' was really a category of functionality rather than one of varna origins. It was only the legal proceedings in Allahabad, Patna and Calcutta between 1880 and 1930 that moved Kayasthas to respond via print, vigorously defending their self-styled *dvija* status. Colonial ethnography seems to have been largely focused on their functionality and occupational status, which itself was a by-product of how much Kayasthas shaped the early rhythms of the colonial state. Here, colonial ethnography was more a by-product of large processes of state-formation. A deeper reading of the evidence suggests that Dirks' larger argument about the centrality of ethnography is rather shortsighted. Colonial ethnography did not always privilege varna categories.

There were also other limits to how much currency Kayastha had as a caste category beyond colonial ethnography and courts. In spite of these debates among Kayastha societies and publicists to define Kayasthas as a 'caste', a few important observation should first be drawn. First, much of this spurt in activity and organization after the 1880s was largely reactionary. The *Kayastha Samachar* was indeed the first periodical to regularly employ the use of the term 'caste' when describing Kayasthas.[182] But the term was inherently contested, as seen in the debates over Kayasthas' varna origins and within the twelve subcastes of Bihar and the Doab. Indeed, Kayastha conferences spent much of their time attempting (and failing) to impose ritual and customary conformity. And while there really was a spurt in activity by organizations such as the Kayasthas Institute of Lucknow and the Kayastha Sadar Sabha,[183] they seem to have been unable to truly fashion a caste identity that gained currency. These *sabha*s and annual meetings found it difficult to corral the very diverse spectrum of regional Kayastha subcastes according to ritual norms. We can see this if we examine the delegate counts of annual meetings and where they were held. For example, in the 1891 meeting in Bareli 1,518 out of the 1,726 Kayastha delegates were from Rohilkhand.[184] This was similar to the 1892 Ajmer meeting, with most attendees coming from the Rajputana region.[185] Not only were these associations limited by region, they were limited by longevity. Kayastha *sabhas* had little real activity and often disappeared within a few years. As the *Hindustan Review* noted: 'but where are they in existence except on paper'?[186] So while Kayasthas themselves did use the term as a marker of identity, it was far from a cohesive one. The long-standing hierarchies – largely based upon occupation and moral consumption – persevered into the early twentieth century. And the case of Bengali Kayasthas was a wholly separate aspect, with many northern scribes resigning their Bengali equivalents to *shudra* status.

We can see, too, that 'Kayastha' as a caste term had little currency when we look at particular Kayastha memoirs and publications. These service families really only started using it once legal proceedings were afoot after the 1870s. In many instances the term does not even come up. For example, the family history of the Ambastha Kayastha family of Lucknow does not mention the term 'Kayastha' anywhere in its text;[187] the term 'community' (*quam*) is used. The scribes and pensmen who constituted the 'Kayastha caste' were also largely seen more by their occupation than their varna origins. Even Sankatha Prashad's 1920 Urdu publication *Quam-i-Kayastha*, which drew heavily upon Kalhana's twelfth-century *Rajataranagini* ('The Rivers of Kings'), largely celebrated the role of Kayasthas as traditional managers of paper, accounts and the state's written knowledge.[188] Prashad used the term 'community' (*quam*) to describe Kayasthas rather than 'varna' and 'jati'. 'Kayastha' was a more accurate term when specifying their occupational professions and looser community of scribes, rather than their caste origins. The legal proceedings between Calcutta and Allahabad illustrated this, given that the question of their *dvija* status was always a footnote to broader legal contestations over property rights and inheritance. Kayasthas largely defined themselves through occupation and physical association with the pen and paper, rather than varna origins and hierarchy. Their long history as scribes – first under the Mughals and then the British – is a great illustration of this.

Notes

1 W. Crooke, *The North-Western Provinces of India: Their History, Ethnology, and Administration* (London, 1897), p. 182.
2 K. Leonard, *Social History of an Indian Caste: the Kayasths of Hyderabad* (Berkeley, 1979).
3 Some of the documents have purportedly survived and are rumoured to be in the possession of various Muslim gentry families in Lucknow and by the Raja of Mahmudabad. Dr Vibhuti Rai and Sri Sampal Rai, Lucknow, 2006, 2007, 2008; Dr Raj and Mrs Naheed Verma, Lucknow, 2006, 2007, 200; Mr Ram Advani, Lucknow, 2003, 2004, 2006, 2008. Also see 'Settlement report and statements of the District of Moozuffernugger for the year 1866', F. Williams, Commissioner, in *Settlement Report of the District of Moozuffernugger* (Allahabad, 1873), p. 4.

4 Capt J. MacAndrew, Settlement Officer, Royal Bareilly, to C. Currie, Settlement Commissioner of Awadh, No. 138, 31 May 1864, in *Papers related to Land Tenures and Revenue Settlements in Oude* (Calcutta, 1865), p. 519. Hereafter *PRLTRSO*.

5 Maj F. Chamier, Settlement Officer, Daryabad, to C. Currie, Settlement Commissioner of Awadh, No. 180, May 1864, in *PRLTRSO*, p. 536.

6 NWPRP, P/220/76, 'Circular order for the Sadr Board of Revenue, No. 4, Appendix No. 7, 1856', 4 March 1856, IOL.

7 Revenue Proceedings, Home Department, No. 3275, 19 October 1861, NAI.

8 *Directions for Revenue Officers in the North-Western Provinces of the Bengal Presidency* (Calcutta, 1858), p. 29. Hereafter *DRONWP*.

9 R. Thullier, *A Manual of Surveying for India: Detailing the Mode of Operations on the Trigonometrical, Topographical and Revenue Settlements of India* (Calcutta, 1851), p. 574.

10 W. Hammond, Sec Sadr Board of Revenue, Appendix XX, 'Instructions by the Sudder Board Revenue concerning the revision of settlement in the Sahaunpore District', n.d., in *DRONWP*, pp. 131–61; also see *PRLTRSO*; also see *DRONWP*, p. 27.

12 M. Reid, Sec to Chief Commissioner, to Settlement Commissioner, Awadh, 18 July 1864, in *PRLTRSO*, p. 462.

13 V. Oldenburg, *The Making of Colonial Lucknow, 1856–1877* (Princeton, 1984). Oldenburg has noted that Lucknow was one of the most highly taxed cities in all India.

14 Thullier, *A Manual of Surveying*, p. 599.

15 J. Perkins, Deputy Commissioner and Settlement Officer, Sultanpur, 18 July 1864, in *PRLTRSO*, p. 457.

16 *Review of the Revenue Administration of the Province of Oudh* (Allahabad, 1886), p. 50.

17 *Settlement Report of the District of Moozuffernugger* (Allahabad, 1873), pp. 90–5.

18 C. Grant, Assistant to the Settlement Dept., Meerut, 9 November 1863, in *Settlement Report of the District of Moozuffernugger* (Allahabad, 1873) p. 152–3.

19 C. Grant, Assistant to the Settlement Dept, Meerut, 9 November 1863, in *Settlement Report of the District of Moozuffernugger* (Allahabad, 1873) p. 152–3. Grant noted that this applied in all areas expect where there were sandy (*bhoor*) soils.

20 *Annual Report on the Operations under Act II of 1878* (Allahabad, 1884), p. 12.

21 H. Evans, *Report on the Settlement of District of Agra* (Allahabad, 1880), pp. 87–8.

22 Ibid., p. 28.

23 W. Hooper, *Final Report of the Settlement of the Basti District* (Allahabad, 1891), p. 67.

24 *Review of the Revenue Administration of the Province of Oudh* (Allahabad, 1886), p. 50.

25 *Report on the Progress of Education in North West Provinces* (Allahabad, 1886), Section vii, p. 49.

26 Ibid., p. 43.

27 A more accurate translation of *mohafiz daftar* would be 'memory/recall office', a testament to the utilitarian functionality *qanungo*s were expected to provide.

28 *DRONWP*, p. 179. Robert Baden-Powell observed that the *qanungo* was 'much relied upon for keeping up what I may call the new system of corrected village records and statistics'. B. Baden-Powell, *The Land Systems of British India* (Oxford, 1892), Vol. II, p. 503.

29 W. Sherring, *Hindu Tribes and Castes* (Calcutta, 1872), Vol. I, pp. 310–11.

30 H. Bellenoit, *Missionary Education and Empire in Late Colonial India 1860–1920* (London, 2007), chapter 5.

31 *DRONWP*, p. 230.

32 W. Neale, *Economic Change in Rural India: Land Tenures and Reforms in Uttar Pradesh* (New Haven, 1962), p. 122.

33 H. Elliot, *Memoirs on the History, Folklore and Distribution of the Races of the North-Western Provinces of India* (London, 1869), Vol. I, p. 180.
34 Elliot, *Memoirs*, Vol. I, p. 36.
35 K.P. Shrivastava, *The Hindu Sociology: Being a Treatise on the Social Position of the Kayastha Community* (Benares, 1913), p. 73.
36 Elliot, *Memoirs*, p. 181.
37 Crooke, *North-Western Provinces*, p. 153.
38 R.V. Russell and R.B.H. Lal, *The Tribes and Castes of the Central Provinces of India* (London 1916), Vol. I, p. 416.
39 J. Nesfield, *Brief View of the Caste System of the North-West Provinces and Oudh* (Allahabad, 1885), p. 47.
40 Ibid., p. 47.
41 Baden-Powell, *Land Systems*, Vol. II, p. 508.
42 *Census of the North-Western Provinces for 1865* (Allahabad, 1867), p. 82; Sherring, *Hindu Tribes*, p. 311.
43 *DRONWP*, p. 230.
44 Elliot, *Memoirs*, p. 181.
45 'Kayastha World', July 1901, *Kayastha Samachar* (Allahabad, 1901), p. 91. Hereafter *KS*.
46 Crooke, *North-Western Provinces*, p. 205; emphasis is the author's own.
47 W. Crooke, *The Tribes and Castes of the North-western Provinces and Oudh* (Calcutta, 1896), Vol. III, p. 2.13; Russell and Lal, *Tribes and Castes*, Vol. III, p. 412.
48 Crooke, *Tribes and Castes*, Vol. III, p. 213.
49 H. Risley, *The People of India* (London, 1915), p. 309.
50 S. Rizvi, *Shah Wali-Allah and His Times* (Calcutta, 1980), p. 174.
51 Crooke, *North-Western Provinces*, p. 182.
52 Bellenoit, *Missionary Education*.
53 S. Sinha, 'Caste conferences & national progress', presidential address delivered at the thirty-fifth session of the All-India Kayastha Conference, held at Delhi on 29 March 1929 (Delhi, 1929), p. 3.
54 B. Misra, *The Bureaucracy in India: an Historical Analysis of Development up to 1947* (Delhi, 1977), p. 320.
55 D.C. Potter, *India's Political Administrators: From ICS to IAS* (Delhi, 1996), p. 118.
56 R.C. Dutt, *Hindu Castes and Sects* (Calcutta, 1896), p. 177.
57 M. Gopal, *Munshi Premchand* (New York, 1964), p. 60.
58 K. Kishore, 'The late Rai Bahadur... his life and times', 1937, unpublished Mss. in author's possession, p. 4.
59 See Bellenoit, *Missionary Education*, chapters 3–5 for more on Nesfield and patronage in the Department of Public Instruction.
60 *Kayastha*, September–October (Agra, 1896), p. 1.
61 Dr Vibhuti Rai and Sri Sampal Rai, Lucknow, 2006, 2007, 2008; Dr Raj and Mrs Naheed Verma, Lucknow, 2006, 2007, 2008; Ms Rakhi Reshmi, New Delhi, 2008, 2009, London, 2010, 2012.
62 *Kayastha*, September–October (Agra, 1896), p. 1.
63 Ibid., p. 3.
64 K. Prasad, *The Kayastha Ethnology, an Inquiry into the Origin of the Chitraguptavansi and Chandrasenavansi Kayasthas* (Lucknow, 1877).
65 Bellenoit, *Missionary Education*, chapter 5.
66 *Kayastha*, January–February (Agra, 1897).
67 *Kayastha*, October (Agra, 1895), p. 6.
68 'Kayastha World', January–February 1901, *KS*, p. 63. Prasad also passed the Bar in 1865.
69 'Kayastha World', p. 63.

70 Sri Sampal and Dr Vibhuti Rai, Raj and Naheed Verma, Sri Ram Advani, Lucknow, 2004, 2006, 2008, 2009. Family Mss. of Sampal Rai, 'Sri Ganeshya Nam', 1915, in author's possession.
71 *Kayastha*, October (Agra, 1895), pp. 4–6.
72 Sri Sampal and Dr Vibhuti Rai, Lucknow, 2004, 2006, 2008, 2009.
73 A.L. Srivastava, *The First Two Nawabs of Oudh* (Lucknow, 1933).
74 Ibid., pp. 256, 262.
75 Ibid., p. 268.
76 Ulrike Stark, in her colourful analysis of the Nawal Kishore Press of Lucknow, has cast doubt on whether Munshi Nawal Kishore was indeed a Kayastha. But Kishore's networks of association and literate family history, coupled with geographic location, would strongly suggest that he was. U. Stark, *Empire of Books* (Ranikhet, 2007), pp. 140–5.
77 *Kayastha*, August (Agra, 1896), p. 4.
78 Ibid., p. 3
79 Mss. of Sri Sampal Rai, 'Sri Ganeshya Nam', 1915, p. 5, in author's possession.
80 Ibid., p. 6.
81 Ibid., p. 8.
82 Sri Sampal Rai, Lucknow, 2004, 2006, 2008.
83 'Sri Ganeshya Nam', p. 8.
84 The author is grateful to Mr Alok Sinha, IAS, Lucknow, who brought this to my attention.
85 'Sri Ganeshya Nam', pp. 5–8.
86 Sri Sampal and Dr Vibhuti Rai, Raj and Naheed Verma, Sri Ram Advani, Lucknow, 2004, 2006, 2008, 2009. Rakhi Rashmi, London, 2010, 2012, 2014.
87 Shrivastava, *Hindu Sociology*, p. 52.
88 Personal communication, Dr V. Rai, Lucknow, 2004, 2006; C. Bayly, *Empire and Information*, p. 245; Sri Sampal and Dr Vibhuti Rai, Raj and Naheed Verma, Sri Ram Advani, Lucknow, 2004, 2006, 2008, 2009. Family Mss. of Sampal Rai, 'Sri Ganeshya Nam', 1915, in author's possession.
89 *A Short Account of the Aims, Objects... and Proceedings of the Kayastha Conference, etc.* (Allahabad, 1893), p. ii.
90 A. Jalal, *Self and Sovereignty: Individual and Community in South Asian Islam Since 1850* (London, 2001), pp. 126–9.
91 Sri Sampal and Dr Vibhuti Rai, Raj and Naheed Verma, Sri Ram Advani, Lucknow, 2004, 2006, 2008, 2009.
92 F. Orsini, *The Hindi Public Sphere: 1920–1940: Language and Literature in the Age of Nationalism* (Oxford, 2002).
93 B.P. Sinha, *Kayasthas in Making of Modern Bihar* (Delhi, 2003), pp. 31–2.
94 F. Robinson, *Separatism among Indian Muslims: The Politics of the United Provinces' Muslims, 1860–1923* (Cambridge, 1974), pp. 30–1.
95 *Sitara-i-Hind*, Moradabad, 28 February 1886, SVN, UPSA.
96 V. Dalmia, *The Nationalisation of Hindu Tradition: Bharatendu Harischandra and Nineteenth-century Banaras* (Oxford, 1997).
97 'Kayastha World', July 1901, *KS*, pp. 250–1; perhaps indicative of the resilience of Kayasthas' looser Indo-Islamic cultural tendencies, the *Kayastha Samachar* started in 1873 as an Urdu publication and only converted to English in 1899.
98 *Kayastha*, August (Agra, 1896), p. 7.
99 L. Carroll, 'Caste, community and caste(s) association: a note on the organization of the Kayastha Conference and the definition of a Kayastha community', in K. Ishwaran, ed. *Contributions to Asian Studies* (Leiden, 1978), pp. 5–6.
100 G.S. Verma, *A Peep into the Origin, Status and History of the Kayasthas* (Bareli, 1929), p. 178; Dr Vibhuti Rai and Sri Sampal Rai, Lucknow, 2006, 2007, 2008; Dr Raj and Mrs Naheed Verma, Lucknow, 2006, 2007, 2008.
101 Crooke, *Tribes and Castes*, Vol. IV, p. 3.

102 R. Owens and A. Nandy, *The New Vaisyas* (Calcutta, 1978), p. 81.
103 E. Blunt, *The Caste System of Northern India* (Allahabad, 1931), p. 237.
104 *A Short Account*, p. ii.
105 Verma, *A Peep*, pp. 179–81.
106 H. Bellenoit, 'Paper, pens and power between empires in north India, 1750–1850', *SAHC* 3, 3 (2012), pp. 348–72.
107 Bellenoit, *Missionary Education*, chapter 5, on the Universities Act and reactions.
108 *Kayastha*, April (Agra, 1896), p. 5.
109 Bellenoit, 'Paper, pens and power'.
110 Bellenoit, *Missionary Education*, chapter 5.
111 Dr Vibhuti Rai and Sri Sampal Rai, Lucknow, 2006, 2007, 2008; Dr Raj and Mrs Naheed Verma, Lucknow, 2006, 2007, 2008.
112 Carroll, 'Caste, community', p. 16.
113 *Kayastha*, August (Agra, 1896), p. 24.
114 *Kayastha*, April (Agra, 1896), p. 5.
115 NWP & O Ed. Procds., No. 314, 1910, UPSA.
116 See, for example, S. Kaviraj, 'The imaginary institution of India', in P. Chatterjee and G. Pandey, eds, *Subaltern Studies VII* (New Delhi, 1992), pp. 41–63.
117 Sinha, *Kayasthas*.
118 *Tulsi Ram vs. Behari Lal*, in *The Indian Decisions: Being a Re-print of All the Decisions of the Privy Council on Appeals from India and of the Various High Courts and Other Superior Courts in India Reported Both in the Official and Non-official Reports from 1875* (New Series) (Madras, 1913), Vol. VI, pp. 959–60.
119 Ibid.
120 One reason Bengali Kayasthas were treated separately seems to have been the differences in legal traditions between north India and Bengal. In the latter the *dayabhaga* was more prominent, representing a more 'reformed' legal tradition compared to the more 'orthodox' *Mitakshara* tradition of Benares. See R. Lingat, *The Classical Law of India* (New York, 1973).
121 *Tulsi Ram vs. Behari Lal*, in *The Indian Decisions*, Vol. VI, p. 959.
122 Prasad, *Kayastha Ethnology*, 27fn.
123 *Raj Coomar Lall and Ors. vs. Bissessur Dyal and Ors*, 4 March 1884, https://indiankanoon.org/doc/362/.
124 Ibid.
125 Ibid.
126 *Asita Mohan Ghose Moulik vs. Nerode Mohan Ghose Moulik*, 8 May 1916, https://indiankanoon.org/doc/120151/.
127 *The Indian Decisions*, Volume V, p. 466.
128 Prasad, *Kayastha Ethnology*, pp. 8–9.
129 *The Indian Decisions*, Vol. 5., pp. 466–7.
130 For differences between the two 'schools' of law, see J. Derrett, *Essays in Classical and Modern Hindu Law: Anglo-Hindu legal problems* (Leiden, 1977), his *Introduction to Modern Hindu Law* (Oxford, 1963) and W. Menski, *Modern Indian Family Law* (Surrey, 2001) for larger discussions.
131 B.R. Ambedkar, *Who Were the Shudras?* (Bombay, 1949), p. 138.
132 Risley, *People of India*, p. 116.
133 Sri Sampal and Dr Vibhuti Rai, Raj and Naheed Verma, Sri Ram Advani, Lucknow, 2004, 2006, 2008, 2009.
134 Dr V Rai and Mr R. Advani, Lucknow, 2004, 2006, 2008.
135 *Hindustan Review*, January 1908, SVN, UPSA.
136 *A Short Account*, p. 12.
137 See *A Short Account*; *Report of the Sixth National Social Conference* (Pune, 1893); *Report of the Seventh National Social Conference* (Pune, 1894); *Kayastha* (Allahabad), series; *KS*, series.

138 Sherring, *Hindu Tribes*, Vol. I, p. 305.
139 H. Wilson, *Glossary of Judicial and Revenue Terms* (London, 1855), p. 272.
140 Risley, *People of India*, p. 194.
141 H. Colebrook, *Miscellaneous Essays* (London, 1837), Vol. I, pp. 181, 182.
142 Ibid., pp. 189–90.
143 Crooke, *Tribes and Castes*, p. 185.
144 Ibid., p. 184.
145 Prasad, *Kayastha Ethnology*, pp. 11–18.
146 Ibid., pp. 19–26.
147 Ibid., p. 13.
148 Verma, *A Peep*, p. iii.
149 Ibid., p. v.
150 Ibid., p. 6.
151 Ibid., p. ii.
152 A. Sharar, *Lucknow: the Last Phase of an Oriental Culture* (London, 1975), 72n.
153 Shrivastava, *Hindu Sociology*, p. 88.
154 J.N. Bhattacharya, *Hindu Castes and Sects* (Calcutta, 1896), p. 175.
155 Ibid.
156 Ibid., p. 180.
157 Dr Vibhuti Rai and Sri Sampal Rai, Lucknow, 2006, 2007, 2008; Dr Raj and Mrs Naheed Verma, Lucknow, 2006, 2007, 2008; Ms Rakhi Reshmi, New Delhi, 2008, 2009, London, 2010, 2012.
158 W. Rowe, 'Mobility in the nineteenth century caste system', in Singer, Cohn, eds. *Structure and Change in Indian Society* (Piscataway, 1970).
159 *Hindustan Review*, June 1907, SVN, UPSA.
160 Risley, *People of India*, p. 309; Premchand's father Ajab Lal was accused of having a 'reputation of being a drunkard who used to beat his wife constantly'. See Gopal, *Premchand*, p. 1; Sarkar, *History of Aurangzeb* (Calcutta, 1924), Vol. V, p 35.
161 K. Jones, *Socio-religious Reform Movements in British India* (Cambridge, 1989).
162 *Hindustan Review*, June 1907, SVN, UPSA; Sinha, *Kayasthas*; Bhattacharya, *Hindu Castes*, p. 186.
163 L.P. Saxena, *A Short History of Temperance Reform in the Kayastha Community* (Agra, 1911), p. ii.
164 Ibid.
165 *Mehra-Nimroz*, Bijanur, 28 September 1894, SVN, UPSA.
166 Stark, *Empire of Books*, pp. 120–2.
167 *Koh-i-Noor*, Lahore, Urdu, 6 November 1894, SVN, UPSA.
168 P.M. Bose, *A History of Hindu Civilisation during British Rule* (Calcutta, 1894), p. 101.
169 Saxena, *A Short History*, p. 2.
170 Leonard, *Social History of an Indian Caste: the Kayasths of Hyderabad.*
171 Lecture given in Lashkar, Gwalior, in Saxena, *A Short History*, p. vii.
172 *KS*, c. 1900.
173 Saxena, *A Short History*, pp. iii–v.
174 V. Gupte, *Ethnographic Notes on Prabhu Kayasthas* (Pune, 1904), p. 50.
175 Sri Sampal and Dr Vibhuti Rai, Raj and Naheed Verma, Sri Ram Advani, Lucknow, 2004, 2006, 2008, 2009.
176 Ibid.
177 Ibid. Family Mss. of Sampal Rai, 'Sri Ganeshya Nam', 1915, in author's possession.
178 N. Dirks, *Castes of Mind* (Princeton, 2001).
179 R. Pant, 'The cognitive status of caste in colonial ethnography', *IESHR* (1987).
180 Crooke, *Tribes and Castes*, Vol. III, pp. 184–213.
181 Risley, *People of India*, p. 40.

182 L. Carroll, 'Kayastha Samachar: from a caste – to a national newspaper', *IESHR*, 10 (July 1973), pp. 280–92.
183 'Kayastha World', January–February 1901, *KS*, p. 63.
184 *Report of the Sixth National Social Conference* (Pune, 1893), p. 3.
185 *Report of the Seventh National Social Conference* (Pune, 1894), p. 362.
186 *Hindustan Review*, February 1904, SVN, UPSA.
187 Family Mss. of Sampal Rai, 'Sri Ganeshya Nam', 1915, in author's possession.
188 S. Prashad, *Quam-i-Kayastha* (Jaunpur, 1920).

Conclusion

This book has attempted to shed new light upon the processes of state formation in India between 1760 and 1860. It has argued that the practice of fiscalism was a defining feature of eighteenth-century Indian statecraft, and that the scribal communities of Hindustan played a pivotal role in regional kingdoms' ability to build up their states. These paper-based revenue administrations allowed Indian rulers in Awadh and Bengal – and later the British – to connect with the agrarian hinterlands via pensmen, to coerce cultivators and extract the fiscal blood in these kingdom's emergent veins. In doing so, it has made a number of key observations. First, it seems that the precolonial period from 1700 to 1760 was far more paper- and procedural-based than scholars have appreciated. It may not have been anchored in law as it would be under the British, but fiscal administration was paper-defined, documented and sophisticated in its scope (and it may have become increasingly paper-intensive after the 1740s). Second, the book has demonstrated that British success in conquering India came largely from its fiscal mastery of an Indo-Islamic tradition that used scribes as interstices between ruling overlords and local structures of power. The British did this much more successfully than other Indian rulers. Yet in spite of the massive ruptures that some elements of British rule brought to its administration, many elements of the precolonial fiscal-administrative world – *qanungo*s, *patwari*s, *khusrah* surveys and paper – survived and came to punctuate the Raj's administration. Lastly, as part of this analysis, this book has tracked the fates of various scribal families, namely Kayasthas, across empires. Kayastha families continued to stud the Raj's administrative apparatus, even if they now had to compete with Brahmins for university spots and service posts, and had to address uneasy questions about their varna rank and twice-born status. The wider social and administrative histories of Hindustan's scribal communities were bound up with, and indeed reflective of, the emergence of modern forms of state organization in India.

New perspectives on the origins of colonial state

One of the major themes this book has engaged with is the question of state formation. It has argued for a new way of interpreting the emergence of the colonial state in India by exmining the central role of fiscalism, paper and documentation.

Scribal paper managers, combined with eighteenth-century patterns of agrarian taxation, were vital for the emergence of modern patterns of governance in South Asia. The origins of these trends can be found in eighteenth-century India's political regionalization, which unleashed aggressive trends in assessment and managing revenue. This doubled in intensity with the Company's agrarian revenue settlements after 1780, and these negotiations and regulations were some of the most important tendrils of the Company's early state. Questions of revenue were, of course, equally matters of legal landholdings, inheritance and personal law. The embryonic systems of police and law, while adopted, changed and sometimes thoroughly gutted, increasingly orbited around the need to secure revenue for Britain's Indian empire. This was particularly the case with colonial law and how it came to anchor fiscal administration. And because of this, government in South Asia by 1850 had become far more paper-oriented and fiscal–legal. The British early on altered the intensity and punctuality of revenue collection and anchored its processes more firmly in political authority. Compared to previous Indian sovereigns, the British were unbending with regard to the regularity, intensity and paper-orientation of land revenue, the 'one great customary source of fiscal wealth in India'.[1] British revenue collection had little patience with the *process* of settlement; it cared more for its expedient *ends*. This was reflected in the more intense legal sanction the Company gave to surveying, property rights and payment enforcement through the courts. It had to be irrefutable and non-contestable. Muzaffar Alam has demonstrated how the Nawabi and Sikh domains were hamstrung by gaps between calculated assessment and what was actually paid as revenue.[2] The British eliminated this gap with bureaucratic intensity, regardless of its impact upon agrarian markets, landholding patterns and, sometimes, the literal stomachs of India's cultivators. The British transformed the late Mughal fiscal-military state into a fiscal–legal–bureaucratic one. This was a marked departure from the practice of eighteenth-century kingdoms and sovereigns, by which the British were able to more successfully weld Hindustan's scribes to political authority – via salary and regulation – than the Mughals' successors. This is where a significant portion of their success lay in their conquest of India and the formation of the colonial state.

The British also built up a much more paper-intensive and paper-obsessed system of administration compared to their predecessors. But this paper also reflected broader racial and cultural dynamics. The British aimed to standardize and make intelligible a system of formerly interconnected officials who were bound together by a shared interest in the moral temperature of the sovereign's administration, wherein paper tempered personal relationships. By enacting such extensive surveys, digests and compendiums, encompassing everything from seed quality to well-digging, the British fashioned themselves as objective administrators. But this came at a significant cost. They lost the religious, cultural and social knowledge that lubricated late Mughal revenue administration. This was a striking example of British removal from the sinews of what the late Chris Bayly called 'affective knowledge'.[3] Fiscally, the British knew so much more by the 1840s. But they reduced the complexities of the agrarian economy to averages, categories and statistics in a fit of relentless taxonomy. It was no surprise that the 1857 uprisings blindsided the British. In a way, British distrust of native officers with any administrative portfolio created the very need for such a voluminous paper monster. This abstract, aloof paper regime did as much to *inform* a more hardened colonial racism as it was informed *by* it.

This book has also engaged with a broader literature on state formation in eighteenth-century India. Seema Alavi, for example, has argued that military organization was vital for the early formation of the Company's state. But this might overly privilege the role of the army as a shaper of change.[4] For one, we must remember that the army's fiscal lifeblood came from agrarian revenue: a third of this revenue paid for the force that was at the end of the day Britain's imperial bullwhip. Agrarian revenue also paid for the infrastructure of the future ICS and the various bureaucratic mechanisms of the colonial state. Likewise, Anand Yang's argument for a 'limited Raj' in Bihar largely ignores the changing value of paper and procedure in the formation of India's new state apparatus. Hindustan's scribes, for example, helped change the fabric of Company administration from within.[5] After 1780 there was a newfound intensity to paper-orientation and changes to the composition of revenue officials. The value of paper itself also changed. In so many cases in the Doab we see less a 'limited Raj' and more a penetrating, paper-obsessed juggernaut, which shook up the north Indian agrarian economy. In this sense the Raj was far from limited. Distant villages, through assessment, surveying and paperwork, felt the effect of political authority like never before, even if it was only that of the district's recognized *patwari* and *qanungo*.

This book has also sought to expand our knowledge of scribal groups only briefly mentioned in Chris Bayly's *Rulers, Townsmen and Bazaars*. While Bayly never explored the histories of north India's pensmen, this book has argued that scribal histories and fiscalism offer a new way of viewing colonial state formation. Like merchant families, they served a sort of 'intermediary' function. They linked ruling fiscal centres (Murshidabad, Faizabad, Lucknow) with agrarian hinterlands and local village economies. Like the commercial families of Benares, these scribes and their fiscal documentation seem to have had a direct and telling impact upon the process of state formation. The eighteenth-century state's strength, this book has argued, was defined by its fiscal reach and authority. And it drew heavily upon a group of scribes who between 1700 and 1780 had become the fulcrum of regional military fiscalism.

Perhaps the most recent work that has touched upon scribes and state formation is that of Bhavani Raman. Raman has argued that British aversion to the skills of memorization and recall effected a new meaning for documentation and that the modalities and juridical value of documents changed under the early colonial state in South India. Raman sees a major change in the value of paper, in that the emergence of a 'certificate regime' transformed the value of governance and administration. This may hold true for Tamil country, but in north India it turned out rather differently. For one, mnemonic traditions were far less prevalent in the Doab's daily fiscal administration. Brahmins were a miniscule minority of

Islamized-Persianized scribes in the north, and the Indo-Islamic ethos of paper, documentation and written record were already established before colonial rule, even if their values would later change. The vast corpus of documentation upon which the Company drew – *hastobud*s, *jamabandi*s and *wasilbaki*s – were existing forms of fiscal information and 'fact'. In this sense, and from the north Indian perspective, there was less change and rupture in the value of paper compared to south India.

So while the nature and impact of British colonial rule remain hotly debated, perhaps the differences are not as wide as the literature would lead one to believe. There is room for newer, fresh approaches. This book sees change and continuity as far more interdependent and almost symbiotic than the simple paradigm of 'British action, Indian reaction' or 'Indian agency, British reaction'. In a way, this dichotomy has hobbled the literature on eighteenth-century India and our understanding of the emergence of the modern Indian state. The paradigm of 'continuity vs. change' is in dire need of reconfiguration. In so many cases, as this book demonstrates, change was made possible by continuity and vice-versa. Concepts of 'British power' and 'Indian resilience' start to look far more suspicious as ways of understanding the transition to colonialism through fiscalism. Revenue collection, the formation of agrarian settlements and, ultimately, the formation of the colonial state's bureaucracy represented neither change nor continuity. They were a finely balanced, symbiotic combination of both. They often worked hand in hand rather than in opposition to each other.

There is also the question of just how modern and premodern the early colonial state was. This book has suggested that the semantics of such categorizations can prove problematic. For one, the Indo-Islamic fiscal traditions were surprisingly 'modern' in the sense that they were paper-driven, moderately procedural and deliberative. Local negotiations and counsel were backed up with paper and 'proof'. The colonial state, though, made fiscal administration more procedural and depersonalized. In a way, it was the essence of the Weberian, rationalist state. But the British also, crucially, stunted so many dynamics in making it comprehensible and manageable. Flexibility in payment amounts (*qist*s) were reduced markedly, bureaucratic 'averaging' reduced the complexities of agrarian revenue and forecasting to unworkable simplicities, and the overall concern for the welfare of the *raiyat* – long a feature of Hindu and Muslim rulers – was wholly jettisoned. Indeed, if we compare the Company's fiscal state to Maratha country and Awadh, we get a deeper understanding of this. In many ways, the Maratha and Nawabi regions were more dynamic and fiscally flexible. But the Company exhibited features of both premodern and modern states. Satish Saberwal and Jan Heesterman have argued that the modern colonial state embraced both premodern and modern political and civic authority, ideologies and practice. They point to an emergent juncture between these two distinct traditions, generating contradictions that have spilled over into the very structure and functioning of the postcolonial state in modern India.[6] This echoes Frank Perlin's argument that the colonial state in India was inherently 'transitional'. It was neither fully 'modern' nor fully 'pre-modern'.[7] In some ways, we see this in north India. The fiscal state drew heavily upon officers of old, injecting their papers with legal value. At the same time, the papers became the basis for the Company's fiscal demands, with substantial numbers of Kayastha families continuing to serve as intermediaries between the ruling authority and the agrarian hinterlands. These fiscal workings were also modern in the sense that they rationally divorced taxing and documentation from personal ties and interactions. The fiscal state was, at best, a stunted transition that ultimately became consumed by its own procedural and paper-regulated logic.

From a fiscal perspective, the precolonial Indian state starts to look somewhat more 'modern'. Stewart Gordon has demonstrated how lean and efficient the administrative machinery was in west India before the 1810s.[8] The Marathas might have been called 'predatory', but their one-quarter tax (*chauth*) seems to have been light on the peasantry. We see similar dynamics in pre-1800 Awadh. Richard Barnett has argued that pre-British Awadh possessed an administrative strength that enabled it to last for so long against the Company's intrusions and machinations. Barnett describes a fiscalism which was light on the peasantry and not extractive enough to engender widespread agitation.[9] It maintained a great degree of stability. Perhaps this is why many aspects of Awadh's pre-1856 administrative fabric were retained and incorporated into North-Western Provinces and Oudh's fiscal apparatus. The *khusrah* surveys and the continuance of the Saxena Kayastha paper managers deep into the late nineteenth century illustrate this perfectly. The precolonial colour of Awadh's revenue administration, moreover, endured for longer than in the neighbouring south and east districts. This might partially explain why overall rates of tax were lower there than in the remainder of the Raj's Doabi territories.[10] From this perspective, the colonial state's regressive and predatory nature come into clearer focus. This is because the Company took the state in radically new directions. It taxed more ruthlessly, more efficiently and was heavy on the peasantry and India's cultivators. It wholly jettisoned the moral modifiers of Hanafi legal sanction and the interconnected constellation of revenue officials. The trumpeting of a 'written administration', 'statistical averages' and legal procedure coexisted, however paradoxically, with these very savage and inflexible tax demands. Indeed, the simmering agrarian discontent across the Doab after 1800 served as a regular illustration of this. The Company's fiscal 'system', in its need to document and tabulate every grain of India's wealth, was by the 1850s personnel-heavy and bloated, even if British administrators claimed to be 'trimming the fat' off the late Nawabi and Mughal corpses. It also had significant, reverberating effects across the countryside and north Indian economy in terms of demographics, migration patterns and the emergence of export-oriented cash-crop planting.

A new history of the scribe

This other main aim of this book has been to shed new light upon the history of the scribe as an active agent of change in India's history. These north Indian pensmen provided essential fiscal documentation and sanction to rulers in the eighteenth and nineteenth centuries, which, in turn, facilitated the emergence of modern paper-driven patterns of governance. Perhaps ironically, the very continuance of these scribes' valuable skills and information assisted the Company in enacting significant change. Here, again, we are brought to the symbiotic relationships between change and continuity. The British were fortunate, for they were able to corral these officers and weld their skills to state prerogatives with a newfound, intense regularity. They, in turn, helped the Company pump out substantial amounts of agrarian wealth, which was the blood in the veins of the colonial state. This wealth funded new law courts, the salaries of the ICS and the soldiers (*sipahi*s) who fought between Spion Kop and Singapore for the British flag. And unlike some Muslim sovereigns, the British had no qualms about utilizing the 'lowly wretch and impossessed' to enforce political authority through the payment of taxes. The Company's administrative 'matter-of-factness' also resonated well with Kayasthas, who by virtue of their own particular precolonial, more vocational-oriented learning experiences adjusted well to this new paper-oriented procedural system. Kayasthas' repository of paper skills meshed well with the procedural fiscal rhythms of Company governance. From one perspective, the subordinate levels of the Raj's bureaucracy by the 1870s distantly resembled Irfan Habib's 'second layer' of Mughal administration.[11]

Of course, this is not to overemphasize the threads that connected the late Mughal and early British empires. These pensmen did experience significant change. As *qanungo*s and *patwari*s, Kayasthas were transformed from Persian-literate gentlemen, who managed revenue and distantly symbolized courtly authority, to clerks who represented the emergent colonial state's bureaucratic, systemic utilitarian authority. Kayasthas became more regularized officers, bound by time sheets, increased paper regulation and, after the 1830s, a new official language of governance. And these Kayasthas had to be pragmatic. They sometimes aspired to reach the commanding heights of Islam's poetic and powerful, but they could only rise so far in the circles of Muslim power. Most did not convert to Islam,[12] and combined with their lack of landed, military and religious prowess this naturally limited their 'administrative worth'. It was much the same under the Raj: a glass ceiling kept the ICS and higher administration firmly in white British hands. And even if they managed to dominate those ICS positions that were technically open to Indians, Kayastha scribes bumped up against racial limits.

But this was far from the whole picture. Scribal skills in paper management, copying and verification, which provided livelihoods and honour, largely remained the same, even if their ends were more firmly anchored to the state. They experienced a qualified change that defied any simple categorization of either change or continuity. They were not a new type of lower administrator but, in a way, a refashioned one. And the effects were incomplete. Kayastha *qanungo*s and *patwari*s were far less common the farther the British travelled west from Benares. Around Delhi, Haryana and the upper Doab *qasbah* townships, lesser Muslim gentry families seem to have fared better than their counterparts farther southeast, where Kayasthas were more concentrated.

In tracking the experiences of Hindustan's paper managers, this book has attempted to build upon the literature on the scribe as a historical actor in India. For example, Karen Leonard has pointed to the continuance of a flourishing Indo-Islamic culture in Hyderabad, demonstrating how Kayastha scribes and pens-men were essential for the Nizam's administration.[13] In Hyderabad, the Nizam's sovereignty and courtly culture continued deep into the early twentieth century. But there were differences from the Doab. In the north this administrative culture had largely been extinguished by the 1830s. Here, we can discern a different *type* of continuity, whereby these scribes continued their skills as paper managers *in spite* of transformational political changes. There was also the question of demographics. Kayasthas were far more crucial for political sovereignty in north India due to their larger numbers. Unlike in Hyderabad, north Indian Kayasthas did not have to significantly compete for service posts via education until 1900.

More recent work by Rosalind O'Hanlon has shed light on how 'social worth' was shaped by competition between Prabhu Kayasthas and Chitpavan Brahmins for service posts in seventeenth-century Maratha domains. O'Hanlon has demonstrated that, because of west Indian Hindu kings' ritual affirmation and Kayasthas' twice-born (*dvija*) status, there were vibrant debates over the social worth of west Indian Kayasthas.[14] We can draw some interesting comparisons with north India here. For one, the Doabi Kayasthas faced far less competition for service posts than their equivalents in the west Maratha lands. Even at the height of Mughal power Kayasthas came to dominate so many subordinate positions within the wider machinery of revenue administration in the absence of service Brahmins. They were able to compete with minor Muslim gentry service families because they partially inserted themselves into an Indo-Islamic culture. In a way, Kayasthas had a relatively open field. This would partly explain why they became so valuable as British power expanded upcountry from Bengal. Also, the debates over Kayasthas' ambiguous *dvija* status did not get off the ground until the 1870s, whereas in the west Maratha lands they seem to have already been current by the late 1600s.

This book has also engaged with Bhavani Raman's recent work on south Indian scribes. Raman has painted a picture of a south Indian scribe's world being transformed by the changing value of paper and attestation in early colonial India. She has argued that changing values in paper, which ate away at the mnemonic traditions of Tamil scribes, led to a wholly altered world for south Indian scribes.[15] Again, comparisons with north Indian offer some interesting perspectives. For one, the social and caste composition of these scribes was different. In the Doab they were rarely Brahmin or high-caste. There was also a less well-entrenched Indo-Islamic administrative tradition in Tamil country, which partially explains the absence of mnemonic traditions that existed in the Tamil south and why the value of paper was bound to change. But in north India paper as an administrative tool *defined* the fiscalism of north India – for both Muslim and British rulers. Raman also seems to ascribe little agency to these scribes, seeing them as passive functionaries in a British-driven colonial state. This book, though, has argued that north Indian Kayasthas were able to shape substantial changes through their fiscal records, land acquisition and identification of further agricultural tracks for cultivation. By 1900 Kayasthas were so prominent as a 'service caste' that their ability to mould north India's governance led to numerous calls from British officialdom to cut their numbers down.

Some comparisons with Rajeev Kinra's recent work might also prove fruitful. Kinra has argued that through the Hindu scribe Chandar Bhan we can gain new perspectives on the values, civility (*akhlaq*) and mystical awareness (*marifat*) associated with Akbar's court. Kinra uses Bhan as an example to illustrate the cosmopolitan outlook of the Hindu scribe.[16] But this focus on Bhan has some limitations. For one, Bhan gives the view from a remarkably elite perspective. He was, after all, the chief secretary (*mir munshi*) of the Mughal court, far removed from the mundane ocean of revenue workings in which *patwari*s and *qanungo*s swam. Bhan was also, unusually, a Persian-literate Brahmin. Muslim sovereigns did not require ritual Brahmanical affirmation, unlike in the west Maratha lands, and north India's Brahmins were markedly absent from the wider workings of fiscal administration, particularly at the provincial and local levels. The gravitation of Kayasthas into the Indo-Islamic cultural-administrative world perhaps further hardened various Brahmin attitudes, associating Kayasthas with the 'immoral consumption' of north India's Turkic rulers.

The 'colonial archive', materiality and the bureaucratic state

In interpreting the origins of the colonial state, this book has sought new ways of viewing the origins of the state's archival depth. It has argued that the Company state's systematic and 'granular' accumulation of fiscal knowledge – soil qualities, leaseholders and seeds – unleashed unprecedented volumes of paperwork, regulation and procedure. The desire to know the 'state of the revenues' as fully as possible generated deep knowledge that was recorded, organized, indexed and made procedural. This was the beginning of the 'colonial archive'. The priorities of soil classification, well identification and the unlocking of the larger mysteries of proprietary rights were all paramount. Soils, grains and prices, after all, all fed into the master matrix of maximizing agrarian revenue, which had been the mainstay of Indian sovereigns since the eighteenth century. And it is here, more so than in the construction of abstract categories such as 'caste' and 'tribe', where the taxonomies of the colonial state came into their own. Horace Wilson's 1855 *Glossary of Judicial and Revenue Terms*, with its merging of the legal and fiscal worlds, is a perfect example.[17] The evidence here strongly suggests that the early formation of the colonial archive was born not so much out of a desire to categorize India along the lines of caste and 'community' but out of the pressing fiscal need to fund the early Company's military-fiscal state. Colonial ethnography and the social categorization of India, which scholars such as Nicholas Dirks[18] and Bernard Cohn[19] saw as crucial in colonial appropriations of Indian knowledge systems, played a relatively minor role. There was little concern with categorizing caste and language. It should also be stressed that the mundane pulse of daily administration more regularly affected the lives of cultivators and intermediaries than abstract racial or caste taxonomies. Categories of caste and ethnicity, which Dirks and Cohn saw as a result of the state's 'investigative modalities', were by-products of this whole process of 'fiscal archivization' rather than preconditions for it.

Of course, this larger accumulation of fiscal and agrarian knowledge – organized and indexed – was still impressive. It was breathtaking in its scope and ambition. The use of statistical averaging to make sense of historical crop yields and assessments was novel. The vast agrarian taxonomy and the formation of the colonial archive was awe-inspiring and voracious. But beneath the surface this taxonomical juggernaut masked crucial shortcomings of the colonial state. For one, paperwork, documented data and procedure gave the British a soothingly misleading sense of mastery. The whole system of paper accountability – whereby even the costs of surveying itself were averaged across parganas – bordered on the absurd. The morass of paperwork, duplications, attestation and deposited copies blinded them to the punishing assessments they made in the first place. Indeed, in the Company's new drive to know as much about India's agrarian economy as possible, their search for information that could be 'categorized' created the very conditions that stunted the long-standing flexibility of revenue collection in India. In a way, the colonial state was seductively hoodwinked by its own paper saturation. This above all reflected weakness, rather than mastery.

If we step back for a moment, a few observations can be made on the emergence of 'bureaucracy' in modern India. We have seen how eighteenth-century India was already moving towards what would later develop into bureaucracy. The Indo-Islamic traditions were well developed and the methods used for collecting revenue – paperwork, procedure and flexibility – were striking not just in administrative manuals (*dastur ul-amal*s) but also in general commentary. This was not wholly different from what the Company created in its Doabi domains. The British used paperwork and procedure in ways similar to their predecessors. But what distinguished the Company's application of fiscalism from previous Indian rulers was its anchoring in law and, tragically, inflexibility when faced with inability to pay. Eighteenth-century fiscal vocabularies of suasion were transformed into vocabularies of legalism. The accumulation of indexed and searchable knowledge, with its anchoring in legal procedure, ensured that the personalized elements of revenue administration noted by Shitab Rai and Muhammad Faiq were rendered unnecessary. The whole 'de-personalization' of fiscal administration by the Company through procedure paperwork rendered it mute to its moral failings. The famines that punctuated the nineteenth century in north India were stark testaments to this inflexibility.

The materiality of paper and its use, which was part of this accumulative body of fiscal knowledge, also *increased* in importance rather than being *changed* irrevocably. The Doab's residual eighteenth-century fiscal practices were becoming increasingly paper-intensive. Paper was part of the administrative fabric of north India by 1700, and its importance increased exponentially for sovereigns wanting to further document and assess their holdings. The Company's fiscalism ratcheted up the intensity and volume of paper in circulation to unthinkable degrees. But the value of paper did not change so much as its organization and systematization. What is more, the Company's paper fiscalism stimulated extant networks of paper production, procurement and refinement across north India, connecting Sialkot to Sylhet. For the first few generations of British rule, it was dependent upon Indian sources and networks of paper for the organization and accumulative sanction it needed. Local collectors also had to compete with market forces, which led to the creation of the category of 'stamped paper' to root out 'fraud'.

Yet the increased materiality of the Company's 'paper raj' also served as a precedent for the eventual ballooning of the fiscal state into the full-blown Raj, with its specialized departments, all backed by paper. The state's increasing functions, such as health, public works and education, all became bureaucratized via processed pulp. Much of this was guided and stimulated by the model of fiscal paper governance set by the Company. Indeed, the whole taxonomical, bureaucratic rhythms of later public works, including roads, a streamlined postal (*dak*) system and even public instruction were spawned from the wider reverberations of fiscalism's orbital weight. Roads, improved written communications and public instruction were all meant to contribute to more efficient, paper-driven and reliable revenue collection over which the colonial state exercised strong control.[20] Fiscal mastery was and would remain the primacy of the Raj. Dadabhai Naoroji's critique of the 'Home Charges' and Congress' anti-tax campaigns were both reminders of how the Raj's fiscal interests were ultimately unaligned with Indian well being.

Bureaucratic organization and the state

Engaging with literature on bureaucratic processes and organization should prove useful for historians of South Asia. In examining the functioning of bureaucracy in contemporary Pakistan, Matthew Hull has demonstrated that paper-based bureaucracies are not static, immovable behemoths. Rather, they are entities that respond to, and are shaped by, local events and characters. Hull sees bureaucratic texts produced through the shaping ethos of a region's culture, society and religion.[21] We see some of these dynamics in colonial India. For one, while the power of procedure and verification were unprecedented in India's history, we see so many instances where the fiscal regime of the Company was shaped by Indian dynamics, not least the role Hindustan's scribes played in colouring the regime, particularly in the Doab and Awadh after 1860. *Jamabandi*s and *hastobud*s served as the statistical bases for revenue demands, while large elements of the *khusrah* surveys – which were themselves a cultural expression of space and value – were incorporated into fiscal sinews of north India. In a way, the Doab's eventual, immovable bureaucracy represented a longer, drawn-out stitching together of various British and Indo-Indian elements.

Our present work here can also be enriched by engaging with the broader literature on bureaucracy and economic formation beyond the South Asian context. David Allen's recent work on the 'institutional revolutions' of modern economies has argued that the emergence of measuring and standardization was crucial in the rise of modern states. He notes that the main aim of modern institutions that measure, quantify and render comprehensible was to eliminate the variability of routine and irregularity.[22] Colonial India was a perfect example, seen in the Company's drive for accuracy, regularity and reliability. 'Averages' and paperwork were to whisk away the vagaries of the monsoon, often at a pen stroke. The British ruthlessly eliminated the numerous gaps and 'irregularities' of the fiscal-agrarian world: between assessment and collection, between knowledge of past and present tax rates and between Indian 'mendaciousness' and British 'truthfulness'. Along these lines, Ben Kafka's recent work sees the emergence of modern paper-oriented bureaucracy as bound up with the drive of modern states to be accountable to their peoples, originating with Revolutionary France. According to Kafka, this produced an exponentially ballooning, almost absurd volume of paperwork, which overwhelmed its managers.[23] India, though, was rather a different case. It saw an explosion of paperwork not to manage its *citizens* but to govern and extract agrarian wealth from its *subjects*. Paper was used as much to subjugate as it was to hold governments accountable. Michael Crozier's classic work on bureaucracy also has strong echoes in the Indian case. Crozier has argued that bureaucratic structures possess a 'maladaptive behavior': that is they cannot adjust and learn from mistakes made.[24] While they keep their composite 'members' such as clerks and administrators content, larger paper- and procedural-based institutions cannot make structural changes that might improve the function and efficiency of the whole structure. One the one hand, the importance of Indian revenues was perhaps the impetus for the Raj's 'maladaptive behavior'. On the other, the whole fiscal-bureaucratic system echoed Crozier's insight that larger bureaucratic structures, in order to maintain the status quo, never learn from 'mistakes'. The famines and dearth that punctuated nineteenth-century north India were the outcomes of statistical averaging, inflexibility and the 'scientific basis' of assessments. This fiscal-status-quo boat would not be rocked until Gandhi's campaigns after 1920.

Alvin Gouldner also offers some interesting perspectives for historians of South Asia. Gouldner's analysis of various strands of bureaucracy has highlighted a concept he calls 'representative bureaucracy', whereby rules and regulations emerge through some common agreement.[25] We see shades of this in colonial India. While not an 'agreement' per se, the ways in which the early Company state significantly drew upon extant scribal communities and their fiscal information were a result of an encounter between Indian paperwork and scribes and British interests and governing forms. They were the product of a fusion of late Indo-Islamic fiscal trends and paperwork and a British obsession with paper verification, the inviolability of procedure, and certainty. This may not have been an 'agreement' but more a 'merging' of various strands in the late eighteenth and early nineteenth centuries.

Of course, the ghost of Max Weber hangs over any discussion on bureaucracy and organizational rationality. Weber's concept of 'rational-legal authority',[26] and the separation of personal from official property rights, does seem to have echoes in the Indian context. This book has argued that the dichotomy between a traditional 'patrimonial bureaucracy' and modern, rationalist bureaucracy in the late-Mughal period looks suspicious. This is partially because eighteenth-century India was already paper-intensive, and regional kingdoms were becoming increasingly so. The British did 'rationalize' this system to some degree between 1780 and 1830. The legal anchoring of fiscalism was a perfect example of this, as was the reduction in the number of subordinate Indian revenue officers whose very job was to negotiate among a constellation of parties and stakeholders. This eliminated the 'moral binding' that defined eighteenth-century revenue traditions and hence rendered it impersonal. But the specific documentation and fiscal intelligence sought out by the British (*jamabandi*s and *hastobud*s held by *qanungo*s) were to a degree already de-personalized. This is precisely why the Company state sought out *qanungo*s and *patwari*s – their utility had long been based in being a statistical 'refugee of the husbandman' rather than as moral adjudicator of rights and wrongs. So the Company's *kaghaz raj* was, in a way, only partially Weberian. But perhaps most importantly, as this book has argued, the whole process of bureaucratization was not simply an appendage of larger changes in state formation in late-eighteenth- and early-nineteenth-century India. Paper, agrarian wealth and their management were the beating heart of state formation. The mastery of fiscalism though paper was central to the rise of the East India Company's empire and the emergence of modern forms of Indian state organization.

Notes

1 W. Hunter, *Readings in Indian History* (Calcutta, 1891), p. 62.
2 M. Alam, *The Crisis of Empire in Mughal North India* (Delhi, 1986), p. 315.
3 C. Bayly, *Empire and Information: Intelligence Gathering and Social Communication in India, 1780–1870* (Cambridge, 1997).
4 S. Alavi, *The Sepoys and the Company: Tradition and Transition in Northern India, 1770–1830* (Delhi, 1995).
5 A. Yang, *Limited Raj: Agrarian Relations in Colonial India, Saran District, 1793–1920* (Berkeley, 1989).
6 See the essays in M. Doornbos and S. Kaviraj, eds. *Dynamics of State Formation: Europe and India Compared* (London, 1998), particularly those by J. Heesterman, S. Eisenstadt and H. Hartman.
7 F. Perlin, 'The pre-colonial Indian state in history and epistemology', in H. Claessen and P. Skalnik, eds. *The Study of the State* (The Hague, 1981), pp. 295–7.
8 S. Gordon, *Marathas, Marauders and State Formation in Eighteenth Century India* (Delhi, 1994).
9 R. Barnett, *North India between Empires: Awadh, the Mughals, and the British, 1720–1801* (Berkeley, 1980).
10 P. Penner and R. Maclean, *The Rebel Bureaucrat: Frederick John Shore as Critic of William Bentick's India* (Delhi, 1983), p. 215.
11 I. Habib, *The Agrarian System of Mughal India* (Delhi, 1999), p. 331.
12 Dr Vibhuti Rai and Sri Sampal Rai, Lucknow, 2006, 2007, 2008; Dr Raj and Mrs Naheed Verma, Lucknow, 2006, 2007, 2008; Ms Rakhi Reshmi, New Delhi, 2008, 2009, London, 2010, 2012.
13 K. Leonard, *Social History of an Indian Caste: the Kayasths of Hyderabad* (Berkeley, 1980).

14 R. O'Hanlon, 'The social worth of scribes: Brahmins, Kayasthas and the social order in early modern India', *IESHR* 47, 4 (2010), pp. 563–5.
15 B. Raman, *Document Raj: Writing and Scribes in Early Colonial South India* (Chicago, 2012).
16 R. Kinra, *Writing Self, Writing Empire: Chandar Bhan Brahman and the Cultural World of the Indo-Persian State Secretary* (Berkeley, 2015).
17 H. Wilson, *Glossary of Judicial and Revenue Terms* (London, 1855).
18 N. Dirks, *Castes of Mind: Colonialism and the Making of Modern India* (Princeton, 2001).
19 B. Cohn, *Colonialism and Its Forms of Knowledge: The British in India* (Princeton, 1996), p. 5.
20 See *Directions for Revenue Officers in the North-Western Provinces of the Bengal Presidency* (Calcutta, 1858), pp. 100–40, in particular.
21 M. Hull, *Government of Paper: the Materiality of Bureaucracy in Urban Pakistan* (Berkeley, 2012).
22 D. Allen, *The Institutional Revolution: Measurement and the Economic Emergence of the Modern World* (Chicago, 2012).
23 B. Kafka, *The Demon of Writing: Powers and Failures of Paperwork* (New York, 2012).
24 M. Crozier, *The Bureaucratic Phenomenon* (Chicago, 1964).
25 A. Gouldner, *Patterns of Industrial Bureaucracy* (Glencoe, 1954).
26 See, for example, M. Weber, *Economy and Society* (*Wirtschaft und Gesellschaft*), G. Roth and C. Wittich, trans. (Berkeley, 1978).

Glossary

Akhbarnavis	newswriter in Mughal India
Amils	collector or official
Audalat	court
Bandobast	'agreed and closed', referring to assessment rates
Dar ul-Insha	Department of Correspondence
Daul	an estimate
Hastobud	'is and was', historical rent roll
Hukum	order
Insha	art of letter writing
Jama	assessment
Jamabandi	revenue agreement
Kayastha	scribal groups in north India
Khazana	treasury
Kist	instalment
Kistibandi	instalment agreement
Khufianavis	secret-letter writer in Mughal India
Khurif	late-summer-to-early-fall harvest
Khusrah	precolonial form of surveying often done by *qanungo*s
Maktab	primary school where Persian was taught
Malguzar	one who takes the wealth, or 'mal' – equivalent to a tax collector
Mansabdars	military officers in Mughal India
Mosibat	disaster
Mauziah	neighbourhood
Mukhtarkar	revenue officer
Nastaliq	Persian variant of the Arabic script
Pargana	lowest administrative subdivision
Patta	lease to cultivate
Patwari	local revenue chief in a village
Qabooliyat	agreement to pay revenue
Qanungo	'of the law', subordinate revenue position
Qasbah	medium-sized urban township
Rabi	spring harvest

Raiyat/mazarian	cultivators, common folk
Raqba	total cultivated land area
Sarkar	official
Siyaqi	accountancy
Shikasta	'broken', version of the Perso-Arabic script
Samghi	ink
Takfif	discount
Wasilbaki	balance statement
Yaddasht	note, memorandum

Bibliography

Archival sources

British Library, London – East India Company Records
Agra Revenue Proceedings, 1834–6
Bengal Board of Revenue Proceedings, Ceded & Conquered Provinces, 1803–22
Bengal Board of Revenue Proceedings, Western Provinces, 1822–31
Bihar & Benares Revenue Proceedings, 1816–22
Ceded & Conquered Provinces Revenue Proceedings, 1804–15
NWP Revenue Proceedings, 1836–77
NWP Sadr Board of Revenue Proceedings, 1836–58
Uttar Pradesh State Record Office, Lucknow
NWP & O Selections from Vernacular Newspapers
NWP & O GAD, Local Self-Government and Municipal Proceedings (select)
National Archives of India, New Delhi
Foreign Department, Political Consultations

Oriental manuscripts

India Office Library, London
Mss. ADD. 6586, Fol. 53–73, 'Opinion of some natives, not names, on the rules to be observed for a proper collection of revenue in Bengal, in 24 articles'
Mss. 7052, 1788, Fol. 1–165, 'Copy of Kishen Chand's (*qanungo* of Rakimpur) answer to queries put to him by the Board of Revenue on the subject of the Dinagipur Hustabud) papers' Add. 6588, 'Khulasatu-i-Siyaq'
Add. 22831, Fol. 6a–19b, 'Dastur ul-Amal-Shahanshahi', (Account of the Provinces of Hindustan'), Thakur Lal, 1778
OR. 1750, Fol. 162, Sanbhu Lal, 'Miftah-i-Khanzain', 1782
OR. 2011, Fol. 111, Chatar Mal, 'Diwan-i-Pasand, nineteenth century
Bodleian Library, Oxford
Narain, *Ta'rikh-i-Jadid*, 'A history of the Nawabs of Oudh from the time of Sa'adat Khan down to the death of Asaf ud-Daula', 1787
Kumar, *Sultan al-hikayat* ('A concise history of Oudh'), 1853

Unpublished Mss. in Oriental languages

Sri Sampal Rai, Lucknow, *Sri Ganeshya Nam*, 1911, Mss. in author's possession

Personal interviews, 2004–14

Ram Advani, Lucknow, 2003, 2004, 2006, 2008
Sampal and Vibhuti Rai Dr, Lucknow, 2004, 2006, 2008
Raj and Naheed Verma, Lucknow, 2004, 2006, 2008
Rakhi Rashmi, New Delhi, 2008, 2009; London, 2010, 2012, 2014
Ajay Srivastava, Annapolis, MD, 2012

European Mss., India Office Library, London

Mss. Eur F218/30, 'Translation of a Persian petition from the native inhabitants of the Subah of Azeemabad to the King', 1772

Unpublished Mss. in European languages

N. Haidar, 'Persian newsletters', unpublished Mss in author's possession
N. Haidar, 'Language, caste and the secretarial class in Mughal India', unpublished Mss. in author's possession

Oriental-language printed works (Persian, Hindi and Urdu)

Fisher, M., 'The imperial court and the province: a social and administrative history of pre-British Awadh, 1775–1856', unpublished PhD dissertation, University of Chicago, 1978
Kishore, N., *Allah Kudae'i* ('Allah is the God') (Lucknow, 1869)
Prasad, C., *Citragupta mahaparivara ka itihasa* (History on Chitragupta and his descendants) (Patna, 1986)
Faiq, M., *Insha-ye-Faiq* ('Composition of Faiq') (Lucknow, 1880)
Narayan, L., *Ruqat-i-Lachmi Narayana* ('Letters by Lakshmi Narayana') (Lucknow, 1880)
Prashad, S., *Quam-i-Kayastha* ('The Kayastha community') (Jaunpur, 1920)
Shauk, D., *Jawahir-i-Manzouma va Merat al-Sarf* ('Treasure of writings and the observance of grammar') (Kanpur, 1878)

Periodicals

Asiatic Researches
Comparative Studies of South Asia, Africa and the Middle East Imperial Gazetteer of India
Indian Antiquary
Indian Economic and Social History Review
International Review of Social History
Journal of Bihar Research Society
Journal of the American Oriental Society
Journal of Asian Studies
Journal of the Asiatic society of Bengal
Kayastha
Kayastha Samachar
Modern Asian Studies
Proceedings of the Indian Historical Records Commission (IHRC)

European-language works to c. 1920

A Short Account of the Aims, Objects and Proceedings of the Kayastha Conference, etc. (Allahabad, 1893)

Agnew, V., *A Report on the Subha or Province of Chhattisgarh written in 1820* AD (Nagpur, 1915)

Allen, C., *Accountant's Manual for Collectors and other Officers in Charge of Treasuries in the North-Western Provinces* (Agra, 1847)

Blochman, H., trans., *The Ain-i-Akbari* (London, 1873)

Butler, D., *Outlines of the Topography and Statistics of the Southern Districts of Oudh* (Calcutta, 1839)

Carnegy, P., *Notes on the Races, Tribes and Castes Inhabiting the Province of Oudh* (Lucknow, 1868)

Chatterjee, T., trans., *Seir Mutaqherin* (Calcutta, 1902)

Connell, C.J., *Land Revenue Policy – Northern India* (Calcutta, 1876)

Crooke, W. *The North-Western Provinces of India: Their History, Ethnology, and Administration* (London, 1897)

Cust, R., *Questions on the Subjects Treated of in the Directions for Revenue Officers* (Agra, 1853)

Cust, R., *Directions for Revenue Officers in the North-Western Provinces of the Bengal Presidency* (Calcutta, 1858)

Elliot, C., *Chronicles of Oonao* (Allahabad, 1862)

Elliot, H. *Memoirs on the History, Folklore and Distribution of the Races of the North Western Provinces of India* (London, 1869)

Ghulam, H., *A Translation of the Sëir mutaqharín* (Calcutta, 1902)

Grierson, G., *Bihar Peasant Life* (Calcutta, 1885)

Gubbins, M., *Report on the Settlement of Zillah Etawah* (Agra, 1844)

Gupte, T.V., *Ethnographic Notes on Prabhu Kayasthas* (Pune, 1904)

Hooper, W., *Final Report of the Settlement of the Basti District* (Allahabad, 1891)

Hoey, W., trans., *Memoirs of Delhi and Faizabad, Being a Translation of the 'Tarikh Farahbakhsh' of Muhammed Faiz Bakhsh* (Allahabad, 1888)

Hooker, J., *The Flora of British India*, 2 Vols. (London, 1871)

Hunter, W., *Readings in Indian History* (Calcutta, 1899)

Hussain, H., trans., *The Mirza Nama* (London, 1913)

Irwin, H.C., *The Garden of India, or Chapters on Oudh History and Affairs* (London, 1880)

Jaffar, S.M., *Some Cultural Aspects of Muslim Rule in India*

Kale, V., *Indian Administration* (Pune, 1915)

Kaye, J., *Memorials of Indian Government: Being a Selection from the Papers of H. St. G. Tucker* (London, 1853)

Maclagan, E., *Punjab Census Report Vol. XIX*, (Peshawar, 1891)

Malcolm, J., *Memoir of Central India, including Malwa, and Adjoining Provinces* (London, 1832)

Martin, M., *The History, Antiquities, Topography and Statistics of Eastern India* (London, 1838)

Martin, R., *The Indian Empire* (London, 1858)

Mill, J.S., *Memorandum of the Improvements in the Administration of India during the Last Thirty Years* (London, 1858)

Millet, A., *Report on the Settlement of the Land Revenue of the Fyzabad Sistrict* (Allahabad, 1880)

Papers Related to Land Tenures and Revenue Settlements in Oude (Calcutta, 1865)
Permanent and Temporary Settlements, North-Western Provinces (Allahabad, 1873)
Prasad, K., *The Kayastha Ethnology, an Inquiry into the Origin of the Chitraguptavansi and Chandrasenavansi Kayasthas* (Lucknow, 1877)
Reports on the Revenue Settlement of the North Western Provinces of the Bengal Presidency, under Regulation IX, 1833 (Benares, 1863)
Rose, H., *Report on the Settlement of the District of Cawnpore* (Agra, 1842)
Russell, H., Lal, H., *The Tribes and Castes of the Central Provinces of India* (London 1916)
Saletore, G., ed., *Banaras Affairs (1788–1810)* (Allahabad, 1955)
Saletore, G., *Ancient Indian Political Thought and Institutions* (Bombay, 1963)
Sarkar, J., *History of Aurangzib, Mainly Based on Persian Sources*, four vols. (Patna, 1912)
Sarkar, J., *The India of Aurangzib* (Calcutta, 1901)
Saxena, L., *A Short History of Temperance Reform in the Kayastha Community* (Agra, 1911)
Selected Reports, on the Revision of Settlement under Regulation IX. of 1833, in the Delhie Territory (Agra, 1846)
Selections from Revenue Records (Calcutta, 1866)
Selections from the Revenue Records of the North-West Provinces, 1818–1820, Preceding the Enactment of Regulation VII, 1822 (Calcutta, 1866)
Sen, J., *History of Elementary Education in India* (Calcutta, 1933)
Settlement Report of the District of Moozuffernugger (Allahabad, 1873)
Settlements of the North-Western Provinces: Dispatch of the Court of Directors, 13 August 1851 (London, 1851)
Shakespear, A., *Selections from the Duncan Records*, two vols. (Benares, 1873)
Sherring, M., *Hindu Tribes and Castes as Represented in Benares* (London, 1872)
Sinha, S., *Caste Conferences and National Progress: Presidential Address Delivered by Sachchidananda Sinha at the Thirty-fifth session of the All-India Kayastha Conference held at Delhi on the 29th March 1929* (Delhi, 1929)
Sleeman, W., *Ramblings and Recollections of an Indian Official* (London, 1844)
Sleeman, W., *A Journey through the Kingdom of Oude 1849–50*, two vols. (London, 1858)
Solvyns, B., *The Costume of Hindostan* (London, 1807)
Spry, H.H. *Modern India: with Illustrations of the Resources and Capabilities of Hindustan* (London, 1837)
Shrivastava, K., *The Hindu Sociology: Being a Treatise on the Social Position of the Kayastha Community* (Benares, 1913)
The Indian Decisions (New Series): Being a Re-print of All the Decisions of the Privy Council on Appeals from India and of the Various High Courts and Other Superior Courts in India Reported Both in the Official and Non-official Reports from 1875 (Madras, 1913)
Thomas, E., *The Revenue Resources of the Mughal Empire in India* (London, 1871)
Thornton, J., *Report of the Settlement of Seharanpore* (Agra, 1840)
Thomason, J., *Report of the Collector of Azimgurh on the Settlement of... Chuklah Azimgurh* (Agra, 1837)
Thomason, J., *Direction for Settlement Officers and Collectors of Land Revenue* (Agra, 1849)
Thomason, J., *Despatches: Selections from the Records of Government, NWP* (Calcutta, 1856)
Thornton, T., *The East Indian Calculator* (London, 1823)

Thornton, E., *Report of the Settlement of the District of Seharanpore* (Agra, 1840)

Translation of a Proceeding Regarding the Settlement of a Village According to the System Pursued in the North-Western Provinces (Agra, 1847)

Tucker, H., *The Trial of Henry St. Geo. Tucker, Esq. for an Assault, with Intent to Commit Rape, on the Person of Mrs. Dorothea Simpson: Held in the Supreme Court of Judicature at Fort William in Bengal* (London, 1810)

Tucker, H., *A Review of the Financial Situation of the East India Company, in 1824* (London 1825)

Verelst, H., *A View of the Rise, Progress and Present State of the English Government in Bengal* (London, 1772)

White, W., *The Prince of Oude* (London, 1838)

Wilson, H., *Glossary of Judicial and Revenue Terms* (London, 1855)

Zaidpuri, G.H., *Riyazu-a-Salatan*, M.A. Salam, trans. (Calcutta, 1904)

European-language secondary works after c. 1920

Ahmad, M., *System of Education in Medieval India, 1526 to 1761* AD (New Delhi, 1987)

Alam, M., *Crisis of Empire in Mughal North India: Awadh and the Punjab, 1707–1748.* (Delhi, 1986)

Alam, M., *The Languages of Political Islam: India, 1200–1800* (Chicago, 2004)

Alam, M. 'The pursuit of Persian: language in Mughal politics', *Modern Asian Studies* 32 (1998): 317–49

Alavi, S., *The Sepoys and the Company: Tradition and Transition in Northern India, 1770–1830* (Delhi, 1995)

Alavi, S., ed., *The Eighteenth Century in India* (Oxford, 2008)

Allen, D., *The Institutional Revolution: Measurement and the Economic Emergence of the Modern World* (Chicago, 2011)

Alvi, S.S., trans., *Mauizah-i-Jahangiri* ('Advice on the Art of Governance') (Albany, 1989)

Asher, C. and Talbot, C., *India before Europe* (Cambridge, 2006)

Baillie, N., *Mohammadan Laws on Land Tax According to the Moohummudan Law: Translated from the Futawa Alumgeeree* (Quetta, 1979)

Barnett, R., *North India Between Empires: Awadh, the Mughals, and the British, 1720–1801* (Berkeley, 1980)

Basu, P., *Oudh and the East India Company* (Lucknow, 1943)

Bayly, C.A., *Empire and Information: Intelligence Gathering and Social Communication in India, 1780–1870* (Cambridge, 1996)

Bayly, C.A., *Rulers, Townsmen and Bazaars: North Indian Society in the Age of British Expansion* (Cambridge, 1983)

Bellenoit, H., *Missionary Education and Empire in Late Colonial India, 1860–1920* (London, 2007)

Bhattacharya, B., *Danasagara of Ballalal Sena* (Calcutta, 1956)

Burton, A., *Dwelling in the Archive* (Oxford, 2003)

Chabra, G., *Advanced Study in the History of Modern India Vol. II, (1813–1920)* (Jullundur, 1962)

Chatterjee, K., *Merchants, Politics, and Society in Early Modern India: Bihar, 1733–1820* (Leiden, 1996)

Chatterjee, K., 'History as self-representation: the recasting of political tradition in late eighteenth century eastern India', *MAS* 32, 4 (1998): 913–48

Chatterjee, K., 'Scribal elites in Sultanate and Mughal Bengal', *IESHR* 47, 2 (2010): 445–72
Cohn, B., *Colonialism and Its Forms of Knowledge: The British in India* (Princeton, 1996)
Cohn, B., 'From Indian status to British contract', *Journal of Economic History* 21, 4 (1961): pp. 613–28
Cohn, B., 'The initial British impact on India: a case study of the Benares region', *Journal of Asian Studies* xix (1960): 418–31
Cohn, B., 'Political systems in eighteenth century India: the Benares region', *Journal of Asian Studies* 19, 4 (1962): 418–31
Cole, J., *Roots of North Indian Shi'ism in Iran and Iraq: Religion and State in Awadh, 1722–1859* (Berkeley, 1988)
Colebrook's Translation of the Lilavati (New Delhi, 1993)
Court, H., trans., *Araish-i-Mahfil* ('The Ornament of the Assembly') (Calcutta, 1882)
Dale, S.F., *Indian Merchants and Eurasian Trade, 1600–1750* (Cambridge, 1994)
Dalmia, V., *The Nationalisation of Hindu Tradition* (New Delhi, 1997)
Dirks, N., *Castes of Mind: Colonialism and the Making of Modern India* (Princeton, 2001)
Doornbos, M. and Kaviraj, S., eds, *Dynamics of State Formation: Europe and India Compared* (London, 1998)
Encyclopaedic Dictionary of Medieval India: Mirat-ul-istilah (Delhi, 1993)
Faruqi, M., *Crafting Traditions: Documenting Trades and Crafts in 19th Century North India* (New Delhi, 2005)
Fisher, M., *The Travels of Dean Mahomet* (Berkeley, 1997)
Ghani, M.A., *Pre-Mughal Persian in Hindustan* (Allahabad, 1941)
Gopal, *Munshi Premchand* (New York, 1964)
Gordon, S., *Marathas, Marauders and State Formation in 18th Century India* (Delhi, 1994)
Guha, R., *A Rule of Property for Bengal: An Essay on the Idea of Permanent Settlement* (Chapel Hill, 1996)
Habib, I., *Medieval India: The Study of a Civilization* (Delhi, 2007)
Habib, I., *The Agrarian System of Mughal India, 1556–1707* (Delhi, 1999)
Hadi, N., *Dictionary of Indo-Persian Literature* (Delhi, 1995)
Haidar, N., 'Norms of professional excellence and good conduct in accountancy manuals of the Mughal Empire', *International Research on Social History* 56 (2011): 263–74
Hanaway, W. and Spooner, B., eds, *Literacy in the Persianate World* (Philadelphia, 2012)
Gilmartin, D. and Lawrence, B.B., eds, *Beyond Turk and Hindu: Rethinking Religious Identities in Islamicate South Asia* (Gainesville, 2000)
Hooker, J., *The Flora of British India*, two vols. (London, 1871)
Hull, M., *Government of Paper: the Materiality of Bureaucracy in Urban Pakistan* (Berkeley, 2012)
Hutton, J., *Caste in India: Its Nature, Function and Origins* (Cambridge 1946)
Jafar, S.M., *Education in Muslim India* (Peshawar, 1936)
Jalal, A., *Self and Sovereignty: Individual and Community in South Asian Islam since 1850* (London, 2001)
Kaul, A., *The Kashmiri Pandit* (London, 1924)
Khan, G., *History of Islamic Education in India and Nadaut ul-ulama* (Delhi, 2004)
Khan, H., trans., *Translation of Maharajah Kalyan Singh's Khulasat-it-Tawarikh* (n.d.)
Kidwai, S., *Gilchrist and the Language of Hindoostan* (New Delhi, 1972)
Lee, C.J., 'How to do things with words: African oral history and its textual incarnations', *Journal of the International Oral History Association* 4, 1–2 (November 2007–November 2008)

Kaviraj, S., 'On the construction of colonial power: structure, discourse, hegemony', in *Contesting Colonial Hegemony: State and Society in Africa and India*, D. Engels and S. Marks, eds (London, 1994)

Khobrakar, V., ed., *English Translation of Tarikh-i-Dilkasha* (Bombay, 1972)

Kinra, R., *Writing Self, Writing Empire: Chandar Bhan Brahman and the Cultural World of the Indo-Persian State Secretary* (Berkeley, 2015)

Kolff, D., *Grass in Their Mouths: The Upper Doab of India under the Company's Magna Charta, 1793–1830* (Leiden, 2010)

Lakhnawi, S.D. and Ashair, S.H., trans., *Shahnama Munawar Kalam* (Patna, 1980)

Law, N.M., *Promotion of Learning in India during Muhammedan Rule* (London, 1910)

Leonard, K., *Social History of an Indian Caste: the Kayasths of Hyderabad* (Berkeley, 1978)

Makdisi, G., *The Rise of Colleges: Institutions of Learning in Islam and the West* (Edinburgh, 1981)

Mallat, C., *Islam and Public Law* (London, 1993)

Mann, M., *British Rule on Indian Soil* (New Delhi, 1999)

Mann, M., *Britischen Herrschaft auf Indischem Boden: Landwirtsschaftliche Transformation und ökologische Destruktion des 'Central Doab' 1801–1854* (Stuttgart, 1992)

Masudi, M., *Culturology of Persian in Kashmir* (Srinagar, 1997)

Mehta, J., *Advanced Study in the History of Modern India: Vol. II, the Mughal Empire (1526–1707)* (New Delhi, 1981)

Messick, B.M., *The Calligraphic State: Textual Domination and History in a Muslim Society* (Berkeley, 1993)

Migdal, J., *State in Society: Studying How States and Societies Transform and Constitute One Another* (Cambridge, 2001)

Mishra, H.K., *Bureaucracy under the Mughals 1556–1707* (Delhi, 1997)

Mishra, P.L., *The Political History of Chattisgarh (1740–1858 AD)* (Nagpur, 1979)

Misra, B., *Judicial Administration of the East India Company in Bengal, 1765–1782* (Delhi, 1961)

Moin, A., *The Millennial Sovereign* (Berkeley, 2014)

Mueller, C., *The Politics of Communication; a Study in the Political Sociology of Language, Socialization, and Legitimation* (New York, 1973)

Muhammed, K., *Tazkirat-ul-ulama: A Memoir of the Learned Men (of Jaunpur)* (Calcutta, 1934)

Mukhopadhyaya, A., *Reform and Regeneration in Bengal* (Calcutta, 1968)

Nanavaty, J., *Educational Thought* (Pune, 1973)

Nurullah, S., *A History of Education in India* (Bombay, 1951)

Ogborn, M., *Indian Ink: Script and Print in the Making of the English East India Company* (Chicago, 2007)

Oldenberg, V., *The Making of Colonial Lucknow, 1856–77* (Princeton, 1984)

Owens, R.L. and Nandy, A., *The New Vaisyas* (Bombay, 1977)

Pandey, A., *The Trial and Acquittal of Raja Shitab Rai* (New Delhi, 2011)

Parekh, B.C., *The Indian Family* (Southall, 1977)

Penner, P., *Patronage Bureaucracy in North India: the Robert M. Bird and James Thomason School, 1820–1870* (Delhi, 1986)

Penner, P. and Maclean, R., *The Rebel Bureaucrat: Frederick John Shore as Critic of William Bentick's India* (Delhi, 1983)

Perlin, F., 'State formation reconsidered', *MAS* 19, 3: 415–80

Pernou, M. and Jaffey, Y., eds, *Information and the Public Sphere: Persian Newsletters from Delhi* (New Delhi, 2008)
Potter, D.C., *India's Political Administrators: from ICS to IAS* (Delhi, 1996)
Prasad, G., *Bureaucracy in India: a Sociological Study* (New Delhi, 1974)
Raghuvanshi, V., *Indian Society in the Eighteenth Century* (New Delhi, 1969)
Rahit, A., *Tarikh Badshan Begam* ('A Persian Manuscript on the History of Oudh'), M.T. Ahmad, trans. (Allahabad, 1938)
Raman, B., *Document Raj: Writing and Scribes in Early Colonial South India* (Chicago, 2012)
Rahman, P., *Islamic Calligraphy in Medieval India* (Dhaka, 1979)
Rizvi, S.A.A., *Shah Wali-Allah and His Times* (Canberra, 1980)
Robinson, F., *Separatism among Indian Muslims: the Politics of the United Provinces' Muslims, 1860–1923* (Cambridge, 1974)
Robinson, F., *The Ulama of Firangi Mahall and Islamic Culture in South Asia* (New Delhi, 2001)
Saletore, G., ed., *Banaras Affairs (1788–1810)* (Allahabad, 1955)
Saran, P., *The Provincial Government of the Mughals* (Allahabad, 1941)
Sarkar, J., *India through the Ages: a Survey of the Growth of Indian Life and Thought* (Calcutta, 1928)
Sarkar, J., *Mughal Administration* (Patna, 1925)
Sarkar, J., *Bengal Nawabs* (Calcutta, 1952)
Sarkar, J., *Persian Records of Maratha History* (Bombay, 1953)
Sharar, A., *Lucknow: the Last Phase of an Oriental Culture* (Delhi, 1989)
Sen, S.N., *Scientific and Technical Education in India, 1781–1900* (New Delhi, 1991)
Siddiqi, A.R., *The Story of Islamic Calligraphy* (Delhi, 1990)
Singh, J., *Verbal Testimony in Indian Philosophy* (Delhi, 1990)
Sinha, B.P., *Kayasthas in the Making of Modern India* (Patna, 2003)
Singha, R., *A Despotism of Law: Crime and Justice in Early Colonial India* (Oxford, 1998)
Spangenberg, B., *British Bureaucracy in India: Status, Policy, and the I.C.S. in the Late 19th Century* (New Delhi, 1976)
Spears, M. *The Wasikadars of Awadh: a History of Certain Nineteenth Century Families of Lucknow* (New Delhi, 2008)
Srivastava, A.L., *The First Two Nawabs of Oudh* (Lucknow, 1933)
Stark, U., *Empire of Books* (Ranikhet, 2007)
Stern, P., 'Rethinking institutional transformations in the making of modern empire', *Journal of Colonialism and Colonial History* Fall (2008)
Stokes, E., *The English Utilitarians and India* (Oxford, 1959)
Stokes, E., *The Peasant and Raj* (Cambridge, 1979)
Sufi, G., *al-Minhaj: Being the Evolution of Curriculum in the Muslim Educational Institutions of India* (Delhi 1941)
Suri, P., *Social Conditions in Eighteenth Century Northern India* (Delhi, 1977)
Tibawi, A., *Arabic and Islamic Themes* (London, 1976)
Travers, R., *Ideology and Empire in Eighteenth Century India* (Cambridge, 2007)
Umar, M., *Islam in Northern India during the Eighteenth Century* (New Delhi, 1993)
Vansina, J., *Oral Tradition: A Study in Historical Methodology*, H.M. Wright, trans. (London, 1965)
Verma, C., *A Peep into the Origin, Status and History of the Kayasthas* (Bareli, 1929)
Weber, M., *Economy and Society (Wirtschaft und Gesellchaft)*, G. Roth and C. Wittich, trans. (Berkeley, 1978)

Yang, A., *Limited Raj: Agrarian Relations in Colonial India, Saran District, 1793–1920* (Berkeley, 1989)
Yasin, M., *A Social History of Islamic India* (Lucknow, 1958)

Index

Note: tables are indicated in bold, figures and illustrations in italics.

adoption and the Kayasthas 173–4
Agra district 100, 159–60
agrarian knowledge and the Kayastha scribal caste 40–1
agrarian output and Mughal revenue collection 19–23, *22,* 25–6, 40–1, 46
agrarian unrest 98
Ahmuty, Richard 132, 143
Akbar, Emperor 40
Alam, Muzaffar 4, 13, 44, 57, 101, 191; on gaps between assessment and revenue 101, 191
Alam, Shah, Emperor 52, 72
Alamgir, Emperor 57
Alavi, Seema 3, 192
alcohol and the Kayasthas 179–80
Ali, Akbar 103
Ali, Maulvi Roshan 15
Ali, Turab 86–7
Allahabad and the British and East India Company 78–80
Allan, Charles 141
Allen, David 199–200
alluvial soils and agricultural yields 121–2
Ambastha Kayasthas 36, 37, 38, 47
*amil*s as intermediaries 71, 73–4, 89, 91, 92
Appadurai, Arjun 118
Arwal paper 143
Asthana Kayasthas 36
Aurangzeb, Emperor 55
Awadh and revenue administration 109, 156–7; precolonial administration of 19–21, 23, 26, 27, 28–9, 194; and *qanungo*s and *patwari*s 55, 58, 82–3, 159

Baden-Powell, Robert 161
Balmukand, Mehta 41
*bandobast*s (revenue contracts) 27–8, 93, 118–19
Baqir Najim-i-Sani, Mohammed 47
Barlow, Robert 86
Barnett, Richard 20, 194
Barrow, Ian 132
Bayly, Chris 2, 4, 118, 191; on British power 3, 105, 110
Benares and British revenue administration 23–4, 67–8, 72–5, 77, 83–4, 85–6, 89, 134–5, 144–5
Bengal and British revenue administration 67–72, **71,** 91
Bengali Kayasthas 59n7, 176, 179, 183
Bhan, Chandar 5, 46, 197
Bhatnagar Kayasthas 36, 37, 38, 161, 166, 180
Bhattacharya, Jogendra Nath 178, 179
Blunt, Edward 35
Bose, Pramatha Nath 180
Bowen, H.V. 125
Brahmins, the 34–5, 37, 192–3, 196, 197; competition for service posts 169–71, 175, 190; rivalry with Kayasthas 36, 40–2, 46–7, 163, 172, 177, 178
British and East India Company, the 2, 3–4, 7, 8, 67, 68; and the agrarian tax base 67, 77–8, 81, 84, 194; and the colonial archive 123–4, 149; and management of revenue 68–71, 82–4, 88, 91–2, 191; and paper administration 8, 67, 81, 134–42, 149, 198–9; *see also* fiscal effects of the British and East India Company; Kayastha scribal caste, the; paper and British colonial administration
British control of revenue collection 77, 107–10, 134, 147–8, 158, 190–1; *see also* British and East India Company, the; fiscal effects of the British and East India Company
British cutting of the administrative apparatus 91–2, 141, 200, 201

bureaucracy and colonial administration 1, 4; nature of 9–10, 16, 148, 181, 198, 199–201; *see also* Kayastha scribal caste, the; paper and the Mughal state

'calligraphic state', the 134
calligraphy 13–14, 134
Campbell, Alexander 81–2
Canoongoes *see qanungo* (registrar), the
Castes of Mind (book) 181
caste system and fiscal violence in revenue collecting, the 23–4
Chalmers, Frederick 157
Chand, Khab 79
Chand, Mir 81
Chand, Rai Nanak 159
Chand, Ratan 102
Chand, Sabha 53
Chatterjee, Kumkum 5, 6, 7, 46, 59
Chaube, Ram Gharib 1
chaudhuris 92, 122
Chitragupta, King (Hindu god) 33–4, *35*, 39, 50
Clive, Robert 24, 69
Cockburn, Andrew 88
Cohn, Bernard 57, 109–10, 147, 197–8
Colebrooke, Henry 176, 177
collection dates and the use of calendars 92–3, *93*
colonial archive, the 120, 125–8, **126, 131**; and knowledge accumulation 118–19, 123–4, 147, 148–9, 197–8; returns for Settlement Officers **127,** 128–31, **129**
'Colonial Register,' the 144–6, **145**
colonial state and the invention of caste categories, the 181, 197–8
Colvin, Auckland 123
competition for service posts 163, 170–1, 196
Connell, James 109
copyists as a bureaucratic class 18
Court of Judicature, Bengal 70–1
Crooke, William 1, 146, 161, 162, 174, 182
Crozier, Michael 200
cultivators' grievances in Mughal India 25–7
Cuthbert, Edward 78–9, 83, 136

Dale, Stephen 16
daphne cannabina (tree) 17, 142
Das, Jagivan 43, 57
Das, Situl 52
Davis, Mike 98
Dayabhaga school of law, the 174
debt defaults in Mughal India 26–7, 28
debt handling and the Hanafi judicial tradition 24–5, 107
debt settlement in British Bengal 70–1, 120
demographic and migration patterns 99–101, 196
Department of Composition *(dar ul-Insha)* of Benares 73
Dhaincha *(aeschynomene cannabina)* 143
Dial, Bhavani 82
diet and cuisine of the Kayasthas 42
Dirks, Nicholas 118, 147, 181, 197–8
Diwan-i-Pasand (Guide to the Treasury) 21–2, *22*
Doab region, the 19, *78,* 86, 94; and soils 121, 122; *see also* Kayastha scribal caste, the
Dumbleton, Charles 136
Duncan, Jonathan 68, 72, 74–5, 134; and the Benares *qanungo*s 75–6, 85–6, 89, 135, 146
Dutt, Romesh Chunder 163

Edmonston, George 102, 103
Edney, Matthew 118, 133
education and learning of the Kayasthas 15, 44–5, 170–1
Elliot, Charles 107
Elliot, Henry 103, 161
enforcement of revenue collection 80–3, 96, 104, 120
ethnology of the Kayasthas 176–9, 181–3
Evans, Henry 159

Faiq, Muhammad 20, 23, 104, 144, 198
Faiz, Faiz Ahmad 16
famines 2, 70, 200
Fasli calendar, the 92–3, *93*
faujdari courts 74
First Two Nawabs of Oudh, The (book) 166
fiscal centralisation in Bengal 70–1
fiscal effects of the British and East India company 104–5, 138–9, 155, 193–4, 198; and taxation 96–100, **97, 98,** 105–8, 109; *see also* colonial archive, the
fiscal security and fiscal intelligence 70, 144–5
Flora of British India, The (book) 124–5
Folktales from North India (book) 1
Ford, Andrew 81
Fowke, Francis 72, 73, 100

fraud and the value of paper 139, 140, 144, 199

Gaur Kayasthas 36, 39
Glossary of Judicial and Revenue Terms (book) 125, 197
Gordon, Stewart 23, 194
Gouldner, Alvin 200
Grant, Charles 159
Great Rebellion and Uprising (1857), the 149, 157, 159, 163, 192
Great Trigonometric Survey, the 100, 132, 133, 168
Gregorian calendar, the 92–3
Guha, Ranajit 3, 83
guidelines for the use of paper 141–2

Habib, Irfan 12, 21, 55, 77, 85, 195
Habibullah, Maulvi Muhammad 172
Haider, Najaf 45, 47
Hamilton, Nathaniel 137
Hanafi judicial tradition, the 24, 107, 131
Harishchandra, Bharatendu 169
hastobuds (rent-rolls) 120, 125, **126,** 199
Heesterman, Jan 193
Hermansen, Marcia 8
Hindu enrolment in *maktabs* 54
Hindustan and scribes 7, 33
'Home Charges,' the 140, 144, 147, 190
Hooker, Jonathan 124–5
Hooper, William 160
House of Timur, the 14
Hull, Matthew 10, 199
Hume, Allan Octavian 155, 162

ICS (India Civil Service), the 163
illegitimacy and inheritance status among Kayasthas 172
Inden, Ronald 36
India in the eighteenth century 2–3
Indian culture under British rule 3
Indian Economic and Social History Review (journal) 5
India Paper Mill Company, the 143
inheritance of *qanungo*-ships 90
inherited property as a revenue source 79
ink production 17–18
Insha 53
Iqbal, 'Allama' Muhammad 16
Islam and the Kayasthas 38–44, 47–50, **48–9,** 195
Islamic law and revenue collection 24–5
Islamic learning curricula 45, 46
Islamic political culture and paper production 17

jagir (feudal land grants) crisis 2
Jalal, Ayesha 41, 169
jamabandis (historical returns) 118–19, 136, 146, 199; and judicial weight of 75, 78, 105, 107, 120; and returns of Settlement Officers 129, **129, 130**; stamped onto paper 138, 139
Jaunpur, the 'Shiraz of India' 15

Kafka, Ben 10, 200
kaghazi (paper-producing) families 141, 149
Karan Kayasthas 36, 39
Karkari Kayasthas 47
karnam (Tamil village accountant) 67
Kash, Mir Panjab 13–14
Kayastha Ethnology, The (book) 176–7
Kayastha Pathshala, the 165
Kayastha Samachar (periodical) 165, 169, 170, 180, 182
Kayastha scribal caste, the *44,* 87, 102–4, 155, 190, 196–7; education and public instruction 15, 44–5, 170–1; in the eighteenth century 4, 6–7; ethnology of 176–9, 181–3; famous Kayasthas and families 50–4, 164–8, 171–2; groups and regional distribution 34–8, *37,* 94–5; and Islam 38–44, 46, 47–50, **48–9,** 195; marital patterns of 38–9, 90–1, 171, 172, 180; under Moghul governance 46–50, 54–9, 67, 76–7; as *qanungos* 77–8, 80–1, 86, 88, 89–91, 94, 95; rivalry with Brahmins 36, 40–2, 46–7, 163, 172, 177, 178; social and cultural history of 156–7, 159–68; surveying and land assessment 86, 133, 157, 158–9; and twice-born *(dvija)* status 165, 172–6, 178, 182, 196; and vegetarianism 39, 180
Keen, Henry 159
Khan, Ali Vardi 19
Khan, Erich 87
Khan, Jawahar Ali 47, 53
Khan, Muhammad Reza 70, 71, 72, 95
Khattris 53, 54
khusrah surveying method 131–4, **133,** 159, 194, 199; accuracy of 99, 158
Kinra, Rajeev 5, 197
Kishore, Jagal 58
Kishore, Nand 82

Kishore, Nawal 51
kists (instalment payments) 82, 99
knowledge state and fiscal colonialism, the 119–20, 148–9, 191–2

Lakhnawi, Shiva Das 49
Lal, Babu Brijmohan 169
Lal, Basti 88
Lal, Brij Bhukhan 161
Lal, Chakkan 90
Lal, Manu 49
Lal, Sanbhu 72–4, 92, 135
Lal, Subhan 100
Lal, Uday 80
lambardar system, the 101, 130
land acquisition and the Kayasthas 102–4
land assessment of agrarian wealth through increases in cultivation and taxation 85–8, 96–100, **97, 98**
landowning in Bengal 3
language adaptation of the Kayasthas 168–70
Lawrence, Bruce 8
legal cases in revenue courts 146
legal debates over caste status of the Kayasthas 172–6
Leicester, William 104
Leonard, Karen 6, 156, 196
Linguistic Survey of India 1
liquidation of defaulters' assets 27

MacDonnell, Antony 169
Mackenzie, Holt 100
madrassa seminary system, the 44, 63n97
Mainwaring, Michael 82
*maktab*s (primary schools) 13, 14, 15, 18, 44–5, 54
Mal, Chattar 21–3, *22,* 92–3
Mal, Todar 40, 46, 87, 106
Malcolm, John 35–6
*malguzar*s (revenue collectors) 26, 27, 28, 70, 80, 129, 144; assessment of as landowners 102, 103–4
Mann, Michal 90, 98
marriage patterns of the Kayastha scribal caste 17, 38–9, 90–1, 171
Martin, Robert Montgomery 79–80, 106–7, 136, 143, 162
Martin, Stephen 95
Mathur Kayasthas 36, 37–8, 51, 82, 166, 180
Mauizah-i-Jahangiri (Advice on the Art of Governance) 47
measurement of land holdings 132
Meerut Collectorship, the 137
mercenary force of the British and East India Company 149
Messick, Brinkley 134
middlemen in the revenue-collection system 91–2, 109
Middleton, Samuel 58, 87
Mill, John Stuart 120, 146
Money, William 87
monsoon season and and Mughal revenue traditions, the 19, 20–1, 124
'moral consumption' of the Kayasthas 179–80
Moreland, Henry 55
Mughals, the 2, 43, 121; and governance of Kayastha scribes 46–50, 54–9, 67, 76–7; and paper 12–17, 19, 25–9, 190, 192–3
Munroe, Thomas 125

nankar payments 85
Naoroji, Dadabhai 140, 147, 199
Narain, Kish 159
Narain, Raja Ram 52
Narain, Rattan 159
Narain, Sheo 82
Narayan, Lakshmi 49, 53–4
nastaliq calligraphy 16
Nawabs, the 77, 81, 91, 121, 156, 157; fiscal power of 20, 26, 166; and patronage 14, 43, 51–3
Nepali trade and the Indian paper economy 142
Nesfield, Jonathan 161
Newnham, Henry 86
Nigam Kayasthas 89
NWP (North-Western Provinces), the 99, 105, 133, 139, 158

O'Hanlon, Rosalind 5, 196
oral history 8–9
outline of the book 7–8, 9–10
over-assessment of lands for revenue collection 99, 100–1, 106–7

Pane, Michael 132
Pant, Rashmi 181
paper: fraud and the value of 139, 140, 144, 199; and the Mughal state 12–17, 19, 25–9, 190, 192–3; production of 17, 142, 143–4; regulations and standardisation of **137,** 137–8, 147–58, 148–9, 191, 200

paper and British colonial administration 4–6, 10, 100, 195, 196; and fiscal power 88–9, 128, 146–7, 191, 201; and the knowledge state 76, 88, 119, 120, 147–8, 192; and the legal status of landholdings 84, 85; *see also* British and East India Company, the
Parshad, Ganga 83–4
Patna (Azimabad) and paper production 17
patronage in the Mughal Empire 14, 15
patwari (village accountant) 56–7, 58, 101, 133, 141, 160, 201; place in the bureaucratic process 75, 89, 91, 108–9, 130, 138; as repository of information 77, 121, 144; and returns to Collectors 129, 130, **131**
Peep into the Origin, Status and History of the Kayasthas, A (book) 177–8
People of India, The (book) 176
Perkins, Jonathan 133–4
Perlin, Frank 193
Permanent Settlement (1793) 3, 27, 68, 69, 71, 88
Persian influence in Mughal India 13, 50–1, 52, 78; and the British 72, 125, 167, 168; and the Kayasthas 39–40, 45–6, 48–9, **48–9,** 56
planning for revenue estimations 106
Plowden, T.C. 80
Poverty and un-British Rule in India (book) 147
Prabhu Kayasthas 42, 196
Prasad, Ganga 161
Prasad, Munshi Kali 164, 165–6, 176–7, 179–80, 182
Prasad, Rai Janti 165
Prashad, Sankatha 183
Premchand 164
price determination of crops 122–3
property rights 128; and land disputes 83–4, 96, 104–5, 146, 157
public instruction in education and the Kayasthas 170–1
pukka and kutcha wells 123

qanungo (registrar), the 59, 89–90, 201; as an inherited position 54, 57, 89, 90; and the British 71, 90, 91, 92, 141, 158; and land assessment 86, 87, 102–3, 123, 159; as a repository of knowledge 40, 67, 77, 80, 95, 121, 144; responsibilities of 56, 128–9, 130–1, **131,** 138; and revenue collection 75–7, 78–80, 81, 82–5, 87–9; and the Saxena Kayasthas 41, 52, 82, 86, 157; status of 94, 105, 108–9, 157–8, 160–2; and taxation 58, 75, 81, 94
qistibandis (instalment payments) 96, 105

Rai, Bhunipat 87
Rai, Daulat 84
Rai, Harsukh 166–7
Rai, Nawal 52
Rai, Nik 50
Rai, Paramasukh 167
Rai, Punjab 88
Rai, Shitab 69, 70, 104, 110n5, 198; and treatment of debtors 26–7, 71, 120
Rai Kayastha family, Lucknow 167–8
rainfall and well surveys 123–4
Ram, Kitcha 81–2
Ram, Lala Sita 164, 169
Ram, Rai 53
Ram, Rai Umid 58
Raman, Bhavani 5–6, 33, 192, 196
'rational-legal authority,' concept of 200
Ravenscroft, George 122–3
Registers of Landed Property 145, **145**
Regulation I (1822) 125
Regulation III (1803) 138
regulation of paper, the 139–40
regulations and standardisations in paperwork and accounting **137,** 137–8, 148–9, 157–8, 191, 200
Regulation VII (1822) 98–9, 100, 101, 125–6
Regulation VIII (1800) 144
Regulation X (1833) 126, 130, 139
revenue agreements between zamindars and *sarkars* 22–3, *22*
revenue collection in the Mughal Empire 12–14, 15, 18–24, *22,* 25–9
Richards, John 21, 98, 101
Risley, Herbert 162, 174, 176, 182
Rivers of Kings, the *(Rajataranagini)* 36
Ross, Alexander 84, 87, 104
Rulers, Townsmen and Bazaars (book) 192
Rumbold, Thomas 69
Russell, Robert Vane 161

Saberwal, Satish 193
Sadr Board of Revenue **131**
Safdarjang 52
Sahay, Bhawani 132
Sahay, Lala 87
Sahay, Suhar 105
Salmon, William 84
Sarkar, Jadunath 14

Sathnami sect of Kayasthas 43
sawakar families 17
Saxena Kayasthas 36, 37–8, 39, 51, 86, 166, 194; and land assessment 77, 82, 123, 133, 157; landholdings of 102, 103; as *qanungos* 41, 52, 82, 86, 157; *see also* Rai, Shitab
scribes and pensmen and fiscal authority 29, 79, 92–3, 192–3, 194–5; *see also patwari* (village accountant); *qanungo* (registrar), the
Settlement Officers 106, **126,** 137, 138, 146, 157; assessments and returns 126, **127, 129,** 129–30
Shah, Muhammad Ali 51, 52
Shah, Raja Adil 80
Shah II, Akbar, Emperor 49
Shankar, Deo 86–7
Sharar, Abdul 40
Shauk, Munshi Daulat Rai 50–1
Sherring, Matthew 161, 176
Shia Nawabs, the 46, 77, 81, 86, 91, 156; and patronage 43, 51
Shore, Frederick 98
shudra status of Kayasthas 174–5, 178
Sialkot and paper production 16, 18
Singh, Amir 82
Singh, Bukhtawar 82
Singh, Bulwant 23, 80
Singh, Chait 73
Singh, Govind 53
Singh, Mahapit 85
Singh, Rai Bahadur 53
Singh, Ratan 52
siyaqi (accountancy) in the Mughal state 15, 55
SLC (School Leaving Certificate) 160
Sleeman, William 137
social and cultural history of the Kayastha pensmen 156 7, 159–68
soil classification 120–2, 125, 197
soldier as tax collector, the 23–4
Srinagar 18
Srivastava, A.L. 166
Srivastava Kayasthas, the 36, 37–8, 39, 40, 47, 176; status of 82, 164, 166
stationery costs 136
stereotyping and the romanticising of Indian agriculture 106–7
Stokes, Eric 77, 83
Stracey, John 136
subgroups of Kayasthas 36–8, *37*; *see also* Saxena Kayasthas; Srivastava Kayasthas
Subrahmanyan, Sanjay 44, 57
Sufism and the Kayasthas 49
Suleiman the Magnificent 24
surveys of Indian agriculture 131–4, **133,** 146, 158, 168
Suryadhvaj Kayasthas 37

Tabatabai, Ghulam Hossein 68, 72, 148
Tagore, Rabindranath 178
taqavi loans 99
taxation and colonial rule 3–4, 6, 7, 105–8, 109; and the agrarian tax base 67, 77–8, 81, 84, 194; and land assessment 85–8, 96–100, **97, 98**; and taxonomy and documentation 124–32, **126, 127, 129,** 146, 176, 198
tazkira (Persian/Urdu writing) 8–9
tehsildars 92, 130, **130**
'Thomas generation,' the 79, 98
Thomason, James 101
Thornhill, Thomas 81, 90
Thornton, Edward 79, 87
Timuri Muslim rule 41, 42
Travers, Robert 70, 95
treasury weekly and monthly returns **137**
Tucker, Henry 97, 106, 140
twice-born *(dvija)* status of Kayasthas 165, 172–3, 174–5, 176, 178, 182, 196

ud-Daula, Asaf 53, 58, 81, 84
Ullah, Shah Wali 49
Universities Act (1904) 170
Upper India Paper Mill Company 166

Valpy, Henry 79
Vansina, Jan 8
Vansittart, Henry 71
varna status 175
vegetarianism and the Kayasthas 39, 180
Verelst, Harry 69, 70, 71
Verma, Gopinath Sinha 177–8, 182
Verma, Ram Saran Das 164–5
violence and revenue collection 23–4

wastelands sale in the Doab 158
wasti pen, the 16
Weber, Max 9, 16, 200
Wilson, Horace 125, 176, 197

Yang, Anand 88, 192

Zaidpuri, Ghulam Hossein 68
zamindars 1, 20, 69, 79; and debt defaults 26, 27; and revenue collection 21, 22, 27, 72–3